Edvard Munch

Frontispiece: Edvard Munch in his open air studio at Ekely

Ragna Stang

Edvard Munch

THE MAN AND HIS ART

TRANSLATED FROM THE NORWEGIAN

BY GEOFFREY CULVERWELL

ABBEVILLE PRESS, INC. ● PUBLISHERS ● NEW YORK

Copyright © 1977 by H. Aschehoug and Co. (W. Nygaard),
Johan Grundt Tanum Forlag, and Ragna Stang, Oslo.
English Translation Copyright © 1979 by Arnoldo
Mondadori, S.p.A., Milan. Munch's pictures are used in
cooperation with the Oslo Kommunes Kunstsamlinger and
other holders of reproduction rights.

Library of Congress Cataloging in Publication Data

Stang, Ragna Thiis.
   Edvard Munch : the man and his art.

   Translation of *Edvard Munch.*
   Bibliography: p. 313
   Includes indexes.
   1. Munch, Edvard, 1863–1944.   2. Artists—Norway
—Biography.   I. Title.
N7073.M8S7313   709'.2'4   [B]   78–31813
ISBN 0–89659–025–9

Design: Fiorenzo Giorgi and Rolf Andersson
Color photography: Istituto Fotografico Scala, Florence,
Oslo Kommunes Kunstsamlinger, and O. Vaering, Oslo

Foreword

The origins of the book were a smaller one on Edvard Munch on which I worked together with my late husband Nicholas Stang, and which was brought out posthumously under his name by the publishing house of Grundt Tanum in 1971. Subsequently the publishers H. Aschehoug & Co, in co-operation with Grundt Tanum asked me to write a larger, richly illustrated book on the artist. In this I have adhered to the basic concept of the earlier work, retaining certain sections, but as work on the new book progressed, so much of the original had to be changed that it was decided to publish the completed work under my name.

The quotations, which once formed part of the main body of the text, have been greatly expanded, and the reference numbers for the ones from Munch himself are given at the end of the book.

Because of these many quotations it has been necessary to add supplementary notes, which are assembled at the back of the book. In these I have included a great deal of material culled from Norwegian museums and libraries, as well as from places that I visited while retracing Munch's footsteps in West and East Germany.

I should like to thank Oslo Kommunes Kunstsamlinger (the Oslo Municipal Art Collection) for their kindness in allowing me to publish the many quotations from their archives. Several of them have already been published in previous works under their direction by scholars such as Johan H. Langaard, Reidar Revold, Pål Hougen, Gerd Woll and Arne Eggum.

Many quotations are taken from an unpublished correspondence between Edvard Munch and Jens Thiis, which I have bequeathed to Munch-Museet (the Munch Museum). All the quotations have been placed so as to relate thematically and chronologically to the main text, which I hope will enhance the reader's enjoyment as well as throwing greater light on Edvard Munch's art and personality. In order to make Munch's writings more readily understandable it has been necessary to make certain careful amendments to his highly idiosyncratic spelling and punctuation. In that and in many other practical matters I have received invaluable assistance from Øivind Blom, the chief editor at Aschehoug. I should also like to thank Rolf Andersson and Arnoldo Mondadori Ltd who undertook the considerable task of realizing the lay-out of the book as I had basically envisaged it. My further thanks go to Oslo Kommunes Kunstsamlinger, Nasjonalgalleriet (the Norwegian National Gallery) and Rasmus Meyers Samlinger (the Rasmus Meyer Collection) in Bergen, as well as to all the private owners who gave permission for new definitive photographs to be taken of their works. Certain of the plates were taken by the photographer at Munch-Museet. I should like to express my gratitude to the many members of the Museum's staff, past and present, who gave me so much help, particularly the librarian Frida Tank, the curators Gerd Woll and Jan Thurmann-Moe, and my two friends, Liv Schjodt and H. G. Dedichen, who acted as 'representatives of the public' and whose comments helped me a great deal.

For this English edition, I should like to express my thanks to the publishers Gordon Fraser Gallery, to Geoffrey Culverwell for the main translation, to Anthony Martin for additional translation and to John Boulton Smith for supervising, editing and checking the text throughout.

RAGNA STANG

Foreword to the English edition

It is sad that neither Ragna Stang nor her husband Nic Stang lived to see the publication of the English edition of the important Edvard Munch book on which both had worked for so long. Nic Stang died in 1971, at the early age of sixty-three. Ragna Stang lived to see the book published in Norway in 1977, but was tragically killed in a car crash the following year. Both were much loved and respected in the Oslo cultural world to which they had contributed so much. Ragna Stang had for many years played a leading part in the development of Oslo Kommunes Kunstsamlinger (the Oslo Municipal Art Collection) through her work first at the Vigeland and later at the Munch museums.

I last saw Ragna Stang in Oslo a few months before her untimely death. Dr. Stang attached great importance to the English language edition of the book, which Gordon Fraser was then starting to prepare. She asked me then to help with the edition in making a number of small alterations, inserting additional material and in generally checking the English version. This the publisher and I have scrupulously tried to do. At the time of Dr. Stang's death there remained a few small points which awaited final consultation with her. We have endeavoured to complete these in the way in which I think she would have wished, and I am most grateful to members of the staff of Oslo Kommunes Kunstsamlinger for their help in doing this.

This book, a landmark in publication of Munch material in English, is a fitting memorial to the work of Ragna and Nic Stang. In writing this foreword I recall with gratitude their help and friendship over the years.

JOHN BOULTON SMITH

Contents

1 Self-Portraits, 9
Self-scrutiny from the difficult years

2 The Home, 29
A heavy family inheritance

3 The Bohemian, 43
Thou shalt paint thy life

4 The Naturalist, 53
We cannot all paint nails and twigs

5 1899—A Year of Decision, 65
There should be no more painting of people reading and women knitting

6 Face to Face With a New Era, 77
Nature lies in the mood of the beholder

7 The Frieze of Life, 101
A poem of life, love and death

8 The Graphic Artist, 125
An art dedicated to mankind

9 The Draughtsman, 153
The keys to his art

10 A Decade of Misfortune and Progress, 167
Often I felt that women would stand in the way of my art

11 Friends and Patrons, 181
My fame forges ahead like a snow-plough

12 Illness and Breakdown, 207
My capacity for work was unimpaired

13 Back Home in Norway, 217
The Norwegian mountains loom threateningly before me

14 The Oslo University Murals, 233
The powerful forces of eternity

15 A New Monumentality, 251
Now it is the turn of the workers

16 The Final Years, 269
The one danger for me is not to be able to work

Abbreviations, 284

Notes, 285

List of Illustrations, 305

Chronology, 311

Bibliography, 313

Index, 316

1: Self-Portraits

My art gave me a reason for living.   Munch to K. E. Schreiner[1]

My art has allowed me to bare my soul.
                    Munch to K. E. Schreiner[2]

Nature is not something that can be seen by the eye alone—it lies also within the soul, in pictures seen by the inner eye.
                    Munch, 1907/8[3]

My pictures are my diaries.   Munch to Ludvig Ravensberg[4]

The notes that I have made are not a diary in the accepted sense of the word; they are partly extracts from my spiritual life, partly poems written as prose . . .   Munch to Ragnar Hoppe[5]

1 **Self-portrait (age 23)**, 1886
  Oil on canvas, 33 x 25 cm.
  Nasjonalgalleriet, Oslo

2 **Sketch for No. 1**
  Brown chalk on paper, 33 x 24.5 cm.
  Rolf E. Stenersen Collection, RES A220

2

< 1

Probing into Edvard Munch's art is like turning the pages of a particularly vivid and moving diary. He only ever painted what he himself had lived through, or at least experienced. His life is mirrored in his pictures, and as Munch the man and Munch the artist are inseparable, we must start by learning something of that life.

'In my art I have tried to express my own life and its meaning. In so doing I hope that I will also help other people to understand their own lives.'[1] There could hardly have been a clearer statement of artistic intent than that.

In this book we shall follow Edvard Munch through times of illness and poverty, and the lonely years of almost universal rejection, a rejection that ended only when his true genius was recognized, first by the outside world and finally by the people of Norway, his homeland. At the same time we shall also try to see him in the wider context of contemporary cultural and social developments. Studying Munch's life is like watching the passing of a single day: from the gloomy dawn of his youth, the shadows of anxiety are gradually dispelled by the warming rays of the morning sun, and culminate in the sparkling colours of the twilight years.

But how is it that nowadays Edvard Munch's art still reaches out and touches people in every part of the world, regardless of race or creed? Lonely as he was, he regarded it as his ultimate mission in life to reach out to his fellow men: he was well aware of his own artistic strength and he saw himself as a prophet, or a 'nabi'[2] to use his contemporary terminology. It is for this reason that his art is a long succession of confessions about himself, the result of his burning need for self-knowledge. The basic aim of all real art is, after all, to intensify people's feelings about the meaning of life.

In illustrating Munch's development as a person and as an artist, his own comments on his philosophy of life and his pictures provide valuable guidelines. He often wrote out his reflections[3] several times, in order, as he himself says, to be sure that it was 'the right Munch speaking. Because you must realize that there are two Munchs.' But there are not just two—there are countless Munchs. And for this reason we are beginning the book with a small selection of his many self-portraits, bearing in mind that often the artists who probe most deeply into their times are the ones who paint the most self-portraits. Generally this does not simply indicate selfish introspection: any artist who wishes to penetrate beneath the superficial realities of life must continually strive to 'know himself' in order to be able to 'help others understand their own lives'. Although Munch the artist reveals Munch the person, at the same time he protects his integrity, thereby retaining an element of mystery that continually possesses our imagination. These 'self-scrutinies', combined with Munch's own comments, give us a fascinating insight into his world; there is the feeling of standing face to face with a genius—a genius who, in all his solitude, never once retreated into his ivory tower.

The person who 'explained' Munch best is Munch himself. And that is why the first chapter of this book has been devoted to what he himself said.

My art had its roots in my search for an explanation of life's inconsistencies. Why was I not like other people? Why was I born, when I never asked to be? It was my rage at this injustice and my continual thinking about it that influenced all my art; these thoughts lay behind all my work, and without them my art would have been completely different.

Munch to K. E. Schreiner[6]

A bird of prey has fixed itself within me; its claws have dug into my heart, its beak has pierced my chest, and the beating of its wings has clouded my brain. Munch[7]

It would be amusing to give a talk to all those who have seen our paintings over the years and have either laughed or just scratched their heads. They are completely incapable of appreciating that there is any sort of reason involved in these momentary impressions of life. All they know is that a tree cannot be red or blue, nor can a face be blue or green—since childhood they have learned that leaves are green and skin is a nice pink colour. They cannot bring themselves to believe that the artist really meant to use those strange colours—it must be some kind of effete intellectual humbug, or perhaps just the product of a deranged mind, preferably the latter.

They cannot get it into their heads that these pictures are the result of serious thought, of suffering—they are the product of sleepless nights, the fruits of physical and mental torment.

Munch, 1890[8]

3 **Self-portrait,** 1881/2
Oil on canvas, 26 x 18 cm.
Oslo Kommunes Kunstsamlinger, OKK 1049

*4 **Self-portrait under Woman's Mask,** 1892/3
Oil on cardboard, 69 x 44 cm.
Oslo Kommunes Kunstsamlinger, OKK 229

*5 **Self-portrait with Cigarette,** 1895
Oil on canvas, 111 x 86 cm.
Nasjonalgalleriet, Oslo

5 >

*The camera will never compete with the brush and the palette,
until such time as photographs can be taken in Heaven or Hell.*
Munch[9]

*When I embarked on the voyage of life I felt like a boat made of
old, rotten wood, whose builder had launched it on an angry sea
with these words: 'If you go under, it will be your own fault and
you will be consumed by the everlasting fires of Hell.'*
Munch to K. E. Schreiner[10]

*What is art? Art grows out of grief and joy, but mainly grief. It is
born of peoples' lives.* Munch, 1905[11]

*Nature is the eternal abundance from which art gains its
sustenance.* Munch, 1907/8[12]

*The fact that Germany has fallen under the spell of my art affords
me a cold feeling of power; and at least it has stimulated interest
in it.* Munch to Jappe Nilssen[13]

*All in all, art results from man's desire to communicate with his
fellows. All methods are equally effective. Both in literature and
in painting the technique varies according to the aims of the
artist. Nature is a means to an end, not an end in itself. If it is
possible to produce the desired effect by changing nature, then it
should be done. A landscape will alter according to the mood of
the person who sees it, and in order to represent that particular
scene the artist will produce a picture that expresses his own
personal feelings. It is these feelings which are crucial: nature is
merely the means of conveying them. Whether the picture
resembles nature or not is irrelevant, as a picture cannot be
explained; the reason for its being painted in the first place was
that the artist could find no other means of expressing what he
saw. The finished work can only give a hint of what was in the
artist's mind.* Munch[14]

7

8

9

*6 **Self-portrait in Hell**, 1895
Oil on canvas, 82 x 66 cm.
Oslo Kommunes Kunstsamlinger, OKK 591

*7 **Self-portrait with Skeleton Arm**, 1895
Lithograph, 45.5 x 31.7 cm.
Oslo Kommunes Kunstsamlinger, OKK 192
Ref. G. Schiefler No. 31

8 Edvard Munch (age 27)
Admission card for Christiania Theatre

9 Edvard Munch (age 22)
Admission card to Société Royale d'Encouragement
des Beaux Arts

10

11

The truth of the matter is that we see with different eyes at different times. We see things one way in the morning and another in the evening, and the way we view things also depends on the mood we are in. That is why one subject can be seen in so many ways and that is what makes art so interesting.   Munch, 1891[15]

My fame is growing. My peace of mind is another matter.
Munch to Jens Thiis, 1907[16]

My fame forges ahead like a snowplough.
Munch to Emanuel Goldstein, 1905[17]

It seems as though my soul can return to this beautiful and thorn-filled world.   Munch to Ernest Thiel, 1906[18]

The drink became stronger, the attacks more frequent. I also fell prey to sudden bouts of anger, and I would start fighting with people.   Munch[19]

12

13

Thinking enhances sensitivity, but diminishes feeling. Wine heightens one's feeling, but weakens one's sensitivity.
Munch to Emanuel Goldstein[20]

For several years I was almost mad—then I found myself staring straight into the hideous face of insanity. Munch[21]

I have been buffeted by dangerous autumn storms before my time—they deprived me of man's best season, the midsummer. Here in the autumn heavy branches were torn from the tree, but I have to admit that I heal very easily and so perhaps these scars will also disappear. Munch to Sigurd Høst, 1909[22]

The catastrophe came exactly seven years to the month after the disaster in 1902 that caused my present condition . . . But if I were stronger, I should become an immeasurably better artist. As we have already discussed, I believe that I have come near to collecting my impressions together to form historical themes. This will give me greater peace of mind and be in itself a very positive development. Munch to Emanuel Goldstein[23]

10 **Head to Head,** 1905
Woodcut, 40 x 54 cm.
Oslo Kommunes Kunstsamlinger, OKK 612
Ref. G. Schiefler No. 230—40 x 54 cm.

*11 **The Blossom of Pain,** 1897
Watercolour, pencil and crayon, 50 x 32.8 cm.
Oslo Kommunes Kunstsamlinger, OKK 2451

*12 **Self-portrait with brushes,** 1904
Oil on canvas, 197 x 91 cm.
Oslo Kommunes Kunstsamlinger, OKK 751

*13 **Self-portrait with Lyre,** 1896/7
Pencil, ink, watercolour and gouache, 68.8 x 53 cm.
Oslo Kommunes Kunstsamlinger, OKK 2460

17

14

*14 **Self-portrait with Wine Bottle**, 1906
Oil on canvas, 110 x 120 cm.
Oslo Kommunes Kunstsamlinger, OKK 543

*15 **Self-portrait at Clinic**, 1909
Oil on canvas, 100 x 110 cm.
Rasmus Meyers Samlinger, Bergen

My motto has become 'Steer clear of everything'. I now confine myself to nicotine-free cigars, alcohol-free drinks, and non-poisonous women (either married or unmarried). You're going to find me an extremely boring uncle.
Munch to Sigurd Høst, 1909[24]

Today I am sending you a large portrait. There may be many others in the future, but in that case you must select one—there are several self-portraits. They are self-scrutinies from the difficult years. I think that the one I am sending off and the one in which I am sitting by the glass are the best two. They were painted during my time at Weimar. (Plate 14)
Munch to Jappe Nilssen, 1909[25]

The alcohol-filled days of pain and happiness are finally over for me; I have turned my back on a strange world . . . Like the old Italian painters, I have decided that women's proper place is in heaven. Roses can inflict too much damage with their thorns. I am beginning to see the resemblance between women and flowers; I enjoy the scent of the blooms, I admire the beauty of the leaves, but I never touch them and so I am never disappointed.
Munch to Jappe Nilssen, 1908[26]

15

I have lived the whole of my life partly in a dream world, partly in reality. People have realized this and have attacked my defenceless body like ravening wild animals, whilst my soul was wandering far away.   Munch to K. E. Schreiner[27]

A silent and resigned melancholy has filled my heart at the thought of losing so many of my beloved children. (Munch had just sold a number of his pictures, which he always referred to as his 'children'.)   Munch to Sigurd Høst, 1909[28]

16

17

18

'Do you get a feeling of sickness?' 'What do you mean?' 'Don't you recognize the smell?' 'The smell?' 'Yes, can't you sense that I am beginning to decay?'
(Exchange between Munch and Rolf Stenersen concerning the painting illustrated in Plate 19)[29]

My soul is like two wild birds, each flying in its own direction.
Munch[30]

People will be able to see from these two note-books that my philosophy of life and my spiritual art had their beginnings during my bohemian period in the middle and end of the 1880s, and developed even more during my stay in Paris in 1889.
Munch to Ragnar Hoppe, 1929[31]

16 **Self-portrait in Bergen,** 1916
Oil on canvas, 90 x 60 cm.
Oslo Kommunes Kunstsamlinger, OKK 263

17 **Self-portrait with Hand Under Chin,** 1911/12
Oil on canvas, 83 x 69 cm.
Oslo Kommunes Kunstsamlinger, OKK 117

18 **Self-portrait with Cigarette,** 1908
Lithograph, 56 x 45.5 cm.
Oslo Kommunes Kunstsamlinger, OKK 227
Ref. G. Schiefler No. 282

19 **Self-portrait during Spanish 'flu',** 1919
Oil on canvas, 151 x 131 cm.
Nasjonalgalleriet, Oslo

20

22

22

21

I know that in Scandinavia in recent years there has been a good deal of opposition to the way I painted my pictures; to their large format and also to the way in which I use art to express my innermost feelings. I noticed this coolness amongst young artists throughout the North and also here in Oslo. But the large exhibition I had in Berlin and the subsequent one in Oslo (1927) silenced their criticisms, at least on the surface. I have a pretty good idea that at the moment my work is going to encounter the same kind of opposition in Sweden.

Munch to Ragnar Hoppe, 1929[32]

My whole life has been spent walking by the side of a bottomless chasm, jumping from stone to stone. Sometimes I try to leave my narrow path and join the swirling mainstream of life, but I always find myself drawn inexorably back towards the chasm's edge and there I shall walk until the day I finally fall into the abyss. For as long as I can remember I have suffered from a deep feeling of anxiety which I have tried to express in my art. Without anxiety and illness I would have been like a ship without a rudder.

Munch to K. E. Schreiner[33]

20 **Self-portrait. Inner Turmoil, 1919**
   Oil on canvas, 151 x 130 cm.
   Oslo Kommunes Kunstsamlinger, OKK 76

*21 **The Bohemian's Wedding, 1925**
   Oil on canvas, 65 x 80 cm.
   Oslo Kommunes Kunstsamlinger, OKK 848

22 Sketch for *Self-portrait. Inner Turmoil* (No. 20)
   Crayon drawing, 31 x 24 cm.
   Oslo Kommunes Kunstsamlinger, OKK 246/2

23 **Self-portrait at Ekely, 1926**
   Oil on canvas, 92 x 73 cm.
   Oslo Kommunes Kunstsamlinger, OKK 318

24

I am like a sleepwalker on top of a roof. Don't waken me roughly or I shall fall and break my body.   Munch[34]

People have again started talking about my having a larger exhibition of my paintings in Stockholm. But I often find these exhibitions rather tiring: they're like being personally held up for judgement or being publicly executed. It's as though I'm being hung on the gallows for all to see.

Munch to Ragnar Hoppe, 1929[35]

With the passing of the years I have become more and more unsuited to the company of my fellow men, even my best friends. Just think—for six years I haven't been to a single party, or even been a guest at the homes of my best friends like Thiis and others.   Munch to Ragnar Hoppe, 1929[36]

I haven't appeared in public since I was last in your house. My hair is now down to my shoulders and my beard reaches my chest. Every morning I can employ a marvellous free model by painting my own skinny body in front of the mirror. I use myself for all the Biblical characters like Lazarus, Job, Methuselah, etc.

Munch to Jens Thiis, 1933/4[37]

24 **Self-portrait: The Night Wanderer,** c.1930
Oil on canvas, 90 x 68 cm.
Oslo Kommunes Kunstsamlinger, OKK 589

25 **Self-portrait eating a 'truly magnificent cod's head',** 1940
Oil on panel, 46 x 34 cm.
Oslo Kommunes Kunstsamlinger, OKK 633

26 **Self-portrait as Seated Nude,** 1933/4
Pencil and watercolour, 70 x 86 cm.
Oslo Kommunes Kunstsamlinger, OKK 2462

27 **Self-portrait,** 1919
Oil on canvas, 100 x 95 cm.
Oslo Kommunes Kunstsamlinger, OKK 449

28 **Self-portrait (after the Spanish 'flu'),** 1919
Black crayon drawing, 43 x 61 cm.
Oslo Kommunes Kunstsamlinger, OKK 2766

25

26

27

28

29

29 **Self-portrait by the Window**, 1949/51
   Oil on canvas, 84 x 107.5 cm.
   Oslo Kommunes Kunstsamlinger, OKK 446

30 **Self-portrait between the Clock and the Bed**, c.1940
   Oil on canvas, 150 x 120 cm.
   Oslo Kommunes Kunstsamlinger, OKK 23

*Thank you for the fish and the lobster—they were delicious . . .
I'm very much looking forward to the enormous cod, both the one
with the magnificent head and the lightly-salted one with the
ivory flesh.* Munch to Christian Gierløff, 1943[38]

*It really has been a terrible winter [1942–3], particularly for me
because it has been so damp. I have asthmatic bronchitis which
settles in my throat and makes it difficult for me to be with
people . . .* Munch to Christian Gierløff, 1943[39]

*I have already experienced death when I was born. The real birth,
which is called death, still awaits me.*
Munch to K. E. Schreiner[40]

We do not pass away—the world passes away from us.
Munch[41]

*Flowers will grow up from my rotting corpse and I will live on in
those blooms.* Munch[42]

*Death is the beginning of life, the beginning of a new crystal-
lization.* Munch[43]

30 >

31

. . . I am afraid that the Germans are going to want to have my house, and in any case I've been told that one should be ready to evacuate. As it is, they have already taken over my property in Hvidsten. I am sure that nobody really realizes just how much work that involved for me; there were sixty years' paintings, graphics and drawings to deal with. I never used waste paper baskets except to store things in, and this made the business of sorting the wheat from the chaff extremely difficult . . . It did, however, have the effect of giving me the chance to renew old friendships and relive past days.

Munch to Christian Gierløff, 1943[44]

32

31 The old artist in Ekely in 1943

32 Edvard Munch in 1938, age 75

2:The Home

33

34

A heavy family inheritance

My mother came of good strong farming stock, but her natural strength was gradually eaten away by the worm of consumption. My father, as you already know, came from a literary family; he had the makings of a genius, but he was also tainted with a tendency towards degeneracy. I arrived in the world on the point of death and my parents had to have me christened at home as quickly as possible. At the time my mother was carrying within her the germ of the tuberculosis that six years later was to deprive five small children of their mother. Sickness and insanity and death were the black angels that hovered over my cradle and have since followed me throughout my life. My father tried to be both mother and father to us, but he had a difficult temperament and an inherited nervousness that led to almost insane bouts of religious obsession, during which he would spend days pacing up and down the room, praying to God. At an early age I was taught about the perils and miseries of life on this earth, about life after death, and also about the agonies of Hell that lay in store for children who sinned. When he was not going through one of his periods of religious fanaticism, he could be like a child and play and joke with us and tell us stories. As a result, it became doubly painful for us when he punished us; on those occasions he would be almost beside himself with anger. It is that nervous anger that I have inherited. Munch[1]

33 **At the deathbed**, c.1915
Oil on canvas, 140 x 183 cm.
Statens Museum for Kunst, Copenhagen

34 **At the deathbed** (also called **Fever** or **The Son**), 1896
Lithograph and indian ink, 39.3 x 50
Oslo Kommunes Kunstsamlinger, OKK 214
Ref. G. Schiefler No. 72.

*35 Drawing for No. 34, 1892/3
Indian ink and crayon, 23 x 18 cm.
Oslo Kommunes Kunstsamlinger, OKK 286

35

The art of the young Munch had two main sources of inspiration. One was his home, to which he felt extremely strong ties of affection all his life, and the other was the bohemian intellectual society of Christiania (the old name for Oslo) during the 1880s. Later on we shall examine how Munch afterwards gravitated towards a similar milieu in Berlin and Paris during the 1890s.

Illness and anxiety played a central part in Munch's life, and therefore also in his art. The process began in his earliest years when as a small and impressionable child he was exposed at close quarters to the full grimness and injustice of death. He also experienced love in all its complexities, either at first hand or through the medium of his friends. He was able to identify so deeply with his friends that he could relive all their experiences as if they were his own. Everyone who knew him personally speaks of the barrier of intense shyness that was so hard to penetrate, but art acted as his means of communication. 'All in all, art results from man's desire to communicate with his fellows. All methods are equally effective.' 'I do not believe in art that does not spring from man's yearning to open up his heart. All art, literature as well as music, must come from the heart: art is the distillation of man's very life-blood.'[4]

These statements closely echo the avowed code of the idealistic young bohemians of the 1880s: 'Thou shalt write thy life.' As late as the 1930s, Munch wrote to his early friend Jens Thiis, who at that time was busy writing a biography for the artist's seventieth birthday: 'You need not look far to find the origin of the Frieze of Life. The answer lies in my bohemian days—it was merely a question of painting one's own life and life as it is lived by others.'[5]

Munch came from a long line of government servants,[6] many of whom had made important contributions to Norway's scientific, literary and artistic development. Some of his ancestors had been officers and clergymen; one officer, an engineer called Jacob Munch, had been, amongst other things, a pupil of David's in Paris and had become Norway's foremost painter of portraits in the Empire style. One of his clerical forbears, Johan Storm Munch, as well as being a bishop was also a poet, and his son, Andreas Munch, a late Romantic lyric poet and dramatist who died in 1884, became an important contemporary figure and was even given the title of Professor. However, the most illustrious member of the family was another professor, Edvard's uncle, P. A. Munch (1810–63), an historian who could rightly be called a genius. His brother Christian (1817–89), was Edvard's father, a regimental doctor who had had a very adventurous youth. As a twenty-one-year-old medical student he had taken part in the famous Norwegian theatrical controversy in Christiania in 1838, coming out in support of Welhaven. The whole affair became so heated that one member of the pro-Wergeland faction shouted out amidst the uproar: 'Down with everything that bears the name Munch!'[7]

He reappears at the age of twenty-six as doctor on an emigrant ship bound for New York, and two years later he was sailing the Mediterranean. In 1861, aged forty-four, he married the twenty-three-year-old Laura Cathrine Bjølstad and set up house in a farm called Engelhaugen, at Løten in the Hedmark district, some 100 kilometres north of Oslo. It was there that their daughter Johanne Sophie was born in 1862, and there too, on 12 December 1863, Edvard Munch himself was born. The family moved back to Christiania in 1864.

Dr Munch was very conscious of his family's intellectual tradition[8] and his children would often gather round the paraffin lamp to read aloud from the

36

38

37

Munch's mother died in 1868, aged thirty. That same year she wrote a farewell letter to her children: *My dear children, Jesus Christ will ensure that you lead a happy life both here and in the hereafter. Love Him above all else and do not grieve Him by turning your back on Him . . . And now, my beloved children, my dear little ones, I bid you farewell, your beloved Daddy will be better able to show you the way to Heaven. I shall be waiting for you all there . . . God be with you now and forever, Sophie, pale little Edvard, Andreas and Laura and you, my dear, sweet unforgettable, self-sacrificing husband.* Laura Munch[2]

39

32

40

It is Christmas Eve and I am thirteen years old. There is blood trickling out of my mouth and fever raging in my veins. Suddenly I feel myself giving a silent scream of terror. Now, any moment now, you will be standing before your Maker and you will be condemned to permanent punishment. Munch[3]

Monday 8 November 1880
I have now been taken out of technical school. I have decided to become a painter.

Wednesday 8 December 1880
I am now busy studying art history.

Tuesday 22 November 1881
Since the end of August I have been attending drawing school fairly regularly.

Sunday 10 December 1881
Yesterday I sent three of my smaller works to an auction house where they sold off a whole lot of paintings. It was pretty much of a disaster as the majority of paintings fetched little more than what it had cost to have them framed. I had to buy one of mine back myself, but the other two fetched 11 and 15.50 krone, 10 krone net.

Extracts from Edvard Munch's diary[4]

36 **Dr. Munch with his wife and children,** c.1895
Charcoal drawing, 48 x 63 cm.
Oslo Kommunes Kunstsamlinger, OKK 2266

37 **Laura Munch with her five children**
(Left: Sophie and Andreas. Right: Edvard and Laura.
On her lap is Inger.)
Photograph

38 **Dr. Christian Munch,** 1885
Oil on canvas, 38 x 28 cm.
Oslo Kommunes Kunstsamlinger, OKK 1056

39 **Self-portrait,** 1880
Oil on panel, 43.6 x 35.4 cm.
Bymuseet, Oslo

*40 **The Death of Hakon Jarl,** 1877
Indian ink drawing made by Munch, age 14
Oslo Kommunes Kunstsamlinger, OKK 35

works of such writers as Walter Scott. They also read extracts from their uncle's book *The old Nordic sagas of gods and heroes* or his monumental *History of the Norwegian people*. In addition to this, their father was a brilliant storyteller with a deep fund of the old sagas and a penchant for ghost stories.

However, the doctor was soon finding it increasingly difficult to make ends meet; his practice was in the poorer part of town, and in those days there was no form of socialized medicine. In 1868, when Edvard was five years old, his mother died of tuberculosis, which was extremely prevalent at the time; nine years later his favourite sister Sophie fell victim to the same disease, dying at the age of fifteen, and disaster struck the family once again in 1895 when Edvard's brother Peter Andreas, a doctor like his father, died aged thirty.

Following the death of their mother, the children were looked after by their aunt, Karen Bjølstad, who took over the running of the household. She encouraged the artistic tendencies of the children, who were all keen young artists, and in fact, when things were particularly difficult, she herself would earn a little extra money by selling small decorations, such as landscapes made out of moss, ferns and pieces of twig, which were then popular as wall ornaments. She was convinced of Edvard's talent[9] from the very first, and it was she who managed to get him out of the technical school where his father had enrolled him, in order to develop his artistic potential. Her success can be gauged by the fact that in the autumn of 1881, Edvard had become a pupil of the sculptor Julius Middelthun at art school.[10]

The death of his wife affected Dr Munch deeply. He lost much of his natural gaiety and his deep religious faith began to take on a darker and more inward-looking quality. Edvard began to have frequent rows with his increasingly pietistic father: after one such argument Edvard returned home late at night to find his father praying for the soul of his son. The artistic result of this was the woodcut entitled *Old Man Praying* (Plate 172), executed as late as 1902. Edvard's portrayal of his father's 'almost insane bouts of religious obsession' does not altogether accord with the description given by a younger relation, the painter Ludvig Ravensberg: 'My old uncle Christian was full of fun; he always reminded me of a patriarch with his long white beard.' He also mentions 'his high degree of learning and his great historical knowledge' and goes on: 'He was P. A. Munch's brother and a lively and witty conversationalist, with the rare ability of being able to make history come alive using the simplest words. He was an extremely entertaining and amusing man. Edvard has inherited a lot from his father.' Ravensberg also speaks of 'the atmosphere of refinement in the house'[11] and the kindness and consideration of those who lived in it.

Although after her sister's death, Karen Bjølstad restored a feeling of security to the shattered household, it was soon shaken by a new tragedy. The illness and death of fifteen-year-old Sophie in 1877 had a devastating effect on the sensitive and vulnerable fourteen-year-old Edvard; she had been his favourite sister, and for the rest of his life he was never to be able to rid himself of the memory of that terrible loss. Two of his major works, *The Sick Child* and *Spring*, which date from the second half of the next decade, show clearly how deeply Munch was affected by the experiences. However, similar sickroom scenes were popular with many artists during this period, which Munch later referred to as 'putetiden', literally 'the time of pillows'.[12] The memories lay dormant for a long time, as the artist himself said, but they surfaced decisively on the death of his father in 1889; they recur in letters and notes, and they are commemorated in his artistic production throughout the 1890s, both in paintings and prints. One of the main subjects is *Death in the Sickroom* (Plate 51), in which Munch shows the dying girl sitting in an armchair. He also uses the theme, with extraordinary attention to detail, throughout a further series of pictures describing the event (Plates 33, 34 and 35). Once again he painted not 'what I see, but what I saw'.[13]

Munch was perfectly clear in his mind as to the major inspirations for his art. He also realized the important part played by his home and the events that he had witnessed there. Even in later years, when he had achieved fame as an artist, he still harked pathetically back to his childhood: 'Sickness and insanity and death were the black angels that hovered over my cradle and

41

I do not paint what I see, but what I saw.   Munch, 1890[5]

I painted echoes of my childhood in the blurred colours of that time. By painting the confused colours, lines and shapes that I had seen in a moment of emotion, I hoped to recreate the vibrant atmosphere like a phonograph. This is how the pictures of my frieze of life were born.   Munch, 1890[6]

[Sophie's] *eyes became red—I could not believe that death was so inevitable, so near at hand . . . The priest arrived in his black robes and his white ruff collar. Was she really going to die? In the final half hour she felt much more comfortable, the pains had gone. She tried to get up and pointed to the armchair by the side of her bed. 'I would so like to sit up,' she whispered. How strange she felt—the room was different—it was as though she was seeing it through a veil—her body seemed to be weighed down with lead—she was so tired.* Munch, 1895[7]

Thursday 5 May 1881
Yesterday I finished the picture for my Munch aunts [Plate 42]. *They treated me to a large cup of hot chocolate in return and even gave me a really beautiful drawing book for me to remember them by.*   Munch[8]

42

*41 The Sick Child, 1896
    Chalk drawing, 42.1 x 40.9 cm.
    Private Collection

*42 The Aunt's Sitting Room, 1881
    Oil on canvas, 21 x 27 cm.
    Oslo Kommunes Kunstsamlinger, OKK 1047

*43 The Dead Mother and the Child, 1894
    Pencil and charcoal, 50 x 65 cm.
    Oslo Kommunes Kunstsamlinger, OKK 301

*44 The Dead Mother and the Child, 1899
    Tempera on canvas, 104 x 180 cm.
    Oslo Kommunes Kunstsamlinger, OKK 420

43

44

have since followed me throughout my life.'[14]

He had been a sickly child, often unable to attend school because of rheumatic fever or some other ailment, and as a result he had a terror of both tuberculosis and insanity. He was haunted by the thought of death throughout his life, but nonetheless he considered illness almost a pre-condition for his work: '. . . I must retain my physical weaknesses, they are an integral part of me. I don't want to get rid of illness, however unsympathetically I may depict it in my art.'[15] Such a dependent childhood and the effect on him of so much human tragedy, made him more and more attached to his home and family. His 'Letter to the family' expresses his concern for them as well as his willingness to help whenever it was within his power.

The Munch household was run on patriarchal lines with good, old-fashioned order and discipline very much in evidence, and Karen Bjølstad ruled over it with a firm but affectionate hand. But the need for strict economy[16] and the fact that the family had no proper mother and lived in a series of modest apartments[17] meant that they certainly remained fairly isolated from the rest of Christiania's *haute bourgeoisie*.[18] From his youth, Edvard was basically at odds with 'polite society', and as he became more and more involved with the bohemians, his antipathy to its moral and social conventions grew. Later on we shall examine the effect that the bohemian leader, Hans Jaeger, had on Munch's life. But it is a fact that hardly any other of his followers fulfilled Jaeger's moral requirements as completely or exposed his own innermost thoughts and his most personal experiences as ruthlessly as did Munch. Only Jaeger himself in his writings could possibly be thought to have achieved the same degree of self-revelation.

Munch's art still touches our hearts and minds today because, by searching the deepest recesses of his own mind, he has arrived at an area of shared experience. His individualism is that of universality.

45

46

45 **Sister Inger, age 14**, 1882
     Charcoal drawing, 34.5 x 25.8 cm.
     Oslo Kommunes Kunstsamlinger, OKK 2361

46 **Sister Laura, age 14**, 1881/2
     Oil on panel, 23 x 18 cm.
     Oslo Kommunes Kunstsamlinger, OKK 1046

*47 **Sister Inger, age 16**, 1884
     Oil on canvas, 97 x 68 cm.
     Nasjonalgalleriet, Oslo

48

48 **Siesta**, 1883
    Oil on paper mounted on panel, 35 x 48 cm.
    Oslo Kommunes Kunstsamlinger, OKK 1055

*49 **Old Aker Church**, 1881
    Oil on cardboard, 21 x 15.5
    Oslo Kommunes Kunstsamlinger, OKK 1043

50 **Aunt Karen in her Rocking Chair**, 1884
    Oil on canvas, 47 x 41 cm.
    Oslo Kommunes Kunstsamlinger, OKK 1108

49

*51 **Death in the Sickroom**, c.1893
Oil on canvas, 136 x 160 cm.
Oslo Kommunes Kunstsamlinger, OKK 418

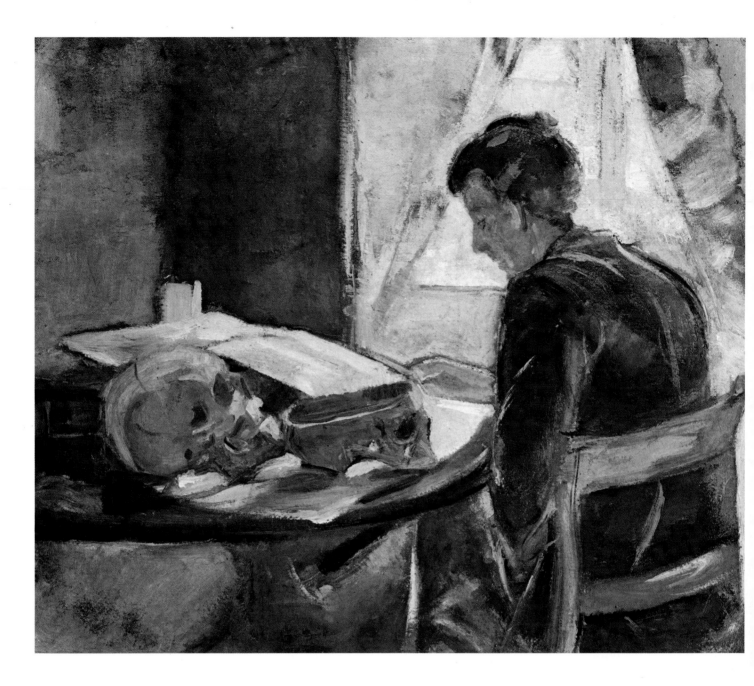

52 **Brother Andreas studying Anatomy,** 1883
(He later became a doctor, but died in 1895, thirty years old)
Oil on cardboard, 62 x 75 cm.
Oslo Kommunes Kunstsamlinger, OKK 202

3:The Bohemian

Thou shalt paint thy life

It is quite true that my ideas developed under the influence of the bohemians or rather of Hans Jaeger. Hans Jaeger gave me his support. Many people have mistakenly claimed that I developed under the influence of Strindberg and the Germans, during my stay in Berlin in 1893/94. My ideas had already been formed by then, and I had been painting my 'Life Pictures' for several years.
Munch to Broby-Johansen, 1926[1]

I am now sitting in 'the Grand' with Hans Jaeger who is going to be put into clink tomorrow. Munch to Arne Garborg, 1888[2]

With his painting of Hans Jaeger, despite its rather crude, un-finished look, the artist has reached the point where he can convince all and sundry of his ability to produce a vivid and brilliant character study, as well as a truly expressive portrayal. The most comforting thing about the exhibition is that this work is one of his last. Andreas Aubert, 1889[3]

*53 **Hans Jaeger**, 1889
Oil on canvas, 110 x 84 cm.
Nasjonalgalleriet, Oslo

54 **Hans Jaeger**, 1896
Lithograph, 46 x 33 cm.
Oslo Kommunes Kunstsamlinger, OKK 218
Ref. G. Schiefler No. 76

54

Edvard Munch often stated that the so-called 'bohemian' movement which flourished in Christiania during the 1880s had a decisive influence on him. We have already quoted in Chapter 2 the letter that he wrote to Jens Thiis on the subject in the 1930s. In 1926 he wrote in similar vein to the young Danish writer Broby-Johansen: 'It is quite true that my ideas developed under the influence of the bohemians or rather of Hans Jaeger . . .'[19] And in his own copy of his little pamphlet[20] on *The Frieze of Life* he jotted down: '*The Frieze of Life* was conceived as a result of conversations and ideas from my bohemian days that I acquired sitting in 'the Grand' or walking about in the long summer nights.'

Although Munch did not himself belong to the inner circle of bohemians, his closest friends did, and he had a great admiration for Hans Jaeger. The portrait which Munch painted of him in 1889 shows a deep understanding of that man's trials and tribulations; it was painted just after Jaeger had been released from jail, and we know that Munch was together with him in 'the Grand' the evening before he was sent to prison[21] for the second time. Jaeger even got permission to have one of Munch's paintings in his cell[22]; the original has unfortunately been lost, but from the description it must have combined elements of *Madonna* and *The Day After*. It is also no mere coincidence that one of the first portraits Munch produced as a lithograph was that of the friend he so admired for, and that one of the last lithographs he published (1943-44), shortly before his death, was a new one of that same bohemian friend (Plate 356).

What then was the ideal for which this extraordinary man and his band of intellectuals and artists were fighting? Basically, their movement, which marks a significant turning point in Norway's cultural development,[23] was fighting to achieve greater human rights and an increase in personal and artistic freedom. The bohemians gained their inspiration from other European centres, such as Paris, where a reappraisal of traditional values was already well under way. In the more southerly countries this kind of moral and intellectual readjustment took place with a relative lack of upheaval, but in the northern capitals, particularly Christiania, 'that Siberian town'[24] as Munch called it, the movement was met with such single-minded and relentless hostility that what elsewhere had been a few gentle ripples on the surface of society, in Norway became a full-scale storm, a life and death struggle in some circles that had far-reaching effects; social, political, and, above all, artistic and intellectual.

Norway was, at that time, very insular and the new ideas swept through the country and its tiny capital like a hurricane. The Dane Georg Brandes acted as intermediary in introducing the latest cultural ideas from Europe into the country and he assisted greatly in the establishment of a truly Norwegian literary genre, not least by direct personal contact with Norwegian poets who, almost without exception, had their works published in Copenhagen. His atheism, however, did much to shock Norwegian middle class sensibilities.

Early in the 1880s the best known Norwegian artists[25] moved from Munich to Paris—and then came home, something that had previously been an extremely rare occurrence. They arrived back in their native country bursting with new ideas that ranged from Impressionism to Anarchism. They had also acquired a liking for the Continental way of life, for café society, the brothels of Paris and free love. The poets too had returned from Paris, and soon Christiania found itself host to a group of people whose way of life came as a rude shock to the complacent middle-class population of a small town boasting in 1885 a mere 135,000 inhabitants.

The majority of these bohemians were writers of varying talents, and naturally enough their idol was Emil Zola. Literature was assessed according to its degree of social usefulness, and the leader of the group, Hans Jaeger, found it necessary to write a foreword to his novel[26] *From the Christiania Bohemians* (1885): he felt obliged to solve, 'without original literary talent', a problem which had concerned him and which he had waited for someone else to solve—'the problem of inaugurating a modern Norwegian literary genre, that of the novel.' And he was sure that the novel, 'both by its structure and its content must act as a powerful antidote to what is at present considered to be acceptable social conduct.'

Certainly the reaction against this autobiographical and revealing novel, which in contemporary eyes was merely pornography, could hardly have been more violent: all copies of *From the Christiania Bohemians* were promptly confiscated and its author given a two-month jail sentence[27].

Jaeger was a highly intellectual man, whose avowed intent was the overthrow of the existing social system: he was a confirmed anarchist who, as well as writing fiction, also produced a book on Kant, and ended his literary career with *The Anarchist's Bible*. Contemporary society also viewed as equally disruptive the whole group of 'angry young men' who made a point of attacking everything that was traditionally held sacred.

The traditionalists' worst suspicions were confirmed the year after the banning of Jaeger's book, when Christian Krohg, in his novel *Albertine*[28], attacked a well-established institution which was commonly accepted by the middle classes: that of official prostitution. They considered it a necessary evil, in that it acted as a protection for their well-brought-up young daughters, whose virtue had to be maintained at all costs. *Albertine* was proscribed, but Krohg, who was not only a bachelor of law but also a member of one of the country's most illustrious families, escaped with a fine. He continued his campaign with a vast painting entitled *Albertine in the Police Doctor's Waiting Room*[29], based on an incident described in the novel. Krohg was in every way one of the central figures of the bohemian movement, and it was he who edited their newspaper *The Impressionist*[30].

There were furious debates over glasses of whisky and soda, ranging from discussions about Determinism, the doctrine to which these Naturalists subscribed, to, paradoxically enough, the right of free men to live (and also take) their lives as they saw fit. This involved freeing themselves from the shackles of the Church and religion, but the discussion that always produced the greatest flow of rhetoric was that concerned with the doctrine of free love.

There were of course other discussions about society itself and man's place in it, as well as plans for the new and more egalitarian system which was to take the place of the old one when that had finally fallen. Their aim was to reveal the human truths that lay behind the façade of contemporary society. It was the painter's duty to paint the realities of the time.

Personal tragedies, syphilis, suicide, alcoholism and hopelessly entangled relationships with women were the price that the bohemians had to pay in order to practise what they preached. They were completely ostracized by the rest of society, but they found little privacy in their own cramped environment, where everyone knew everything about everybody else.

Munch was finally introduced into bohemian society by his artist friends and their teacher, Christian Krohg. He made many close friends there and soon adapted to their restless life-style. It would indeed have been strange if the young Munch had remained unaffected by this group of deeply committed young rebels, however few in number they may have been.

Nevertheless, the shy and retiring Munch felt, and indeed was, the odd man out. One of the many bohemian writers, and an avid practitioner of the group's ideals, was Herman Colditz, and this man's attempt at writing a totally honest autobiography makes him an invaluable source of information. In his book, *Kjaerka, a Studio Interior*[31] (1888), he paints a picture of Edvard Munch (Nansen), whom he calls a 'repulsive idiot' who 'spends the whole day boring people with his endless talk about paintings' (see quotation on page 48. An extract from a novel by Herman Colditz).

It was a very tough environment for such a sickly young man, and the

55

And then there was Hans Jaeger—possibly the thing that saddens me most. I almost hated him. Deep down I thought he was right —but even so! Munch, 1889/90[4]

At that time I myself had the opportunity of buying the Hans Jaeger portrait, which Munch was unhappy with and which he was going to overpaint because of the cost of the canvas; that is to say, about six to eight kroner, but money was scarce in those days and I could see no way of getting my hands on such an enormous sum. Jappe Nilssen, 1911[5]

*55 **Two Bohemian Friends**, c.1890
Pastel
Private Collection

*56 **Gunnar Heiberg**, c.1890
Crayon drawing, 73.5 x 59.5 cm.
Private Collection

57 **Tête-à-tête** (Jensen-Hjell and Inger), c.1884
Oil on canvas, 65.5 x 75.5 cm.
Oslo Kommunes Kunstsamlinger, OKK 340

*58 **A Fight In the Studio**, 1881/2
Oil on cardboard, 47 x 63.5 cm.
Oslo Kommunes Kunstsamlinger, OKK 628

56

57

58

59

We [Munch and Vigeland] were often together in the 90s; I remember sitting in 'the Grand' with him one Christmas Eve until ten o'clock, then he went home to his sister etc. and I went up to Pilestredet and went to sleep on the floor.
> An extract from the diary of Gustav Vigeland, the Norwegian sculptor, dating from the 1930s[7]

His Girl Kindling the Stove shows a marvellously intense depth of feeling . . . Edvard Munch's picture reveals qualities which can never be taught, but it has shortcomings that can easily be rectified if the will to do so is there . . . (see Plate 68)
> Gunnar Heiberg, 1883[8]

An extract from a contemporary novel by Herman Colditz, Kjaerka, a Studio Interior, written in 1888. In an imaginary conversation, Nansen (Edvard Munch) discusses Moen (Gustav Wentzel): What irritates me is the way in which he sits and struggles over those dreadful pictures of his; I can do in days what he takes months to do, and get results that are a thousand times better. His trouble is that he doesn't paint with his head— God knows, he might just as well be mending a hole in a pair of gumboots. He says that I don't work; but I work until I make myself ill and unable to sleep at night if I'm really involved in something—I become a complete nervous wreck—I really do suffer . . .[9]

The first picture of a woman in love I gave to Hans Jaeger. He had it on the wall of his cell, number 19. He describes it beautifully in The Impressionist. I did it in 1888, it was a big picture and certainly a very fine one.   Munch to Jens Thiis, 1933[10]

Hans Jaeger describes this lost painting, which he calls Hulda, as being of a woman . . . life-size, naked to the hips and lying back on the bed with both hands behind her head and her elbows stretched out on either side . . . her dark hair hanging dishevelled over one shoulder.[11]

Since that picture has been hawked round exhibitions for years without finding a buyer, it occurs to us that the drunken girl should long ago have slept it all off, and that in any case Nasjonalgalleriet is not the right place for her to do it in . . . After all that we have seen and experienced of Thiis since he became director, he is clearly not the level-headed and unbiased man that we had hoped he would be in his new and demanding post.
> An extract from an article in the newspaper Aftenposten in 1909, after Jens Thiis had bought The Day After for Nasjonalgalleriet.[12]

principles preached by those around him were diametrically opposed to those prevailing in Dr. Christian Munch's puritanical middle-class home. Their heathen way of life both fascinated and repelled the young Munch. He may well have been appalled by their godlessness, but he listened nonetheless to their needle-sharp discussions concerning the latest ideas like, Determinism, Socialism and Anarchism, and their talk of freedom for women and of free love. He also participated, in his rather distant way, in some of the more heated debates. Everyone who knew Munch speaks of his ability to observe and to listen, and, despite his apparent remoteness, he could suddenly cut in on a conversation with his ironic, often self-mocking comments and his concise use of paradox, putting the whole discussion into perspective. His sensitive nature certainly reacted to the fate of his friends[32], very few of whom lived to see old age. 'Thou shalt write thy life' was the first of their commandments, and their ninth and last was 'Thou shalt take thy life', an order which many of them were to obey. Munch witnessed many personal tragedies and he saw at first hand many of his friends being gradually destroyed by life. The bohemians' plea for full artistic freedom must have echoed his own sentiments entirely, and their fight for spiritual freedom would also have appealed to him, but he was still deeply attached to his home, as well as being very close to his family, of whom he was always very proud. As a result he can therefore have felt little inclination to follow the bohemians' second precept: 'Thou shalt sever thy family roots'. He always retained a certain shy, somewhat aristocratic attitude towards his companions' rather uncouth life-style. And yet it is clear that the colourful way in which they lived attracted the voyeur in him, and also provided the raw material which enabled him to become what he wished to be—and what he indeed became—in his own words a portrayer of 'the modern life of the soul'.

*59 **The Day After, 1894**
  Oil on canvas, 115 x 152 cm.
  Nasjonalgalleriet, Oslo

60 Detail of No. 59
  (The first version, from 1886, was destroyed in a fire)

61 **The Painter Jensen-Hjell**, 1885
Oil on canvas, 190 x 100 cm.
Private Collection

62 **Sigbjorn Obstfelder**, 1896
Lithograph, 36 x 27.5 cm.
Oslo Kommunes Kunstsamlinger, OKK 818
Ref. G. Schiefler No. 78a

63 **The Hands**, 1895
Lithograph, 48 x 29 cm.
Oslo Kommunes Kunstsamlinger, OKK 196
Ref. G. Schiefler No. 35

64 **Inheritance**, 1897/99
Oil on canvas, 141 x 120 cm.
Oslo Kommunes Kunstsamlinger, OKK 11

62

63

64

Whether anyone has covered themselves with glory or dishonour through this purchase is still to early to judge.
Jens Thiis replying to the *Aftenposten* article in another newspaper, *Verdens Gang*.[13]

Hans Dedekam complains that *the Art Gallery, apart from the pictures that it bought at the exhibition, has been unable to secure an example of Munch's latest colour period.*[14]

It does not even have a properly prepared ground; it is just daubed straight onto the canvas. It almost looks as though it has been painted with the colours that were left over on the palette from another painting. Various of these splotches have landed on the face, amongst them a speck of white which represents the one and only eye, which the painter has neglected to depict, giving us instead the impressionistic effect of the white reflection from a monocle. It is Impressionism carried to its extreme. A travesty of art. SS on the portrait of Jensen-Hjell, 1885[15]

Werenskiold went white with anger because I had exhibited that picture. Munch to Henning Gran[16]

. . . Munch writes poetry with colour. He has taught himself to see the full potential of colour in art . . . His use of colour is above all lyrical. He feels colours and he reveals his feelings through colours; he does not see them in isolation. He does not just see yellow, red and blue and violet; he sees sorrow and screaming and melancholy and decay. Sigbjørn Obstfelder, 1893[17]

At that time there must have been a lot of things to attract the eye of a painter . . . the strange light that illuminated all those night-time meetings that took place in every imaginable sort of café, the lips mouthing defiant words, heedless of restraint or consequence, often overbearing and brutal as only Norwegians can be, vast shadows of misery, impotence and shabbiness— spirits straining for fulfilment, striving in vain to be great, complete, unique. And at the centre of all the faces there would be Jaeger, whose logic was as sharp as a scythe and as cold as an icy blast, but whose one burning ambition nevertheless must have been for all men to be able to emerge from the darkness and every-where enjoy as rich and fulfilling a life as possible, wherever they lived. Sigbjørn Obstfelder, 1896[18]

65

66

Copying Nature. We can never hope to duplicate Nature anyway —therefore it is better to express one's own feelings. How could one possibly paint real grief—tears that well up from the depths of a person's soul, like those of the woman I saw crying in the hospital for venereal disease, her arm clutching a pale, naked, sickly child. She had just discovered that her newborn child was doomed to die. Her contorted face, the swollen lips, her bloated crimson chin. Her eyes were mere slits from which rivulets of tears were flowing—and her reddish purple nose.

That anguish-racked face had to be painted the way I saw it then against the green walls of the hospital. And the inquiring, suffering eyes of the child I had to paint just as I saw them then staring out of the tiny, pallid, yellow body—as white as the white sheet on which it lay. So I had to ignore a lot of other things such as the effects of truth to light, which is relative. Large areas of the picture were like a poster—wide expanses of nothingness. But I hoped to make the best parts, the ones meant to convey the picture's true message of pain, something even more sublime.

And then the public all laughed at the picture, saying that it was blatantly immoral, and I was once more destined to be mocked and martyred. I knew that the accusation of immorality would cause me pain, even though I had intended it to be a highly moral work. And I knew that I would be branded like a common criminal. Munch[19]

When someone comes to describe that era, who will be able to do so? It would have to be a Dostoevsky, or a mixture of Krohg, Jaeger and perhaps myself, to be capable of depicting that Russian period in the Siberian town which Christiania was, and for that matter still is. It was a time for blazing new trails, and a testing time for many. Munch[20]

The Bohemians' Nine Commandments

1 Thou shalt write thy life.
2 Thou shalt sever thy family roots.
3 Thou canst not treat thy parents harshly enough.
4 Thou shalt not touch thy neighbour for less than five kroner.
5 Thou shalt hate and despise all such peasants as Bjørnsterne Bjørnson.
6 Thou shalt never wear celluloid cuffs.
7 Thou shalt never cease from causing scandal at the Christiania Theatre.
8 Thou shalt never show remorse.
9 Thou shalt take thy life.

The following extracts are taken from the autobiographical notes which Munch made for a projected novel in which he calls himself Nansen and his female admirer Fru Heiberg: *Nansen sat in a heap in the middle of the sofa. How tired he felt—and how lonely. He had wandered the streets until he was nearly dropping, and then finally he had dragged himself up there. Sick, sick and lonely. How he longed to lay his tired head on a nice, soft, woman's breast—breathe in her perfume—listen to her heartbeat. Feel her soft, round breasts up against his chin.[21]*

Nansen is visiting one of the girls at Vika and thinking of Fru Heiberg: *Come back this evening, then, she said. Perhaps, he replied. She really was too revolting. And the mental picture of Fru Heiberg was far more sedutive, far more tempting than ever. He clenched his teeth. He suddenly felt an overwhelming feeling of hatred—he did not exactly know against whom—but he felt it as strongly as if she had rejected him.[22]*

You are like a woman passing between two lines of men who are stretching out their hands towards your naked body. Munch[23]

65 **Young Man and Whore** (Edvard Munch and Rose), c.1895
   Watercolour and charcoal, 50 x 47.5 cm.
   Oslo Kommunes Kunstsamlinger, OKK 2445

66 **The Hands,** 1893
   Oil on canvas, 89 x 76.5 cm.
   Oslo Kommunes Kunstsamlinger, OKK 192

4:The Naturalist

We cannot all paint nails and twigs

Naturalism was a religion, and we were its fanatical adherents. We firmly believed that a wet Wednesday afternoon in Lakke-gaten was infinitely more poetical, from an artistic point of view, than A Bridal Procession in Hardanger.   Frits Thaulow[2]

It would certainly be wrong to ignore Krohg's influence on me completely—what I mean to say is that I could not possibly be thought of as one of his pupils . . . He was an excellent teacher, and just the great interest he showed was enough to encourage me —and during that short time [when Munch attended Krohg's art school in 1882] *I certainly learnt quite a lot from him.*
Munch to Jens Thiis, in the 1930s[3]

67 **Sister Inger,** 1892
   Oil on canvas, 172 x 122.5 cm.
   Nasjonalgalleriet, Oslo

68 **Girl Kindling the Stove,** 1883
   Oil on canvas, 97 x 66 cm.
   Private Collection

68

In 1882, when Munch was nineteen, he and six other young painters,[33] all roughly the same age, rented a studio opposite the Parliament building.[34] The studio next door belonged to Christian Krohg, who was a civil servant's son, a lawyer and a writer, and was the most important artistic figure in Christiania during the 1880s. Even though the young painters regarded him as 'an old academic',[35] they were still grateful for any advice that the controversial thirty-year-old artist might give them.

Munch claims in an undated letter to Jens Thiis that Krogh had only given him instruction for three months. But there is evidence to suggest that his memory is at fault and that Krohg advised him for much longer than that. In later life Munch tended to stress the part played by Hans Heyerdahl in his artistic development, saying: 'It would be true to say that I owe more to Heyerdahl than Krohg.'[36] Admittedly he did also add that 'as a teacher he (Krohg) was excellent', but he was loathe to accept that he had ever been a pupil of Krohg's.

It is quite certain that as an artist, and possibly to an even greater extent as a person and a writer, Krohg had a special significance for the young Munch. He stood at the very heart of the bohemian movement and the storms of protest caused by his novel *Albertine* and the painting associated with it have already been discussed. An interesting footnote to this incident is that Munch always maintained strenuously that he had painted one of the figures in *Albertine*.[37]

When Munch exhibited one of his earliest paintings (*Girl Kindling the Stove*), Krohg used words like 'superb'[38] and 'overwhelming'. Later on he was to spring repeatedly to Munch's defence, saying that the young artist was without doubt the representative of the 'Third generation'[39] and that he expected great things of him. He called him 'an Impressionist[40]—the only one we have', but always with a slight note of envy. In 1891 he defended Munch's painting *Evening*,[41] also known as *Melancholy*, making particular mention of the yellow boat that appears in it. He said that he had seen in a flash that the picture 'almost threateningly presages a new form of artistic vision'. Even by 1891 he saw that Munch had affinities with Symbolism. Munch 'makes Nature subservient to mood and rearranges it to better express its essential qualities'.[42]

The fact that in the summer of 1889 Munch became godfather to Christian Krohg's son, Per,[43] at Åsgårdstrand shows the close relationship that had developed between teacher and pupil. Krohg's influence can be clearly seen in several paintings that Munch did in the 1880s, such as *Morning* (1884) (Plate 73), not only in their naturalistic composition but also in his choice of subject. His main concern, however, was with purely artistic problems, particularly those of colour, and although his pictures bore traces of naturalist influence, they lacked the social awareness of Krohg's 'Seamstress' paintings. These works of social realism were so called because the critics unfeelingly called all girls of a certain class 'seamstresses',[44] regardless of whether or not they sewed. Nevertheless, the reddish-haired girl whom Munch has depicted in his painting would have come from exactly that kind of background. He shows her sitting deep in thought, half-way through putting on her stockings, contemplating the long day that lies ahead of her; and yet, unlike Krohg, Munch is not trying to make any kind of social statement. On the contrary, the scene has a bright, happy feeling, with the glow of early morning shining in on the white bedclothes and bathing the fair-skinned young girl in light. He is concerned with the artistic possibilities of the subject, not the girl's unhappy place in society. The clear morning light casts

69

70

56

We were all very fond of Krohg and thought him an outstanding painter. As a teacher he was excellent, and we all gained a great deal of encouragement from the interest he showed in our work . . . I painted several of my best heads before he corrected me.
Munch to Jens Thiis, in the 1930s[4]

Munch's art heralds almost menacingly a new view of art, serious and severe. It is related to Symbolism, the latest direction in French art.   Christian Krohg[5]

Something that I have always had and which Krohg lacks—which makes me the complete opposite of him—is a nervous, broken way of handling colour.   Munch to Jens Thiis[6]

We, the generation of Norwegian painters to which I belong, are not Impressionists—unfortunately. We can only stand on the Mount and look into the Promised Land.   Christian Krohg[7]

But neither can one achieve mastery by dreaming. Just because someone like Munch shows signs of possessing an outstanding gift for painting, which some people would even consider to merit the word genius, there is no reason why he should be spared the hard task of making himself intelligible to others. If a person has something valid to offer, he must find a means of expressing it in a way that more than just a handful of individuals can understand . . . Munch does have the potential for genius. But there is also a danger that his talent will be wasted . . .
Andreas Aubert, 1886[8]

an unreal warmth over such mundane objects as a carafe and a glass. The simple external reality has to compete with an overall mood, the artist's sole concern, which he creates by the juxtaposition of his own imaginary colours in great luminous blocks. Already in this early work we can see how Munch assembles colours and details in the subject itself at the middle of the picture.

Even this 'straightforward' seamstress offended both the critics and the general public, who found 'the subject and its treatment in extremely poor taste',[45] and criticized it on the grounds that it was 'just like a sketch', words that were to dog Munch for years to come: they were even used to describe pictures that he had taken months, even a year, to complete. A few people, though, amongst them the best known artists of the older generation, were able to understand the true merits of his use of colour, and one of them, Frits Thaulow, bought the painting for 100 kroner.

Thaulow, who was a distant relation[46] of Munch, also became an important figure in the young artist's life when, in the summer of 1883, he invited him to join the group of young painters who attended his 'Open air Academy' at Modum.[47] Thaulow was a self-proclaimed Naturalist, and together with Erik Werenskiold and Christian Krohg he worked hard to provide greater opportunities for artists in Christiania. He believed that young Norwegian artists should have a chance to see contemporary French art, and he sent several of them to Paris at his own expense.[48] In fact, he himself had close connections with French art, being, amongst other things, brother-in-law to Paul Gauguin.[49]

In March 1884 Thaulow wrote to Munch's father[50] and suggested that Edvard should go to France 'to see the Paris Salon'. Even before his trip to Paris, the work that Munch had done that year (1884) showed a considerable widening of the twenty-one-year-old's talent. In the portrait of his sister Inger (Plate 47), he has achieved an extraordinary feeling of space, and he has also succeeded in giving the figure an almost three-dimensional quality by the use of subtle shading between her Confirmation dress and the background, by his treatment of the hands, and by the meticulous attention to detail in his painting of the head, which shines out at us in three-quarter profile.

But the work that really caused a sensation and created the first full-scale scandal was his portrait of the painter Jensen-Hjell (Plate 61). The sheer size of the painting (c. 190 × 100 cm) was in itself a gesture of defiance that typified the cheerful, supercilious character of the elegant, yet shabby, arrogant and self-assertive bohemian. The free, impressionistic style, the almost impudent dash of white on the monocle that represented the eye, the subject's casual bearing, 'as though he were a Spanish grandee'[51] in Jens Thiis's words, were all bound to produce some kind of reaction. Some called it a travesty of art;[52] other said: 'The picture has made people laugh just like a caricature does; perhaps that is its sole purpose.' The whole thing was 'A

71

*69 Country Road, 1891–92
     Oil on canvas, 85 x 91 cm.
     Oslo Kommunes Kunstsamlinger, OKK 1111

 70 Evening, 1888
     Oil on canvas, 37 x 75 cm.
     Private Collection

 71 Drawing for No. 69
     Indian ink, 17 x 24 cm.
     Oslo Kommunes Kunstsamlinger, OKK 129

moral scandal, a disgraceful episode for which the selection committee, who have allowed this kind of picture to appear in public, must also be held responsible.'

In 1882 Krohg had painted his full-length portrait of Johan Sverdrup. To pay such a provocative tribute to the Left's controversial leader, who had not as yet become Prime Minister, was bad enough, but that painting was considered quite outrageous. Undoubtedly, though, the portrait of Sverdrup (and the example of Manet) provided Munch with the inspiration for his portrait of Jensen-Hjell, the forerunner of a whole series of full-length portraits. It is also interesting to note that in this painting he has already discovered the basic technique which he was to use in the majority of his work, namely the neutral, empty background with a strongly defined line between the floor and the wall, with possibly the hint of a corner. When Munch in later years called these portraits 'the guardians of my art' perhaps this portrait of his bohemian friend should not be considered to be representative. But at that time the only protection Munch had was that of his close friends and one or two of the older painters, who realized that he was the best of his contemporaries.

During these years of penury Munch adopted the strategy of painting portraits on condition that the sitter paid for the paints and the canvas—and

72 **Spring Day on Karl Johan Street**, 1891
Oil on canvas, 80 x 100 cm.
Bergen Billedgalleri

73 **Morning**, 1884
Oil on canvas, 96.5 x 103.5 cm.
Rasmus Meyers Samlinger, Bergen

E.Munch 1884

73

Everything about your son confirms me in my belief that he possesses a rare artistic talent, something that interests me greatly. It is for this reason alone, and not because we are related, that I am keen for him to have a chance to see the Paris Salon . . . I can arrange a return trip there, using a ship from Antwerp, for 300 kroner, a sum of money which, if used intelligently, will be sufficient for a stay, whose sole purpose will be that of studying art. I wrote to your son's teacher, Christian Krohg, and he has replied that a trip to Paris would be of great benefit to Munch, and would do much to foster his development, helping him to concentrate more. Frits Thaulow to Munch's father, 1884[9]

The North's most interesting painter.
The German artist Fritz von Uhde, describing Munch to Thaulow[10]

also a decent evening meal at 'the Grand'. It was a method of payment that Munch often made use of in order to give himself the necessary motivation. And he also had a favourite waiter whom he paid in paintings: little else is known about this man, but he must certainly have amassed a considerable art collection.

In the spring of 1885 Munch went to Paris at Frits Thaulow's expense and stayed there a couple of weeks. It is hard to say what effect this short stay had on him, or whether it affected his choice of subject or his method of painting. At best, we can only guess at what he saw; he himself wrote home[53] to say that he had been to 'the Salon and the Louvre', but we should bear in mind that he had almost certainly seen examples of French Impressionist painting before his trip—Paul Gauguin, for example, had shown three pictures[54] at the same autumn exhibition as Munch in 1884. It would also seem likely that Frits Thaulow, as well as telling his young protégé about his brother-in-law, would also have shown him examples of his work. Some years later Munch was to be given the nickname of 'the Norwegian Bizarro',[55] a pun on the Norwegian mis-spelling of 'Pissarro' but we have now no way of knowing whether he was acquainted with the work of that artist at the time. Even in the 1880s, the heyday of Naturalism in Christiania, Impressionism and its theories were comparatively well known.

Munich was no longer the artist's Mecca; now it was Paris. But, even so, until 1885 Munch had basically been a naturalistic painter, at the same time striving to capture reality and achieve technical proficiency. There was no future, however, in doctrinaire Naturalism.

Thaulow, himself a Naturalist, had already realized this in 1883, when he suggested that Munch should 'have a chance to see the Paris Salon', by which he meant primarily a chance to see modern French art. In *The Dance*[56] and *Tête-à-Tête*, both painted before his trip to Paris, Munch has succeeded in capturing a fleeting moment in time. The rapid flecks of colour from the rapid brushstrokes, the fragmented contours, both give a feeling of life and shimmering movement.

1886 was the year of Munch's great breakthrough, when he painted three pictures that have always been regarded as among his greatest. Today only one, *The Sick Child*, still survives in its original version;[57] the other two, *The Day After* and *Puberty* were both lost in fires, the first in a storeroom and the second in a student's lodgings.[58]

A letter that Munch sent to his aunts, in which he made no attempt to hide the fact that he was very glad to get 750 kroner from the insurance company for five paintings which had been burnt, gives a good indication of the low state of his finances. Besides, he knew that the pictures could be replaced, and he painted them all again. *The Sick Child*, for example, the original version of which is now in Nasjonalgalleriet in Oslo, he painted no less than six times,[59] sometimes doing several versions in the space of a single year, although there are few other subjects that he re-worked so often. That work marked a turning point in his career, and each time he repeated it, it was with variations. Towards the end of his life he painted it again, because he wanted to renew his contacts with the past and 'rid myself of a slight feeling of flatness in my art'.[60]

Leif Østby[61] has analyzed *The Sick Child* and shown how the squareness of the canvas is repeated in the pillow and the shape that the figures make with the fold in the bedspread, and how the diagonals intersect at the point where the hands meet. Detail is reduced to a minimum, and perspective is unimportant; it is the figures themselves which must create a feeling of space. Colour contrasts and the interaction of flat surfaces further contribute to the illusion; at the age of twenty-three, Munch had already anticipated the techniques of Cubism. It is no mere coincidence that the artist, long after the heyday of Cubism, himself used the work 'cubistic' to describe his early work.

The Sick Child marks the point at which Munch finally solved the technical problems of his art, and he repeated his success in the five other versions that he painted, as well as in engravings of the same subject. It may seem surprising that, in the catalogue, he called the painting which had caused him so much work, a 'Study', but that was almost certainly done in anticipation of those critics who he knew very well would call anything he did 'unfinished' and 'sketchy'.

To the astonishment of the public, who greeted his work with derision, and also to the amazement of the critics, *The Sick Child*, a picture 'executed with none of the necessary preparation', was hung in a very prominent place. 'If one looks at it from a distance[62] one can just about distinguish the vague outline of what the picture shows, but it is like peering through fog . . . The nearer one gets to it, the further away it seems, until finally all one is left with are random blobs of colour . . . the ravings of a madman. It's almost impossible to walk by the picture without seeing someone standing there laughing at it.' But the cruellest and most insensitive criticism of this moving and deeply-felt portrayal of a young redhaired girl's encounter with death was that the picture 'is completely devoid of any spiritual meaning'.[63]

That young girl's farewell to life is paralleled by another painting which Munch completed in the same year and in which he depicts a young girl's anguished first meeting with the mysteries of adult life that she senses lie before her. In *Puberty*[64] he has not painted the expectation but the very real agonies of uncertainty that torment her slim body, as she sits with her knees together and her thin arms hiding the first stirrings of womanhood. Her only surroundings are the linen sheets, flecked with blood, and the sketchy outline of the bed on which she is seated; our whole interest is instinctively

The only influences in The Sick Child *and* Spring *were the ones that came from my home: those pictures were my childhood and my home. Only someone who knew the conditions at home could understand why there can be no conceivable chance of any other place having played a part in their birth; my home was to my art as the midwife is to her children. I remember it well—those were the days of pillows, of sickbeds, of feather quilts. But I firmly believe that scarcely any of these painters has ever experienced the full grief of their subject as I did in* The Sick Child. *Because i was not just I who was suffering then: it was all my nearest and dearest as well.* Munch to Jens Thiis[11]

When I first saw the sick child—her pallid face and the vivid red hair against the white pillow—I saw something that vanished when I tried to paint it. I ended up with a picture on the canvas which, although I was pleased with it, bore little relationship to what I had seen. I painted the scene many times in the space of one year, scratching it out, just letting the paint flow, trying endlessly to recapture what I had seen the first time—the pale, transparent skin against the linen sheets, the trembling lips, the shaking hands. Munch[12]

With The Sick Child *my painting took a whole new turn. That picture marked a complete breakthrough in my art, and provided the inspiration for the majority of my later works. No other painting in Norway has ever caused such a violent outburst of moral indignation. On the opening day, when I went into the room where it hung, there were crowds of people packed round it—and there were sounds of derisive laughter.*

When I went out into the street, the young Naturalist painters were standing there, together with their leader, Wentzel, the most fêted artist of the day . . . 'Pretentious rubbish!' he screamed in my face. 'Congratulations on a truly great painting,' said Ludwig Meyer, one of the very few who had anything good to say about the picture at all. Aftenposten *really went to town with their insults and abuse.* Munch[13]

What delicate colours! One wants to whisper 'Hush, quiet!' to the people talking round one—Munch should have called his picture Hush!*.*

Jaeger on the subject of *The Sick Child*, the day before he was due in jail to serve a sixty-day sentence.[14]

For Munch's own sake I would have preferred it if his sick child had been rejected. Not because it reveals his talent any less clearly than his earlier work, but because it shows that he is slowing down his own self-development. In its present form, that Study *is merely some sort of half-finished sketch. He has tired himself out in its execution, and the result is an abortion, a failure like those that Zola described so well in* L'Oeuvre.

Andreas Aubert in *Morgenbladet*, 1886[15]

74 **The Sick Child**, 1885/86
Oil on canvas, 119.5 x 118.5 cm.
Nasjonalgalleriet, Oslo

75 Detail of No. 74

76 **Line Dedichen,** 1884
   Pencil drawing, 23 x 17 cm.
   Private Collection

76

< 75

drawn to the young girl herself and her eyes, opened wide in fear, which meet our own. As is so often the case with Munch's portraiture, he has chosen to show the subject head-on, thereby deepening our understanding of her character and enabling us to gain a great insight into her mood.

The light shines in from the left, and the young girl casts a forbidding shadow over the white bed and wall, a shadow that perhaps seems even more menacing in the later lithograph and engraving. As in the case of *The Day After*, the original of *Puberty* has been lost, but both pictures were re-painted by Munch at the beginning of the 1890s.

It seems incredible that *Puberty* (Plate 103) could have been painted by a young man, but it argues much for Munch's powers of understanding and his ability to identify with the emotional states of others. As we have already seen, he was able to write about his dying sister's sufferings with great perception (page 34), and this rare gift of understanding is revealed not least in his many interpretations of woman and man's relations with her.

The Day After (Plate 59) was first painted in 1886, but, although the original has been lost, an old photograph[65] of it shows that the later version differs quite considerably. The picture of the young girl asleep, dead to the world after the previous night's party, is beautifully painted and drawn, and the artist has included several clues to what has happened. The bottles and glasses on the table in the foreground, as well as the untidy bed, give the work a much more defined quality than *Puberty*, but although the upper part of the girl's body and her sleeping, yet deeply expressive face, are very carefully portrayed, her skirt and legs are fairly sketchily painted.

The painting *Hulda*[66] that Hans Jaeger had with him in his cell and about which he quarrelled with the prison chaplain, was an early version of this theme. In *The Impressionist* Jaeger writes that she was 'life-size, naked to the hips and lying back on the bed with both hands behind her head and her elbows stretched out on either side . . . her dark hair hanging dishevelled over one shoulder.' Munch himself says that the first painting which Jaeger had on his wall was the first version of *Loving Woman*,[67] later to become known as *Madonna*.

In these pictures, not least in *The Sick Child* (Plate 74), we can see how Munch was gradually growing away from the Naturalists. Even the young artists had difficulty in following him, and a remark by one of the true 'realists', Gustav Wentzel, who at that time was well on the way to full recognition, indicates the position. He and Munch met one day on the stairs, and Wentzel blurted out: 'Shame on you, I had no idea that you were going to start painting that kind of thing. That sort of rubbish.' 'Well,' replied Munch, 'we cannot all paint nails and twigs.'[68]

Munch continued to do paintings of friends, literary men, but the days of summer inspired him also to paint *The Meadow of Flowers*, now in Nasjonalgalleriet, Oslo, and *Evening at Vrengen* (Plate 78), a painting of his sister Laura in the peace of a summer's evening. In the latter the composition is new,[69] with the figure of his sister appearing in the forefront of the left-hand corner, truncated, a technique that Western artists had copied from Japanese coloured woodcuts. The yellow hat of the title by which the picture is also known dominates this highly evocative scene, which is in shades of blue, yellow and mauve. However, despite the harmonious and peaceful atmosphere that Munch has created, the influence of Krohg and his style of painting can be clearly detected. And yet Krohg was well aware that Munch was beginning to assert his artistic independence, and he wrote: 'Deep down, Munch's art has always been the same, and now it is beginning to assert its true contempt for realism.'[70]

His brief trip to Paris[71] in 1885 succeeded in making Munch aware of the great paintings of the past, but, apart from that, he learned little that he could not have learned at home. But in 1889 he returned once more, to stay for several years, and he also travelled south to the sun and blue seas of Nice, 'a fairly large town on the Mediterranean, which is a favourite spot for artists because of its natural beauty', as he himself says in a rather sarcastic reply to Bjørnson,[72] who begrudged the young bohemian Munch his State scholarship.

Many years were to elapse between the day Jaeger took Munch's painting of *Hulda* to prison with him, and the day that Munch finally fulfilled

77

78

Jaeger's commandment to 'paint thy life'. Before that could happen, he had to find his way out of the cul-de-sac of Naturalism and develop his own individualistic way of painting, and, ironically, the men who helped him in this were themselves naturalistic painters: Krohg, Werenskiold and Thaulow.[73] These three were the first to recognize the full extent of Munch's talent and his artistic potential, giving him their wholehearted support and protecting him from the bigotry of the critics and the condemnation of the public.[74]

77 **Arrival of the Mailboat**, 1890
Oil on canvas, 98 x 130 cm.
Private Collection

78 **Evening at Vrengen**, 1888
Oil on canvas, 75 x 101 cm.
Private Collection

5 : 1899 - A Year of Decision

There should be no more paintings of people reading and women knitting

And I am living with the dead—my mother, my sister, my grandfather and, above all, with my father. All the memories, even of the smallest details, come flooding back. I see him now as I last saw him while he was still alive, that day, four months ago, when he said good-bye to me on the quayside. We were rather shy with each other—reluctant to show just how deeply we felt the sorrow of parting, and how fond we were of each other. My father did not want me to know how he grieved for me, how he lay awake at night agonizing over my way of life, heartbroken because I did not share his beliefs.   Munch, 1890[1]

In Spring—*with the sick girl and her mother sitting by the open window, bathed in the sunlight which streams through it—I took my leave of Impressionism and Realism.*   Munch, 1890[2]

Those at home, my aunt, my brother and my sisters, believe that death is but a sleep, and that my father can see and hear . . . He could not understand my aims in life and I could not understand the things that he valued most highly . . . Did you know what things grieved me, did you realize why I sometimes treated you so harshly? I was not alone. She was with me, she was in my blood.
Munch, 1889[3]

*79 **Moonlight (Night in St. Cloud)**, c.1893
Pastel, 80 x 75 cm.
Private Collection

*80 Léon Bonnat's Studio

80

It often happens that the strands of a person's life are drawn together and converge at a certain point, only to separate again and go off in different directions.

Edvard Munch reached that point in 1889. He broke loose from the past, and both his artistic and his private life took on a whole new turn. Family ties were loosened as a result of his father's death in November, and it was also during that period that Munch began to feel himself able, and willing, to look back seriously at the difficult years of his childhood and to portray the traumas of his early years. The way forward was revealed to him one *Night in St. Cloud*, but to start with he was completely captivated by and caught up in his new French surroundings.

A number of Norway's best and most highly-regarded artists[75] supported the controversial twenty-six-year-old in his efforts at obtaining a State scholarship.[76] Munch himself made great efforts to further his own cause and show what he stood for—and where he stood. In April he opened his first one-man exhibition,[77] in which he exhibited a total of 110 paintings—a representative selection of everything he had done up to that time.

Included in this exhibition were most of the works that we have already dealt with, but there were also several new ones, two of which deserve particular mention. One is the portrait of Hans Jaeger (Plate 53). He shows the leader of the bohemians sitting in the corner of a sofa, a glass of drink in front of him, tired, shivering and disillusioned, a wry smile playing on his lips. He is alone, an outcast from society, and yet he seems strangely at peace, his self-confidence overcoming his feelings of resignation. He may be a loser, but he knows what he stands for.

The whole painting is beautifully executed, particularly in the characterization of the sitter: it typifies the mood of pessimism prevailing at the time. And yet that picture, in a way, marks Munch's final break with Jaeger and his circle of friends. In Paris he gradually began to reject the Naturalism of the 1880s and fall under the spell of the two great new literary and artistic movements of *fin-de-siècle* France: Symbolism and Mysticism.[78]

The other masterpiece from that crucial year is *Spring* (Plate 81), a picture in which Munch himself felt he had finally said goodbye to conventional realism. It was certainly with this painting that he hoped to gain his scholarship and prove that he was capable of doing other things besides the 'unfinished sketch' as people had called *The Sick Child*. It has even been suggested that he was trying to do a sort of academic 'demonstration piece'. But, whatever his motives, we cannot help but admire the different elements in the painting, such as the still life on the table and the way in which the light plays on the curtains and on the pot plants on the window sill. The way in which he has positioned the two figures and the intensity of their interaction give further proof of his genius. Munch was himself ill when he painted this masterpiece of the mother and her sick daughter bathed in the life-giving light of spring, and the whole scene vibrates with the intense insight of one who understands the true meaning of illness.

Inger on the Beach, or *Evening*, as it was originally called (Plate 82), was definitely no academic 'demonstration piece'. *Morgenbladet* called the picture, one of the high points of Norwegian art, 'complete rubbish'.[79] It was also called 'a hoax perpetrated on the public', while another newspaper spoke of 'the casually strewn stones,[80] which seem to be made of some soft, shapeless substance'. And yet we are able to share the experience of the young girl in her white dress and her yellow hat, sitting on the boulders at the water's edge. We can appreciate the warmth of the stones set against the

67

coldness of the sea, the simplification of colour and form, and respond to the juxtaposition of colours and the rhythm binding the whole scene together. Everything that the artist has shown, he himself experienced. Munch painted the scene before his trip to Paris, where he was to listen to the Symbolists' new, simplified form language, perhaps to Gauguin himself.

Paul Gauguin's son,[81] Pola, said of *Spring* that a change of direction was inevitable after such a complete work; it was impossible for Munch to make any further progress along that particular route. Realism had become a diversion, and in *Inger on the Beach* we can see how he eschews any kind of roundabout way—the vivid impressions of his mind go straight to the canvas. The painting was finally bought by Erik Werenskiold, an act which caused a sensation at the time.

Despite all the harsh words, the critics reacted much more positively to that painting, especially in view of what they had said about *Spring* and the portrait of Jaeger. At last Munch began to attract a definite following of admirers and people who believed in him. The most responsible of the critics, Andreas Aubert,[82] wrote rather belatedly 'on request' a strange piece about the picture, full of reservations, despite the fact that he could 'see traces of genius in his talent' and greatly admired the painting's 'fineness, composition and intensity'. He ended by recommending Munch for the scholarship,[83] but 'on the express condition that he find someone capable of teaching him how to draw from life and also that he submit examples of his work after the space of a year'. Surprisingly, Munch fulfilled both of these conditions, and in July he received the scholarship.

That summer he rented the house at Åsgårdstrand for the first time—the house that was to become his 'summer refuge' for the next twenty years. His stays there were to have a deep and lasting influence on his landscape painting, introducing him to the mysterious half-light of the Norwegian summer night and the soft, sinuous curve of the shoreline, a line which, in his own words, was to wind its way through *The Frieze of Life*, bringing unity to the whole.

His first stay in the sleepy and idyllic little fishing village, which only came to life during the hectic summer months, was to be an uneasy one.[84] Åsgårdstrand had long ceased to be the home of prosperous shipowners and sea captains, but it was soon playing host to a variety of artists and writers from the capital. However, despite all the parties and various emotional involvements, Munch succeeded in completing one major work, *An Evening Talk*, now in the Statens museum for Kunst, Copenhagen. The scene shows Munch's sister Inger, her hands clutching a shawl tightly to her body against the cool evening air, talking to the critic Sigurd Bødtker by the verandah steps, whilst in the background the fjord stretches far away into the distance, its waters finally blending with the blue of the sky. It is a rich, thickly painted summer picture, with a bold use of colour and an almost impressionistic feel to it.

We can also see Munch's impressionistic style in his *Military Band on Karl Johan Street*[85] (Plate 90), a painting which he completed before his visit to Paris. It shows a new technique of composition, and a much tighter style. In the sunlit street the band seems to be an impenetrable mass of marching men, advancing relentlessly along the almost deserted thoroughfare, while the whole scene is framed by the dramatic half-figures in the foreground.

By the beginning of October Munch was living in a small hotel in Paris with two other artist friends.[86] He was now a mature artist, face to face with his own times.

Following advice that he had been given, he began to attend the extremely demanding art school run by Léon Bonnat,[87] a strict academic of the old school who had given instruction to a number of the best Norwegian artists,

81 **Spring,** 1889
   Oil on canvas, 169 x 263.5 cm.
   Nasjonalgalleriet, Oslo
   Illustrated on previous page

82 **Inger on the Beach,** 1889
   Oil on canvas, 125 x 162 cm.
   Rasmus Meyers Samlinger, Bergen

70

82

83

and it is clear that Munch really worked hard in order to get the most out of
his stay. Even on the stairs, Bonnat's pupils were faced by the work of one
of the most highly-esteemed artists of the time—a large canvas by Puvis de
Chavannes[88] called *Doux Pays*—whilst in his apartment, their teacher taught
them to appreciate the great works of the past by analysing the many old
masters that hung on his walls.

'Bonnat likes my drawings very much,' Munch wrote home.[89] But when it
came to painting he soon found himself at loggerheads with his teacher: it
was a classic conflict between an academic and a rebel who wanted to paint
things as he, and he alone, saw them. The final break is reputed to have come
after an argument as to whether the white wall behind the model had a
greenish or reddish tinge!

At the turn of the year he moved to St. Cloud, on the outskirts of Paris,
where he formed a very close friendship with the Danish poet Emanuel
Goldstein.[90]

The death of his father had a profound effect on the young Munch. He
made many notes during that autumn and winter of 1889, and we can see

It is even harder to see any merit in Herr Edvard Munch's Evening [Plate 82, Inger on the Beach], which shows a lady holding a yellow straw hat sitting on a pile of stones by the sea- shore . . . Presumably here, too, the lighting is to blame for the painting's sketchy, insubstantial quality; the aimlessness of the scene reaches its high point in the seated woman, a completely lifeless and expressionless figure, as unreal in colour as in shape. The same goes for the artist's depiction of the casually strewn stones, which seem to be made of some soft, shapeless substance . . . All in all, the picture seems to us to have so little artistic merit that we find its inclusion in the exhibition extremely hard to justify. Aftenposten, 5/10/1889[4]

A long beach stretches out towards the interior of the picture and ends in a beautiful and harmonious line. It is sheer music. It winds slowly away towards the stillness of the water, interrupted only by small, subtle features, such as the roof of a house, and a tree, but the artist has not allowed any detailed treatment of the branches to interfere with the line of the painting.
Christian Krohg[5]

Munch is the first painter who turns towards idealism, who dares to make nature, his model, etc. subservient to mood, and to re- arrange them to better express their essential qualities. A truly enchanting picture! Christian Krohg, 1891[6]

You may well not believe me, but there will come a time when you will laugh if someone makes the same objections that you are making now, and you, naturally enough, with the typical fickle- ness of the public, will have forgotten that you ever said such a thing and you will deny it hotly. Christian Krohg[7]

It happened sometimes that I came across a landscape which I wanted to paint, perhaps when I was feeling depressed or perhaps when I was in a good mood. I would go away and fetch my easel, put it up, and paint what I saw. I often produced good paintings that way, but they never turned out the way I wanted. I never succeeded in painting the scene in the way I had seen it, in the mood that I was in at the time. This often happened, and so, when it did, I began to scratch out what I had painted and try to recall my original mood, striving to recapture that first impression.
Munch[8]

But, all the same, I think that we are like two clocks, which were adjusted in St. Cloud and ever since have kept roughly the same time. Emanuel Goldstein to Munch, 1892[9]

84

83 **Evening (Melancholy), 1891**
  Crayon, oil and pencil, 73 x 101 cm.
  Oslo Kommunes Kunstsamlinger, OKK 58

84 **Landscape in St. Cloud, 1890**
  Oil on canvas, 46 x 38 cm.
  Oslo Kommunes Kunstsamlinger, OKK 1109

how, during this difficult period of his life, he was beginning to view his problems from a distance, to understand more fully the patterns in his personal life and evaluate the true significance of his emotional involve- ments. We have already remarked on his gradual alienation from Jaeger and the materialism of the bohemians, and now, under the influence of the new ideas that he had encountered in Paris and with the strict religious atmosphere of his home gone, Munch began to develop a mystical and pantheistic philosophy and a completely different attitude towards life and art.

It was not long before the endless philosophical discussions with his friend Goldstein gave Munch the idea of committing his thoughts to paper.[91] He was later to say of these jottings that they were 'not a diary in the accepted sense of the word; they are partly extracts from the life of my soul, partly poems written as prose . . .'[92]

Goldstein, a couple of years later, wrote in a letter of their 'phonographic quality',[93] and it seems likely that he and Munch had plans to produce a magazine together. These reminiscences from the winter of 1889/90 obviously drew their inspiration from similar writings by Jaeger,[94] and Munch resumed them in 1892 and again later in his life. He eventually rewrote them, expanding and adding to them, and he collected the majority of them in two small booklets under the titles *Origins of the Frieze of Life* and *The Frieze of Life*.

They are important documents, and provide evidence of his fight against Naturalism and all that it implied. One particular extract, which stands out as representing the core of his beliefs, has been described by some art historians as 'Munch's Manifesto',[95] a description which he himself never used. Many scholars have tried to place an exact date on this testament to

85

88

85 **Man and Woman**, c.1890
Ink drawing, 30.2 x 28.5 cm.
Oslo Kommunes Kunstsamlinger, OKK 365A
(On left hand side of the drawing and on the back Munch wrote
several important notes dealing with, amongst other things, the
forthcoming Frieze of Life)

86 **Dr. Munthe reading**, 1882
Pencil drawing, 26 x 20.6 cm. Private Collection

87 **Karen Bjolstad knitting**, 1882
Pencil drawing, 19 x 13 cm. Private Collection

*88 **Emanuel Goldstein**, 1908/9
Lithograph, 27.5 x 24.5 cm.
Oslo Kommunes Kunstsamlinger, OKK 272
Ref. G. Schiefler No. 276

89 **Death at the Helm**, 1893
Oil on canvas, 100 x 120 cm.
Oslo Kommunes Kunstsamlinger, OKK 880

86

87

Extract from Munch's *Manifesto*, 1889. *A strong, bare arm—a
powerful, sunburnt neck—and a young girl laying her head on the
firm muscles of the man's chest. Her eyes are closed, and she
listens open-mouthed to the words that he is whispering into her
long, flowing hair.*

*I should depict the scene as I then saw it, but in a blue mist.
This couple, at that moment, were not themselves: they were
merely one link in the endless chain that joins one generation to
the next. People should understand the sacred, awesome truth
involved, and they should remove their hats as in a church. I
ought to exhibit a whole group of such pictures. There should be
no more paintings of interiors, of people reading and women
knitting. In future they should be of people who breathe, who feel
emotions, who suffer and love.*

*I felt it my duty to paint that scene—it seemed so natural.
Their bodies would take shape and the colours would come alive.*
Munch[10]

*What if modern literature were generally to concern itself more
with the spiritual aspects of life and less with engagements,
dances, trips to the country and misfortunes like that? . . . we
need books which deal more with the individual, and which will,
in that respect, probably bear more relationship to the attitudes
of grown-up people nowadays. We had little experience of the
secret impulses that exist unheeded in the hidden areas of the
soul, or the disorderly confusion of our senses; nor were we able
to take a close look at the fragile world of fantasy within us, or
follow its thoughts and emotions as they wandered through the
unknown. We knew little of the endless, boundless journeys of the
heart and the mind, the mysterious operations of the nervous
system, the whisperings of our blood, the prayers of our bones:
the whole subconscious life of the soul was a closed book.*
Knut Hamsun in *Samtiden*, 1890[11]

*An old fisherman has gone out in his boat on the deep blue sea . . .
the sun is beating down . . . and the sulphurous sail hangs limply
down, as though wilting in the heat. The old man sits slumped,
his hands resting on his lap, his head hanging exhausted on his
chest . . . But at the helm, just where the colours are at their most
venomous, there sits the yellow figure of death, a grinning
skeleton looking at his prey . . .* Franz Servaes[12]

89

Munch's artistic 'conversion', but space here precludes a detailed discussion of the subject. There is, however, definite evidence that he wrote a great many notes during that cold winter in St. Cloud, notes which could almost be called 'confessions of his art'. They are in many ways similar to what he later allowed to be published, albeit in a somewhat revised form. He systematically rejected his earlier philosophy and formulated a new artistic creed: 'There should be no more paintings of people reading and women knitting. In future they should be of people who breathe, who feel emotions, who suffer and love.'

That statement, which gives clear notice of Munch's intention to practise what contemporaries called 'mood painting', has almost a religious ring to it. For the time being, however, not only was he overwhelmed by his new surroundings but he also had a burning desire to master different painting techniques, and for this reason it was to be some time before he was able to carry out his intended programme. But even so, in the peace of St. Cloud he painted a picture which clearly indicated what was to come, called *Moonlight* (*Night in St. Cloud*, Plate 79).

Blue is the predominant colour, with the other tonal shades blending into

90

it in a manner reminiscent of the work of Whistler,[96] and the result—to use the terminology of the time—is a true 'mood painting': a romantic, almost symbolic representation of a moment of quiet reflection. The closed window shuts out the world, while the twin cross shapes give an uneasy reminder of death. Is that Munch perhaps trying to portray his own feelings following the death of his father?

During the autumn months he had come into contact with the works of the French Neo-Impressionists, and he strove to achieve the same illusion of depth as they did by the use of accentuated lines leading towards the 'interior' of the painting, without actually resorting to the use of conventional perspective.

His friends back in Norway were full of admiration for what was, in every respect, a 'new' painting, and the Norwegian poet Vilhelm Krag wrote a poem in praise of it.[97] *Night in St. Cloud* is unique amongst Munch's works from the period around 1890, but in many ways it anticipates his *Frieze of Life*, and the other paintings which he produced in Berlin after 1892.

One sunny spring day I heard the music coming down Karl Johan Street, and it filled me with joy. The spring, the sun, the music, all blended together to make me shiver with pleasure. The music added colour to the colours.

I painted the picture, but I let the colours reverberate with the rhythm of the music. I painted the colours that I saw at that time.

Munch[13]

90 **Military Band on Karl Johan Street**, 1889
  Oil on canvas, 102 x 142 cm.
  Kunsthaus, Zurich

6 : Face to Face with a New Era

Nature lies in the mood of the beholder

A great wave swept over the world—Realism. Nothing existed which could not be demonstrated or explained by means of physics or chemistry—painting and literature consisted solely of things that could be seen by the eye or heard by the ear—it was concerned only with the external shell of Nature. People had become content with the discoveries they had made—they ignored the fact that there were other things to be discovered, even broader avenues to be explored. They had found bacteria, but not what they consisted of. Munch, 1892[1]

The mystical will always be with us—the more it is discovered, the more inexplicable it will become. The new movement, the signs of whose progress can be detected everywhere, will express all those things that for a generation have been suppressed—the whole of that important mystical facet of human nature. It will give free expression to all those subtle nuances that hitherto have only been hinted at in hypotheses. A whole mass of things that cannot be rationalized—newborn thoughts that are still not properly formed. Munch, 1892[2]

*91 **Rue Lafayette,** 1891
Oil on canvas, 92 x 73 cm.
Nasjonalgalleriet, Oslo

92 **Rue de Rivoli,** 1891
Oil on canvas, 80 x 63 cm.
Fogg Museum, Cambridge, U.S.A.

92

1889 was the year of the great Paris World's Fair in honour of the hundredth anniversary of the Revolution. Artists were in the forefront of those who wished to display their talents at this world exhibition, one of whose main attractions was the great Eiffel Tower, itself a symbol of what man could achieve with modern techniques. There was a 'Centennial Exhibition' of post-Revolutionary art, a 'Ten Years' Exhibition' showing contemporary art —and also art forms that were still in their infancy. In the latter there were several works by members of the Norwegian artists' colony in Paris. One man[98] was even reported as having said of the Scandinavians that 'the Norwegian school will soon be renowned throughout Europe'. But amongst the artists named, no mention was made of the one Norwegian artist who really was to achieve universal fame: Edvard Munch. His sole exhibit was the five-year-old *Morning* (Plate 73), and it is probable that this painting was shown only because its owner, Frits Thaulow, lived in Paris.

It was a time of cultural reassessment,[99] when many of the old accepted values and conventions were being called into question. But, above all, it was a period of intense literary activity, and it was in literature and in the many journals and periodicals, which seemed to spring up overnight and then disappear almost as quickly, that the new ideas of the time were first formulated. Broadsheets and pamphlets are always at their most prolific during times of upheaval.

Many of the new theories and concepts that first appeared during the 1880s were inspired by the works of Baudelaire,[100] particularly his work on the philosophy of art and the extraordinary anthology of poems which he had published a generation earlier, *Les Fleurs du Mal*, parts of which were subsequently banned. In this work Baudelaire confronted the Romantic reader of the day with the morbid and the macabre, combined with an evocative sensuality and a deeply-felt lyricism. In a time of ever-increasing Naturalism he preached that the true origins of art lay in man's imagination; it was there that he would find the true harmony which cannot be discovered in the complex and constantly changing world of reality. In a single, fleeting moment of inspiration, an artist can bridge the gap between the disordered and haphazard reality of the human world and the hidden world of beauty beyond it which only our senses can apprehend.

Followed to its logical conclusion, this theory is, in fact, a commendation of those individualistic, subjective artists who take it upon themselves to interpret the world and their surroundings as they see them at any given moment. A form of acute sensory perception which can be applied to any object, however mundane.

Poets such as Stéphane Mallarmé,[101] whose portrait Munch painted during a subsequent visit to Paris, and Verlaine[102] and the Belgian Maurice Maeterlinck,[103] were the main protagonists of the literary Symbolist movement. Their—and Baudelaire's—ideas were expounded in a number of intellectual journals and gradually permeated the whole of society, becoming a decisive factor in the development of contemporary art. It was their ideas which lay behind the struggle of the 'Decadents' against Naturalism: that was the name they themselves had adopted and it was under that banner that they published their two journals, *La Décadence* and *Le Décadent*. They sought to reveal the strange and undiscovered areas of man's consciousness, the dark, half-understood side of his inner mind. And in the middle of the 1890s (1896), Sigmund Freud published his theories on *angst*, the basic anxiety that he maintained lay at the back of the human mind, tormenting contemporary society with feelings of uncertainty and insecurity. Later on he developed this theory to conclude that we are all 'Symbolists' in our dream-lives and that we all conceal or interpret the innermost secrets of our psyche by means of symbols.

Already in 1886, three years before Munch arrived in Paris, the Greek Jean Moréas[104] had written the Symbolists' literary manifesto and participated in the publication of their periodical *Le Symboliste*. In a short time, like so many others, he was using his talents as a poet to express, in blank verse, man's deepest sensory experiences, using a completely new form of language and rhythmical cadences.

Painting was particularly influenced by the new movement. Two years before Munch arrived in the French capital, Gauguin[105] and a number of his artist friends had returned to Paris from Pont-Aven in Brittany. Within a couple of years a number of these followers of Gauguin were to group themselves together under the name of the 'Nabis', the Hebrew word for 'Prophets'.[106] They rejected all forms of Naturalism and Impressionism, both old and new, trying to achieve a synthesis of line and form, emphasizing the flatness of their paintings and concentrating on the decorative elements. By the time the Nabis had formed their group, the Symbolist movement was already firmly established in Paris, led by artists such as Odilon Redon, Gustave Moreau,[107] Puvis de Chavannes, and the Belgian Félicien Rops. As a theorist and teacher Moreau was the most important of them, continually urging artists to express their innermost spiritual thoughts in their work. As a painter, he himself tended towards the exotic and the mystical, making extensive use of subjects from Classical mythology and the Bible. His use of bright, almost enamel-like colours, and the strong literary undertones of his work combined to make him a truly 'revolutionary' painter.

From all these theories and influences it was only a short step to a truly religious form of mysticism. Rosicrucianism[108] was initially a feature mainly of the literary scene, but it soon spread to embrace the artistic also. 'Artists and authors are . . . the people who assist at the birth of ideas,' according to its credo: 'they can reveal, at a stroke, the workings of the subconscious . . . theirs is a labour of love in the realms of paradox which lie between the dream world and the real world.'[109]

Some artists became totally immersed in mysticism, haunted by a longing for distant lands and far-off days, experimenting in the occult in an effort to satisfy deep religious longings. Others found solace in nature, interpreting it in their own intensely personal way.

Even though there are traces of these themes in Munch's paintings from the 1890s, he was the least 'literary' artist of them all. In contrast with that of his contemporaries, his work contains very few purely literary elements, and few other artists succeeded as well as he in combining the symbolic with the purely artistic. Although the subject matter of his art is of great importance, the private ordeals of his troubled life lie at its heart, and are communicated to us with a directness that is timeless.

During his prolonged stays in France Munch became increasingly familiar with the artistic and intellectual trends of the day. When he returned to Paris as a famous, or rather notorious modernist, following the furore he had caused in Berlin in 1892 and his productive stay there, he became similarly involved in the French scene.

Munch was no theorist in the French manner, and, because his formal art education had been such a haphazard affair, his knowledge of the theory of art was sketchy. His ideas were primarily those of a painter, and these, combined with his own fantasies, were the essential elements of his work. While he was 'going to school' and painting impressionistic pictures, he spent his second winter in Nice, and in the opening months of 1891 he made a great many entries in his 'little violet book'. As well as being statements of his artistic beliefs they were also confessions of a deeply personal nature. They reveal a colour sense that is far removed from the analytical approach of the Impressionists, and an attitude to reality that differs radically from the doctrines of conventional realism.

Munch succeeded in putting into artistic practice the ideas that lay behind the theories of the Symbolists and other groups. His goal as a painter was to bring them to life in a strictly subjective way and somehow capture the

93

94

LE MORT JOYEUX

95

reaction that he, and he alone, had experienced when first confronted by his subject.

During these years, when he was dividing his time between Paris, Nice and Åsgårdstrand, his art became subject to many external influences, not least those of Neo-Impressionism. One American scholar (Deknatel)[110] has likened his impressionistic paintings to 'a calm and untroubled island among his other works'. Nevertheless, none of these pictures conform with the artistic 'plan of action' which he had formulated that night out in St. Cloud, and another group of works from the same period reveal a change in Munch's choice of subject matter and also in his technique of composition and his use of colour. And yet, at the same time, he was playing the part of an 'art for art's sake' aesthete: in an exhibition that year in Norway he even called the portrait of his sister Inger *Harmony in Black and Violet*. That kind of title would seem to be more in keeping with a painter like Whistler than the Munch of the 1890s that we know—a painter and poet with a message for the world.

Despite illness and financial problems, these were productive years for Munch—as yet he had not fallen under the spell of printmaking. He painted several street scenes in Paris: in one letter he wrote 'I am living in a beautiful room with a balcony', and it was from this balcony that he painted *Rue Lafayette* (Plate 91). The intense, almost blinding light seems to melt the shapes of the people, the carriages and the horses in a blaze of colour, reminiscent of a carefully arranged firework display. Both here and in the more summarily executed *Rue de Rivoli* (Plate 92) everything is in motion: as someone once said, it is as though one is in the age of the motor car rather than the horse and carriage. But the flickering, multi-coloured turmoil of *Rue Lafayette* is held in check by the long line of perspective formed by the

93 **Stéphane Mallarmé**, 1896
Lithograph, 51.2 x 28.9 cm.
Oslo Kommunes Kunstsamlinger, OKK 221
Ref. G. Schiefler No. 79b

94 Sketch for Charles Baudelaire's *Les Fleurs du Mal*, 1896
Indian ink drawing, 28 x 20.5 cm.
Oslo Kommunes Kunstsamlinger, OKK 402

95 **In the Open Air**, 1891
Oil on canvas, 66 x 120 cm.
Oslo Kommunes Kunstsamlinger, OKK 495

railing, finally coming to rest in the gently swirling pattern of the balcony floor.

Back in Norway, he put his new skills into practice once more when he revisited Karl Johan Street, where the last of the bohemians were still spending their time. The shimmering light of his *Spring Day on Karl Johan Street* (Plate 72) recalls the pointillist technique of Seurat, while *A Rainy Day on Karl Johan Street* harks back to the work of the early Impressionists.

In the winter of 1891, a year which had been particularly fruitful from an artistic point of view, Munch returned to Nice, 'the city of happiness, health and beauty'[111] which gave him the necessary strength to fight against the infirmities that even then haunted him. Amongst the many paintings from this period is *Night in Nice* (Plate 96), the first work by Munch to be bought by Nasjonalgalleriet.[112] It was painted from the roof of the villa where he was staying, and shows a night-time scene in varying shades of blue. And yet the moon, shining on the villas and their roofs, brings to light subtle tones of mauve and pink and golden red in the windows. The technique is one of restrained Impressionism, and yet the outlines are boldly, almost overpoweringly, defined, rather in the manner of the iron railing in the sunlit *Rue Lafayette*.

It was not far from Nice to the gaming tables of Monte Carlo, and like all inveterate gamblers Munch had his infallible system. However infallible it may have been, Munch generally managed to break even, but never seemed to be any better off. His painter friend Christian Skredsvig,[113] who was in Nice at the same time as Munch, could not understand this—until he discovered that Munch, having collected a day's winnings, would then go and squander it in some other sleazy gambling den. But the future painter of 'the modern life of the soul' was just as interested in his surroundings and in his fellow men clustered round the roulette wheel as he was in the game itself.

In one of these paintings (Plate 97) we can see him taking notes, bringing his system up to date, while the other players sit round the table, gambling. In another,[114] the main figure is the man in the foreground leaving the table, ruined and resigned, turning his back on his fellow gamblers who carry on their gaming regardless.

But, at the same time, Munch was also working on the technique that he had first used, even before his travel scholarship, in *Inger on the Beach* (Plate 82), whereby all extraneous detail is reduced to a minimum in order to reveal the essential truth of the subject. After several summers at Åsgårdstrand he became so familiar with the shoreline that he could recall it and relive it whenever, and wherever, he was, seeing its simplified shapes and colours in his mind's eye, but without losing the sharply observed details.[115]

In Paris and Nice Munch painted the first versions of *The Kiss* and *Melancholy*, but we shall come back to those later. The most significant move that he made during these years was to embark on the series of paintings that were later to be known as *The Frieze of Life*, a succession of images of 'love and death' that reflected the many hardships that Munch had experienced even before reaching his thirtieth birthday.

His protector and refuge when the world went against him, which it almost invariably did, was Christian Skredsvig, who wrote of Munch's ambition 'to paint the memory of a sunset'.[116]

In Norway, as in the rest of Europe, there was a great feeling of uncertainty amongst the people, an anxiety that was reflected in both art and literature. And it was during this period that Munch painted a group of pictures whose basic theme is contemporary 'angst', but which also illustrate very well how, even in his most expressive paintings, he never lost touch with the basic 'truth experience' that inspired them. In all his versions of *The Scream* (Plate 107) and *Angst* (Plate 108) we find the same diagonal composition and the same landscape. And yet, despite the fact that both scenes are firmly rooted in a deeply-felt reality, the way in which Munch has simplified the people and their surroundings gives them a timeless and universal relevance: they become ageless symbols.

Back in Norway he detected the same 'angst' in the deathly faces[117] of the crowds of good bourgeois hurrying towards the same red sunset in the *Evening in Karl Johan Street* (Plate 128).

I feel that I am drifting further and further away from the kind of thing that the public likes—I feel that I will end up being even more outrageous.   Munch, 1891[3]

Thank you for the portrait. It is extremely penetrating, and I recognize myself very clearly in it.

Stéphane Mallarmé to Munch[4]

I am finally in Nice, the city that I have dreamed of for so long . . . It is more beautiful here than I have ever dreamed. The Promenade des Anglais is most impressive—with the wonderfully blue water on one side. The sea is such a fleeting shade of blue that it looks as though it has been painted with naptha. But how lonely it is—I have long since stopped listening to the footsteps on the stairs, as I know they are never for me.

Munch to Emanuel Goldstein, 1891[5]

When [Munch] got the scholarship for the third time, it was rumoured that it was because he had been in poor health and he was still unwell. But the few extremely modest scholarships that we are able to provide are not intended to be used as some kind of sickness benefit; to use them as such is an abuse of the system.

Bjørnstjerne Bjørnson in *Dagbladet*, 1891[6]

. . . which incontrovertibly places him in the forefront of the younger generation. He must stay at their head. He should have an art scholarship for the whole of his life.
  . . . here is the germ of the art that will supplant our fine, upstanding, meticulous realism.
  Do you really think that Werenskiold would buy pictures from Munch to hang on his sitting room walls and look at every day if they were of no merit ?

Frits Thaulow's reply to Bjørnstjerne Bjørnson, who was trying to prevent Munch being granted an art scholarship.[7]

A large room. Over there by the gaming table, a cluster of people—their backs are bent. A few arms and faces lit up by the lamp. Beyond lie other rooms—the same hush, the same bunch of people round the bank. It is like an enchanted castle, in which the devil is having a party. That is the gaming hell of Monaco.

Munch, 1892[8]

The gaming table is a strange and fickle animal—it has its own whims—roulette is its nerve centre. Today, when I experienced the workings of that mysterious creature, I made notes and jotted down my impressions so as to be able to investigate its habits.

Munch, 1892[9]

96 **Night in Nice**, 1891
    Oil on canvas, 48 x 54 cm.
    Nasjonalgalleriet, Oslo

97 **Gaming Tables at Monte Carlo**, 1892
    Oil on canvas, 75 x 116 cm.
    Oslo Kommunes Kunstsamlinger, OKK 50

During these years Munch was continually analyzing the world about him, just as the Impressionists did, but, at the same time, he was looking inwards into his own soul and reliving past experiences. His thoughts even strayed to the subject of death, with which he had come face to face on several occasions in his own family. He no longer treated it as something belonging to the past, something that could be treated objectively, as he had, despite his personal experiences, when he painted *The Sick Child* and *Spring*. He was going to be a poet and a prophet, and, like them, he would communicate with his fellow men through the language of his own experience.

He gradually became more and more involved in the themes of *The Frieze of Life*, a work in which he sought to express his deepest thoughts in the simplest possible terms, and which was to take up all his energies as a man and as an artist into the new century.

Munch himself realized that he was about to make a complete break with the past: he was finally turning his back on realism and the doctrines of French Impressionism.

THE EXHIBITION AT TOSTRUP'S BUILDING[118]

We have already seen how, in 1889, Munch completed many of his major works, held his first one-man exhibition, and travelled to France, where his encounter with that country's new ideas and new techniques of painting had a decisive influence on his art.

1892 was a similar year in many respects, and, it could be argued, an even more important one. That year he opened his second one-man exhibition in his home town, on the strength of which, despite the damning comments of his critics, he was offered a chance to exhibit his works in Berlin. The Berlin exhibition caused a tremendous furore and closed after eight days, but Munch became Germany's 'artist of the moment' and for a number of years Germany became his second home.

Much happened in the three years that separate his two exhibitions in Christiania. He had reached his twenty-ninth year, hardened by the bitter experience of life and the critics' cruel remarks, but encouraged by the understanding of some of the older artists. Three times he had been granted a State scholarship, on the last occasion despite protests by Bjørnstjerne Bjørnson. In France he found himself confronted by a whole stream of new ideas which had challenged his opinions and modified his technique.

He gradually formulated his ideas about the past and the future, and, after the death of his father, he felt a deep responsibility for his family. It was clear

100

In a first floor room on Louisenstrasse, in North Berlin, the red light of a spirit lamp burned throughout the night . . . This was the home of the Przybyszewskis . . . He was a full-blooded Pole, who wrote avant-garde works of fiction in German and suffered from hallucinations. She was Norwegian, very slim, with the figure of a 14th century Madonna and a laugh that drove men wild.

Her name was Ducha, and she drank absinthe by the litre without getting drunk . . . There was a piano by the door, an extraordinary instrument, which one could shut off by means of a handle, so that even if Stachu [Przybyszewski] started hammering away on it, nobody else in the building would be disturbed . . . This piano was, in a way, the focal point of their poky little flat. One man would dance with Ducha, while the other two sat at the table and watched; one would be Munch, and the other, as often as not, Strindberg. The four friends there were all in love with Ducha, each in his own way, but they never let it show. Stachu was perfectly happy with the situation. Munch called Ducha 'Lady' and always addressed her very politely and correctly, even when he was drunk. The country to the west, the Paris of Huysman and Rops, provided the basis for Stachu's dissertations on pathological eroticism . . . Strindberg spoke about chemical analysis, while Munch just sat and listened. A couple of years later Ducha went to Tiflis (Tbilisi), where she met her end: a wild young Russian held a revolver to her forehead, and when she burst out laughing, he calmly pulled the trigger, killing first her and then himself . . . Julius Meier-Graefe[10]

98 Dagny Juell, at the beginning of the 1890's

99 **Julius Meier-Graefe,** 1895
Oil on canvas, 100 x 75 cm.
Nasjonalgalleriet, Oslo

100 **Girl by the Window,** 1891
Oil on canvas, 96 x 65 cm. Private Collection

101 **Dagny Juell Przybyszewska,** 1893
Oil on canvas, 148.5 x 99.5 cm.
Oslo Kommunes Kunstsamlinger, OKK 212

98   99

to him that he should not marry,[119] because of the tuberculosis that ran in the family and also because of a history of mental illness, but the main reason was that he was convinced that art was to be his whole life. The 'spiritual diary entries' of this period, as he himself called them later on, are crammed with thoughts about the meaning and function of art, but they also contain much autobiographical information. He calls himself Brandt, and it is clear that he had plans to write a 'Christiania novel',[120] possibly—judging by his use of language—along the lines of the one written by Jaeger.

A magazine that Munch and Goldstein hoped to publish together never came to anything,[121] nor did Munch's planned novel. He considered 'paint thy life' more important than 'write thy life'. But it is clear that his time in France after his father's death greatly helped him to mature, whilst his friendship with Goldstein also had a profound effect on him.

The Munch who opened the second exhibition on 14 September 1892 at the jeweller Tostrup's building was altogether more self-assured and more confident than the old Munch. The exhibition itself contained most of the same paintings that were to be shown in Berlin later that autumn, and which were to set light to the glowing embers of discontent[122] that smouldered beneath the surface of German art, bringing into the open the basic conflict between the traditionalists and the modernists.

The majority of the pictures had already been seen by the Norwegian public, and had stirred up a massive controversy. Of the new works, most were impressionistic ones that he had done in Paris, such as *Rue Lafayette* (Plate 91), with a few examples of 'mood painting' or 'blue painting', like *Night in St. Cloud* or *Night in Nice* (Plate 96). He also included pictures of the gaming tables at Monte Carlo, where he had been such an eager participant, and a few pictures with the most up-to-the-minute titles, like *Harmony in Black and Violet* (Plate 67), the portrait of his sister, Inger, painted in 1892.

There were no 'people reading and women knitting', but then neither were there any of the kind of paintings that he had earlier promised: the sort which would 'make people take their hats off, like they do in church', i.e. the paintings that were later to appear in his *Frieze of Life*. Certainly, the first version of *The Kiss* (Plate 124), completed in 1891, was included in the exhibition, and so was *Jappe on the Beach*, or *Jealousy*, as it was called in the catalogue. There was also another picture which bore many similarities to *The Scream*, namely *Despair* (Plate 111), at that time exhibited under the title of *Mood at Sunset*.

The reaction of the critics was much as before. *Aftenposten* spoke of 'delirium' and 'feverish hallucinations',[123] and 'bits of beach that look like dismembered whales and old saddles'.[124] *Morgenbladet* felt that 'the artist is playing games with people's taste'.[125] *Verdens Gang*, however, admired his 'courageous refusal to compromise[126] and his steadfastness in the face of such frequently uninformed criticism'.

A few days after Munch had opened his exhibition in Tostrup's Building, the Danish painter J. F. Willumsen also opened an exhibition in Christiania, in Abel's Art Gallery. We know that the two artists, who were roughly the same age, met each other at their respective exhibitions, and we also know that Willumsen visited Munch at home, as well as borrowing money from him to pay for his ticket back to Copenhagen. They were also ranked together by the critics.[127]

Willumsen was a great friend of another Danish painter, Johan Rohde,[128] and some months later Munch wrote to Rohde telling him of his plans to paint a 'series' of pictures, the first time that he actually described them in this way.

Then, out of the blue, Munch received a letter[129] from a fellow artist who had seen his exhibition, saying that he had 'particularly liked it . . . May I therefore take the liberty of asking you, if you have not already made any previous arrangement about your pictures, whether you would be willing to show them (in Berlin) and under what conditions.'

The writer of the letter was a Norwegian artist called Adelsten Normann, a member of the Düsseldorf school and a fine exponent of this type of painting, who was also on the board of the Verein Berliner Künstler. Why he should have taken such a timely interest in Munch is something of a

102

. . . [Dagny] *was a poor advocate of the doctrine of free love that her husband is said to have preached in his books. In reality the couple did not indulge in that kind of practice. We, their close friends, know that they lived happily together with their two children each summer up at Kongsvinger.*
Munch, on the death of Dagny, 1901[11]

When a friend once asked Munch who had written about him most sensibly, he unhesitatingly replied: *Julius Meier-Graefe.*

In connection with the picture Lovers in the Waves *(the lithograph), which D has bought, I should like to make it clear that the subject or the inspiration for that picture is a model that I had in Berlin in the 1890s. I also used her for the big lithograph,* Madonna. *I let Przybyszewski have one of the sketches to illustrate a collection of poetry. It bore a certain resemblance to Dagny . . .*
When we discussed whether it was in fact Dagny or the girl I had used as a model, we were completely mistaken. On the other hand, there is a definite likeness . . . Munch[12]

She was conscious of it, but she could not understand it . . . She could not think, all she could feel was an uncontrollable trembling throughout her body. She clasped both her hands between her knees, leaned her whole body forward and drew in her feet. She sat huddled up in this position on the edge of the bed and listened to this frightening, unknown thing, racked with anxiety. What could it be? There it was again! It terrified her. It made her tremble. The whole house was full of ghosts.
From Stanislaw Przybyszewski's *Underveis (On the Way)*[13]

102 Vignette for Przybyszewski's collection of poetry *The Vigil*, 1894
Charcoal drawing, 61.5 x 47.1 cm.
Oslo Kommunes Kunstsamlinger, OKK 2449

103 **Puberty**, 1894
Oil on canvas, 150 x 111 cm.
Nasjonalgalleriet, Oslo

86

103 >

104

mystery, but it has been suggested that the highly-respected German artist Fritz von Uhde[130] may have had a hand in the affair. The latter had already visited Oslo in 1888, when he had seen examples of Munch's work and had told his friend Frits Thaulow that Munch was 'the North's most interesting painter'.

That extremely complimentary remark is, in itself, rather surprising, when one considers that von Uhde's naturalistic representations of Christ, which were ranked amongst the great masterpieces of the day, could hardly be further removed from Munch's style of painting, but we know that von Uhde would have had the chance to see four of Munch's pictures at an exhibition in Munich the previous year, although they had aroused very little interest: in fact, the critics had never even mentioned Munch's name in their reports. It is also strange that the decision to invite Munch to Berlin in 1892 was unanimous, as he was one of the twenty-nine Norwegian painters who had declined to take part in the 50th anniversary exhibition of the Verein Berliner Künstler. Instead, the Norwegian painters ended up in the Glaspalast in Munich.

104 **Mother and Daughter**, 1897
Oil on canvas, 135 x 163 cm.
Nasjonalgalleriet, Oslo

*105 **The Voice**, 1893
Oil on canvas, 90 x 119 cm.
Oslo Kommunes Kunstsamlinger, OKK 44

106 **Eyes**, 1894/95
Charcoal drawing, 41.5 x 50.3 cm.
Oslo Kommunes Kunstsamlinger, OKK 329

THE BERLIN SCANDAL

However unexpected it may have been, Munch did receive a unanimous invitation to show his works in the German capital. It was the first time that anyone had had a one-man exhibition in the Verein Berliner Künstler, and it was also the first exhibition in the newly-opened round room in the Architektenhaus.

On 4 October Munch closed his show in the Tostrup Building, and on the same day he received a letter from Adelsten Normann telling him to send off his paintings as quickly as possible. One month later, on 5 November, Munch was able to open his exhibition of what the advance publicity called 'Ibsen'sche Stimmungsbilder'[131] ('Ibsen-like mood paintings').

Never in its fifty-year history had the Verein Berliner Künstler shown such paintings, and never had it been at the centre of such controversy. Radical German art of the period was mainly represented by the naturalistic pictures

of Max Liebermann and von Uhde. Far to the south, in Munich, there were one or two artists who had been influenced by Impressionism, but in the Berlin of Kaiser Wilhelm and Anton von Werner,[132] Impressionism was a dirty word. Unlike the people of Munich, very few Berliners had ever had a chance to see an impressionistic picture, even if they had wanted to. In fact, apart from a small number of artists, hardly any Germans visited Paris at all, so great was anti-German feeling in the French capital.

A fierce controversy broke out immediately. The universal reaction was one of shock and horror, and criticism was universally violent.

The conservative *National-Zeitung*[133]—which even got his name wrong, calling him 'E. Blunch'—wrote that he had sold 'his body and soul to the rule of French Impressionism, and like all his fellow countrymen [!] he is trying, wherever possible, to beat the French at their own game of breaking all the old-established rules of art'. All traditional values and artistic ideals are ignored by 'Blunch and all his friends'. Another critic demanded that the exhibition be closed immediately. But the most bitter attack was made by the editor of *Kunst-Chronik*, the highly respected art historian Adolf Rosenberg.[134] He called Munch's pictures 'Naturalistic excesses, the like of which have never been seen in Berlin before. What this Norwegian has achieved in the way of shapelessness and crudeness of painting, and brutality and coarseness of feeling, makes the sins of the French and Scottish Impressionists pale into complete insignificance, let alone the Munich Naturalists.' In conclusion he wrote: 'There is no point in wasting words on Munch's paintings, as they have got absolutely nothing to do with art.'

It was to be more than ten years before Munch's art was mentioned again in *Kunst-Chronik*.

There is no need to quote any more of the critics, as they were almost all equally damning, even in the liberal *Berliner Tageblatt*. But the editor of that paper, Theodor Wolff,[135] who was later to become so famous, felt compelled to defend Munch in front of his colleagues. He only went to the exhibition for a laugh, he quite frankly admitted, 'but, so help me God, I did not laugh . . . Because in the middle of all those demented visions and utter abominations I really felt that I could detect fine, hyper-sensitive feelings.' During those stormy times Munch found one more person who supported him: the artist Walter Leistikow,[136] two years his junior, who, albeit under a pseudonym, came out in his favour in *Freie Bühne*. They later became firm friends.

'Art in Danger' was the theme of a telegram in *Frankfurter Zeitung*, and, in the days that followed, the debate about Munch's *réputation scandaleuse* raged throughout Germany, and was even taken up in the pages of French magazines. It was a debate that would be carried on for years. Naturally enough, back in Norway, *Aftenposten* was watching events in Berlin with interest, and the paper weighed in with an article entitled 'Munch's Berlin fiasco'.[137] It spoke of 'the depths of depravity and tastelessness that Naturalism can lead to' and of how people stood and laughed, unable to make head or tail of the pictures. They were obviously referring to what Rosenberg had said about the exhibition, and the extraordinary use of the word 'Naturalism' shows just how little Prussian Berlin knew about modern art. A scandal was inevitable.

The kind of schemers who always seem to haunt artistic circles began to collect signatures for a petition, and soon they had gained enough to force a general meeting of the Verein Berliner Künstler. A meeting was called for 11 November, and amidst stormy scenes it was decided, by 120 votes to 105, to close down the exhibition. And so, on the following day, it was duly closed.

The 105 who had voted against the motion promptly marched out of the hall to another meeting place, where they formed a new association, but without formally resigning from the old one. One of them, the sculptor Max Kruse,[138] has given a dramatic account of the effects of the exhibition. It had, he said, 'shown us that pictorial art can be called on to express all mankind's most heart-felt emotions. All the old-established ideas about Art were completely overturned, and, contrary to accepted practice, colour and form became secondary to the need of the artist to express his deepest feelings.'

Kruse also suggests that the exhibition paved the way for the Secession

I went up to visit him one day . . . He was in the middle of a painting. On the edge of the bed sat a naked girl model. She did not exactly seem to be an angel, but, nevertheless, she looked innocently chaste and shy . . . It was precisely those qualities tha[t] had persuaded Munch to paint her. And as she sat there, the dazzling rays of the spring sun flooded over her, while the shado[w] of her head hung fatefully behind her. That was how he painted her, with all his heart, and in that picture—he called it Puberty *—he achieved something lasting, something universal, and profoundly true to life.* Adolf Paul[14]

Your eyes are as large as half the heavens when you stand close t[o] me, and your hair is flecked with gold dust. I cannot see your mouth—only that you are smiling. Munch[15]

Munch does not practise art for art's sake, which would just be [a] game for him, but for the sake of the terrible anxiety that haunt[s] him. Akseli Gallen-Kallela (Axel Gallen) on Munch[16]

The terror of life has pursued me ever since I first began to thin[k] Munch[17]

Have you seen a screaming sky? No! I can tell you I have! It w[as] as though the sky had opened a thousand mouths and screamed colour down on to the world. The whole sky was a never-ending mass of dark red stripes on a black ground. Rivulets of blood . . no! a puddle in which the red glow of evening was reflected, together with a dirty yellow. Stanislaw Przybyszewski[18]

And for several years I was almost mad—at that time the terr[ify]ing face of insanity reared up its twisted head. You know my picture The Scream. *I was being stretched to the limit—natur[e] was screaming in my blood—I was at breaking point. Then a young blonde girl with a smile as fresh as spring came to my rescue. You know my pictures and you know that I felt it all. A[nd] that I gave up hope of ever being able to love again.* Munch[1]

For a long time he had wanted to paint the memory of a sunset red as blood. No, it really was congealed blood. But nobody els[e] would have experienced it as he did. Everybody else would hav[e] thought of clouds. He spoke sadly of the sight that had filled h[im] with terror. Sadly, because the paltry resources at the artist's disposal were never adequate . . . 'He is striving for the impossible, he is despairing at his religion' I thought to myself, [I] advised him to paint it, and he produced his extraordinary wo[rk] The Scream. *Christian Skredsvig[20]*

I was walking along a road one evening—on the one side lay t[he] city, and below me was the fjord. I was feeling tired and ill—[I] stood and looked out over the fjord. The sun went down—the clouds were stained red, as if with blood.
I felt as though the whole of nature was screaming—it seem[ed] as though I could hear a scream. I painted that picture, paint[ed] the clouds like real blood. The colours screamed. The result w[as] The Scream *in the* Frieze of Life. *Munch[21]*

I stopped and leaned against the railing, half-dead with fatig[ue]. Over the grey-blue fjord the clouds hung, as red as blood and tongues of flame. My friends drew away. Alone and trembli[ng] with fear I experienced nature's great scream. Munch[22]

There are no clouds in the evening red,
No reflections of the day that's dead.
There are tongues of flame, and rivers of blood,
A fiery sword, a hot, crimson flood.
The anguish of judgement, the torments of death.
Vilhelm Krag in *Dagbladet*

*107 The Scream, 1893
Oil, casein and pastel on cardboard, 91 x 74 cm.
Nasjonalgalleriet, Oslo

111   112

t, 1894
a canvas, 94 x 74 cm.
Kommunes Kunstsamlinger, OKK 515

t, 1896
rcolour and indian ink, 37.0 x 32.3 cm.
Kommunes Kunstsamlinger, OKK 259·

t, 1896
lcut, 46 x 37.7 cm.
Kommunes Kunstsamlinger, OKK 568
j. Schiefler No. 62

air, 1892
a canvas, 92 x 67 cm.
ska Galleriet, Stockholm

icream, 1895
graph, 35 x 25.2 cm.
Kommunes Kunstsamlinger, OKK 193
j. Schiefler No. 32

movement, as it took place in the middle of a fierce dispute between Anton von Werner and the Academy, which was controlled by members of the younger generation. The only part the powerful von Werner had played in the exhibition was to put his signature to the original invitation.

As soon as they had seen the pictures the artists dashed back to the assembly hall, and von Werner announced that the exhibition was closed— it was a travesty of art, merely a manifestation of filth and brutishness. 'We explained that one could not throw out a guest, to which Werner replied: ''That is a matter of complete indifference to me, the exhibition stays shut!'' Then all hell broke loose, with people shouting and screaming, and finally fights began to break out. We, the younger members, wanted to get out of the hall, while the older ones tried to stop us leaving. Finally, we formed ourselves into a wedge and charged through the line of men trying to restrain us. We left Wilhelmstrasse flushed with victory . . .'

There was a much larger crowd than they had expected, and it included faces that must have taken them completely by surprise. It would have been unthinkable to form a new association on that basis. Max Kruse's final words were 'It is always easier to destroy than to build.' And that, briefly, was 'der Fall', otherwise known as 'die Affaire Munch'.

Berliner Tageblatt[139] was quite right when it made the observation that 'One must not jump to the conclusion that all those who voted against the closure of Munch's exhibition are necessarily in favour of the kind of art that he represents', a remark that is substantiated by a statement[140] put out by the 105 breakaway members of the Verein. In it, they reasserted the one argument that Munch's defenders had put forward, namely that he had been invited as a guest and by closing down his exhibition the rules of hospitality had been broken. This action was a disgrace, regardless of whether they 'in any way approved of the style of painting shown in Munch's pictures'. The whole affair had been, above all, a fight for intellectual and artistic freedom,[141] and the right to have one's case heard properly.

Although their efforts were almost completely in vain, Munch did at least become a famous, or rather notorious, artist in Germany,[142] the country which, at that time, was the first stop for Scandinavian artists trying to establish a reputation in the world. He had become, more than almost any other artist, 'the man of the moment' in a wide cultural field. Directly after the Berlin controversy he received invitations to exhibit in Düsseldorf and Cologne, the first in a long line of exhibitions which he was to hold throughout Germany in the coming years.

In July 1893 Walther Rathenau[143] bought his first Munch, *A Rainy Day in Christiania*, and in the same year Munch appears amongst the artists exhibiting in the Freie Berliner Kunstausstellung.[144] This was an exhibition

113

of rejected works, and it also included two pictures by 'the Norwegian' [!]
August Strindberg, who unfortunately is not only a poet, but also has
ambitions to be a painter'. Munch's pictures were described as
'Schmierereien' (daubs).

It is interesting to note that, included in this exhibition of rejects were
works by the young Käthe Kollwitz,[145] in which the critic Julius Elias thought
he detected the influence of Munch. We have no evidence that Munch and
Käthe Kollwitz ever met, either then or later, but it is highly probable that
they did. We do know, however, that Elias bought Munch's impressionistic
picture *The Dance* for 100 marks, and that the two of them subsequently
became friends.

MUNCH'S BERLIN DAYS

Munch found life very difficult in Norway, and not only financially: he felt
that he was being persecuted and made fun of by his fellow countrymen. It
therefore seemed perfectly natural to settle in Berlin, even after the scandal
that he had caused in 1892. Of course, he was also subjected to insults in
Germany, but at least he was not totally ignored. He would be able to lead his
own life in the big city, and he had a circle of friends who admired his art
and who gave him great inspiration for his work, either by discussing the
latest ideas and theories with him or just by providing him with the necessary mental stimulus. Their goals were different from those of materialistic
and bohemian Christiania, but their life style was similar, and indeed, many

*Once, when I talked to Munch about that picture [Sunset], he said
that he had not painted Nature, but a memory, not just a straightforward scene, as it would appear to the outside world, but a
subjective image, which had slowly but surely become indelibly
etched on his retina and his memory, and which always appeared
in glaring colours behind his eyelids, whenever he closed his eyes.*
Gustav Schiefler, 1893[24]

*Like a lyric poet, his work often has strong musical affinities. He
has paintings, which, like symphonies, do not need, and should
not have, titles. The Scream ought never to have had a title. The
spoken word only distorts the picture's power.*
Sigbjørn Obstfelder[25]

*Nature seemed to be stained with blood, with people passing by
like priests.* Munch to Gustav Schiefler[26]

*During the past year, I discovered Kierkegaard for the first time,
and there are certain marked similarities. I now understand why
people have compared my work to his so often. I never understood the reasons before.* Munch to Ragnar Hoppe[27]

108 **Angst**, 1894
Oil on canvas, 94 x 74 cm.
Oslo Kommunes Kunstsamlinger, OKK 515

109 **Angst**, 1896
Watercolour and indian ink, 37.0 x 32.3 cm.
Oslo Kommunes Kunstsamlinger, OKK 259

110 **Angst**, 1896
Woodcut, 46 x 37.7 cm.
Oslo Kommunes Kunstsamlinger, OKK 568
Ref. G. Schiefler No. 62

111 **Despair**, 1892
Oil on canvas, 92 x 67 cm.
Thielska Galleriet, Stockholm

112 **The Scream**, 1895
Lithograph, 35 x 25.2 cm.
Oslo Kommunes Kunstsamlinger, OKK 193
Ref. G. Schiefler No. 32

110

< 108

111

movement, as it took ____ the ____
von Werner and the Academy, which was ____
younger generation. The only part the powerful von Werner had played in
the exhibition was to put his signature to the original invitation.

As soon as they had seen the pictures the artists dashed back to the
assembly hall, and von Werner announced that the exhibition was closed—
it was a travesty of art, merely a manifestation of filth and brutishness. 'We
explained that one could not throw out a guest, to which Werner replied:
"That is a matter of complete indifference to me, the exhibition stays shut!"
Then all hell broke loose, with people shouting and screaming, and finally
fights began to break out. We, the younger members, wanted to get out of
the hall, while the older ones tried to stop us leaving. Finally, we formed
ourselves into a wedge and charged through the line of men trying to restrain
us. We left Wilhelmstrasse flushed with victory . . .'

There was a much larger crowd than they had expected, and it included
faces that must have taken them completely by surprise. It would have been
unthinkable to form a new association on that basis. Max Kruse's final words
were 'It is always easier to destroy than to build.' And that, briefly, was 'der
Fall', otherwise known as 'die Affaire Munch'.

Berliner Tageblatt[139] was quite right when it made the observation that
'One must not jump to the conclusion that all those who voted against the
closure of Munch's exhibition are necessarily in favour of the kind of art that
he represents', a remark that is substantiated by a statement[140] put out by
the 105 breakaway members of the Verein. In it, they reasserted the one
argument that Munch's defenders had put forward, namely that he had been
invited as a guest and by closing down his exhibition the rules of hospitality
had been broken. This action was a disgrace, regardless of whether they 'in
any way approved of the style of painting shown in Munch's pictures'. The
whole affair had been, above all, a fight for intellectual and artistic
freedom,[141] and the right to have one's case heard properly.

Although their efforts were almost completely in vain, Munch did at least
become a famous, or rather notorious, artist in Germany,[142] the country
which, at that time, was the first stop for Scandinavian artists trying to
establish a reputation in the world. He had become, more than almost any
other artist, 'the man of the moment' in a wide cultural field. Directly after
the Berlin controversy he received invitations to exhibit in Düsseldorf and
Cologne, the first in a long line of exhibitions which he was to hold throughout Germany in the coming years.

In July 1893 Walther Rathenau[143] bought his first Munch, *A Rainy Day in
Christiania*, and in the same year Munch appears amongst the artists
exhibiting in the Freie Berliner Kunstausstellung.[144] This was an exhibition

113

of rejected works, and it also included two pictures by 'the Norwegian' [!] August Strindberg, who unfortunately is not only a poet, but also has ambitions to be a painter'. Munch's pictures were described as 'Schmierereien' (daubs).

It is interesting to note that, included in this exhibition of rejects were works by the young Käthe Kollwitz,[145] in which the critic Julius Elias thought he detected the influence of Munch. We have no evidence that Munch and Käthe Kollwitz ever met, either then or later, but it is highly probable that they did. We do know, however, that Elias bought Munch's impressionistic picture *The Dance* for 100 marks, and that the two of them subsequently became friends.

MUNCH'S BERLIN DAYS

Munch found life very difficult in Norway, and not only financially: he felt that he was being persecuted and made fun of by his fellow countrymen. It therefore seemed perfectly natural to settle in Berlin, even after the scandal that he had caused in 1892. Of course, he was also subjected to insults in Germany, but at least he was not totally ignored. He would be able to lead his own life in the big city, and he had a circle of friends who admired his art and who gave him great inspiration for his work, either by discussing the latest ideas and theories with him or just by providing him with the necessary mental stimulus. Their goals were different from those of materialistic and bohemian Christiania, but their life style was similar, and indeed, many

Once, when I talked to Munch about that picture [Sunset], he said that he had not painted Nature, but a memory, not just a straightforward scene, as it would appear to the outside world, but a subjective image, which had slowly but surely become indelibly etched on his retina and his memory, and which always appeared in glaring colours behind his eyelids, whenever he closed his eyes.
Gustav Schiefler, 1893[24]

Like a lyric poet, his work often has strong musical affinities. He has paintings, which, like symphonies, do not need, and should not have, titles. The Scream ought never to have had a title. The spoken word only distorts the picture's power.
Sigbjørn Obstfelder[25]

Nature seemed to be stained with blood, with people passing by like priests. Munch to Gustav Schiefler[26]

During the past year, I discovered Kierkegaard for the first time, and there are certain marked similarities. I now understand why people have compared my work to his so often. I never understood the reasons before. Munch to Ragnar Hoppe[27]

114

◄14

*Remarkable water formations in blue and violet, and those bits
of beach that look like dismembered whales and old saddles.
There are giant octopuses with long tentacles spreadeagled on the
field, which are supposed to represent treestumps and roots, and
there is a moon that can reflect itself in four mirror images, one on
top of the other, like a necklace of gold coins suspended over the
extraordinary stone configurations that the eagle-eyed impressionist has detected . . .   Aftenposten, 1892[28]*

◄13 **The Mystery of the Beach**, 1892
    Oil on canvas, 100 x 140 cm.
    Private Collection

114 **Melancholy (The Yellow Boat)**, 1892/93
    Oil on canvas, 65 x 96 cm.
    Nasjonalgalleriet, Oslo

of the Christiania set were themselves now settled in Berlin.

Their favourite meeting place was a little tavern in the heart of the old
centre of the city, called 'Zum Schwarzen Ferkel', by the Unter den Linden.
Also in this street was the elegant Café Bauer, another of their haunts, which
they used as a *poste restante*. It was August Strindberg who first discovered
the tavern and, with the permission of the owner, named it after the old
black wineskin that hung outside.

It had a very un-German, or at least very un-Prussian, atmosphere, and
there were endless heated arguments and frequent clashes of temperament
among the young men who congregated there. Nor was it conducive to peace
to have in their midst an extremely attractive and much courted woman.
Dagny Juell[146] was the daughter of a Norwegian country doctor and later the
wife of the man who, along with Strindberg, was the leader of the group: the
Polish-German author Stanislaw Przybyszewski. She was called Ducha by
her husband—or Aspasia, after Pericles' famous mistress. Ducha was herself
a writer of considerable talent, and her husband with the difficult Polish
name, whom they called Stachu, was a very engaging character who seemed
to embody the spirit of the time. But it must be remembered that although
we are dealing with a very small group of people, nevertheless they
epitomized the decadence of *fin-de-siècle* Europe.

That same year, the twenty-four-year-old Przybyszewski published a pamphlet *Zur Psychologie des Individuums*, in which he analysed Chopin and Nietzsche. A man of many parts, Przybyszewski was an outstanding interpreter of Chopin's music. Later on he turned his attention to the Swedish poet and critic Ola Hansson,[147] who was eight years his senior.

The art historian Meier-Graefe has given us a description of what life in Berlin was like for Munch and his friends (see page 84). Together with Przybyszewski and two others he published the first book on Munch as early as 1894. It was a defence of Munch's art, called *Das Werk des Edvard Munch*.

Like Strindberg and so many of his contemporaries, Przybyszewski was a mystic, obsessed by the occult, who dabbled in black magic and revelled in the idea of being a 'Satanist'. One of his books, written, incidentally, in Norway, was entitled *Satans Kinder* (*Satan's Children*).

This band of fellow thinkers, mainly composed of Scandinavians, Jewish intellectuals, and rebels such as Hermann Schlittgen, the chief illustrator for the paper *Fliegende Blätter*, was soon joined by the violently temperamental Richard Dehmel,[148] whom Strindberg called a 'wilder Mann'. At the age of thirty he was on the threshold of his big breakthrough as a lyric poet, and he it was who held the 'Künstlerabend' which Jens Thiis described so vividly. It took place in Dehmel's villa outside Berlin, at Pankow, which at that time was still surrounded by countryside, and it lasted a whole day and night, possibly longer, according to Thiis. Among the other guests were the satanic Stachu and his wife, Munch, the Finnish painter Akseli Gallen-Kallela, born Axel Gallen[149] (who, despite the fact that he was a very different type of painter, exhibited with Munch in Berlin), the Norwegian sculptor Gustav Vigeland,[150] and Norway's most remarkable lyric poet of the day, Sigbjørn Obstfelder.

It was Munch who first introduced Hermann Schlittgen[151] to his 'Ferkel' friends, and the German later recounted how he had shared rooms with Munch during these years—continually moving from boarding house to boarding house. These small hotel rooms also served Munch as studios, both in Berlin and Paris, as well as during his travels round Germany to places such as Weimar. On one of these Weimar visits, Munch and Schlittgen were returning from a splendid breakfast with Count Harry Kessler,[152] when Munch suddenly exclaimed to his friend: 'That is how I must paint you. Full-length, and in the same high spirits as you are now.' The resulting work today hangs in Munch-Museet in Oslo, and is called quite simply, *The German* (Plate 123). In many such hotel rooms he would paint the things that had inspired him during the day or the memories of the past that still weighed heavily on his mind, and skilfully and accurately etch out designs on his copper plates. Despite the hectic atmosphere of the milieu in which he lived, Munch was incredibly productive during these years—and it was also during this time that he formulated the philosophy of life which shines so clearly through his art. Although it was intensely personal, perhaps Jens Thiis was right when he said that 'his art is a display of temperament that seems like a view of life.[153]

The most renowned—and the most difficult—of the Ferkel fraternity was, not surprisingly, August Strindberg,[154] who in 1892 was on the threshold of a new marriage, and also building up the so-called 'Inferno crisis'[155] which was later to erupt in Paris. His genius was so similar to Munch's own that friction between them was inevitable, as well as a kind of love/hate relationship; the situation being further complicated by their conflicting loyalties to Ducha. Munch shared with him that eventful and chaotic winter of 1892 in Berlin, and also experienced the dramatic 'Inferno crisis' in Paris, the most disordered period of Strindberg's turbulent life. The Paris episode was in 1896, when Munch and Strindberg both belonged to a circle not dissimilar to that which they had frequented in Berlin. It included a number of artists (in most cases friends of Gauguin), several writers, and the composer Frederick Delius[156] who was to remain a lifelong friend of Munch's and who left some amusing recollections of the two of them and Strindberg at that time.

There are several small instances offering insight into the relationship

115

In light nights shapes take on fantastic colours—on the beach lie stones like trolls. Munch[29]

It was evening. I walked along by the sea—the moon shone between the clouds. The stones reared up over the water, like the mysterious magic inhabitants of the ocean, there were large white heads, laughing—some up on the beach, others down in the water. The girl walking by my side seemed like a mermaid, with shining eyes, and her flowing hair gleamed in the light from the horizon . . Munch[30]

They admired the water and the column-like reflection of the moon. The little stone in the distance looked just like a head to them—it moved and glittered. Munch[31]

Out in the still water, a boat—a yellow boat, parallel to the horizon—a masterly repetition of the line in the background. Munch should be grateful that the boat is yellow. Had it not been, then he would never have painted the picture . . . The latest word now for colour is 'resonance'. Has anyone ever heard such resonant colour as in this picture?

. . . Sometimes it seems closer to music than painting, but, in any case, it is brilliant music. Munch should be paid a composer's salary. Christian Krohg, 1891[32]

It is as though the embittered, sketchily painted, pallid face and the suffering eyes are radiating a malevolent force that has blighted the whole landscape with sombre, doom-laden colours— a melancholy shade of mauve, a sulphurous yellow, a venomous green. Even the shoreline seems to twist and turn with hopeless yearning. The whole landscape expresses a mood.
Jens Thiis, 1933[33]

*115 **Madonna**, c.1894
Oil on canvas, 95 x 75 cm.
Private Collection

116 **Madonna**, 1894/95
Oil on canvas, 91 x 71 cm.
Nasjonalgalleriet, Oslo

116 >

between the painter and the famous and controversial poet. Munch once told a friend that Strindberg, as a joke, 'used to trip me up and leave me lying flat out in the street'. When it happened again, Munch threatened to give him a good beating—'and then he stopped that little trick'. And when, some years later, Strindberg sat for his portrait, the poet never said a word on arrival: he merely laid a revolver on the table[157] in front of him—and stayed silent throughout the whole session. Strindberg considered it a deep insult that Munch has mis-spelt his name 'Stindberg' at the bottom of the famous litho-graph, and, worse, he was offended by the naked woman that Munch placed in the border round the portrait, 'the woman that he detested'.

They went their separate ways, but remained bound together by the group of friends that they had shared. Their uneasy 'co-operation' is illustrated in a strange correspondence that they had in connection with an article that the magazine *Quickborn*[158] wanted to publish, text by Strindberg with illustrations by Munch. The article was published in 1899, but there was little connection between the text and the illustrations. An episode that occurred shortly after the turn of the century shows very well how the 'demonic' Strindberg lived on in Munch's mind. It happened when Munch was painting a woman's portrait on the beach at Warnemünde,[159] and the wind blew away his easel: he immediately packed away all his equipment, exclaiming—'That wind is Strindberg, trying to disrupt my work!'

They finally succeeded in achieving a kind of *modus vivendi*, largely by maintaining a respectful distance from each other. The portrait of Strindberg (Plate 118), which Munch painted that stormy autumn of 1892 in Berlin, he later presented to the Nationalmuseum in Stockholm as a token of the respect he felt for his friend. Also, in the later lithographic portrait mentioned above, Strindberg's name was corrected and the naked woman on the border was replaced by a decorative linear motif. Strindberg was neither the easiest nor the most grateful of Munch's sitters: when Adolf Paul remarked that he found the Berlin portrait 'a good and expressive likeness', Strindberg retorted, 'To Hell with *likeness*![160] It should be a stylized portrait of a poet! Like the ones of Goethe!'

Besides the people already mentioned, there was a constantly changing, floating population of Scandinavian poets and artists in Berlin. The irrepres-sible Danish poet Holger Drachmann[161] (Plate 120) arrived from Copenhagen on one occasion, and caused a considerable commotion at the Ferkel. As a result of a thundering row that had broken out round Strindberg, who was about to leave for Munich to visit his current fiancée, the mood amongst all the aspiring geniuses at the tavern was extremely tense, and Drachmann tried to calm things down by poking gentle fun at them all. Of Munch, the burly and self-opinionated poet said: 'I am certainly not like Munch, who arrived here and created a *succès de scandale*, which so delighted him that he finds himself unable to appreciate anything purely on its own merits.' Munch promptly got up, handed back a letter of recommendation that Drachmann had given him for an exhibition in Hamburg—and left.

But the Dane was not a man to bear grudges, and in a subsequent *Berlin Letter* (1894), published in the Danish newspaper *Politiken*, he wrote a tribute to Munch's perseverance in the face of that city's continued hostility, ending with the words: 'He struggles hard. Good luck with your struggle, lonely Norwegian.'

And struggle he did. At the time that Drachmann wrote his *Berlin Letter*, Munch had more friends than buyers: it was not until the beginning of the twentieth century that, after numerous exhibitions, his fortunes changed and the slow but sure growth in his reputation eventually led to a great improvement in his finances. The hard times were over when, in 1902, he first exhibited his *Frieze of Life* at the Seccession in Berlin.

For me, his Madonna picture represents the essence of his art. She is the Earth Mother. The woman who gives birth in pain. I think one would have to go to Russian literature to find a similarly devotional conception of woman, a similar glorification of the beauty of pain. Sigbjørn Obstfelder, 1896[34]

Woman who surrenders herself—and finds the pain-filled beauty of a Madonna. Munch[35]

. . . I hope that Munch is strong enough to master the gigantic task of painting a cycle of pictures that embrace every aspect of life, the first section of which, Love, *is almost completed.* Stanislaw Przybyszewski, 1894[36]

There were things there that came from deep within him, from his very heart, works from his own soul—things that he had seen, experienced, and felt. Anyone who can talk, paint or sing with such depth of feeling, has the natural gifts of a poet. He sees the world that he loves with a poet's eye. Walter Leistikow on Munch in *Die Freie Bühne*[37]

They sat crammed together in the little wine tavern on Unter den Linden, which Strindberg had discovered and which soon became the meeting place for a large number of young artists, many of whom have gained considerable reputations as poets and painters with the passing of the years. Here sat Strindberg and Dehmel, Hartleben and Leistikow, Holger Drachmann, Gunnar Heiberg, Christian Krohg, and countless others who at the time were burst-ing with new ideas . . . Right at the centre was Przybyszewski, his large eyes burning in his pale face, young, enthusiastic, brim-ming over with courageous optimism. Nervous and moody, sometimes up in the skies where the stars shone just for him, sometimes down on the brink of despair, face to face with a blank wall . . . He could suddenly jump up ecstatically and rush head-long to the piano, with such speed that he seemed to be summoned by some inner voice. And in the deathly hush that followed the first chord, Chopin's immortal music would reverberate through the tiny room and suddenly turn it into some marvellous auditorium. And he himself became so totally absorbed and interpreted the artistry of his fellow countryman with such consummate skill that we all became transfixed, spellbound, oblivious of time and place until the final echoes died away. Munch at the time of Przybyszewski's death in 1929[38]

The newspapers are being extremely abusive—though I have been highly praised in a couple of them. The young, however, are all very pleased at my pictures . . . An important art dealer here has suggested that I exhibit my work at Cologne and Düsseldorf in his premises there, and I shall do so, if the conditions are favourable. You have probably only seen unfavourable reviews— the conservative press has seen to that. If that is the case, I must send you the favourable ones that I have. Munch, writing to Karen Bjølstad, 1892[39]

This whole uproar has been most enjoyable. I could not have asked for better publicity . . . I have never had so much fun. It is incredible that anything as blameless as painting could have caused such a furore . . . Munch, writing to Karen Bjølstad[40]

One must not jump to the conclusion, adds the Berliner Tageblatt, that all those who voted against the closure of Munch's exhibition are necessarily in favour of the kind of art that he represents. In that aspect Munch's supporters are negligible, even amongst the young. The central question is one of principle. The opposition's main contention is simply that in art everyone should be allowed to have their say. Dagbladet, 1892[41]

17

119

117 **Walter Leistikow and his Wife**, 1902
Lithograph, 52.2 x 86.8 cm.
Oslo Kommunes Kunstsamlinger, OKK 243
Ref. G. Schiefler No. 170

118 **August Strindberg**, 1892
Oil on canvas, 120 x 90 cm.
Nationalmuseum, Stockholm

119 **Henrik Ibsen at the Grand Café**, 1906/10
Tempera on canvas, 116 x 181 cm.
Oslo Kommunes Kunstsamlinger, OKK 717

120 **Holger Drachmann**, 1901
Lithograph, 58.6 x 44.8 cm.
Oslo Kommunes Kunstsamlinger, OKK 240
Ref. G. Schiefler No. 141

121 **Knut Hamsun**, 1896
Drypoint, 27.9 x 18.3 cm.
Oslo Kommunes Kunstsamlinger, OKK 40
Ref. G. Schiefler No. 52

122 **Stanislaw Przybyszewski**, 1895
Pastel and oil, 62 x 55 cm.
Oslo Kommunes Kunstsamlinger, OKK 134

120

121

118

122

It is as if the subject had been secretly spied on in his study, and captured at a highly characteristic moment. His head and the upper part of his body are set against the warm background in an extremely vivid and life-like way. The impression conveyed is that of a violent temperament, combined with supreme arrogance and a feeling of bitter anger at the world.

Adolf Paul on Munch's portrait of Strindberg[42]

He had a little room in the Hotel zum Elefanten . . . in front of the bed lay a miserable piece of carpet, the sum total of the room's adornment. The canvas arrives, two metres high. It has been decided that we shall begin at ten o'clock in the morning, and I arrive at the exact time. Munch is still lying in bed. He looks at his hands and says: 'I'm still too nervous. I must first wait until I'm in a more peaceful frame of mind.' He orders a bottle of port from the waiter. 'Please come back in half an hour.' When I come back, the bottle is empty. 'Right, I'm fine now.' He starts to draw me. The room is so cramped that he can hardly take a step backwards. After each sitting, the waiters had to take the picture down to the courtyard so that he could judge the effect . . . The tatty little carpet on which I stood became a beautiful Oriental rug in the picture, while Munch changed the drab yellow of the walls to a fine lemon yellow, and my coat became a pure shade of ultramarine . . . Herman Schlittgen[43]

*123 **The German** (Hermann Schlittgen), 1904
Oil on canvas, 200 x 120 cm.
Oslo Kommunes Kunstsamlinger, OKK 367

123

7: The Frieze of Life

A poem of life, love and death

As I have already mentioned, I got the idea for the majority of these pictures from my early childhood, more than thirty years ago, but I have become so preoccupied with the task that I have been unable to leave it alone ever since. This is despite the fact that I have had no external encouragement to go ahead, let alone support from anyone conceivably interested in seeing the whole series assembled in one room. Munch[1]

The frieze is intended as a series of decorative pictures, which, gathered together, would give a picture of life. Through them all there winds the curving shoreline, and beyond it the sea, while under the trees, life, with all its complexities of grief and joy, carries on. Munch[2]

When I had placed them together, I felt that individual pictures had a thematic connection with each other. As soon as they were together, an echo ran through them all and they seemed totally different from when they were on their own. It was like a symphony. And that was how I found out how to paint friezes. Munch[3]

I intended that the frieze should be given space in a room that could provide the right architectural surroundings for it, so that each section would come into its own without damaging the overall effect, but unfortunately nobody so far has considered carrying out this plan. Munch[4]

These [pictures], which now seem incomprehensible, I believe, when finally brought together, will be more easily understood—they will deal with love and death. Munch to Johan Rohde[5]

In Ibsen's When We Dead Awaken, *the sculptor's resurrection work became split up and unfinished, and the same thing happened to my work.*
Some of the pictures ended up in Rasmus Meyer's collection in Bergen, and others in the Oslo National Museum. I was given no support in completing the project during the time that I was working on it. It was destroyed by chaos and adversity. Now, for the first time, I have gathered the leftovers together so as to form an approximation of what I had planned twenty years ago. It is just a body without a head. Munch, 1929[6]

Moreover, I had had the whole Frieze of Life *ready for a long time —prepared many years before I arrived in Berlin.*
Munch to Jens Thiis, c.1933[7]

The pictures are for the most part notes, documents, rough drafts, themes. That is their strength. Munch[8]

124 **The Kiss,** 1892
Oil on canvas, 99 x 81 cm.
Oslo Kommunes Kunstsamlinger, OKK 59

After having taken his controversial Berlin exhibition to a number of other German towns, Munch returned with it to the capital in December 1892, and in February 1893 he took it to Copenhagen.[162] The Danish painter Johan Rohde helped him to hang the works, and it was in connection with this that Munch wrote him a letter in which he mentioned for the first time that he was 'continuing with studies for a series of pictures' and that it had also occurred to him that several of [his] 'pictures which are with Kleis' belonged to the series.

When he wrote his 'manifesto', he did not use the word 'series'; instead he said, 'I shall paint a *number* of such pictures.' As we have already seen, it was to be some years before Munch actually carried out his intended programme, but now, three years later, it seemed as though the idea of completing the series had at last begun to take a serious hold on his mind. He had had the chance to see large exhibitions of his art shown in spacious surroundings, and he had become aware of the underlying connection between them. 'These pictures, which now seem incomprehensible,I believe , when finally brought together, will be more easily understood—they will deal with love and death.'

When in the December of that same year (1893), Munch once more rented premises on Unter den Linden,[163] he was able to show twenty-five pictures, the majority of which were new. The exhibition also included a series of six pictures entitled *Die Liebe*, which were to form the nucleus of 'his most important work', later called by Munch *The Frieze of Life*.[164]

To all intents and purposes, Munch spent the rest of his life struggling with the *Frieze of Life* pictures. He rearranged them in different ways, changed their titles, and continually added new works, some of them painted specifically for the series, others already painted, but which he thought 'belonged'. And every time that he had to sell a picture that he considered formed part of the frieze, he would make another version 'for my constantly plundered frieze of life'.

It is for this reason that a great number of his *Frieze of Life* pictures exist in several versions. He did not make copies; he repeated the works in order to 'renew my links with my earlier period',[165] to prevent himself from losing sight of his original goals. His dream was that his *Frieze of Life* should finally come to rest in 'a room whose architectural design would provide them with an appropriate setting'. But he doubted whether his plans to bring 'these storm-tossed pictures'[166] together would ever materialize.

Let us now examine the six paintings that he first exhibited under the title of *Die Liebe* ('Love' series) in 1893. It is quite possible, with regard to the title if nothing else, that Munch drew inspiration from Max Klinger's[167] much admired graphic series *Eine Liebe*, which dates from 1887. Klinger was one of the few artists that Munch mentions by name in his correspondence—and always in highly complimentary terms. Perhaps his teacher, Christian Krohg, had awakened his interest in the series.

But even in the titles, *Eine Liebe* and *Die Liebe*, there is a basic difference: Munch is dealing with a universal theme, whereas Klinger is recounting a particular love story in anecdotal form. Klinger's story does not concern us: we are merely passive witnesses to the faithless wife's fear that she is pregnant, and the dream that she has of her husband's anger and her own suicide. In Munch's work, however, the young girl's anguish does not centre on her fear of having lost her virginity but on the agonies of uncertainty that she feels concerning the years that lie ahead. In the first picture of the series, which at that time was called *Sommernachtstraum* (Summer Night's Dream), but later came to be known as *The Voice*, she is not really listening to the voices of the other young people out in the boats: it is her own inner voice that she hears in the still of the pale summer night. With wide-open, staring eyes, she stands alone, her mind torn between anxiety and longing for the new life that awaits her; unconsciously she offers herself up to the future, and yet turns her back on temptation, while in the background there lurks the threat of sex, symbolized by 'the moon's golden pillar that stood in the water and flickered'.[168]

Nor does the next picture, *The Kiss*, tell us, like Klinger's, the story of two lovers living in fear of the husband's unexpected return. Munch shows a symbolic meeting of the sexes, an encounter that represents the kind of universality which he dreamt of portraying in his *Frieze of Life*. The two figures melt into one another in a faceless, mouthless, armless embrace. Munch has captured that moment in which two people surrender themselves, and their individuality, totally.

The third picture in the poem of love was originally called *Liebe und Schmerz*, but now goes under the title of *Vampire*. The first title *Love and Pain* could in fact have been used as a name for the whole *Frieze of Life*, and it sums up very well a great deal of Munch's work: for him love was always inextricably bound up with suffering—and with death.

When, in his next picture, he showed a *Loving Woman*, he also showed the halo of suffering that surrounds her head. Even here—at the very moment of conception—the woman is alone. Later he was to paint a number of pictures on that theme, also including in his overall scheme a marvellous lithograph, *The Tree of Knowledge*, the latter work being accompanied by an explanatory text that reflects one of Munch's major philosophical preoccupations: 'Now the hand of death touches life'.[169]

The theme of the fifth picture,[170] at that time called *Jealousy*, is also loneliness: it is the feeling of being an outcast, of being completely alone in the world, that inspired the original title of the work. Its composition was almost identical to that of the painting which Munch had shown in the autumn exhibition in 1891 and which had inspired Christian Krohg to write his famous article 'Thank you for the yellow boat'. In the intervening period, Munch had done a lot of work on the subject, as he wanted to use it as a vignette[171] for his friend Emanuel Goldstein's collection of poetry, called *Alruner* (*Mandrakes*).

In the picture that Krohg described, the man is shown in profile in the bottom right hand corner of the scene, sunk in *Melancholy*, as the work later became known. But in the version that most probably formed part of the 'Love' series, Munch has made one small, but extremely significant alteration: the man has now turned and is facing us head-on. It is a device that Munch often used to intensify the expressive force of his pictures. The man's eyes stare reproachfully out at us from his pallid face, his back turned on the couple standing on the jetty, while behind him there stretches a landscape that no longer has the lyrical quality of *Evening*; it is blighted by his evil thoughts. Munch has 'moulded Nature in accordance with his mood'.

In the sixth, and final picture in the 'Love' series, the anguish of loneliness reaches its peak in *Despair*, or, as it later came to be known, *The Scream*.

We have observed how, in each picture of the series, Munch has expressed the dominant theme in such a way as to allow universal identification. Whether we like it or not, we are all obliged to make some kind of value judgement, because the artist is dealing with something that each of us has either experienced in the past or will experience in the future. The pictures either make us aware of our problems or confirm their existence. We are compelled to acknowledge their intrinsic truth because, to quote Munch's own words, they help one 'to gain a true understanding of life'. If we refuse to accept them, it is either because we dare not or perhaps because we are not yet sufficiently 'whole' human beings. The last picture in the series, *The Scream*, is perhaps the one which, of all Munch's works, will have the most profound effect on future generations—but it is probably with our present generation that it strikes the deepest chords. Rarely has the blind panic of human loneliness been portrayed with such force; even Nature has become an evil power that overwhelms the sexless, hopeless, tiny little embryonic being, stranded under the flaming, swirling skies of sunset which presage the

Munch 1892

125

126

127

125 **The Kiss,** 1892
  Oil on canvas, 72 x 91 cm.
  Nasjonalgalleriet, Oslo

126 **The Kiss,** 1894/95
  Pencil drawing, 18.8 x 28.8 cm.
  Oslo Kommunes Kunstsamlinger, OKK 362

127 **The Kiss,** 1895
  Drypoint and aquatint, 32.9 x 26.3 cm.
  Oslo Kommunes Kunstsamlinger, OKK 21
  Ref. G. Schiefler No. 22

128

end of the world.

    Whatever art historians may say about the 'Art Nouveau influence' and the 'artistic Zeitgeist' revealed in these sinuously sweeping lines, the picture still retains its original emotive force because Munch the poet used all his nervous energy to express in paint that for which words were inadequate. Colour and line become endowed with symbolic and evocative powers; it is they that transmit the intangible echoes of the soul.

    Nasjonalgalleriet in Oslo possesses a copy of the painting, from 1895, which has, written in the sky, the words 'could only have been painted by a madman'.[172] The handwriting is very reminiscent of Munch's own, and the majority of scholars are convinced that it was indeed he who wrote this extraordinary inscription—perhaps before the paint had dried—and they point to it as evidence that Munch at some stage began to doubt his own sanity. Quite possibly he did write those words, but the main interest of *The Scream* lies not in what it says about Munch, but in what it says about you and me.

    It is works like *The Scream* that have played such an important part in the development of European art—and continue to do so today. It is not hard to see why Munch has been called one of the fathers of Expressionism.[173]

    Even in *The Scream* Munch was drawing on his own personal experience.

This series of pictures is, in my opinion, one of my most important works, if not the most important. Nobody here in Norway has ever remotely understood it. It was, above all, in Germany that people first understood it most fully. But in Paris, too, it gained a measure of understanding; as early as 1897 it was hung in the place of honour on the main wall of the last and most important room in the Salon des Indépendants—and it was the work of mine that people understood best in France. Munch[9]

Was it because she took my first kiss, that she took away my life's breath. Was it that she lied—she deceived—that one day suddenly the scales fell from my eyes and I saw a Medusa's head and I saw life as a thing of terror. Munch, c. 1890[10]

Everybody who passed by looked at him, stared at him, all those faces, pallid in the evening light. He tried to concentrate on some thought, but he could not. All he felt was an emptiness in his head . . . His whole body trembled, and sweat ran down him. He staggered, and now I am falling too. People stop, more and more people, a frightening number of people . . . Munch[11]

I can see behind everyone's masks. Peacefully smiling faces, pale corpses who endlessly wend their tortuous way down the road that leads to the grave. Munch[12]

I can see . . .
I must have arrived on the wrong planet.
It's so strange here! Sigbjørn Obstfelder[13]

In my art I have tried to explain life and its meaning to myself. I also intended to help others to understand life better.
Munch[14]

A German once said to me: 'But you could rid yourself of many of your troubles.' To which I replied: 'They are part of me and my art. They are indistinguishable from me, and it would destroy my art. I want to keep those sufferings.' Munch[15]

Strindberg's rather troublesome Finnish admirer, Adolf Paul, visited Munch while he was working with a model in his room. He tells of how the model had long, flame-red hair that fell over her shoulders like congealed blood: *'Kneel down in front of her,' he shouted at me. 'Place your head against her.' I obeyed. She leaned forward over me and pressed her lips against my neck, her red hair spilling out over me. Munch started painting, and before long he had completed his* Vampire. Adolf Paul[16]

In my portfolio I have got the first rough drafts of The Kiss *and* Vampire. *They date from the years 1885–86.* Vampire *is the one that really makes the picture literary, but in fact it is just a woman kissing a man on the neck.*
Munch to Jens Thiis, c.1933[17]

129

128 **Evening on Karl Johan Street**, 1893/94
Oil on canvas, 85 x 121 cm.
Rasmus Meyers Samlinger, Bergen

129 **Evening on Karl Johan Street**, 1896
Hand-coloured lithograph
Private Collection

His artist friend, Christian Skredsvig, with whom he lived in Nice in 1892, tells how Munch 'had wanted to paint the memory of a sunset.[174] As red as blood.'

The memory that he wanted to paint was of an evening back in Norway, and he has recalled it so accurately that the locality is easily recognizable—there are even parts of the wooden railing[175] still standing today. The exact site is out on Nordstrand, with the city of Oslo and Holmenkollen hill in the distance, and there is another earlier picture which possesses an almost identical landscape in the background. It also contains the same two figures which appear in *The Scream*, but this time one of them is a thinly-disguised self-portrait. The painting was entitled *Despair*, and when Munch next exhibited his 'Love' series in 1894 in Stockholm,[176] under the Swedish title of *Kärlek*, both pictures appear in the catalogue: No. 67 was 'sick mood'[177] (*Despair*) and No. 68 was *The Scream*. The *Frieze of Life* now comprised fifteen paintings, and the series was exhibited in 1895 both in Berlin[178] and at Blomqvists Lokale in Christiania. Some of the works were also shown at the 'Salon des Indépendants'[179] in Paris in 1896 and 1897.

In 1902 Munch was invited by the distinguished German artist Max Liebermann[180] to show examples of his work at the Secession in Berlin, together with other painters, amongst whom were his friends Leistikow and von Hofmann.[181] By this time the 'Love' series had almost quadrupled in size, and the twenty-two works were now assembled in a carefully thought-out cycle, sub-divided into four sections and called *Aus dem modernen Seelenleben* (*From the Modern Life of the Soul*). The four sections were called 'Love's Dawning', 'The Rise and Fall of Love', 'The Terrors of Life' ('Livsangst') and 'Death'.

The title *From the Modern Life of the Soul* strikes us as being very literary in concept, and it is far from certain that it was Munch's own idea, as he himself was very little concerned about what titles his pictures had. And yet the reference to the 'life of the soul' is what he approved; as late as 1929 Munch wrote to the Swedish art historian Ragnar Hoppe[182] that it gave him much pleasure that his lecture was intended to 'deal with the spiritual content of my art'. The word 'spiritual' ('soul painting') was to recur constantly in discussions of Munch's art from that period.

At about the same time that Munch wrote his St. Cloud 'manifesto', the Norwegian author Knut Hamsun, four years his senior, was working on his famous article 'From the subconscious life of the soul', published in *Samtiden* in 1890 (see page 74).

Several of Munch's close literary friends were wrestling with similar problems during that era of Neo-Romanticism and Symbolism—not least of

130

them Strindberg—and a good deal has been written about how Munch was influenced by his literary friends; Krohg even went as far as calling him 'our fourth greatest poet'.[183]

But can Munch be considered a literary painter? He himself stated that he was afraid of being accused of painting 'Gedankenmalerei'[184] (literally, 'Thought painting'). Munch is not a literary painter inasmuch as he paints what he has seen, not what he has thought. What distinguishes Munch from so many of his Symbolist contemporaries—and saved him from the gimmickry of other would-be Symbolists—is, as has already been emphasized, the fact that he never painted things that he had not personally lived through or 'at least experienced'. This enabled him to develop his genius for identifying not only with the very young girl and her jealous friend, but even with the woman making love, at the moment of embrace. It differs from Ibsen's gift for understanding women's problems, being altogether more intuitive—and it bears no relation at all to Strindberg's bitter outpourings. Munch is often accused of having been influenced by his Berlin friends where women were concerned, by Przybyszewski's 'Satanism' and Strindberg's hopelessly one-sided opinions. But we have already noted that the basic concept of his 'Love' series had been formulated *before* he met them, and, in any case, there are preliminary sketches and drawings still in existence which show that he had already begun to wrestle with the subject before his 'Ferkel' days. There was probably a great deal of truth in his own

Munch derives most of his sensory impressions from past images or fantasies, things that only poets normally use as a basis for their work . . . in this way he stands nearer to contemporary literature than contemporary pictorial art.

Paul Scheerbart, 1895[18]

It has interested me greatly that you wish to hold a lecture on the subject of the exhibition, and that you want to draw attention to the spiritual aspects of my art. Nowadays, to my irritation, it is often described as literary, and, with even less justification, it has also been called German 'Gedankenmalerei' ('Thought painting')—remarks that are not intended to be complimentary. I have an extremely high opinion of good German art, but not the sort that is quite rightly reviled as 'Gedankenmalerei'.

Munch to Ragnar Hoppe[19]

The painter Paul Hermann says that Munch used him as a model on several occasions—'even for Jealousy, as well'.

Paul Hermann was a painter who used the name Henri Héran, because his own could be confused with the French illustrator Herman Paul.[20]

131

*130 **Vampire**, c.1893
   Oil on canvas, 78 x 98 cm.
   Oslo Kommunes Kunstsamlinger, OKK 292

131 **Vampire**, 1895/96
   Lithograph and woodcut, 38.2 x 54.5 cm.
   Oslo Kommunes Kunstsamlinger, OKK 567
   Ref. G. Schiefler No. 34

assertion that Jaeger and his bohemian friends played a more important part in his artistic development: after all, Munch had come into contact with them much earlier on in his life. And his sketches are positive proof that many of his greatest works were already lurking 'behind the retina' prior to his days in Berlin.

It would be perfectly correct to say that Munch, in his paintings and his graphic work, but most of all in his drawings, shows signs of misogyny. But in many cases he is dealing with specific experiences: his sphinxes and harpies, his Salomes and his female birds of prey all show the characteristics of particular women. They represent his own personal traumas, when he had experienced 'the love that moves mountains'. It may be that he was telling the truth when he said 'I have never loved', but his extreme sensitivity to the human condition renders him capable of 'explaining' it to us. No misogynist could ever have portrayed the apotheosis of a woman at the peak of sexual ecstasy with so much insight, or given the scene such an aura of sanctity by the inclusion of a halo. When he later painted his *Death of Marat* with the almost defiant figure of Charlotte Corday standing by the corpse, he is portraying an event which had actually happened; he is not indulging in the same kind of blanket condemnation of women as many of his contemporaries. The pain felt by the men in *Ashes* and *Separation* is the pain of despair, not that of burning hatred. It is the inevitability of life's misfortunes that he is 'explaining' and recounting: love must die, some day it must turn

132

to ashes. With great awareness and with great sensitivity he portrays the loneliness of the two people on the beach—so near to each other and yet so far apart.

Often the symbolic force of Munch's work is strengthened by various technical devices. He uses shadow, for example, to heighten the young girl's feeling of fear in *Puberty*, or to deepen the mystery of the summer night in *Moonlight*. The two lovers in *Consolation* cast sinister shapes, while *The Mad Woman* hesitates uncertainly at the sight of her own silhouette. We have already seen how he made use of 'the moon's golden pillar' to underline the agonies of uncertainty suffered by the girl in *The Voice*, and he frequently portrays the full moon (and its 'pillar' reflection) in his landscapes as a means of bringing Nature to life. Hair is another symbol he often uses with very realistic effect; he shows the woman's hair entwined round the button of a man's coat, while in other pictures it seems to represent the invisible bonds, which connect a man to a woman as in *Separation*. Flowers came to symbolize Art, which feeds on the life-blood of an artist, and the artist has Munch's own features. There can certainly be no more deeply felt self-portrait than *The Blossom of Pain* (Plate 11). Foetuses and embryos make one think of life to come, but in the *Madonna* lithograph they are harbingers of death. Some of these symbols were later overpainted by Munch; for example, those in the original 'frame' of the *Madonna* painting,[185] which were retained in the

132 **Jealousy**, 1895
Oil on canvas, 67 x 100 cm.
Rasmus Meyers Samlinger, Bergen

133 **Jealousy**, 1896
Lithograph, 46.5 x 56.5 cm.
Oslo Kommunes Kunstsamlinger, OKK 202
Ref. G. Schiefler No. 58

134 **The Virginia Creeper**, 1898
Oil on canvas, 119 x 121 cm.
Oslo Kommunes Kunstsamlinger, OKK 503

133

A similar situation to the one portrayed in *Jealousy* is described in Przybyszewski's book *The Vigil* for which Munch did the title vignette. The central character (Przybyszewski) says to his beloved: *You must kiss him now—you must. I give my woman to the artist, I, the king. . .[21]*

One day when I talked to Munch about the art that had impressed him most deeply, he named Edgar Allan Poe's Tales of Fantasy [Tales of Mystery and Imagination] *and Dostoyevsky's* Prince Myshkin [The Idiot] *and* The Brothers Karamazov. *These two deeply poetic writers are also his kindred spirits. No one in art has yet penetrated as far as they have into the mystical realms of the soul, towards the metaphysical, the subconscious. They both view the external reality of the world as merely a sign, a symbol of the spiritual and the metaphysical.*   Hans Dedekam, 1892[22]

Just as Leonardo da Vinci studied human anatomy and dissected corpses, so I try to dissect souls.   Munch[23]

Tall, thin-faced, with piercing eyes—surrounded by golden hair, like a halo. A strange smile through her tightly-drawn lips. A certain Madonna-like quality. Suddenly I was filled with an inexplicable feeling of anxiety—I shivered. Then she went away, and I began the Dance of Life. *In the evening I dreamed that I kissed a corpse and I jumped up, racked with fear. I had kissed the sallow, smiling lips of a corpse—a cold, clammy kiss.*
Munch[24]

I have begun a new picture, The Dance of Life. *One light summer's night, in the middle of a meadow, a young priest is dancing with a woman with flowing hair. They stare into each other's eyes, and her hair wraps itself round his head. The background is a mass of whirling people—fat men biting women on the neck. Caricatures and strong men entwining women.*
Munch[25]

The Storm *provides a good illustration of the way in which Munch advanced the frontiers of painting . . . Munch has intentionally enveloped the whole scene in the darkness of night. The figures say nothing: the central element is the natural language of the Storm itself. Munch understands this language, his pantheistic soul speaks it clearly and fluently. Is it his fault if so-called connoisseurs of art cannot get by without a translation?*
Willy Pastor[26]

The men of old were right when they said that love was a flame— because when it is burnt out, all that remains is a pile of ashes.
Munch[27]

graphic version of the work.

One picture that Munch himself saw as an important link in the *Frieze of Life* was *Man and Woman in a Wood* (*Metabolism* Plate 144): he maintained that it was 'as vital as a buckle is for a belt'.[186] This remark might seem difficult for us to understand, looking at the picture today, but X-rays have shown that originally there was an embryo painted on the tree-trunk,[187] and amongst Munch's many possessions discovered after his death was the painting's original frame, in which the inevitability of decay is symbolized by a carved design of bones and skulls. As we see them today, they are just two naked people who radiate a feeling of life and vitality that Munch never originally intended.

What, then, was the message that this picture was intended to convey, the picture Munch considered so all-important for *The Frieze of Life*? In its original frame it would have provided the key to understanding his whole philosophy of life—a series of beliefs, bearing no relation to conventional religion,[188] which first found expression as early as the 1890s. He had arrived at a pantheistic belief in a hidden life force, whose existence was inextricably bound up with the cyclical renewal of Nature. It is a belief that shines through many of his works, and one that he maintained throughout his life. It found expression in his graphic work, as, for example, when he shows the dead woman giving life to the new generation through a tree of fruit, or in his painting *Fertility* (Plate 146).

As early as 1894 the first book on Munch appeared. Called *Das Werk des Edvard Munch*, it was written by four of his friends, one of whom, Przybyszewski, was also its publisher. The other three participants were the authors and art historians Franz Servaes, Willy Pastor and Julius Meier-Graefe. The book is important, not only because it enables us to date Munch's paintings from that period, but also because we know that the authors had had long discussions with the artist before writing it. The work is sub-titled 'Eighteen themes from the modern life of the soul' and was primarily an attempt to justify Munch to his detractors. In the year the book was published Munch opened his exhibition in Stockholm, the catalogue of which included a translation of a large section of Przybyszewski's article on the 'Love' series, which would seem to suggest that Munch appreciated the

134

135

Pole's rather fulsome description of his work.

All in all, it would seem that Berlin in the 1890s, and its lively coterie of intellectuals centred on *Pan* magazine,[189] played an important part in Munch's development, helping him to formulate the ideas which hitherto had only existed in embryonic form in his mind. Certainly, the years between 1892 and 1895 were extremely productive ones for him. And much of the credit for this sudden burst of artistic activity must go to the literary milieu in which Munch found himself, although it is hard to decide quite who benefited most from whom. His Berlin friends readily admitted that they drew great inspiration from *the Light from the North*,[190] but the interminable discussions over glasses of wine in 'Zum Schwarzen Ferkel' also provided much-needed stimulus for Munch, involved in the serious business of realizing his 'Frieze of Life, that embraces both Love and Death'. We have seen how, by 1893, he had already finished the 'Love' series, and in the following years he painted a succession of major works, each of which was destined to form part of his poetic *From the Modern Life of the Soul* until finally the whole work, a symphony in four movements, was completed.

Later on we shall see how, with the help of the new medium of graphics, he returned once more to the themes of *The Frieze of Life*. On single sheets of paper he would blend the concrete and the abstract, the tangible and the intangible, expressing them both in an easily accessible language.

The 'Love' series was a kind of prelude, an overture to the four movements of *The Frieze of Life*, which Munch revealed to a wider public at the Berlin Secession in 1902. The reaction was predictable: a mixture of indignation and admiration, of contempt and respect. But by this time Munch had established a reputation amongst people whose opinions mattered, at least in Germany: it was to take several years before his fellow Norwegians began to appreciate the true extent of his genius.

*135 **The Dance of Life**, 1899/1900
Oil on canvas, 126 x 191 cm.
Nasjonalgalleriet, Oslo

136 Detail of No. 135

136 >

138

The burnt-out or burnt-down people shown in the picture entitled Ashes *will certainly not add to the beauty of Nasjonalgalleriet walls.* Aftenposten, 1909[28]

I do not paint the image of nature—I take from it—or draw from its rich cornucopia. Munch[29]

The trees and the sea form perpendicular and horizontal lines, which are repeated endlessly in different combinations. The beach and the people give a feeling of swelling movement and life—strong colours echo harmoniously throughout the pictures.
Munch[30]

Through them all [the pictures] *there winds the curving shore-line, and beyond it the ever-moving sea, while under the trees, life, with all its complexities of grief and joy, carries on.*
Munch[31]

Two people never love each other—at the same time.
Gunnar Heiberg in *Love's Tragedy*[32]

I do not think that a frieze need always have that sameness and uniformity that so often makes decorative paintings and friezes so appallingly boring, with the result that it could almost be said of them that they are the sort of paintings that never get noticed. I maintain that a frieze can easily be made to have the same qualities as a symphony, which can soar into the light and sink down to the depths. Its strength can be modulated. Likewise different strains can echo and re-echo within the main theme, interspersed by drum-beats. Munch[33]

137 Detail of No. 135

138 Sketch for *The Dance of Life*, 1898
Indian in, charcoal and (bluegreen) crayon, 35.9 x 45.8 cm.
Oslo Kommunes Kunstsamlinger, OKK 2392

It is interesting to see how Munch had developed the themes of the 'Love' series. The pictures, which were hung in the place of honour in the entrance hall, were divided into four groups, the first comprising roughly the same pictures that had made up the original series, with pride of place being given to a new and extremely impressive landscape: *Starry Night*. The painting contains no human figures, but it would have been unthinkable for Munch to have tried to express the spiritual life of modern man without including a landscape in some prominent position. And, not surprisingly, the landscape that he portrayed was his beloved Åsgårdstrand, the place to which his mind returned constantly, whether he was painting 'in a garret in Nice, or some dark room in Paris or Berlin'.

In *Starry Night* (Plate 140) Munch has adopted a soft, sombre tone to portray the lonely and moody landscape, with its vast, brooding tree, the sweeping curve of the beach, and the deep blue sea mirroring the starry skies above.

In the next picture, *Eye to Eye* (Plate 145), we witness the meeting of a man and a woman. Their pale faces stare mutely at each other; even in this, the first encounter, we have a feeling of impending unhappiness. The scene contains many elements that were to recur throughout the frieze, such as the woman's hair brushing against the man's chest, warning of their future fateful involvement, and the tree at the very centre of the scene, the Tree of Life, which is destined both to draw them together and separate them from each other. The house with the light shining through its windows is also something that Munch often used to great effect, as, for example, in his dramatic portrayal of *The Storm* (Plate 139). This incident can also be pinned down to an exact locality—outside Kjøsterud farm at Åsgårdstrand. The people huddle together, terrified by the forces of Nature; so violent is the storm that the gusts of wind seem to control the artist's brush strokes. Only one woman, a pale and solitary figure, has the courage to break loose from the crowd of people and come towards us, while behind her stands the mysterious, locked house, its lights blazing in the summer night. The scene

139

obviously made a deep impression on Munch, and fifteen years later, when his fevered mind had itself fallen prey to uncontrollable storms, he returned once more to portray it in a frenziedly vivid woodcut (Plate 278).

The same house reappears in *The Virginia Creeper* (Plate 134), with the blood-red leaves giving it an eerie, almost haunted quality. Surely some drama must lurk behind the sinister mood that pervades the bleak landscape, with its skeletal trees and the house engulfed in the blood-red flames of the creeper. Against the background of the harsh, threatening colours of the house, a man comes forward to meet us, his tormented eyes staring straight into ours. What happened in that locked house during the autumn night? We shall never know, but Munch often made use of houses to create a certain mood, just as he did landscapes.

We have already seen how, in *The Scream*, Munch intensifies the feeling of anguish and suffering by having the figure turn towards us, drawing us into

140

The whole mystery of development condensed into one scene. The many-faceted nature of woman is a mystery to man. Woman, who is at the same time a saint, a whore and a hapless devotee.

Munch[34]

All the others add up to one—you are a thousand.

Gunnar Heiberg[35]

It happened in 1895. I had an exhibition that autumn at Blomqvist's, and the pictures had stirred up a fierce controversy. People even wanted the police to boycott the premises. One day I met Ibsen down there. He came up to me and said, 'I find it very interesting. But believe me—the same thing will happen to you as happened to me: the more enemies you make, the more friends you will have.' I had to accompany him round, and he insisted on seeing every picture. There was a lot of the Frieze of Life *on show . . . He was particularly interested in* The Three Stages of Woman, *which I had to explain to him. 'That one is the dreaming woman—that one, the woman that enjoys life to the full—and the nun is the one standing there palely against the trees.' He then enjoyed himself greatly looking at my portraits, in which I had emphasized the characteristics of the sitters almost to the point of caricature. Some years later Ibsen wrote* When We Dead Awaken, *in which the sculptor's work was never finished, but disappeared abroad. I recognized many themes that resembled the pictures in the* Frieze of Life, *such as the man sitting hunched up amongst the stones, sunk deep in melancholy, and the jealousy-ridden Pole, with a bullet in his head.*

The three women—the white-clad Irene, dreaming about life, Maja, naked and full of life's joys, and Irene's brooding nurse, the sorrowing woman with the pale face that stares out from the tree trunks. These three women reappear in Ibsen's drama—just as they frequently do in my art. Munch[36]

I envisaged the frieze as a poem of life, love and death. The subject of the largest painting, the man and woman in the wood, perhaps lies somewhat outside the range of ideas expressed in the other pictures, but its role in the frieze is as vital as a buckle is for a belt. It is a picture of life, as well as of death, it shows the wood feeding off the dead and the city growing up behind the trees. It is a picture of the powerful constructive forces of life. Munch[37]

41

39 **The Storm,** 1893
Oil on canvas, 98 x 127 cm.
Museum of Modern Art, New York

40 **Starry Night,** 1893
Oil on canvas, 135 x 140 cm.
Private Collection

41 **Ashes,** 1894
Oil on canvas, 121 x 141 cm.
Nasjonalgalleriet, Oslo

the main body of the painting and changing us from passive spectators to active participants. It is this same feeling of involvement that is achieved in *The Virginia Creeper.*

The same malevolent, triangular face stares out at us in the new picture with the old name—*Jealousy* (Plate 132). The mood is even more intense than in the *Jealousy* from the 'Love' series: the man is being tortured by jealousy at the sight of his woman standing with another under the Tree of Knowledge. A passionately deep red cloak envelops her pale pink flesh, while the man beside her, who bears Munch's unmistakeable profile, is wearing a nondescript black garment. It is not the man but the woman who is beset by passion—she is the evil one, the temptress. And in the left-hand side of the picture there stands a blood-red, flame-shaped bush, a symbol of the cruelty of love's eternal mystery.

Love dies and is turned to *Ashes* (Plate 141)—all that is left for the man is emptiness and despair, while the woman tears at her red hair and dumbly

117

cries her misery. Behind them stands the dark and threatening pine forest, while the middle ground is dead and barren, and from the cold stones in the foreground there slowly rises a flame-like border.

In the same year that Munch completed *Ashes* (1894), he also finished his *Three Stages of Woman*, or *The Sphinx*,[191] to give it the original title, and once more it is Åsgårdstrand's 'curving shoreline' that wends its way through the picture. The virginal young girl in the white dress looks longingly at the 'ever moving' sea, while under the 'crown of trees' the cheerful prostitute stands, brazenly flaunting her nakedness, and the nun in her black habit stares glumly in front of her. All three women are separated from the man on their right by the fiery, blood-red bush, and he, by his movement, is clearly signalling that he is about to desert them all.

Munch struggled endlessly with the problems of portraying this subject, which meant a great deal to him personally, before finally painting the picture in 1894. The following year he exhibited it back in Oslo at Blomqvist's Lokale, where Ibsen was particularly intrigued by this picture of 'The Virgin, the Prostitute and the Nun'. That meeting made a great impression on Munch and he often claimed that his painting had influenced Ibsen in his play about the sculptor Rubek (*When We Dead Awaken*), and Pål Hougen,[192] in his brief but penetrating analysis of the relationship between the two men, has uncovered several pieces of evidence that would seem to suggest that Munch was right in what he said. Later on we will examine the influence that Ibsen had on Munch.

The three women from *The Sphinx* reappear in *The Dance of Life*, painted in 1899 (Plate 135). It would, in fact, be more correct to see them not as three different women, but as the personification of what Munch himself called 'Woman, who is at the same time a saint, a whore and a hapless devotee'. The whole painting is permeated by the golden light of the moon spilling out onto the sea, emphasizing the underlying atmosphere of sexuality, which is represented by the carefree couple in the background dancing happily together and the innocent young girl approaching the pair of dancers at the centre of the picture with a mixture of curiosity and wonder. Totally absorbed in each other, they whirl round in the dance of life, the red dress of the girl wrapping itself round the dark suit of the man, while her copper hair spreads out against his heart. The man on the right with the green face leers brutishly at his partner, who tries to fend him off, until finally we come to the ageing woman standing alone, a bitter and disillusioned spectator of a dance in which she no longer participates. The whole painting reflects the irreversible laws of destiny.

Occasionally, as in *The Scream*, Munch endows line and colour with an expressive force of their own that far exceeds the usual bounds of painting. He achieves this to a certain degree in *Evening on Karl Johan Street*, but in *Angst* (Plate 108) the effect is almost overwhelming. The sickly, yellow faces in the spring evening have a kind of mystical quality that makes one think instinctively of death—and of the vision of death that one finds in the works of contemporary poets, such as Obstfelder[193] and Maeterlinck.[194] Just as some of their poems have the expressive quality of paintings, so Munch's art often possesses the powers of poetry—but without falling into the category of 'literary painting'. *Evening on Karl Johan Street* (Plate 128) could easily be used as an illustration for his friend Obstfelder's poem *Jeg ser* ('I can see'). The small figure that we see in silhouette is Munch himself: he is the one who is not like the others, who breaks away from the crowd and wends his own lonely way, turning against the macabre tide of living dead 'who wend their tortuous way down the road that leads to the grave'.[195] The colours create an extraordinarily disturbing mood, particularly in the way that Munch juxtaposes his favourite deep violet with a sinister shade of pale yellow. Even the Parliament building (the Storting) with its empty, staring windows, presents an uncharacteristically threatening aspect. And yet, almost like a prophecy being fulfilled, there came a time when the people of Oslo saw it in the same sinister light that bright spring day when the black and red swastika flag fluttered against the deep blue sky, when the memory of Munch's painting sent a cold shiver down the spine, heightening feelings of hopelessness and despair.

In *Angst*, the sky and the whole landscape are filled with the same

The breath of life is, if you wish, the same as the soul or the spirit. It would be foolish to deny the existence of the soul, and one cannot deny the existence of a life-force.

We must all believe in immortality, and also, for that matter, that it is possible to claim that the breath of life, the spirit of life, lives on after the body is dead . . . What becomes of the spirit of life, the power that holds a body together, the power that fosters the growth of physical matter? Nothing—there is no evidence in nature to suggest that anything does. A body that dies does not vanish—its substance is transformed, converted. But what happens to the spirit that inhabits it?

Nobody can say where it goes to—to try and assert its non-existence after the body has died is as ridiculous as insisting on trying to demonstrate how or where that spirit will continue to exist. Munch[38]

I felt it would be a pleasurable experience to sink into, to unite with—to actually become that everlasting, ever-stirring earth, perpetually bathed in sunlight . . .

I would become one with it, and plants and trees would grow up out of my rotting corpse . . . I would be 'in' them, I would live on—that is eternity. Munch[39]

In all my work people will see that I am a doubter, but I never deny or mock religion. Munch[40]

142 **The Three Stages of Woman**, 1894
   Oil on canvas, 164 x 250 cm.
   Rasmus Meyers Samlinger, Bergen
   Illustrated on previous page

143 **Red and White**, c.1894
   Oil on canvas, 93 x 130 cm.
   Oslo Kommunes Kunstsamlinger, OKK 460

143

sweeping waves of colour as *The Scream*, but the loneliness of the figures becomes even more terrifying, as theirs is the loneliness of people in a crowd. In their solitude they are caught in an inexplicable cosmic dread.

'The camera will never compete with the brush and the palette, until such time as photographs can be taken in Heaven or Hell,'[196] says Munch in his little pamphlet on *The Origin of the Frieze of Life*. This statement encapsulates one of the most basic tenets of his artistic philosophy: for him, art was the means of exploring the mystical boundaries of man's psyche. He penetrated deeper and deeper into the mind, passing from the conscious to the sub-conscious, but the deeper he plumbed the more 'angst'-ridden he became. And this 'angst' was not only centred on life, as in the 'Love' series, but also on death, a theme which began to obsess him in the 1890s and continued to do so right up until the end of his life.

He once told his friend Schreiner, 'I have lived the whole of my life partly in a dream world, partly in reality.' He also recounted how he was continually being pursued by feelings of anxiety and insecurity, for which he had only one cure: painting. Munch instinctively tried to 'paint out' his fears in such works as *The Scream*, and in the same way he portrayed death in order to exorcize his own bitter memories of it. He often discussed the part played by illness in his life, and he was himself convinced that when he 'paints sickness and grief, it is . . . a healthy reaction which people can learn a lot from in leading their own lives'.[197]

Munch found it hard to forgive Johan Scharffenberg[198] for having said in

145

144 **Metabolism or The Transformation of Matter, (Man and Woman in a Wood)** c.1898, but overpainted later, c.1918
Oil on canvas, 175 x 143 cm. (excluding painted frame)
Oslo Kommunes Kunstsamlinger, OKK 419

145 **Eye to Eye,** 1893
Oil on canvas, 137 x 110 cm.
Islo Kommunes Kunstsamlinger, OKK 502

the Students Association that his art was sick, because he belonged to a sick family, and many years later he wrote: 'I do not think that my art is sick—despite what Scharffenberg and many others believe. Those kind of people do not understand the true function of art, nor do they know anything about its history.'[199] Munch often asserted that his mental problems were of vital importance to him: 'without illness and anxiety I would have been like a rudderless ship.'

Munch underwent several key experiences in his life, which he returned to constantly, the majority of them being incidents that he had witnessed as a child, when he was at his most vulnerable. The memory of his dying mother was an image that he persistently tried to come to terms with. Perhaps he relived the sense of childish helplessness when he painted the memory of his mother, who died when he was so young, or when he recalled the death of his beloved sister Sophie. It was his anxiety in the face of death that made him portray it so often, and prompted him, at the age of thirty-two, to include the arm of a skeleton beneath his own portrait.

One of the main pictures in *The Frieze of Life* is *Death in the Sickroom* (Plate 51), but the remarkable thing about it is that it does not portray death, or even the dying moments of the young girl; it is the effects of death on the living that Munch is concerned with. The figures in the painting do not cling to each other for consolation—quite the opposite: they draw away from one another, either sunk in deep despair or staring blankly towards us, numb with grief. The one who should have helped, her doctor father, seeks sorrowing refuge in prayer, while the brother, who is studying to become a doctor, just leaves the room. Her aunt, who has been looking after her since the mother's death, leans helplessly on the dying girl's chair, while Munch

123

146

himself half turns away from us despairingly. Despite its deceptive simplicity, the painting's composition is extraordinarily effective. The figure of the father in the background, his hands clasped together in prayer, is echoed in the person of Inger, who faces us head-on, her sorrowing eyes dominating the whole scene. The profile of her other sister, Laura, who is slumped in a chair in the foreground, is mirrored in the profile of Edvard, as he moves slowly towards the dying girl, while the bowed head of the grief-stricken aunt is itself reflected in the melancholy figure of the brother as he steals out of the room. The pyramid formed by the figures in the foreground rears up against the flatness of the background, bringing a great feeling of perspective to the desolate room, while the sickly green and yellow colours fill it with an icy chill. The whole scene is portrayed with a strength of feeling that strikes us like a cold gust of wind. He returned to the subject on other occasions (*At the Deathbed* and *Fever*), each time resolving its artistic and emotional problems in a different way, finally achieving the greatest degree of simplification in the lithograph completed in 1896.

*146 **Fertility**, 1898
Oil on canvas, 120 x 140 cm.
Private Collection

8 : The Graphic Artist

An art dedicated to mankind

We need something more than just photographs of nature. Nor should we content ourselves with painting pretty pictures to hang on sitting room walls. Let us try and see, even though we ourselves may not succeed, if we cannot lay the foundations of an art dedicated to mankind. A style of art that will fire man's imagination. An art that springs from our very hearts.   Munch[1]

Munch's graphic work is] the revelation of a technical genius that makes Munch one of the greatest graphic artists of all time, and perhaps the greatest of his contemporaries.   Thor Hedberg[2]

Some people pretend that they are capable of more than they really are: Munch is crafty, he does quite the opposite.
Max Liebermann[3]

147 **The Lonely One**, 1896
Mezzotint and drypoint on zinc, 28.7 x 21.7 cm.
Olso Kommunes Kunstsamlinger, OKK 816
Ref. G. Schiefler No. 42

148 **Death and the Maiden**, 1894
Drypoint, 29.3 x 20.8 cm.
Oslo Kommunes Kunstsamlinger, OKK 3
Ref. G. Schiefler No. 3

148

In 1894 Munch produced his first graphic work—an etching of the German art critic Mengelberg,[200] who had written praising his painting. At the time he was still living in Berlin, and during his ten years as a painter he had already produced a number of very important works. We have no idea who it was that encouraged him to lay down his brushes and take up the burin, but it may have been Mengelberg himself. However, we have already mentioned that Max Klinger's series of engravings from the 1880s may well have given Munch inspiration for the 'Love' series, as he was a notable graphic artist of the time. Many similarities have been noted between the two artists' work,[201] and Munch himself expressed great admiration[202] for that German artist in particular. It is also possible that the young Käthe Kollwitz, who, by 1890, had already embarked on her career as a graphic artist could have interested Munch (four years her senior) in the new medium. His friend, the Ibsen authority Julius Elias,[203] in his review of the exhibition of rejected works in 1893, had, in fact, hinted at a connection between Munch and Käthe Kollwitz. We also know that Köpping,[204] the graphics professor, stood firmly by his beliefs and resigned from his post in 1892 in protest at the way that Munch had been treated.

It is impossible to say what effect Hermann Struck,[205] who subsequently published his famous book on engraving, in which an original etching of Munch's was included, had on the Norwegian artist as early as 1894, but he is another possible influence.

The young Munch seized with both hands this opportunity of reaching a far wider public by means of graphics. There was no need now for a picture to disappear on to the wall of some private owner, as did paintings : by means of a copper plate, a stone or a piece of wood he could spread his message to a far greater number of people. He had been forced to accept the bitter truth that his paintings were by no means easily saleable, but Munch had never intended to make any compromises. It had hardly ever occurred to him to tailor his art to public taste, but graphics gave him the chance to reach a much wider range of people without 'deserting the goddess of art'.

He began by engraving a couple of portraits, but quickly changed to making engravings and lithographs of subjects similar to those of *The Frieze of Life*: *Death and the Maiden*, *The Sick Child* and *Puberty* were the titles of some of his first works. Munch never thought it important to number his graphic work, and he had himself no idea of the size of the various editions. He spread his works around like confetti, by means of exhibitions and commissions, and by giving countless numbers of them to friends and people who had helped him. The prints that he left to the city of Oslo in his will, approximately 17,000 of them, represent only a fraction of his total production. When one considers the astronomical sums that collectors pay nowadays, it is strange to read of his plans to hold an 'auto-da-fé'[206] of all his graphic work on the grounds that far too many of them had been sold.

During the difficult years around the turn of the century Munch was fortunate in getting to know a number of people who, apart from acting as his patrons, also became close friends. Later on we shall see just how important men like the Swede Ernest Thiel, and the Germans Albert Kollmann and Max Linde, became for him.[207] In 1902 he came into contact with the magistrate Gustav Schiefler,[208] an avid collector of prints, who tells the story of how, after seeing some of Munch's work, he longed to meet 'that magician'.[209] The magistrate became so interested in Munch's prints that he set himself the agreeable task of producing a *catalogue raisonné* of the artist's entire production, and in 1907 the first section of this work was published, the second part coming out in 1927. The books sold out quickly, and it was not until 1974 that this indispensable work was reissued by a Norwegian publisher.

At a time when Munch was feeling completely alone and threatened by the world, when he was dragging himself from hotel to boarding house, visiting spa after spa to find some way of calming his nerves, his only connections with normal middle-class life were two houses in Hamburg and Lübeck, one the home of Schiefler, the other of Linde. There he found people who offered him warmth and understanding, who admired his work and who also provided him with commissions.

It would seem that Munch had fallen completely on his feet, to judge by the technical skill of his first graphic works, but if we examine his work in that field closely we can see that it took much hard work before he had explored the full potential of the various media. He tackled the problems with great enthusiasm, making use of every possible method available and experimenting until he found the right technique. And by means of this tireless experimentation he succeeded in opening up whole new vistas for graphic artists: he himself said 'All means are equally good'.[210] But he was not experimenting for the sake of experimenting; he was striving to find a means of communicating with his fellow men. Undoubtedly, in the process he either ignored or broke the rules governing conventional contemporary graphic usage, but he had had no formal training in the art, and therefore he simply had to 'get on with it'.

But it was precisely in this unconventional learning process that he blazed new trails, making simplifications that no one else had ever considered. He drew inspiration, as did many of his European contemporaries, from Japanese woodcuts, at that time very much in vogue. But instead of using the very elaborate Japanese method of printing, which involved as many as twelve blocks, he took a single block of wood and cut it up with a saw[211] into small pieces, which he was then able to colour as he wished. The white line that appeared round each block of colour was an added bonus, and he was able to achieve almost endless permutations by repositioning the various individual pieces. The whole process became an adventure for him, and he was able to explore all the possibilities of the medium while working on it. For example, he combined different techniques in one work: overlaying lithographs on woodcuts and vice versa, making use of a cut-out paper moon, complete with 'golden pillar', in some prints and omitting it in others (see page 139). He also embellished his prints with watercolour, pastel and oil paint on occasion, combining the traditional fineness of the engraver's art with unexpectedly soft, almost velvety effects. He even made use of the natural grain of the wood, as in his woodcut of *The Kiss*, whose monumental uncluttered style made it a landmark in the history of the woodcut. Munch was no intellectual snob, and he sometimes used ordinary office machines, normally intended for business letters or songsheets, while at other times he used a hectograph. The fact that a hectograph print only lasted for a short time was of no consequence to him—it could always be livened up with water colour or pastels. He was constantly learning new things, sometimes quite by chance, sometimes after endless experimentation, and sometimes merely as a result of a mistake or a stroke of luck, but he always remained very conscious of the material with which he was dealing and he always altered his style to suit the medium.

Graphics were gaining very much in popularity, and artists were beginning to recognize them as an art form in their own right. It is true that men such as Goya and Daumier had used lithography, and also that Millet had produced some striking etchings earlier in the century, but there then followed a period of decline, when prints were mainly used for illustrations, or to provide reproductions of other artists' works in books and magazines, or simply as posters. However, towards the end of the 1880s and throughout the '90s painters began to realize that graphic art was not just the domain of printers, but a valid art form that could hold its own with conventional painting. These *peintres graveurs* began to publish their works in folios, which were intended for a specific collectors' market, and they also started signing them to increase their value. Another practice which began during

149

*149 **The Three Stages of Woman**, 1895
Drypoint, etching and aquatint, 28.5 x 33 cm.
Oslo Kommunes Kunstsamlinger, OKK 20
Ref. G. Schiefler No. 21

*150 **Puberty**, 1894
Lithograph, 40 x 27.5 cm.
Oslo Kommunes Kunstsamlinger, OKK 189
Ref. G. Schiefler No. 8

151 **The Sick Child**, 1894
Drypoint with roulette, 36.1 x 26.9 cm.
Oslo Kommunes Kunstsamlinger, OKK 7
Ref. G. Schiefler No. 7

150

this period was that of numbering each edition so that the purchaser could be sure what he was buying.

Pan magazine launched an original print of Munch's, while *La Revue Blanche* published *The Scream*, and the famous French dealer Vollard included Munch's *Angst* in his *Album des peintres graveurs*, an honour which the artist shared with Bonnard, Renoir and Vuillard, amongst others. His friend Meier-Graefe[212] published a portfolio of 8 engravings in 1895, and in 1903 Dr. Max Linde[213] commissioned a series of lithographs of his home (Plate 239) and his family, while six years later, in 1909, Munch himself published his *Alpha and Omega* series (Plates 279–81). Much earlier on, he had had plans to publish a suite under the title of *The Mirror*, but this idea never came to anything.

Of his earliest etchings, two examples are particularly noteworthy: the beautifully sensitive portrait of *The American Woman* and *Death and the Maiden* (Plate 148), a brilliant simplification of his painting of the previous year. His engraving of *The Girl in a Nightdress Standing by a Window* shows how hard he was trying to achieve the effect of painting in his early graphic work: his main preoccupation is with the trembling moonlight that fills the room, and with the varying tones of shadow, the same problems that faced him in his engraving of *Moonlight* (*Night in St. Cloud*).

Amongst the other paintings that he reproduced graphically in Berlin, printed in mirror image, was *The Day After*, perhaps somewhat simplified and heavy-handed when compared to the original. Naturally enough, he also did a version of *The Sick Child*, which he interpreted in a beautifully balanced and highly sensitive drypoint (Plate 151). This square picture has become one of Munch's most important works, because, under the etching, he has sketched a summery landscape (perhaps his idea of the perfect landscape). He was to return to the *Sick Child* theme in his first coloured lithograph, the masterpiece published by Clot in Paris (Plate 173).

In fact, every subject that had any significance or meaning for Munch reappears in his graphic works, not only in different versions, but also in different media.

His prints were to provide an accompaniment for his paintings, but at the same time they were not intended to be merely reproductions of his painted work. Graphics for Munch were as important as paintings; they demanded another artistic language, which in due course he was both to master and enrich. In some prints he was able to achieve a greater degree of precision or an even greater feeling of expressiveness than he could have in a painting of the same subject. It is because of this that we are able to see the gradual process of the painter learning from the engraver and vice versa, until finally they both arrived at the 'crystallization' that he had so striven towards. In a sense he condensed all his skills as a painter into his graphic work, only to transfer them back when, after his excursion into the world of prints, he returned once more to painting. It was a kind of artistic cross-fertilization.

Munch was always true to himself, and often we can see how he remained true to a certain formula, once he had discovered it. The six paintings that he did of *The Sick Child* provide clear evidence of this. But, as he himself said, he never copied; he merely used the earlier versions to ensure that he remained faithful to the essential qualities of the originals. He had become like an icon painter, striving to express the objective in a subjective way.

We have already discussed how Munch used his own form of symbolism in his paintings; although variable, this is always recognizable and always capable of interpretation. This is even truer of his graphic works, because the demands made on him by the materials he used forced him to submit to a form of discipline that he had never encountered in painting. He found that he had to simplify and condense, qualities which proved to be of great benefit in his painting, as there too he had been endeavouring to reduce things to the barest essentials. As a result, he succeeded in achieving greater clarity, greater maturity and, when he finally embarked on a large work, a greater sense of the monumental.

I am happy to hear that you are going to take up etching again. I believe that the essence of your art lies in printmaking.
Max Linde[4]

The things that destroy modern art are large exhibitions and huge art emporiums, and the fact that the pictures must look nice and decorative on a wall. It is not art for its own sake, nor does it claim to convey any message. Munch[5]

. . . never before had I experienced such power . . . a series of truly remarkable and stirring pictures . . . It was an unforgettable experience . . . From that moment I longed to get to know the magician that had created them.
Gustav Schiefler on the subject of his first encounter with Munch's etchings in 1902[6]

The sign of a great artist (not just a second-rate one striving to prove himself) is that he can deal with the technical craft problems with careless ease or simply make light of them, because the great artist's guardian angel will always place the right expressive medium in his hands. Gustav Schiefler, 1907[7]

He often carries a copper plate in his pocket, on to which he will etch some scene that particularly catches his imagination of the moment—a landscape, a waitress in a wine tavern, a couple of men playing cards, or a serious portrait.
Gustav Schiefler, 1907[8]

152 **Gustav Schiefler**, 1905
Drypoint, 23.2 x 18.5 cm.
Oslo Kommunes Kunstsamlinger, OKK 112
Ref. G. Schiefler No. 238

*153 **Harpy**, 1900
Lithograph, 36.5 x 31.5 cm.
Oslo Kommunes Kunstsamlinger, OKK 239
Ref. G. Schiefler No. 137

152

154

155

. . . he anticipated the doctrines of Cubism long before Picasso, a remarkable indication of the instinctive self-assurance that led to his artistic development. Gustav Schiefler[9]

Munch dared to paint the life of the soul, to give form to ideas, sensations, and memories which people were aware of from their readings of the literature of modern psychoanalysis, but which they thought could only be expressed semantically. Then we saw that the brush and the engraver's burin were capable of delving even deeper. Gustav Schiefler[10]

It is the quality of intensity and spontaneity that makes Munch's art so dear to me, and makes it the one that I can best see myself in, the one in which I can feel my own heartbeat, my own breathing. It is that spontaneity that has made Munch a greater psychologist than one could ever be oneself, even with the most intensive private studying. It is as though he had seized on the dark unmapped areas that lie within us all, but which also contain our finest qualities—seized on them and instinctively set them down on a canvas, almost without being aware of the fact himself. In my opinion, Munch has something of the quality of an Aladdin in his art. Harald Hals, 1895[11]

I have recently turned up a number of notes that I made during the last forty years, which are like entries in a spiritual diary. They follow close on the heels of my etchings and paintings, and they could well be added to the engravings of my Frieze of Life *as a sort of commentary—they are almost poems written as prose.* Munch to Ragnar Hoppe, 1929[12]

The last time, we discussed how many of the old engravings could be reprinted. It is possible that I still have a number of the plates and stones in store, but I think that it is out of the question to print any more. Quite simply, I feel that I have already produced too many and, on the contrary, I would rather be like Rembrandt (would that I resembled him in other respects!) and make an 'auto-da-fé' of engravings. I will publish the prints of recent years in very small numbers. I do not consider them to be graphic enough. Munch to Ragnar Hoppe[13]

156

154 **The Lonely Ones,** 1899
Woodcut, 39.5 x 53 cm.
Oslo Kommunes Kunstsamlinger, OKK 601
Ref. G. Schiefler No. 133

155 **The Lonely Ones,** 1899
Woodcut, 39.5 x 53 cm.
Oslo Kommunes Kunstsamlinger, OKK 601
Ref. G. Schiefler No. 133

156 **The Lonely Ones,** 1895
Drypoint, 15.5 x 21.4 cm.
Oslo Kommunes Kunstsamlinger, OKK 19
Ref. G. Schiefler No. 20

157 **Melancholy,** 1896
Woodcut, 33.3 x 42.2 cm.
Oslo Kommunes Kunstsamlinger, OKK 588
Ref. G. Schiefler No. 116

157

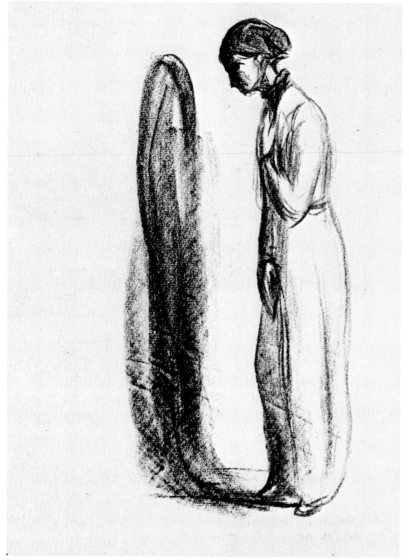

158

159a

b

*Home meant need—and a sister in the mental asylum. That calls
for a brother's help.*   Munch[14]

*Now you own a print that, because of its alleged immorality,
could not be shown in Christiania.*
       Munch on the subject of *The Kiss*, which he gave to
       Schiefler.[15]

158   **The Insane Woman (Melancholy),** 1908/9
      Lithograph, 25 x 12 cm.
      Oslo Kommunes Kunstsamlinger, OKK 281
      Ref. G. Schiefler No. 286

159   a, b, c, **The Kiss,** 1897/98
      Woodcut
      Oslo Kommunes Kunstsamlinger, OKK 577–580 (Variations of
      the same subject)
      Ref. G. Schiefler No. 102

160   **The Kiss,** 1895
      Drypoint and aquatint, 32.9 x 26.3 cm.
      Oslo Kommunes Kunstsamlinger, OKK 21
      Ref. G. Schiefler No. 22

c

160 >

161

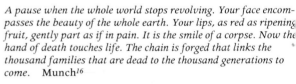

162

A pause when the whole world stops revolving. Your face encompasses the beauty of the whole earth. Your lips, as red as ripening fruit, gently part as if in pain. It is the smile of a corpse. Now the hand of death touches life. The chain is forged that links the thousand families that are dead to the thousand generations to come. Munch[16]

163

161 **Madonna,** 1895–1902
Lithograph, 55.5 x 35.3 cm.
Oslo Kommunes Kunstsamlinger, OKK 194
Ref. G. Schiefler No. 33

162 **Madonna,** 1895
Lithograph
Oslo Kommunes Kunstsamlinger, OKK 194 (This version is hand-coloured and is dedicated to Przybyszewski)

163 **Madonna,** 1895
Drypoint, 36 x 26.5 cm.
Oslo Kommunes Kunstsamlinger, OKK 15
Ref. G. Schiefler No. 16

164 **Madonna,** 1895–1902
Lithograph, 60.4 x 44.5 cm.
Oslo Kommunes Kunstsamlinger, OKK 194
Ref. G. Schiefler No. 33

I went to Dannenberger the printer at Lassally's and saw how Munch's graphics were printed. I was rather surprised when I saw the woodcut colour-plate. It had been sawn into small pieces, which were stained with red and green colour. Then the square was reassembled rather like a child's jigsaw, placed in the press, and suddenly a multi-coloured print with a sort of veined pattern appeared. Erich Büttner[17]

Moonlight glides over your face, which is full of the earth's pain and beauty . . . like a corpse (sic) we glide out on to a vast sea.
Munch[18]

Man and woman are drawn to each other. Love's underwater cable carried its currents into their nerves. The cable strands bound their hearts together. The woman's hair has wound itself around him and penetrated to his heart. Munch[19]

166

138

167

168

165 **Women on the Beach,** 1898
Woodcut, 45,4 x 50.8 cm.
Oslo Kommunes Kunstsamlinger, OKK 589
Ref. G. Scheifler No. 117

166 **Women on the Beach,** 1898
Woodcut (Block), 45.5 x 51.3 cm.
Oslo Kommunes Kunstsamlinger, OKK 589

167 **Women on the Beach,** 1898
Woodcut, 45.5 x 50.8 cm.
Oslo Kommunes Kunstsamlinger, OKK 589
Ref. G. Scheifler No. 117

168 **Lovers in the Waves,** 1896
Lithograph, 31 x 41.9 cm.
Oslo Kommunes Kunstsamling, OKK 213
Ref. G. Scheifler No. 71

169

170

The moon was yellow. A golden pillar stood in the water and flickered, melting in its own glory, and gold floated out over the sea. When our eyes met, unseen hands wove invisible threads that passed from your eyes to mine and bound our hearts together.
Munch[20]

When you went over the sea and left me, it was as if there were still invisible threads uniting us. It was as though something was tearing at an open wound. Munch[21]

One evening I came to have a discussion with my father on the subject of how long unbelievers are tormented in Hell. I maintained that no sinner could be so great that God would let him suffer for more than a thousand years. Father said that they would suffer for a thousand thousand years, but I would not give up the argument. I became so irritated that I finally left the house, slamming the door behind me. After I had walked the streets for a bit, my anger subsided, and I returned home to make my peace with him. He had gone to bed, and so I quietly opened his bedroom door. My father was on his knees in front of the bed, praying. I had never seen that before. I closed the door and went to my own room, but I could not get to sleep: all I could do was toss and turn. Eventually I took out my drawing block and began to draw. I drew my father kneeling by his bed, with the light from the bedside lamp casting a yellow glow over his nightshirt. I fetched my paint box and coloured it in. Finally I achieved the right effect, and I was able to go to bed happy, quickly falling asleep.
Munch[22]

171

172

169 **Attraction,** 1896
Lithograph, 39.5 x 62.5 cm.
Oslo Kommunes Kunstsamlinger, OKK 208
Ref. G. Schiefler No. 66

170 **Separation,** 1896
Lithograph, 41 x 62.5 cm.
Oslo Kommunes Kunstsamlinger, OKK 210
Ref. G. Scheifler No. 68

171 **Attraction,** 1896
Lithograph, 47.2 x 35.5 cm.
Oslo Kommunes Kunstsamlinger, OKK 207
Ref. G. Schiefler No. 65

172 **Old Man Praying,** 1902
Woodcut, 45.8 x 32.5 cm.
Oslo Kommunes Kunstsamlinger, OKK 607
Ref. G. Schiefler No. 173

173

The lithographic stones, on which the large head was drawn, lay next to each other in rows, ready for the printing process. Munch arrived, stood in front of the stones, closed his eyes tightly and, stabbing the air with his finger, said: 'Print . . . grey, green, blue, brown.' Then he opened his eyes and said: 'Right, it's time for a glass of schnapps now.' The printer kept on working until Munch came back and once more, still with his eyes closed, ordered: 'Yellow, pink, red.' And he repeated the same process a couple of times more.

The painter Paul Hermann on how the lithograph of
The Sick Child was executed.[23]

173 **The Sick Child,** 1896
Lithograph, 42.1 x 56.5 cm.
Oslo Kommunes Kunstsamlinger, OKK 203
Ref. G. Schiefler No. 59

174 Detail of a different version of No. 173
Oslo Kommunes Kunstsamlinger, OKK 203–18

174 >

175

Was this really love? He felt anxious. How could it be, that within the space of an hour a woman could insinuate her way int[o] his heart like some sort of foreign body.
Stanislaw Przybyszewski[24]

Before I set eyes on you, holy maiden, you lived in chaste and blameless innocence in my mind, like a vision of purity, untouche[d] by the darkness of motherhood. Stanislaw Przybyszewski[25]

We thought about how to publish his works; the large lithograph[s] and woodcuts would be printed on expensive paper and issued as a series, a sort of graphic life-frieze. Gustav Schiefler[26]

For a long time I have been planning to get together a large work involving writing and pictures. Munch to Ragnar Hoppe[27]

It is impossible to publish any new prints, at least of the older works. The majority of them have been destroyed, and the ones still in existence have been ravaged by old age. And besides, I decided long ago not to produce any new prints because I find th[at] too many have already been published.
Munch to Ragnar Hoppe[28]

176

144

175 **Nude Girl,** 1896
Mezzotint and drypoint on zinc, 14.5 x 12.7 cm.
Oslo Kommunes Kunstsamlinger, OKK 29
Ref. G. Schiefler No. 39

176 **In Man's Brain,** 1897
Woodcut, 37.2 x 56.7 cm.
Oslo Kommunes Kunstsamlinger, OKK 573
Ref. G. Schiefler No. 98

177 **The Three Stages of Woman,** 1899
Lithograph, 46.2 x 59.2 cm.
Oslo Kommunes Kunstsamlinger, OKK 238
Ref. G. Schiefler No. 122

178 **The Voice,** 1896
Woodcut, 37.8 x 56 cm.
Oslo Kommunes Kunstsamlinger, OKK 572
Ref. G. Schiefler No. 83

177

178

179

He has great inner strength, and like his dead friend Sigbjørn Obstfelder he belongs to the group of men that Vilhelm Ekelund calls 'soul preachers'. **Ragnar Hoppe, 1929**[29]

*179 **Evening (Melancholy),** 1896
Woodcut, 37.6 x 45.5 cm.
Oslo Kommunes Kunstsamlinger, OKK 571
Ref. G. Schiefler No. 82

*180 Detail of another version of Plate 179

People's souls are like planets. Like a star that appears out of the gloom and meets another star—they shine brightly for a moment and then disappear completely into the darkness. It is the same when a man and woman meet—they glide towards each other, the spark of love ignites and flares up, then they vanish, both going their own separate ways. Only a few come together in a flame that is large enough for them to become one. Munch[30]

181 **Moonlight,** 1896
Woodcut, 41.2 x 46.7 cm.
Oslo Kommunes Kunstsamlinger, OKK 570
Ref. G. Schiefler No. 81

182 **The Maiden and the Heart,** 1896
Etching and drypoint, 23.4 x 23.7 cm.
Oslo Kommunes Kunstsamlinger, OKK 37
Ref. G. Schiefler No. 47

183 **The Maiden and the Heart,** 1899
Woodcut, 25.2 x 18.4 cm.
Oslo Kommunes Kunstsamlinger, OKK 602
Ref. G. Schiefler No. 134

183 >

184

184 **Encounter in Space,** 1899
Woodcut, 18.1 x 25.1 cm.
Oslo Kommunes Kunstsamlinger, OKK 603
Ref. G. Scheifler No. 135

185 **To the Forest,** 1915
Woodcut, 51 x 64.6 cm.
Oslo Kommunes Kunstsamlinger, OKK 644
Ref. G. Scheifler No. 444

186 **Kiss on the Hair,** 1915
Woodcut, 15.5 x 16.8 cm.
Oslo Kommunes Kunstsamlinger, OKK 643
Ref. G. Scheifler No. 443

186 >

185

187

Perhaps there are two people from Chaos, interwoven destinies, meeting out there in space, while the glittering eyes of the stars look on.   Sigbjørn Obstfelder[31]

His plates were often etched in a café, even on the street.
Max Linde[32]

188

187 **Tingel-Tangel,** 1895
Lithograph, 41 x 62.8 cm.
Oslo Kommunes Kunstsamlinger, OKK 198
Ref. G. Schiefler No. 37
(This hand-coloured version is from a private collection)

*188 **Man's Head in Woman's Hair,** 1896
Woodcut, 54.6 x 38.1 cm.
Oslo Kommunes Kunstsamlinger, OKK 569
Ref. G. Schiefler No. 80

152

9 : The Draughtsman

The keys to his art

But the high spot of the evening came when Edvard, grown up Edvard (15–16 years old at the time), showed his sketch books, his drawings and small oil paintings . . . we all sat spellbound. In his little paintings I could see many of the districts and the strange houses that we had passed on the way. There was Telthus Street climbing up the steep hill to Old Aker church, the yellow house with the trees that stood on the riverbank beyond Grüner's bridge . . . And then there were all the drawings of the family going about their daily life in the house.

The painter Ludvig Ravensberg[1]

It was not difficult to persuade my father that I might become a painter; it was only that he was afraid of the models. My aunt took a lively interest in our attempts at drawing and she was probably the one who contributed most to my becoming a painter, at least at this early stage. Munch to Jens Thiis[2]

Right at the centre of the chaos there stands a Munch (munk-monk), staring at everything helplessly with a child's frightened eyes. Why? he asks. Why? It is me . . . a blood-red sun shines over the whole scene, and the cross is empty. Munch[3]

89 **Seated Model**, 1896
    Charcoal, pencil and watercolour, 62 x 47.7 cm.
    Oslo Kommunes Kunstsamlinger, OKK 2459

90 **Madonna**, 1893
    Charcoal and pencil, 73.7 x 59.7 cm.
    Oslo Kommunes Kunstsamlinger, OKK 2430

90

All Doctor Munch's children used to draw busily by the light of paraffin lamps during the long winter nights in their gloomy apartments, and for Edvard, drawing soon became a major interest. At the age of thirteen he made a fantasy about *The Pretenders*, the earliest evidence that we have of his interest in Ibsen. It may well be that their father had read it aloud to the children, who were already familiar with their uncle's account of those dramatic events. We shall later see how Munch became so totally involved in Ibsen's fantasy world that he began to identify with many of his characters, amongst them Duke Skule in *The Pretenders*.

However, as is to be expected, the majority of his drawings as a child and as a teenager were of his immediate family. He portrays an apparently harmonious family life, and in his drawings and early paintings[214] we catch glimpses of Doctor Munch, either reading or resting on the Biedermeier sofa under the family portraits, and Aunt Karen, busy knitting or just sitting in the rocking chair. He often drew (and painted) the view from the windows in Fossveien, showing Telthus hill leading up to Old Aker church or Grüner's gardens, a fine tree-filled park of the day. But the majority of Munch's early drawings show that he spent a lot of time in the environs of the city. He took notes down by the river Aker and up in Nordmarka, and he used these notes as the basis for his first paintings. He also found his way to the square in front of the Royal Palace, where he drew the firework display that celebrated the crown prince's wedding in 1880. We also know that Munch enrolled in the Royal School of Drawing in August 1881, and that he was allowed to miss out the beginners' classes and go straight into Julius Middelthun's[215] lectures, where he was given the chance to draw nudes from life.

The family's financial circumstances being very poor, the young Edvard therefore felt that it was his duty to contribute to the running of the household, but he suffered many disappointments in his efforts to sell his paintings (see page 33). In his diary[216] we can follow Munch's humiliating progress from publisher to publisher, as he tried to get his drawings accepted by the illustrated magazines.

Several purely academic drawings from his time at the School of Drawing and at Bonnat's studio have survived, but more interesting is his progress after he gave up depicting 'people reading' and 'women knitting', showing how his major works gradually developed. It is as if we were present at the birth of an artist when we see a germ of inspiration in one work gradually develop in subsequent works, until the original concept has taken root and finally blossoms. Often the original idea is a perfectly simple one, as in *Farewell* (Plate 192), a straightforward drawing of man kissing a woman in travelling clothes saying good-bye[217]; and yet we sense that that scene was the original inspiration for *The Kiss* (Plates 124–5), which Munch was to paint again and again for the *Frieze of Life* series, as well as including it in a beautiful etching (Plate 160) and, finally, in a starkly expressive woodcut (Plate 159).

In effect, Munch's graphic work from 1894 onwards meant a revival of his skill as a draughtsman; right up to 1903 he engraved directly on to the copper or stone plate. And the inspiration for all his prints came as we have seen either from within himself or from other works that he had already completed: despite the fact that he was an avid visitor of museums and art galleries, we have yet to find a single shred of evidence that he took notes during these visits or that he ever painted or drew even one copy of any of the masterpieces that he came across.

191

In Chapter 1 we saw a number of his self-portraits, in which he analyses
and reveals much of his own personality. Naturally enough, there are also a
good many drawings of himself, some of which are purely figurative and
give us an idea of what he looked like at various stages of his life, but there
are others in which he subjects himself to the most searching self-scrutiny
with remarkable objectivity. He was always scrupulously honest with his
public. Sometimes, however, his message is not totally clear, as, for example,
when he gives his own unmistakable features to a hermaphrodite figure with
large breasts (Plate 270). He is unafraid of sharing his deepest misgivings
with us. The symbolism is far simpler in *The Blossom of Pain* (Plate 11), in
which the suffering artist gives his own life-blood to the growing flower that
represents his art. His drawings of female nudes say much about his attitudes
towards woman. When he draws her half-naked, with a halo of suffering
round her head, he immediately makes us think of the Madonna, even if what
he is showing us is a portrait of an extremely worldly woman (Plate 190). His
subtle blue watercolour of a standing woman (Plate 196) betrays some
susceptibility on the part of his coquettish model, and in a number of nude
studies done after 1912 he reveals the happy relationship he enjoyed with
the young model, who evidently gave the ageing master new strength, as
well as renewing his confidence in himself. He paints and draws himself as
The Seducer, and, not without a touch of self-irony, he portrays her as the
dancing Anitra and himself as the ageing Peer Gynt, strutting around like a
young cock trying to impress the girl (Plate 216). Munch identified himself
with Peer Gynt on several occasions, as well as with other characters of
Ibsen. It is hardly surprising that he particularly identified with Oswald, the
sickly artist of good family who moves away from home in *Ghosts*, and he
drew a picture of himself as Oswald,[218] including in it the old sofa from his

192

194

191 **The Empty Cross,** 1901
   Indian ink and watercolour, 43.1 x 62.7 cm.
   Oslo Kommunes Kunstsamlinger, OKK 2452

192 **Farewell** (The original inspiration for *The Kiss*), 1890 (92?)
   Pencil drawing, 27 x 20.5 cm.
   Oslo Kommunes Kunstsamlinger, OKK 2356

193 **At the Window,** before 1889
   Crayon drawing, 27.3 x 24.5 cm.
   Oslo Kommunes Kunstsamlinger, OKK 2379

194 **An Evening with the Family,** 1884
   Pencil drawing, 34.7 x 48.3 cm.
   Oslo Kommunes Kunstsamlinger, OKK 2365

195 **Inger Munch,** 1882
   Pencil drawing, 25.6 x 19.2 cm.
   Oslo Kommunes Kunstsamlinger, OKK 2377

195

193

196 **Blue Standing Nude,** 1920's
  Watercolour, 51 x 35 cm.
  Oslo Kommunes Kunstsamlinger, OKK 1072

197 **Standing Nude,** c.1900
  Tempera, coloured chalk and charcoal, 65.4 x 29 cm.
  Oslo Kommunes Kunstsamlinger, OKK 1131

198 **Charwomen in the Corridor,** 1906
  Gouache and coloured chalk on paper, 71.6 x 47.5 cm.
  Oslo Kommunes Kunstsamlinger, OKK 534

199 **Girl with her hands in front of her Mouth,** after 1912
  Charcoal drawing, 40.8 x 26.9 cm.
  Oslo Kommunes Kunstsamlinger, OKK 519

198

199

childhood home; he even shows the portraits of his own grandparents
hanging on Mrs Alving's sitting room walls. It was Max Reinhardt who in
1906 gave Munch the task of doing 'eine Anregung für die Inscenierung' (a
sketch to give him ideas for the staging of Ibsen's *Ghosts*), a commission which
he duly carried out. The set designer Ernst Stern saw an oil painting for
Ghosts in Reinhardt's studio and said that he thought that it was rather short
on detail, to which Reinhardt replied: 'Perhaps, but the armchair says everything! Its blackness completely captures the whole mood of the play. So do
the sitting room walls in Munch's picture.' He also added: 'The colour is like
that of diseased gums. We must find some wallpaper of the same shade. That
way the actors will be in the right setting.'

Pål Hougen,[219] in his analysis of Ibsen's influence on Munch, cites several
pictures that show how the artist related himself to a number of Ibsen's
characters. He depicted Duke Skule with his own features, and, living as he
did by himself out in the big house at Ekely, he probably did not find it
difficult to identify with John Gabriel Borkman. We can understand why he
used Tulla Larsen as a model for Hedda Gabler, when we see later what a
deep effect the denouement of his affair with her and the disastrous pistol
shot had on Munch's mind.

200

The Frieze of Life *deals with the curse of inheritance. It has a sort of Oswald atmosphere to it.* Munch[4]

A hundred times I have heard Reinhardt reiterating that he never received such strong inspiration from any other painter as he did from these Munch pictures.

Arthur Kahane, Reinhardt's partner[5]

200 **Girls Bathing**, c.1935
Watercolour and crayon, 59.8 x 57.4 cm.
Oslo Kommunes Kunstsamlinger, OKK 1570

201 **Girls on the Beach**, c.1920
Watercolour, 23.8 x 28.9 cm.
Oslo Kommunes Kunstsamlinger, OKK 310

*202 **Max Dauthendey**, 1897
Black crayon drawing, 40 x 60 cm.
Oslo Kommunes Kunstsamlinger, OKK 672

203 **Lady with a Blue Hat**, after 1920
Watercolour, 66.5 x 52 cm.
Oslo Kommunes Kunstsamlinger, OKK 699

201

202

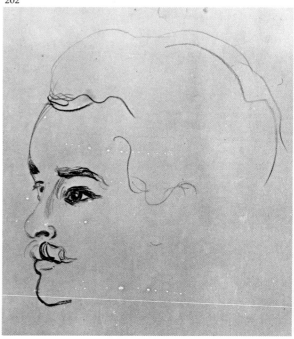

204

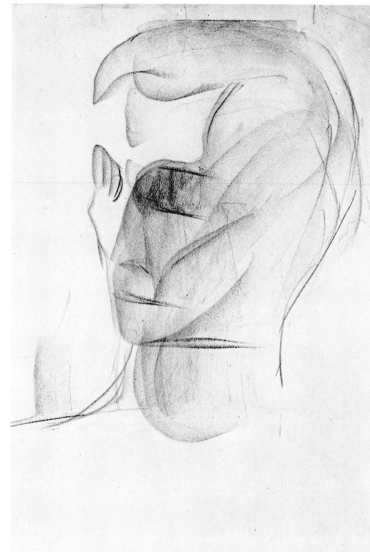

205

204 **Kneeling Nude,** after 1910
Crayon drawing, 35.6 x 26.5 cm.
Oslo Kommunes Kunstsamlinger, OKK 897

205 **Portrait of a Man,** c.1912
Crayon drawing, 40 x 27 cm.
Oslo Kommunes Kunstsamlinger, OKK 733

206 **Ottilie Schiefler,** 1907/8
Watercolour and pastel, 49.4 x 38.5 cm.
Oslo Kommunes Kunstsamlinger, OKK 660

207 **Munch and the Woman in Green** (mirror image), 1920/30
Pencil drawing, 51.5 x 23.2 cm.
Oslo Kommunes Kunstsamlinger, OKK 1642

208 **Half-length Female Nude,** after 1910
Crayon drawing, 40 x 27 cm.
Oslo Kommunes Kunstsamlinger, OKK 910

209 **Stones at Åsgårdstrand,** after 1912
Crayon drawing, 29 x 42 cm.
Oslo Kommunes Kunstsamlinger, OKK 2382

206

208

207

209

163

210

211

212

214

210 Sketch for Ibsen's *Ghosts*, 1906
    Drawing, oil and pencil on paper
    Kunstmuseum, Basel

211 Oswald from Ibsen's *Ghosts*, 1920
    Lithograph, 39 x 50 cm.
    Oslo Kommunes Kunstsamlinger, OKK 421
    Ref. G. Schiefler No. 487

212 Draft for Ibsen's *Ghosts*, 1906
    Tempera on cardboard, 69 x 90 cm.
    Rolf E. Stenersen Collection

213 **Ibsen and Jappe Nilssen,** late 1920's
    Indian ink drawing, 17 x 20.8 cm.
    Oslo Kommunes Kunstsamlinger, OKK 195/145

214 Sketch for Ibsen's *Ghosts*, 1906
    Oil and pencil on paper
    Location unknown

215 Sketch for Ibsen's *Hedda Gabler*, 1907
    Watercolour and pencil, 57.5 x 45.5 cm.
    Oslo Kommunes Kunstsamlinger, OKK 1584

215

213

165

216

217

216 **Anitra's Dance**, 1913
Crayon drawing, 35.5 x 26 cm.
Oslo Kommunes Kunstsamlinger, OKK 1645

*217 **Peer Gynt and the Button Moulder** (Edvard Munch and
Albert Kollmann), 1929/30
Pencil drawing, 21.9 x 28.2 cm. (mirror image)
Oslo Kommunes Kunstsamlinger, OKK 1635

10 : A Decade of Misfortune and Progress

Often I felt that women would stand in the way of my art

Walking here [at Åsgårdstrand] *is like walking amongst my pictures. I get such a strong urge to paint when I am walking in Åsgårdstrand.*   Munch to Rolf E. Stenersen[1]

Liebermann thinks that it is my best picture.
  Munch to Andreas Aubert about *Girls on the Jetty*, 1902[2]

He painted that subject not less than seven times, and he also made an etching and a lithograph and woodcut of it (Plate 342). A related subject, *Ladies on the Jetty* (Plate 296), he painted five times.[3]

218 **Girls on the Jetty**, 1899
  Oil on canvas, 136 x 126 cm.
  Nasjonalgalleriet, Oslo

219 **Girls on the Jetty**, 1900
  Oil on canvas, 84 x 129 cm.
  Private Collection

219

It would take too long to provide a detailed account of Munch's restless and rootless existence between the end of the 1890s and 1908, the year in which he finally collapsed and was admitted into a psychiatric clinic in Copenhagen. Were we to try and follow him from one temporary studio to another, we would come up with an endless list of third-rate boarding houses and hotels in Berlin, Paris, Hamburg and Warnemünde. As a result of his bronchitis and general ill-health he also spent time in sanatoria in Switzerland, Thuringia and back home in Norway, but despite this unsettled life he remained a surprisingly prolific artist.

In 1896, for example, he produced no fewer than forty-five different prints,[220] some of which were milestones in the history of graphic art. His graphics and his paintings had a mutually beneficial effect on each other, and his painting had begun to assume the monumental quality that is mirrored in his graphic work. In his splendid painting of *Mother and Daughter* (Plate 104), for example, we can see the basis for his freely executed woodcut of *Women on the Beach* (Plate 165), completed in the following year. *The Generation Gap* would have been an equally apt title for this subject of the young girl, locked in her own world, and her powerfully-built mother, each unable to communicate with the other. The models for this scene were Munch's sister Inger and his aunt Karen, but the artist has told us something universal about the loneliness of two different generations. He has also given us a vivid insight into the plight of his unfortunate sister Laura[221] whom he shows totally isolated in *Melancholy*[222] (Plate 233). She sits shivering in her old woman's shawl, with the wintry landscape outside clearly visible through the curtainless windows, her dead eyes staring bleakly out towards us. The brilliant red of the table cloth completely drains the living colour from the tulips on the table, while its wandering swirls echo the confusion in her own mind. Another work from roughly the same date is *Inheritance* (Plate 64), his portrayal of the weeping mother holding her syphilitic child in her arms; another example of Munch's extraordinary talent for identifying with the unfortunates of this world. Bitterly he recalled how people stood and laughed when it was exhibited in Paris—'I was once more destined to be mocked and martyred.'[223]

Another similar subject, which also illustrates his rare powers of perception, is *The Dead Mother and the Child*. Yet again he is trying to free himself from the unhappy childhood memories with which he still struggled, whether in his drawings (Plate 43), his etchings or his paintings (Plate 44). In the Bremen version the lost and uncomprehending child does not cry out its pain and fear: it holds its hands to its head in nameless terror, an inner scream ringing in its ears. How old is the child? Edvard was five when his mother died.

As well as these pictures, which all have to do with his own life and his family, he also painted, at about the turn of the century, several Norwegian landscapes that contain no human interest and in which his conscious attempts at simplification achieve a masterly feeling of the monumental. From a guest house in Ljan,[224] to the south of Oslo, he painted a number of winter scenes, in which the detail is suppressed. The blue-black spruces and fir trees stand out against the blue moonlight on the snow and create an almost ghostly atmosphere. The jagged outline of the spruce forest in the distance contrasts strongly with the flatness of the frozen water in the middle ground and the marvellously twisted shapes of the trees in the foreground, while two or three stars flicker feebly in the clear winter night (*White Night* Plate 222). Its summer counterpart is *The Island* (Plate 221), which includes a

220

strangely-shaped fir tree in the foreground that sets off the whole picture, while the white smoke that swirls gently through the trees in *Train Smoke*[225] (Plate 220) imparts a feeling of life and movement. Munch's process of stripping a scene down to its barest essentials reaches its zenith in *Birch Tree in the Snow* (Plate 224), which was completed in the same year. The birch stands bleakly at the centre of the picture, just a black and white trunk covered with a silky sheen of bark, and behind it he ranges the snowdrifts, stones, the symmetrical hill with the large white patches of snow and, in the farthest distance, the gloomy forest of spruce trees.

The painting entitled *Fertility* (Plate 146) could well be regarded as the temporary finale of Munch's *Frieze of Life*, and in it he achieves his greatest feeling so far of the monumental. Apart from that, the image of the pregnant woman carrying the fruits of the earth to the man standing under the Tree of Life is highly symbolic, but the symbolism is not intrusive and the whole mood of the scene is much more life-accepting than hitherto, a quality that is apparent to an even greater extent in *Adam and Eve* (Plate 223).

The earliest version of *Girls on the Jetty* (Plate 218) dates from 1899. He was to paint variations on this theme no less than twelve times,[226] and subsequently also reproduced it in a woodcut. As in *Rue Lafayette* (Plate 91), Munch makes use of a handrail to accentuate the perspective—our eyes instinctively follow it in towards the landscape in the background, even though we are unable to make out precisely where the railing ends and the road, which leads past the large sleeping house into the small town beyond,

220 **Train Smoke**, 1900
Oil on canvas, 85 x 109 cm.
Oslo Kommunes Kunstsamlinger, QKK 1092

221 **The Island**, 1900
Painting
221 Private Collection

222 **White Night**, 1901
Oil on canvas, 116 x 111 cm.
Nasjonalgalleriet, Oslo

170

223

actually begins.

The composition of this first version shows clearly how Munch has applied the same technique of elementary simplification that we have already seen in landscapes of the period. He has achieved a perfect sense of equilibrium in the way that the sharp diagonal of the handrail is matched by the white horizontal line of the wall, while the dark, brooding mass of the linden tree is mirrored in the water below the swirling lines of the shore. Munch specialized in the portrayal of still summer nights, and in this painting he has succeeded, by the use of subtle shades of pink, deep green and blue, in recapturing that mood as never before, the whole effect being further enhanced by the small, watery gold shape of the moon. Against this mellow and restrained background, the green, red, and white dresses of the girls ring out as a fanfare of colour, and we are reminded of the question once posed by Christian Krohg: 'Has anyone ever heard such resonant colour . . . ?'[227]

The first decade of the century was characterized by Munch as being the most fateful, the most unhappy[228] and yet also the most rewarding of his life. It began disastrously with a stay in the tuberculosis sanatorium[229] at Follebu, followed by a trip south to Berlin and Florence, a journey on which he was accompanied by the rich and beautiful young Mathilde (Tulla) Larsen[230] (Plates 226–8). During their journey he became increasingly unbalanced and disturbed, and yet all the evidence shows that Tulla was extremely fond of Munch and that there was even talk of marriage. This, however, for Munch was something to be afraid of, and on several occasions he stated that it would be criminal for him to marry. Whether his tendencies towards illness were the real reason for this refusal or whether he merely used them as an excuse, will never be known for certain. But we do know that he always felt

223 **Adam and Eve**, 1908
Oil on canvas, 130 x 202 cm.
Oslo Kommunes Kunstsamlinger, OKK 391

224 **Birch Tree in the Snow**, 1901
Oil on panel, 60 x 68 cm.
Private Collection

225 **Avenue in the Snow**, 1906
Oil on canvas, 80 x 100 cm.
Oslo Kommunes Kunstsamlinger, OKK 288

224

225

marriage would threaten his chances of realizing his true potential for artistic self-expression. It was a struggle that he was to have not only with Tulla Larsen but all the other women who tried to tie him down and break into his own private world. It was also a struggle that left him, quite literally, maimed, when, one day near the end of his turbulent affair with Tulla Larsen, who had threatened to shoot herself, a revolver went off and severed the top two joints of one of the fingers on his left hand. He felt pain in the finger, right into old age, whenever he held a palette, but the worst scars were those left on his mind by the whole incident, and the finger became a permanent reminder of his unhappy relationship with Tulla Larsen.

She had tried constantly to effect a reconciliation, even going so far as to pretend that she was at death's door as a result of illness. Even though the whole thing was an obvious theatrical exercise, Munch had been prepared to do anything to avoid a scene, and so they had returned together to his little house at Åsgårdstrand, where the incident with the revolver took place. Soon the whole affair began to assume vast proportions in Munch's mind, shattered as it was by excessive drinking and the nervous exhaustion engendered by his nomadic life. He became obsessed by feelings of persecution, the causes of which are to some extent understandable. He had, after all, been subjected to a considerable amount of abuse as an artist by his fellow countrymen and, although it was only natural that Tulla's friends should take her part, Munch's feelings of isolation became almost paranoid. He felt that people in Norway were joining in a conspiracy against him and so once more he returned to his restless wanderings on the Continent.

The year after his traumatic experiences with Tulla he entered into another relationship with a woman, this time an English violinist called Eva Mudocci.[231] He did one lithograph (Plate 232) which illustrates how deeply he felt for her, and they wrote a number of letters to each other that suggest, at the very least, an extremely close relationship. However, yet again, the relationship did not last, as can be seen in Munch's lithograph of *Salome* (Plate 231), in which Eva leans against the anguished head of the artist, smiling sweetly. It is hardly surprising that she was offended by it.[232]

These two lithographs say much for Munch's ambivalent feelings towards Eva Mudocci. One portrait, which is much more than a mere likeness, shows his feelings of devotion, and Munch called this lithograph *Madonna (The Brooch)*. The other shows his feelings of inferiority, a fear of being dominated that almost borders on hate: Eva has been transformed into the blood-thirsty *Salome*, who craves his head and has got it. The two images also reveal a great deal about his complex attitude towards women generally.

We have already seen how important erotic themes are in Munch's art, most particularly in his *Frieze of Life*, but when compared to the work of many of his contemporaries and personal friends, Munch's reveals a much subtler and much more expressive treatment of that particular aspect of human nature. This applies to Strindberg, for example, and even more so to Przybyszewski, whose outpourings on the subject of women are hard to read nowadays without smiling. Scarcely any of his artistic contemporaries possessed enough sensitivity or insight to pay homage to womankind as Munch did when he surrounded the head of the woman in love with a halo of pain. He constantly strove to unravel the mysteries of woman: she who was 'at the same time a saint, a whore and a hapless devotee'. Munch had learned a lot about the realities of love, but whenever he portrayed all that was good about it, there is always an underlying feeling of melancholy. Love goes hand in hand with pain—even with death. At the very moment of total fulfilment the smile of a woman is the smile of a corpse. And when Alpha leans over the dead Omega,[233] 'the expression on her face terrifies him. It is the same one that she had at the very moment when he had loved her most in the wood'.

Munch often allows Death to take the place of the lover,[234] a concept that has captured the imagination of countless artists down the ages. But for Munch Death was not a frightening lover—quite the opposite: women surrender themselves willingly to his embrace (Plate 148).

Again, the works that we know were inspired by Munch's own personal experiences often reveal much about the artist. The incidents that lay behind

I wait some time before completing a work so that I have to rely on my memory for its impressions. I find Nature somewhat overwhelming when I have it directly in front of me.
Munch to Ragnar Hoppe[4]

Pretty good. But one cannot paint that kind of thing from nature; one must try to paint it out of oneself.
Munch to Jens Thiis, when he saw *The Island* for the first time in twenty years.[5]

I have always put my art before everything else. Often I felt that women would stand in the way of my art. I decided at an early age never to marry. Because of the tendency towards insanity inherited from my mother and father I have always felt that it would be a crime for me to embark on marriage. Munch[6]

I have never loved. I have experienced the passion that can move mountains and transform people—the passion that tears at the heart and drinks one's blood. But there has never been anyone to whom I could say—Woman, it is you I love—You are my all.
Munch[7]

226 **Sin (Nude with Red Hair)**, 1901
Lithograph, 49.5 x 39.7 cm.
Oslo Kommunes Kunstsamlinger, OKK 241
Ref. G. Schiefler No. 142

227

228

227 **Mathilde (Tulla) Larsen**, c.1898
Oil on canvas, 119 x 61 cm.
Oslo Kommunes Kunstsamlinger, OKK 740

228 **Female Nude with Red Hair**, 1898/1902
Oil on canvas, 120 x 50 cm.
Oslo Kommunes Kunstsamlinger, OKK 469

29

29 **The Violin Concert**, 1903
Lithograph, 48 x 56 cm.
Oslo Kommunes Kunstsamlinger, OKK 254
Ref. G. Schiefler No. 211

30 Photograph of Eva Mudocci

30

his painting of the *Death of Marat* (Plate 266), for example, were so horrific in Munch's eyes that he maintained that they contributed to his own near-insanity. He saw himself lying bleeding like Marat, while the avenging woman stood coolly and self-righteously in front of the corpse. It was not possible for Munch, when he came to give his own artistic interpretation of the event, to treat the woman who had caused it with impartiality: he had to paint 'from the heart'. Art was his way of defending himself and he used it to come to terms with, and conquer, not only anxiety and death but woman too. The *Alpha and Omega* series (see page 214), completed while he was in the psychiatric clinic in Copenhagen, was the result of this self-defence mechanism. In it he tried to analyse himself and his situation and thereby overcome his illness,[235] depicting Alpha in his own likeness, with Omega as the faithless woman with whom he is hopelessly infatuated and who indulges in unnatural relationships with the animals of the island, even the pig and the donkey, deceiving Alpha with each one in turn. The hybrids born to Omega of these unions (Plate 281) finally end by attacking Alpha and tearing him to pieces. This extraordinary, poetic fable provides us with the key to his views concerning women, but it is a sick and naive philosophy. Eli Greve[236] has called the work a caricature of the *Frieze of Life*, and certainly we find in it no trace of the tenderness which flows like a life-giving stream throughout the *Frieze*. And yet it gave Munch the strength to live through an extremely difficult period of his life and come to terms with the problems facing him. *Alpha and Omega* had helped Munch cross over 'that chasm'.[237]

But what was it that had brought him to the edge of that 'chasm'? He himself maintained that it was his unhappy love affair and the pistol shot, but he also admitted that other events had also contributed to his mental problems. If we are to analyse the reasons for the inevitability of his collapse, it must in all honesty be said that that one unfortunate incident with a woman appears to have assumed a significance in his mind far greater than it really warranted. He felt that he was being hounded not only by Tulla but her friends as well—these friends being the same ones that had fought so hard on his behalf during the early years; people such as Gunnar Heiberg, who had been one of the major influences on his work, and Christian Krohg, who had played such a vital part in his early development. Because they were such old friends Munch could not forgive them for taking Tulla Larsen's side. He remained true to himself, his art and the majority of his old friends, and yet his ravings about 'bohemian society'[238] were so bigoted and so illogical as to suggest that the roots of his persecution mania must lie far back in the early days in Christiania. But if we are to discover their origins, we must first summarize briefly what has already been said.

The harsh, boorish criticism that Munch first encountered as a very young man had made him feel an outsider in Christiania very early on. Despite his circle of close friends and admirers, the Establishment was implacably opposed to him. The abuse that he was subjected to hurt him deeply, as he came from a highly cultured home and had been brought up to respect his superiors and lead a truly Christian life. The fact that he was ostracized on moral and ethical grounds caused him particular grief, perhaps mainly because it caused such sorrow to his family. Strangely enough, the fact that his art was called into question seems to have affected him less. At least there he had the support of his teachers and a small circle of admirers.

Munch was deeply attached to his family. However strained his relationship with his father was on occasion, they never really became alienated, and his death had such a deep effect on Munch that he changed his whole philosophy of life—and of art. As a result he broke away from Naturalism, and also from Jaeger, who had been almost like a second father to him: 'I almost hated him.'[239] Munch writes of how fond he was of his father, but in the next sentence he mentions an affair that he had with a married woman and bursts out 'but she was in my blood'. Both his attitude to Jaeger and to that woman show the ambivalence of his relationship with his father, but throughout his life he sent regular, and sometimes considerable, sums of money home, even when he himself was in financial difficulties.

He was always on good terms with his sisters, particularly Inger, even though he sometimes found her rather over-protective. He, in turn, felt deeply protective and sympathetic towards his other sister, Laura, who suffered from periodic bouts of depressive illness, and his countless letters to his aunt Karen bear witness to deep-seated feelings of gratitude and filial devotion. During periods of difficulty the letters were particularly frequent, and they acted as a kind of umbilical cord between the wandering Munch and his home. He preserved them all carefully and carried them with him wherever he went.

These four people,[240] to whom he felt so deeply attached, led a life completely different from that of his bohemian friends, a fact that must have caused him a great deal of mental strain. In fact, he must have felt on occasion that he was leading a Jekyll and Hyde existence, when, after violent parties with his bohemian friends round café tables, he returned home to say grace at the dinner table. Nonetheless, he never felt tempted to obey the bohemians' 2nd Commandment: 'Thou shalt sever thy family roots'.

As he grew older, Munch's father became increasingly religious. He had his own private battles to fight, this old seamens' doctor who had not always led a perfect life as a young man. He knew very well what it was to have a bad conscience and he often spoke to his son of the agonies of Hell.

One cannot help but wonder whether Munch did not retain some of the Puritan qualities in which he had been brought up to believe. He cannot be called a Christian,[241] and yet, throughout his life he always showed a deep respect for religious values. Perhaps it was this very conflict between the two different life-styles that gave his art its intensity.

The three women in his family who treated him with such tenderness and such concern almost certainly expressed anxiety when they discovered who his girlfriends were. But as we shall see, they never blamed their beloved Edvard: it was always the women who were at fault, and the family always took Edvard's part.[242] Although they meant well, their actions did little to salve his conscience or resolve the inner conflicts that tormented him.

His stock explanation for each of his disastrous affairs was that his tendency towards illness made it impossible for him to marry. Undoubtedly he really believed what he said, but perhaps his fear of disease and mental derangement had become a fixation with him: he could never blot out the memory of the black angels who had hovered over his cradle. But as he grew older he must have succeeded in mastering his morbid obsession with illness, and he still produced extremely good work right up until the last days of his life, when at almost eighty he finally laid his brushes down. The deaths of his mother and sister, however, were ghosts that he never managed to exorcize, and the memory of his own illness and his feeling of being 'different' stayed with him throughout his life. The endless newspaper discussions about his degenerate art and his madness, combined with the young Scharffenberg's disgraceful comments to the Students' Association about the insanity in Munch's family, made him overreact and become even more terrified. He grew to rely on his art to give him the courage to look death and illness in the face. And it was through his art that he was able to see into the dark side of man's nature: intuitively, he had discovered what Freud was later to discover empirically.

The happy, glowing state of marriage may suit many people, not least you and Nørregaard. You have preserved your youth as in a sealed jar . . . that is all very fine, but why should all the furies of Hell descend on a poor painter because he has the misfortune not to be able to marry—but he has only managed to steal a small caress. All the same I hope that in the after-life there are milder geniuses than on this earth. Munch to Sigurd Høst[8]

He wanted to paint a perfect portrait of me, but each time he began on an oil painting he destroyed it, because he was not happy with it. He had more success with the lithographs, and the stones that he used were sent up to our room in the Hotel Sans Souci in Berlin. One of these, the so-called Madonna *[The Brooch], was accompanied by a note that said 'Here is the stone that fell from my heart'. He did that picture and also the one of Bella [Edvard and me [The Violin Concert Plate 229] in the same room. He also did a third one [Plate 231] of two heads—his and mine—called* Salome. *It was that title which caused our only row.*
Eva Mudocci to W. Stabell[9]

Your face embodies all that is tender in the world. Your eyes are as dark as the green-blue sea—they draw me irresistibly to you. A painfully soft smile plays on your mouth, as if you wanted to ask me forgiveness for something.

Your lips are sensual—like two blood-red serpents. There is piety in your face as it glows in the light of the moon. Your hair is brushed back from your flawless forehead. Your profile is that of a Madonna—your lips part gently as if in pain. Anxiously I ask you are feeling sad—but you just whisper, I am in love with you . . . Munch[10]

231 **Salome, 1903**
Lithograph, 40.5 x 30.5 cm.
Oslo Kommunes Kunstsamlinger, OKK 256
Ref. G. Schiefler No. 213

232 **Madonna (The Brooch), 1903**
Lithograph, 60 x 46 cm.
Oslo Kommunes Kunstsamlinger, OKK 255
Ref. G. Schiefler No. 212

231

232 >

233 **Melancholy**, c.1899
Oil on canvas, 110 x 126 cm.
Oslo Kommunes Kunstsamlinger, OKK 12

11: Friends and Patrons

Edvard Munch's art cannot be immediately and instinctively understood, but nevertheless it grips us and stirs our imagination into a turmoil . . . It cannot be denied that his pictures make a deep impression on all those that see them, either because he has purposely tried to strike terror in our hearts by his choice of subject, or because he wishes to charm us by their beauty. In them all there burns the spark of life, which ignites within us . . . Edvard Munch is a person of today, and as such he lives an intensely agitated inner life . . . The man and his work are indeed inextricably bound together; the one serves to clarify and illuminate the other. His work lays bare thoughts that are felt, experienced . . . he is impulsive from an intellectual, not an emotional, point of view. He is anything but sentimental. His art is conceived and born of an idea, or rather of the expression of that idea: just like in Maeterlinck's dramas or other literary works, Munch, by means of his skill as a painter, opens his soul to us, revealing its most secret corners.

E. Gérard in *La Presse*, 1897[1]

234 **Ludvig Meyer's Son Karl,** 1895
Oil on canvas (Detail of No. 243)
Private Collection

235 **Herbert Esches's children,** 1905
Oil on canvas, 147 x 153 cm.
Private Collection

235

Having briefly summarized the effect that these fateful years had on Munch's mind, let us now examine what effects they had on his work. He himself said, 'My fame forges ahead like a snow-plough'.[243]

In 1897 he bought his little house at Åsgårdstrand,[244] the place that he returned to almost every summer. It became his main tie with his homeland, as he spent most of his winters in either Berlin or Paris, exhibiting in a number of German towns, and also at the 'Salon des Indépendants' in Paris in 1896 and 1897. Strindberg wrote articles about him in the leading magazine of the day, *La Revue Blanche,*[245] which also published his print of *The Scream*, while Vollard included *Angst* among the hundred prints in his *Album des peintres graveurs.* The memory of the Paris exhibitions lived on in Munch's mind for a long time. It would appear that the majority of the French, then as later, viewed him as a Germanic and philosophical artist— and also reacted against his use of colour. One unnamed critic, for example, while discussing Munch's exhibition at Bing's 'Salon de l'Art Nouveau', spoke of 'doubts as to whether it is possible to discover any new plan or idea in his work, or any sense of fulfilment'. Another critic remarked that the exhibition 'has definitely nothing to do with art'.

Those kind of comments could just as well have been written in Oslo or Stockholm, but one review that did stick in Munch's memory was that of Edouard Gérard in *La Presse.* He kept the cutting with him until he died and used it in the catalogue of his exhibition in Oslo in 1897, subsequently reprinting it in the *Frieze of Life* booklet that accompanied his show at Blomqvist's Lokale in 1918.

The fact that Munch set so much store by this review indicates that he himself thought it 'correct'. It also shows what a literary interpretation he must have placed on his work of that period, as well as revealing how his admirers saw his art. He was not just a painter: they saw him as a prophet, a 'Nabi'.

In 1902 Munch finally broke loose from the memory of his praying father, the sickrooms with their dying invalids, and his friends in Oslo, and tried to make his own way in the world. That does not mean, however, that he in any way forgot the subjects from that all-important decade of his life while he was planning his *Frieze of Life*. When he had completed the themes 'from the modern life of the soul' in the *Frieze*, Munch began to turn towards subjects that he considered more relevant to 'life as it is lived'. *Adam and Eve* (Plate 223) was painted during these restless years, but it contains no symbolism, no *Fall from Grace*. Adam is a young man in a blue sailor suit, complete with jersey and peaked cap, who is eyeing his Eve up and down, as she stands under the apple tree in a typically close-fitting Edwardian dress with a straw hat tilted coquettishly on her head.

We can see how Munch expresses his *joie de vivre* in the paintings of girls and boys bathing that he completed in the 1890s: it is as though the brooding neurotic was also searching for realism and harmony throughout the period, and it is this sense of harmony that comes to the fore in his first version of *Girls on the Jetty* (Plate 218), completed in 1899. The girls were to become women in subsequent versions of this subject, which was repeated, with variations, right up to the 1930s. In all of them Munch has succeeded in conveying a wonderful midsummer feeling of peace and quiet—both in the landscape and in the people. It was to cost him much pain and suffering, however, to achieve that same inner peace himself.

Between 1902 and 1908, the year of his nervous breakdown, Munch finally achieved his great breakthrough in Germany. When Max Lieberman invited

236

him to exhibit his *Frieze of Life* in Berlin in 1902, Munch gradually formed a circle of friends and sponsors there who fought tirelessly on his behalf: one of these was Albert Kollmann,[246] a 'spirit from the time of Goethe',[247] and Munch believed that he owed his success in Germany to Kollmann.

This strange spiritualist and mystic, who in an extraordinary way always materialized wherever Munch found himself, had long played a modest but important role in German artistic life. He was a great sponsor of new artists and he took his work so seriously that he used to go round to their studios and show them French Impressionist paintings to help them develop their technique. But after he had seen Munch's exhibition in 1902 it was the Norwegian—together with Ernst Barlach—who was his major preoccupation. He came to see Munch's work, and he stayed. Max Liebermann once said of him: 'He understands painting better than all the professors and art experts put together'. His friend, the lyric poet Theodor Däubler, declared that 'Munch was not always the first he mentioned, but he always finished up with him in his dissertations', and he also told the story of how the seventy-five-year-old aesthete suddenly appeared at the large international art exhibition in Cologne in 1912, in which Picasso and Munch were the only two living artists to have their own 'rooms of honour'. He 'sat every day, for hours on end, in the Munch room, over a period of several weeks', according to Däubler, and Munch's biographer, Curt Glaser, gives us further evidence of Kollmann's devotion to the artist: 'He introduced him to many of his

236 **Albert Kollmann,** 1902
Drypoint, 18.8 x 14.1 cm.
Oslo Kommunes Kunstsamlinger, OKK 69
Ref. G. Schiefler No. 159

237 **Friedrich Nietzsche,** 1906
Oil on canvas, 201 x 160 cm.
Thielska Galleriet, Stockholm

238 **The Banker Ernest Thiel,** 1907
Oil on canvas, 191 x 101 cm.
Thielska Galleriet, Stockholm

Thiel's purchase gave me financial freedom during the two years that I needed it most.   Munch to Jens Thiis[5]

I am thinking of painting Ibsen and Bjørnstjerne Bjørnson in the same decorative way as Nietzsche, that is, not using the photographic technique that most painters use in their portraits. I would also like to do the same for Strindberg and Drachmann. I must find myself a steady source of income: if I am to be able to live and paint in comparative peace I shall have to abandon my former bohemian life. I am painting and working flat out.
Munch to Ernest Thiel[6]

238

237

friends, he widened his circle of admirers, and wherever he had an exhibition Kollmann turned up and stood expectantly behind each visitor, waiting for some glimmer of appreciation, some favourable comment.'

In his letters Munch does not hide the fact that Kollmann's hero-worship could be rather tiresome on occasion. One young German painter friend[248] of his tells what happened one day in an inn in Weimar: 'A small, thin man in black gets up from the opposite side of the table and gives a little nod to Munch. When asked who it was, Munch replied: "I'll tell you who that is all right, that is the Devil! Girls like him, and he will do anything to help me. If ever I'm short of money, wherever I may be in the world, a trap-door opens and the Devil comes up to me and says: Munch, here's some money, and then he goes away without saying anything more . . ." Some years later I discovered that the Devil's name was Kollmann.' Subsequently, Munch was to draw himself and Kollmann and call the picture *Peer Gynt and the Button Moulder* (Plate 217).

The eye specialist Max Linde had already written his book with the rather ambitious title *Edvard Munch und die Kunst der Zukunft*[249] (*Edvard Munch and the Art of the Future*), and had also bought one of his works[250] from him, when Kollmann introduced the two of them.[251] Dr. Linde himself tells of the 'stimulating meeting with that shy but fine and brilliant artist'. His highly-cultured and extremely hospitable middle-class home[252] in Lübeck became a sure place of refuge for Munch during some of the most difficult years of his life, but there are many anecdotes that bear witness to the fact that Munch was not the most suitable guest to have in such a narrow-minded and bigoted town. His relations with the Linde family, however, were always very friendly, as can be seen from the letters that he wrote to Linde[253] right up to the latter's death in 1940 at the age of 78. The doctor had lost everything as a result of inflation, and he had had to sell his art collection, but their friendship weathered all these storms. Munch always remained faithful to the past, whether it concerned his work or the people who had not 'betrayed' him.

Throughout Munch's life there were two other people who maintained close ties with him—despite his bouts of excessive drinking and despite their having to pay his bar bills when he was short of money. These were Herbert Esche,[254] a stocking manufacturer in Chemnitz, and his wife—particularly the wife. 'He is a trifle strange and fanciful, but he is a good fellow,'[255] wrote their mutual friend van de Velde, who had built the Esches' house, in which, Munch wrote in 1905, 'I have painted the whole family'.

Frau Esche became rather worried when, after spending a great deal of time sprucing up her children to pose for their portraits, nothing happened,

240

239

239 **Max Linde's House,** 1902/3
Etching, aquatint and drypoint on zinc, 44 x 60.5 cm.
Oslo Kommunes Kunstsamlinger, OKK 88
Ref. G. Schiefler No. 189

240 **Dr. Max Linde,** 1904
Oil on canvas, 133 x 81 cm.
Rolf E. Stenersen Collection, RES A74

*241 Munch between Jan Preisler and Milos Jiránek, 1905

242 **Count Harry Kessler,** 1904
Oil on canvas, 86 x 75 cm.
Private Collection

I beg you not to forget Dr. Max Linde and his household—they helped me out of that chasm into which my fellow countrymen finally pushed me a couple of years ago . . . Nor should his book with the bold title Edvard Munch und die Kunst der Zukunft *be allowed to fade into obscurity. Neither must that spirit from the time of Goethe, Albert Kollmann, be forgotten: he is like the ghost and the conscience of art, haunting the many stages of German art and finally settling on me, a foreigner. You can see his 'Old Italian' face at my exhibitions.* Munch to Jens Thiis[7]

I dare not tell him [a German painter who wanted to go to Åsgårdstrand to write about Munch] *that in Norway I must almost feel grateful to be allowed to sit on a bit of rock—or that I can never feel totally secure there.* Munch[8]

I am glad that I am going away to Weimar, as I have on three occasions threatened people with a pistol purely on impulse. Apart from that, the fact that Germany has fallen under the spell of my art affords me cold comfort, but at least it has stimulated interest in it. I am now going to paint Count Kessler in Weimar, and so all that is missing is a commission from the Duke.
Munch to Jappe Nilssen, 1904[9]

I have just arrived back from Prague, a visit that has helped heal many of the wounds inflicted on me by the beloved city of my birth. As the guest of the Manés group of artists, I was treated like royalty . . . The mayor's coach and horses were placed at my disposal. Munch to Jens Thiis[10]

Munch's work exploded in our hearts like a hand grenade. It shook us to the very foundations; all our hopes and longings were suddenly realized. We were delirious with the feeling, which we had then and still have now, that an artist had arrived in our midst. An artist of our time and our mind. Emil Filla[11]

Munch stood at the beginning of the road that lay ahead of us. Just as we had plucked up enough courage to express ourselves independently in our art, we had the good fortune to meet with Munch. Vačlav Spala[12]

In Prague there was a lot of glory, but little money—here in Hamburg money plays a more important role.
Munch to Karen Bjølstad[13]

I am fussing over what is almost my last child, the 'Bathing' picture, like an anxious mother, and I would very much like to have someone else's opinion of it. Munch to Jappe Nilssen[14]

241

242

but Linde explained Munch's way of working to them:[256] 'Munch can go for weeks without actually putting brush to canvas, merely saying "Ich male mit meine Gehirne" in his broken German ["I'm painting with my senses"]. He carries on like that for a long time, just absorbing, until suddenly he will give shape to what he has seen, pouring his whole body and soul into his work. Then it is only a matter of days, even hours, before his pictures are ready. He puts everything he has into them. That is why his pictures have such a feeling of greatness, of genius.'

While he was in this sort of 'artistic trance' Munch worked out how to best exploit the possibilities of the canvas, and he painted Esche standing, in oil and pastel, and seated, by means of squeezing tubes[257] of paint directly on to certain areas of the canvas, which were almost certainly the first ones to be covered. When Esche complained, Munch explained that it was a technique that he had learnt from Van Gogh,[258] a statement that Esche later discovered to be untrue. His other complaint was that the oil paint was never going to dry properly.[259]

Munch had a very close relationship with both the Linde and Esche families,[260] as can be seen from the letters that they exchanged. In 1903, however, a new patron appeared in the shape of the Swedish banker Ernest Thiel.[261] Munch was later to remember him as the man who came to his assistance when he needed it most.[262] Thiel was also of great help to Gustav Vigeland,[263] when he too was going through a difficult period in his life.

Thiel was a great admirer of Nietzsche and had even translated his works into Swedish, and in 1905 he commissioned Munch to paint a portrait of 'the person to whom I shall be eternally grateful'. From his letters we know that Munch was very happy to paint the poet-philosopher's portrait,[264] but spoke constantly of the need to overcome his nervous disposition and find somewhere where he could enjoy perfect peace. At the same time, he was amazed at his own capacity for work: 'it has, strangely enough, never been greater.

243

Probably some nerves have stopped functioning.'[265]

It was an unusual task, as well as a difficult one, for Munch to have to paint a dead person. He spent a long time in Weimar, studying Nietzsche's writings and the surroundings in which he had lived, but he ended up by painting the philosopher in an open air setting (Plate 237), leaning against a railing and staring out over 'a melancholy landscape'.[266] Munch felt a feeling of kinship[267] with Nietzche, himself a victim of illness, who had once said 'that no deeper knowledge exists than that perceived in illness and all that is truly healthy must first be purified through sickness'.

It was most probably his work on the Nietzsche portrait that gave Munch the idea of painting a whole series of portraits of different writers.[268] All that remain, however, of this projected series are a number of sketches.

During these years he also painted a number of very fine child portraits. It is true that he had painted children before, for example, his charming portraits of Ludvig Meyer's children (Plate 243), but in the large portrait of Dr Linde's sons he achieves a far higher degree of expressiveness. The boys are portrayed with extraordinary care and with a deep understanding of their individual characters, but at the time that Munch painted their picture he had already been living with them for some considerable time and had also completed the 'Linde portfolio', comprising 14 etchings and 2 lithographs of the Linde house and its residents: the children knew him, and he was used to them. It is interesting to note that Munch's great child painting period corresponds almost exactly with the most traumatic days of his life. As already mentioned, he was in the habit of spending his summers at

244

Åsgårdstrand during these difficult years, and while he was there he painted several pictures of young girls against the yellow exterior of his house, with the swirling Jugendstil lines of the garden wall in the background. One of these pictures (Plate 244) particularly captures our imagination, not only because of the joyful way in which Munch has portrayed their little dresses and hats, but because he has depicted the four girls as miniature people. The eldest of them wears a serious and responsible expression, the youngest seems rather shy and unsure of herself, while the two on the right, freely painted in their triangular dresses and multi-sided hats, form a little group of their own. Munch was also to paint some enchanting pictures of children during his time in the clinic[269] in Copenhagen.

He took up Dr Linde's request for a frieze for his children's large nursery[270] with great enthusiasm. At last he would have the chance to decorate a large room; and he set busily to work in Norway on the basis of the measurements that Linde had sent him. His German patron would rather have had Munch working in close contact with him in Lübeck, and his letters to Åsgårdstrand are full of doubts as to whether the finished work would be suitable for the children's room. In fact, as it turned out, Linde refused to accept the frieze when it was finally completed, and Munch had to keep the pictures himself. It was a bitter disappointment for him, even though Linde bought 'the latest large *Summer Night* painting, for 4000 Marks'.

He subsequently got the chance to find a place for at least part of the frieze, when, in 1906, Max Reinhardt decided to open his revolutionary new intimate theatre, the Kammerspiele, with a performance of Ibsen's *Ghosts*,[271] 'in honour of Ibsen and in the spirit of his work'. The only artistic adornment in the theatre before then was a bust of Ibsen by the German sculptor Max Kruse, quoted earlier (page 90).

243 **Ludvig Meyer's children, Eli, Hakon and Karl,** 1895
Oil on canvas
Private Collection

244. **Four Girls in Åsgårdstrand,** 1904–05
Oil on canvas, 87 x 110 cm.
Oslo Kommunes Kunstsamlinger, OKK 488

189

245

246

I am happy to hear that you have already completed some rough sketches for the children's room. I would ask you please to keep the subjects childish, by which I mean in keeping with a child's nature, in other words, no kissing or loving couples. The children as yet have no knowledge of such things. I thought it would be best to choose something with a landscape, as landscapes are neutral and also will be understood by the children.

Max Linde to Munch, 1904[15]

245 **The Bathers Triptych**, 1907/9, Youth, Manhood, Old Age
Oil on canvas, c.206 x 425 cm.
Oslo Kommunes Kunstsamlinger, OKK 704, 705, 706

246 Edvard Munch painting on the beach at Warnemunde. On the right is his large *Men Bathing* picture.

247 Detail of No. 244

247 >

248

Initially the cautious Reinhardt merely asked Munch for a sketch—'something that would inspire him with his stage sets'. One of those who participated in the venture, Arthur Kahane,[272] remarked that, in view of Reinhardt's policy of 'not just finding the best man, but also the only man, for each of his productions, his only possible choice could be Munch'. The artist and the theatre manager soon became close friends, and Munch was given the reception room on the second floor to work in: 'And that was the origin of the cycle of paintings that have since become famous as the *Reinhardt Freize*,[273] a splendid by-product of his work for *Ghosts*.' The frieze became somewhat of a trial for Munch: as late as September 1907 he wrote that 'the frieze is going to destroy me'.[274] During the time he was working on it, Munch led a typically theatrical existence 'working by day, drinking by night',[275] but 'he continued to be an outsider, an enigma to us'.

However, the room that he was decorating, intended for use as the foyer, turned out to be extremely unsuitable for this purpose, and so it was locked up, being opened only once a year for dancing at Carnival time. After the *Reinhardt Frieze* had hung there relatively unnoticed for six years, the pictures were dispersed, until finally, after passing from one place to another, eight of them came to rest in the Nationalgalerie, Berlin.[276] Munch-Museet in Oslo possesses a number of sketches and preliminary studies for the frieze, and both these and the finished works are done in tempera, whereas the Linde pictures are in oils.

*248 **Max Linde's Sons**, 1903
Oil on canvas, 144 x 179 cm.
Behnhaus, Lubeck

249 **Girls Watering Flowers**, 1903/4
Part of the Linde Frieze
Oil on canvas, 100 x 80 cm.
Oslo Kommunes Kunstsamlinger, OKK 54

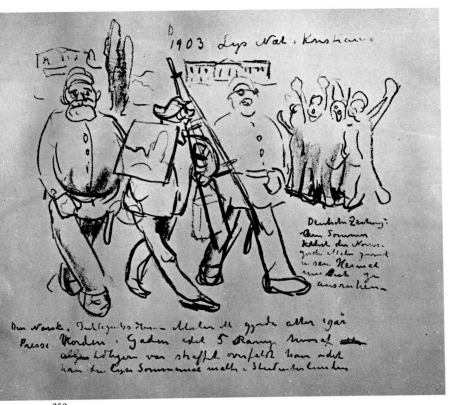

Dr Linde's worries about Munch painting 'kissing or loving couples' for the children's room were not unfounded. Munch was, in fact, painting preliminary studies at night in the park by the Royal Palace in Oslo. And on one occasion he was set upon by a gang of ruffians, and Munch wrote to Linde, in his remarkable, fractured German: *I threatened a group of hooligans with a revolver, and the police took me and all my painting equipment to the police station. I was then allowed to leave, in triumph. It was very exciting, but not good for my angina.*[16]

I have recently taken on a daunting task—I am painting a frieze for the Kammerspiele. I find providing decoration for a definite place both difficult and unfamiliar—and almost impossible in this case, when the theatre is so small and already decorated in fine Biedermeier style. Can you imagine—a combination of me and Biedermeier! Munch[17]

252

One particularly pleasant interlude amongst all Munch's troubles was provided by the exhibition that he held in Prague[277] in 1905. It consisted of 75 paintings and 50 of his graphic works, and it was a great success. Munch was lionized by all the young Czech painters, and he never forgot the warmth and respect that they showed him.

His time in Weimar was also a happy one. He painted several portraits of his patron there, Count Harry Kessler[278] (Plate 242), who offered Munch a studio in the Akademie. The Grand Duke had named Kessler director of the local museum, and the count had plans to start an art centre in the old city, famous for its connections with Goethe,[279] and it was for this reason that one of the most famous architects of the day, the Belgian Henry van de Velde,[280] had been invited to the handicraft school as professor (1901–14). He it was who played perhaps the greatest part in shaping the Jugendstil in Germany. Munch became very friendly with him and in addition painted his portrait, but there were also a number of his German fellow artists whose friendship Munch valued highly, amongst them Ludwig von Hofmann.[281] And yet, the portrait of himself that he painted while he was in Weimar in 1906, the *Self-portrait with Wine Bottle* (Plate 14), shows the face of a deeply unhappy man.[282]

In the summer of 1907 Munch rented a little house at Warnemünde, 'a German Åsgårdstrand',[283] where he managed to enjoy a few months of peace and complete a number of works. He still painted his own deep emotional experiences, but he also began to experiment with subjects in which the artist played a more important role. His new-found friendships, and the commissions he had done for other people, encouraged Munch to think of other things besides himself. It is as though, in his fight against illness, he was searching more or less consciously for subjects that related to Munch the painter rather than to Munch the person.

Many of the landscapes from this period show that, as in his days as a student in Nice and during the carefree summer days back in Norway, he was once more exploring the world around him, whether he was at Åsgårdstrand, a health spa in Thuringia or in Weimar. He could be attracted by a park, by the moist furrows of a newly-ploughed field or a tree with a house in the background, and he would paint it as he saw it, without projecting his own mood into it. He discovered the city, painting his large

250 **Munch being arrested in Palace Park**, drawn in 1903, lithograph from 1911, 40 x 44 cm.
Oslo Kommunes Kunstsamlinger, OKK 334
Ref. G. Schiefler No. 343

251 **Loving Couple in the Park**, 1903/4
Part of the Linde Frieze
Oil on canvas, 92 x 171 cm.
Oslo Kommunes Kunstsamlinger, OKK 695

252 **Young People on the Beach**, 1903/4
Part of the Linde Frieze
Oil on canvas, 90 x 175 cm.
Oslo Kommunes Kunstsamlinger, OKK 35

195

253

254

253 **Trees on the Beach**, 1903/4
Part of the Linde Frieze
Oil on canvas, 93 x 167 cm.
Oslo Kommunes Kunstsamlinger, OKK 14

254 **Summer in the Park**, 1903/4
Part of the Linde Frieze
Oil on canvas, 92 x 171 cm.
Oslo Kommunes Kunstsamlinger, OKK 13

255 **Girls Picking Apples**, 1906/7
Part of the Reinhardt Frieze
Tempera on canvas, 87 x 159 cm.
Oslo Kommunes Kunstsamlinger, OKK 696

picture of Lübeck's harbour and the Holsten Gate, and even went so far as to depict the houses, streets and washing lines of the small town of Warnemünde.

He returned once more to scenes of everyday life, such as people working, and he painted *The Mason and the Mechanic* in clear, harmonious colours, with the black-garbed mechanic standing out sharply against the white mason, who almost seems to melt into the picture.

It seems as though Munch was using his work to fight his way clear of all his troubles: he wanted to take part in life, to be as vital as the splendid naked men he painted on the beach at Warnemünde. He was no longer interested in boys and girls bathing, it was the male physique in all its glowing strength that fascinated him now. He did many preparatory studies, as well as several completed works, but his greatest tribute to the male body is the so-called *Bathers Triptych*[284] (Plate 245). Jens Thiis once wrote, in connection with an exhibition in Brussels: 'I have taken the liberty of christening the picture *Triptyque de l'Homme*. 1. Youth. 2. Manhood. 3. Old Age.' It is tempting to believe that Munch wanted to provide a grandiose counterpart for his old subject: *The Three Stages of Women*—the noble, triumphant man.

The main picture, whose dimensions (c.206 x 225 cm.) are also impressive, is a paean to health and vitality, and shows two splendidly developed men in the peak of condition walking determinedly towards us. The sense of direct confrontation in their posture is heightened by the way their figures cut through the horizontal lines of the almost skyless landscape. There are no aesthetic subterfuges, no attempts at making man subordinate to nature, no thought of trying to beguile us with softness of line. In the bright light of the sun the men stride purposefully towards us after an invigorating bathe, while the youngster on the left approaches us somewhat hesitantly, but with both feet planted firmly on the ground, and the old man in the right hand

255

It has hardly ever happened before that an artist's change from one means of expression to another has had such an effect on his contemporaries, as Munch's had at around the turn of the century.   Gustav Schiefler[18]

256 **Mothers and Children,** 1906
Oil on canvas, 96 x 101 cm.
Private Collection

257 **Mason and Mechanic,** 1908
Oil on canvas, 90 x 70 cm.
Oslo Kommunes Kunstsamlinger, OKK 574

258 **Weeping Woman,** 1906/7
Part of the Reinhardt Frieze
Tempera on canvas, 93 x 143 cm.
Oslo Kommunes Kunstsamlinger, OKK 53

258

painting stands with his arms folded, radiating an aura of calm. Throughout his life, Munch's art had dealt extensively with women and the female body, but since the compulsory studies of his student days he had scarcely ever portrayed the male form for its own sake. Perhaps this tribute to health and virility was part of his struggle against illness.

This more or less conscious new direction in Munch's art, which is here only lightly indicated, reveals his attempts at breaking out of the restricting circle of Self,[285] although this obviously does not mean that he completely achieved it. He soon returned to his old themes, and the sweeping shoreline of *The Yellow Boat* reappears in *Young Men and Women on the Shore* of the *Linde Frieze* (Plate 252). There is a new, bold use of colour, but it is still peoples', young peoples', loneliness and lack of communication that he is portraying.

259

*259 **Children in the Street,** c.1915
Oil on canvas, 92 x 100 cm.
Oslo Kommunes Kunstsamlinger, OKK 836

260 Detail of No. 259

260 >

261

I felt compelled to break up the flat areas and line—I felt that they were becoming mere mannerisms. I subsequently painted a number of pictures with broad, distinct lines, sometimes a metre long, or brush strokes that went vertically, diagonally, horizontally. The surface had been broken. Munch to Jens Thiis[19]

261 **Man with Sledge,** c.1912
Oil on canvas, 65 x 116 cm.
Oslo Kommunes Kunstsamlinger, OKK 761

*262 **Amor and Psyche,** 1907
Oil on canvas, 120 x 99 cm.
Oslo Kommunes Kunstsamlinger, OKK 48

262 >

263

263 **The Fisherman and his Daughter,** c.1902
Oil on canvas, 49 x 67 cm.
Stadelsches Kunstinstitut, Frankfurt

264 **The Murderer,** 1910
Oil on canvas, 95 x 154 cm.
Oslo Kommunes Kunstsamlinger, OKK 793

265 **Village Street in Elgersburg,** 1905
Oil on canvas, 100 x 105 cm.
Oslo Kommunes Kunstsamlinger, OKK 548

264

266 **Death of Marat,** 1907
Oil on canvas, 152 x 149 cm.
Oslo Kommunes Kunstsamlinger, OKK 4

My and my beloved's child, the Death of Marat, *which I carried within me for nine years, is not an easy painting. Nor, for that matter, is it a masterpiece—it is more of an experiment. If you like, tell my enemy that the child has now been born and christened and hangs on the wall of L'Indépendants (the Salon des Indépendants).* Munch to Christian Gierløff[20]

2: Illness and Breakdown

My capacity for work was unimpaired

*y one consolation during that time was that I felt my capacity
*r work was unimpaired. When I had painted my portrait of
*acobson, I said, 'I have remained true to the goddess of art, and
w she is true to me'. Munch[1]

*painted the doctor's portrait full length. When I was painting it
*was master. I felt that the man in whose hands I had been, was
*w in mine. My art was in no way weakened—far from it. I
*ave stayed faithful to the guardian spirits of art, I thought, and
*at is why they are not deserting me now. The pictures that I
inted then are amongst my best. Munch[2]

*7 **Dr. Daniel Jacobson**, 1909
Oil on canvas, 204 x 112 cm.
Oslo Kommunes Kunstsamlinger, OKK 359

*8 Photograph of the model, the portrait and the artist

*8

In 1907, the year after he had completed his *Self portrait with Wine Bottle*
(Plate 14), Munch painted his own interpretation of the event that he considered had caused the world to turn against him: the disturbing *Death of
Marat*[286] (Plate 266), which also illustrates his desire for artistic re-birth.
Until then, it would be fair to say, Munch's art had been an interpretation of
his whole life since childhood, but from that moment on, to quote Eli Greve,
'his art is his life—the only means of living that he knows.'

Munch felt that he had to break up the flat areas and line,[287] and he
painted a number of pictures with exaggeratedly broad brush strokes, sometimes as much as a metre long. We first fully encounter this new attitude
towards colour and technique in the painting entitled *Amor and Psyche*
(Plate 262), in which the man and woman stand obliquely facing each other,
between them a mysterious source of light, which illuminates the woman
while leaving the man's back in shadow. It is almost unbelievable how
Munch has achieved the characterization of the two figures by means of long,
vigorous strokes of colour, which vary from reddish brown to blue and the
palest of yellows, and which give a feeling of pulsating life in their subtle
twists and turns.

He uses a similar technique in his *Death of Marat*, but there the horizontal
lines are equally important. The figure of the murderess, painted in flowing,
almost parallel lines of colour, stands like a statue, while her victim, modelled
in rapid brush strokes, lies limp and dead, his feet pointing slightly away
from us. And echoing through the whole painting is the sound of that pistol
shot at Åsgårdstrand and the memory of the woman who had wounded him.

The re-living of the past which that painting involved proved very hard
for Munch: he wrote to Ernest Thiel, 'it is taking me a long time to recover
from that picture'.[288] And throughout this period he lived up to Schiefler's
description of him, 'paying no heed to time or place, or those around him,
merely goading himself on at a *tempo furioso'*—a state of affairs that was to
last until 1908.

He tried desperately to fight his way out of the vicious circle of depression.
In the very year of his breakdown, in the bitter cold of Hamburg, he wrote
to Thiel, who had sent him money for a trip to Paris, that he was seeing
'almost nobody, as I find being sociable a great strain. It is very hard for
someone like me, who is used to having friends around him and enjoying a
bit of a party, to give it all up, but it is absolutely unavoidable.'[289]

After a riotous three days and nights spent in a haze of alcohol with a
Norwegian author[290] in Copenhagen, Munch finally admitted himself to
Daniel Jacobson's clinic in the autumn of 1908. Sometime between seven and
eight months later, he returned once more to Norway, but this time it was to
be for ever. He was restored in mind and body, both as a man and as an artist,
a transformation that must have been achieved only through a combination
of his extraordinary will power and his amazing capacity for work. But his
growing fame on the Continent must also have made him aware of his own
worth and encouraged him to take better care of himself. All he wanted to do
at that time was to live for his work. 'The way in which I finally decided to
cure myself was a fairly brutal one . . . I hope that it ushers in a new era for
my art.'[291]

Munch saw his stay in the hospital as the end of a whole period of his life.

We have already mentioned some of the causes of Munch's nervous
breakdown: his disgraceful treatment at the hands of the Norwegian press, a
perhaps subconscious feeling of guilt concerning his family, his turbulent

emotional life and what he saw as betrayal by his friends. All this culminated in persecution mania, which in turn drove him to excessive drinking—'I drank like one possessed',[292] he wrote to his friend Jappe Nilssen. He became involved in brawls[293] and a number of fights, which were greatly elaborated in the newspapers. The smallest incidents began to assume enormous dimensions in his mind; he began to suffer from chronic insomnia, but he dared not go home. After each violent outburst, such as the time he ran amok and assaulted several complete strangers in a hotel in Hamburg, he became more frightened. And in order to drown his fears, he drank more, which then led to even more violence: he himself used the word 'hallucinations',[294] when later describing these black-outs. He began to wake up numb in his hands and feet, and with his eyes cut and bleeding.

Eventually he ran into his friend Emanuel Goldstein and begged, 'Please take me to the clinic.' For eight days he did nothing but sleep. A telegram to his friend Christian Gierløff came too late for him to catch the night train, but the following day he arrived at Daniel Jacobson's psychiatric clinic, situated in a quiet street of the Danish capital. 'In front of the door sat a pretty young nurse on sentry duty, who "smiled like a lily", and inside the white room sat another little nurse, reading a book at a table with flowers on it; she looked up and "smiled like a lily of the valley". In the white bed lay Munch. So wide awake, so tired, he glanced towards the door, smiled wanly and whispered: "Here lies Hamlet. And here comes Fortinbras from Norway." "Good morning Shakespeare, what have you been up to?" "I am finished— please sort this out for me." Then the matron arrives, smiling like an arum lily. Yes, Munch, this is a good place. Stay here.'[295]

Gradually Munch began to overcome his restlessness at Jacobson's clinic. His haggard features started to fill out and he regained his ironic sense of humour, writing light-hearted letters about his condition to friends back in Norway. It was also during this time that he painted his brilliantly-coloured, slightly malicious portrait of Daniel Jacobson (Plate 267). He said to the patient in the next room that he had painted the doctor looking 'just as conceited and pleased with himself as he really is'. But, nonetheless, he also managed to portray his strength, his authority and his self-assurance. One day the doctor said to Ludvig Karsten, who had come to visit Munch, 'In all seriousness, I am really worried about him. Just look at the picture he has painted of me. It's stark, raving mad.' But when Karsten was shown the painting, he fell to his knees, and clasping his hands together, exclaimed: 'My God—it's pure genius!'[296]

The portrait reveals a mixture of healthy 'patient protest' and simple high spirits. The figure of the doctor faces us head on, but it seems almost to melt into the surrounding room. When Munch later recounted how the painting had originated, he said, 'I placed him, standing imposingly with his feet wide apart, in a fiery inferno of colour. Then he begged for mercy and became as tame as a lamb.'

He also painted a full-length portrait of his friend Helge Rode,[297] which reveals a very penetrating characterization of the subject, particularly in his stance. Rode, who was an intellectual writer of great sensitivity, was also an enthusiastic admirer of Munch's and even wrote a poem in his honour.

That Munch was going through a period of complete reassessment is reaffirmed in a number of drawings[298] connected with his etching of *The Rag Picker* (Plate 276), who, in his endless wanderings round the town, has become lord of the grey streets through which he carries the burden of his misfortune. It is also revealing that, during this period, Munch restarted work on his lost oil painting of *The Lonely Ones*. But, now, it was mainly the external things of life that inspired his art: he even made portrait engravings of the nurses who had looked after him (Plate 274), as well as other works showing them performing their duties in the clinic.

He did several charming paintings of the children of friends[299] who came to visit him, and he rejoiced in the feeling that his Muse[300] had not forsaken him. He was not a true alcoholic inasmuch as his creative abilities were not impaired, and his nervous breakdown, for all its seriousness, had clearly not been due to some hereditary defect, as he himself had feared, but was the result of a series of misfortunes, finally accelerated by an uncontrollable

I paint and think in the present. I live in the past and the future
Munch, 1909[3]

The crunch had to come some day . . . But when it did, it was fairly dramatic—after a trip to Sweden followed by four days i[n] a mass of alcohol with Sigurd Mathiesen. I had a real blackout and also some minor form of heart attack, I believe. My brain h[as] become damaged by my continual obsessions. I am having shoc[k] treatment and massage and I feel very well in the peaceful atmosphere here—surrounded by extremely kind nuns and a ve[ry] capable doctor. Munch to Jappe Nilssen, 1908[4]

When in 1908 we looked through Munch's portfolio at Warnemünde, he showed me a number of pencil drawings, which he called The First People. *They dealt in a sort of bitterly humoro[us] way with the faithlessness of woman, and they were so amusing that I pleaded with him to publish them in a proper graphic series. They were finally published as* Alpha and Omega, *after [he] had recovered from a serious illness in a Copenhagen clinic.*
Gustav Schiefler[5]

My mind is like a glass of cloudy water. I am now letting it star[t] to become clear again. I wonder what will happen when the dre[gs] have settled on the bottom? I was never mad, as Goldstein thought; it was a web of events and intrigues, woven over many years, combined with the disappointments and the drinking tha[t] resulted from them, which brought about my nervous breakdo[wn].
Munch to Jappe Nilssen[6]

269

270

269 **The Poison Flower** (the first illustration of the *Alpha and Omega* series), 1908
Lithograph, 30 x 18.5 cm.
Oslo Kommunes Kunstsamlinger, OKK 304
Ref. G. Schiefler No. 309

270 **The Sphinx,** 1909
Chalk, 43.3 x 63 cm.
Oslo Kommunes Kunstsamlinger, OKK 2453

bout of drinking.

During his convalescence he paid several visits to the zoo, where he made a number of highly effective animal studies, or perhaps one should say character studies of animals. It was the animals' personalities, their feral qualities, that he was trying to capture, and later in his life he frequently returned to the subject of animals.

We have already discussed how Munch used his art as a sort of defence mechanism to help him over his various crises. It was with this in mind that Dr Linde advised Munch 'to do a series of drawings on the subject of his experiences in the unfamiliar realms of love. It will have a healing effect.' And so Munch embarked on the fable of *Alpha and Omega*, with its brutal and naive philosophy of women, starting with his drawing of the three-headed *Poison Flower* (Plate 269), a negative paraphrase of his *Three Stages of Woman*. According to Munch, the fable deals, 'in jest and earnest, with the age-old story, which must be repeated once more, of man, who since time immemorial has allowed himself to be beguiled by the faithless breed of women'.[301] And, as if to underline the message, he placed the couple on a desert island.

Munch himself upheld the success of Dr. Linde's cure, when he said, 'A strange feeling of peace came over me while I worked on that series—it was as though all the pain was leaving my body.'

211

271

272

273

You continue along alcohol's uncertain road, with all its ups and downs. I have forsaken the companionship of drink—I will not run the risk of being paralysed in my arms and legs. The road is certainly a strange one, with its continual bouts of deathly oblivion followed by the bitter-sweet reawakening to life. I have lost something remarkable, something inexplicable, something that combines both joy and pain, of that I am sure.
Munch to Jappe Nilssen[7]

This time I have been given such a serious reminder that I will find the power to stay away from that poison—it would be the same as dying. Munch to Jappe Nilssen[8]

I must be made of stern stuff—I feel quite well.
Munch to Ernest Thiel[9]

Pluck up courage, Munch, and come and see us. There are a lot of good friends here who will more than compensate you for the enemies that you have, who in any case are afraid to show their faces. Come up and bask in some of the glory. You have scored a major triumph—a complete and overwhelming victory.
Jappe Nilssen[10]

If anyone had said that [that Munch should receive the Order of St. Olav] *five or six years ago, he would have been committed to an asylum.* Max Linde to Munch[11]

As regards that honour, you know that I never set much store by such things—nevertheless, on this occasion, I feel that it was as if a hand were reaching out to me from my homeland.
Munch to Jappe Nilssen[12]

I shall now try and look up to that frightful country—but I am not going anywhere near the Christiania fjord.
Munch to Sigurd Høst[13]

271 **Caricature. Prof. Jacobson passing electricity through the famous painter Munch, charging his crazy brain with the positive power of masculinity and the negative power of femininity,** 1908/9
Pen and ink, 27.3 x 21.2 cm.
Oslo Kommunes Kunstsamlinger, OKK 1976

272 **Caricature of Heiberg and Bodtker,** 1907/8
Lithograph, 22.5 x 32.5 cm.
Oslo Kommunes Kunstsamlinger, OKK 252
Ref. G. Schiefler No. 208

273 **Omega and the Tiger,** 1908/9
Lithograph, 24.5 x 46 cm.
Oslo Kommunes Kunstsamlinger, OKK 311
Ref. G. Schiefler No. 317

274 **The Nurse,** 1908/9
Drypoint, 20.5 x 15.2 cm.
Oslo Kommunes Kunstsamlinger, OKK 128
Ref. G. Schiefler No. 269

275 **Mandrill,** 1909
Lithograph, 26 x 14.7 cm.
Oslo Kommunes Kunstsamlinger, OKK 286
Ref. G. Schiefler No. 291

274

275

In 1908 Jens Thiis became the first director of Nasjonalgalleriet, in Oslo, an event that was to play an important part in ensuring Munch's recognition amongst his fellow countrymen. Even though Thiis was among Munch's circle of friends, he had fortunately avoided any close involvement in the Tulla Larsen affair, which enabled him to write a reassuring letter to the artist a week before his admittance to the clinic: 'My dear friend, how can you feel so alarmed? I am sure that there is nobody here who wishes you any harm. Everyone I know or come into contact with, speaks of you with warmth and sympathy, even those whom you mistrust.'[302] And of Krohg, the arch enemy, he said, 'he must surely be old enough now not to go round acting the fool just because of one postcard, written in the heat of the moment.'

Norwegian reaction to his work began to undergo a significant change while he was in the clinic; even in 1907 peoples' opinions had mellowed considerably since his last exhibition in Oslo. But the major exhibition organized by Jappe Nilssen and Thiis in 1909, which comprised 100 paintings and 200 graphic works, proved to be a total triumph for Munch—apart from a few carping criticisms and a debate in the newspapers that resulted from Nasjonalgalleriet's purchase of five major works from the show. One major consequence, however, of this very far-sighted purchase was that Olaf Schou presented the gallery with sixty works by Norwegian artists, including several pictures by Munch.

The good middle-class people of Oslo found it much easier to recognize Munch now that, the previous autumn, he had been made a Knight of the Order of St. Olav. Not surprisingly, Munch felt somewhat embarrassed at having such a high honour thrust on him, and he wrote rather self-deprecatingly: 'The Order of Olav created quite a stir for me in the clinic— the nurses thought it was such a lovely brooch'.[303] It was a natural enough reaction in one who had been all but banished from his homeland; it was the authorities' way of compensating him for all the years of conflict and vicious persecution that he had undergone.

While the exhibition was in progress, Munch received an ecstatic letter from Jappe Nilssen: 'Never before has an exhibition attracted such crowds or sold so many works. So help me God, every second picture has got a red ticket on it. The place is black with people.'[304] Suddenly Munch realized what it was to have friends with whom he could share happiness, and when they were finally able to telegraph him the financial results of the exhibition (60,000 kroner), the happy patient invited Nilssen and Thiis, together with the painter Ludvig Ravensberg, to a party in a private room at the Grand Hotel[305] in Oslo, where they had a telephone on the table, with an open line to Munch as he lay, flushed with success, on his sick bed.

On the boat back to Norway, Ravensberg urged Munch to take part in the competition for the decoration of the assembly hall of Oslo University, which was to celebrate its 100th anniversary in 1911. And when he arrived back home Munch found the place that was to provide him with all the inspiration he needed for this monumental work: 'This is where I'm going to live,' he exclaimed as he stood in the little white port of Kragerø, and that same day he found 'Skrubben',[306] the house that was to become both his home and his studio. It was while he was thinking of his new life in Norway that he wrote to Sigurd Høst: 'I am looking for a home. I want to live on the open sea; I've no intention of dying amongst the other half-dead fish in the suffocating waters of the Christiania fjord.'[307] In Kragerø he was to spend many peaceful and extremely productive years, possibly the most contented of his life. He grew to know the small town and its inhabitants, and as late as 1942 he was to write to Gierløff, who was living there at the time, about 'this pearl among coastal towns . . . I will always remember with gratitude the consideration that I was shown when I first came ashore. I knew then that I had arrived in a town with a long tradition of culture and a deep respect for art—even though its people were completely bewildered by my work.'[308] A year later he remembered a remark he had wanted to make to some friends who lived on the top of a hill: 'I am like Jonah, who was thrown ashore out of the whale's belly, and when he saw that the land was good he stayed there.'[309]

He invited all the friends who had stuck by him to come and stay—people

213

like the Germans Kollmann, Schiefler and Curt Glaser, as well as his Norwegian friends. In Kragerø he was able to relax and enjoy the friendships for which he had such a boundless capacity, sitting with a glass of the non-alcoholic beer that had become his favourite drink, while old Børre, who later appeared in allegorical form in his *History*, went down into the town to get wine for the guests. Slowly and methodically he painted those of the 'lifeguards of his art'[310] whom he had not as yet painted, men such as Jappe Nilssen and others, as part of the monumental overall scheme that he had embarked on as far back as the 1890s.

The Munch who painted the tormented self-portraits of the restless years bears little relation to the Munch who painted himself in the clinic in 1909.[311] He used the same vigorously sweeping brush strokes as in the *Death of Marat*, in shades of brilliant red and mauvish-blue. The mood is one of determined extroversion: he is preparing himself to reconquer the world and the people he sees in it. The man in the portrait knows that soon his troubles will all be behind him: he feels now the same self-confidence that he had felt fourteen years earlier, when he painted himself in Paris holding a cigarette, but this time he portrays himself in a lithograph (Plate 18), staring triumphantly out of a swirling mass of cigarette smoke.

Now he had even managed to conquer Norway.

276

THE FABLE OF ALPHA AND OMEGA[312]

Alpha and Omega were the first people on the island. As Alpha lay in the grass, sleeping and dreaming, Omega took a piece of straw and tickled him so that he awoke. Alpha was in love with Omega, and that evening the two of them sat close together, watching the moon's golden pillar shimmering and flickering round the island.

They went into the wood, where they came across all sorts of weird animals and plants; although it was strangely dark in there, they also found a lot of beautiful flowers. On one occasion Omega became afraid and threw herself into Alpha's arms. For many days there was nothing but sunshine on the island.

One day, Omega lay at the edge of the wood soaking up the sun, while Alpha sat further back in the wood in the shade. Then a large cloud appeared on the horizon and gradually spread across the sky, casting shadow over the island.

Alpha called for Omega, but she did not hear him. Then he saw that she was holding the head of a snake in her hands, staring into its glittering eyes: a large snake that had slithered out of its hole and coiled round her body. Then suddenly the heavens opened and it began to rain, and Alpha and Omega became frightened.

Then one day Alpha met the snake and he fought with it and killed it, while Omega looked on.

Once Omega met a bear, and she shivered when she felt its soft coat against her body. When she placed her arm around its neck it sank into the animal's soft fur.

She also met a laughing hyena, which had a rather rough coat. But he was impervious to her usual blandishments, and so she plaited a laurel wreath with her soft hands, and slowly leaning her beautiful face towards the animal's head, placed the garland around his neck.

The tiger pressed his wild and frightening head against Omega's dear little face, but she was not afraid. She placed her tiny hand between the tiger's jaws and gently stroked his teeth.

When the tiger encountered the bear on his way through the island, he detected the scent of Omega—the fragrant pale apple blossom that she loved more than anything else, and which she kissed every morning at sunrise. The animals fought and tore each other apart.

Just as on a chessboard, the position changed as a result of one move. Omega clung to Alpha. Inquisitively and uncomprehendingly, the other animals craned their necks forward to see what was happening.

Omega's eyes began to alter. Normally they were light blue, but when she stared at her beloved they became black, flecked with crimson, and then she would sometimes hide her mouth behind a flower. Then her desires started to change. One day Alpha saw how she sat on the beach kissing a donkey that lay in her lap. And so he got hold of an ostrich and placed his head against its neck, but Omega did not look up from her passionate embrace. Omega became depressed and saddened because she could not possess all the animals of the island, and she sat down on the grass and wept bitter tears. Then she got up and ran distraught round the island until she met a pig. She knelt down and buried her body in its long, black bristles, and she and the pig looked at each other.

276 **The Rag Picker**, 1908/9
Etching on zinc, 60 x 44 cm.
Oslo Kommunes Kunstsamlinger, OKK 131
Ref. G. Schiefler No. 272

277 **The Big Cod**, 1902
Etching, 11.8 x 17 cm.
Islo Kommunes Kunstsamlinger, OKK 75
Ref. G. Schiefler No. 165

278 **Stormy Night**, 1908/9
Woodcut, 21.7 x 32.5 cm.
Oslo Kommunes Kunstsamlinger, OKK 622
Ref. G. Schiefler No. 341

279

280

281

But Omega was unhappy. One night, as the moon's golden pillar flickered in the water, she ran away on the back of a deer across the sea to the pale green country that lies in the shadow of the moon, and Alpha was left alone on the island.

One day her children came to him; a new generation of creatures had grown up on the island, and they called him 'Father'. There were small snakes and monkeys, piglets, beasts of prey and things that were half-man, half-animal. He fell into a deep despair and ran along the beach. He heard a scream in the air and held his hands to his ears. The sea, and heaven and earth began to tremble. He was tormented with anxiety.

One day the deer came back with Omega.

Alpha was sitting on the beach, and she came to him. He feels the blood throbbing in his ears. The muscles swell up in his body and he strikes Omega dead. Then he bends over her dead body, and the expression on her face terrifies him. It is the same one that she had at the very moment when he had loved her most in the wood.

As he stands staring at her, all her children and the animals of the island attack him from behind and tear him to shreds. The new generation takes over the island.

279 **Alpha Asleep,** 1908/9
Lithograph, 25 x 44 cm.
Oslo Kommunes Kunstsamlinger, OKK 305
Ref. G. Schiefler No. 310

280 **Omega and the Donkey,** 1908/9
Lithograph, 23.5 x 35 cm.
Oslo Kommunes Kunstsamlinger, OKK 315
Ref. G. Schiefler No. 320

281 **Omega's children,** 1908/9
Lithograph, 25.5 x 50 cm.
Oslo Kommunes Kunstsamlinger, OKK 319
Ref. G. Schiefler No. 324

216

13 : Back Home in Norway

E. Munch, 1917

218

The Norwegian mountains loom threateningly before me

Munch had hesitated before finally deciding to return to Norway,[313] but when he settled in Kragerø, the many large rooms of the old manor house 'Skrubben' were before long filled with canvases. To these he soon added a number of very fine landscape paintings, including *The Sun* and *History*. It was a stroke of luck that the chance of such an important commission as that of providing murals for Oslo University should present itself at that particular moment, and Munch immediately began to prepare his entry for the competition, which had to be submitted by 15 May, 1909. It took, as it transpired, several years of hard work before he finally won through, but this will be dealt with more fully in the next chapter.

Munch was now forty-six, with many years of experience behind him. He had lived a reckless life, pushing himself to the absolute limits of endurance, and had suffered for it, but at last he had had his art recognized by his fellow countrymen, albeit long after it had been accepted in Germany, his second home. So it was ironic that, just as people were beginning to appreciate the old Munch, a new Munch was emerging. This change had begun to occur even before the breakdown. We have already seen how his large pictures of bathers had marked the dawning of a new era in his art, but Munch was constantly developing, and a number of his Warnemünde pictures show a much more spontaneous treatment, not only of people, but above all of nature. We have also seen how his new painting techniques made possible an artistic renewal, and how the self-portrait from the clinic (Plate 15) shows a new mood of self-confidence and a new feeling of vigour and vitality. It is a strange paradox, however, that the period during which Munch's art was predominantly introverted and 'spiritual' was while he was leading a highly volatile life, surrounded by people, whereas he achieved his greatest feeling of extroversion and immediacy vis-à-vis both nature and people at a time of self-isolation, when he became known as 'the hermit of Skrubben'. He admitted that he was essentially a loner, but he was not anti-social, in the usual sense of the word—he was basically much too fond of life. The fact that he lived in his own private world, did not prevent him from inviting old friends, friends that he could trust, to visit him. But there were other old friends that he likened to 'old teeth, which are best removed as time goes on'.[314] He got on well with the people of Kragerø, even if it was a rather distant relationship, but the people to whom he really came close were those who helped him in his daily life: Inga Sterk, who kept house for him, Stina Krafft, who sewed his enormous canvases together, and Lars Fjeld, who helped him get them on to the stretchers. It was Fjeld who attached cords, four to five metres long, from the centre of *The Sun* to the edge of the canvas, painted them, lifted them from the canvas surface and then let them flick back into place, thereby providing Munch with an outline to follow while painting the vast spectrum of radiating rays of the sun. In Kragerø Munch also found models to inspire him: people like Ellef Larsen, and, above all, Børre Eriksen (Plates 305 and 307), the seventy-year-old retired seaman who had sailed all over the world, 'that wonderful model who gave me the inspiration for my work', for *History*.

At 'Skrubben', Munch gained new energy, old friends came to visit him and many a bottle was drunk, but he himself confined his drinking to 'vørterøl (non-alcoholic beer), that foaming nectar of the gods'.

It was not only people, however, who inspired him to new artistic heights: nature played the most important part. Munch had already painted some very good landscapes, from places such as Åsgårdstrand, Ljan, and Nordstrand, but hitherto landscape had merely served as the background for the

...2 Winter in Kragerø, 1912
Oil on canvas, 132 x 131 cm.
Oslo Kommunes Kunstsamlinger, OKK 319

283

shifting moods of mankind. Now his relationship with nature was a much more direct one. He became enthralled by Kragerø's majestic surroundings; the rocks and small islets that led out towards the open sea, the sheer cliffs and the bleak outcrops of granite in which a solitary fir tree had taken root. In *Winter in Kragerø* (Plate 282) that tree rears up like a silent monument, its position in the painting chosen with great care and accuracy, while the triangular shapes in the foreground, underlined rather than hidden by their snowy covering, lead the eye up the trunk of the tree until finally it comes to rest in the dark pyramid of the topmost branches.

Munch portrayed these stark scenes round Kragerø, and also the rich, luxuriant countryside round Hvitsten, in the same straightforward and positive way. Judging by the mood of happiness that shines through these paintings, he must have been intoxicated by the idea of gradually re-discovering his own lost homeland.

This change of style does not really represent a break in his artistic development: rather the pictures of his maturity show a broadening of his knowledge of life. Munch, the searcher of the soul, became the painter of observation and, on a purely artistic level, he was hardly ever greater than during the first twenty years after his home-coming. As he himself said, 'The molecules that make up my soul are at peace.' He had always been an

Here I wander through ten rooms filled with sketches and paintings, while sleet storms rage outside, but loneliness and bad weather do not affect me as deeply as the cruelties of mankind
Munch to Ernest Thiel[5]

I do not think that it is such a bad idea in the case of a beautiful structure like the Eidsvold Monument. What do you mean about me doing the wall decorations and Vigeland the sculpture?
Munch to Jens Thiis[6]

4

3 **Winter Landscape from Kragerø**, 1915
   Oil on canvas, 103 x 128 cm.
   Nasjonalgalleriet, Oslo

4 **The Cliff at Kragerø**, 1910/14
   Oil on canvas, 91 x 112 cm.
   Oslo Kommunes Kunstsamlinger, OKK 579

extremely perceptive observer, but now it was not the labyrinths of man's mind, with all their joys and sorrows, that he was trying to explore: from now on the sun-filled pictures of his old age became more and more concerned with the pleasures and richness of life. The sombre shades of his youth gave way to much brighter tones, and his brush strokes took on a livelier, more joyful quality, as they swept over the canvas in long, bold strokes. Yet many of his pictures still show that their basic inspiration was a sudden mental image, even though the method of composition is simpler and more straight-forward. Munch saw the galloping horse (Plate 325); he noticed its speed; he experienced a feeling of excitement when he saw the children pressing themselves against the rock in fright, as the dark horse with its flailing mane and wild eyes almost filled the narrow track, and he admired the way in which the driver kept his balance. He has portrayed a whole succession of images in one spontaneous and vigorously painted scene.

He recorded the time that he saw Kristofer Støa carrying a spade over his shoulder, as he came home from work at the head of a group of *Workers in the Snow* (Plate 328). Perhaps the sight of these workmen, whose dark clothing made them stand out starkly against the white of the snow, reminded Munch of the naked men whom he had seen advancing up the beach out of the sea at Warnemünde (Plate 245). It is certainly true that they approach us in the

285

same direct and deliberate way, but these men are even more imposing. It is almost as if Munch is not telling us simply about his friend and model Kristofer and his men, but about the relentless advance of the working classes. We shall see how he later took up these working themes from Kragerø again, and dreamed of depicting them in Oslo Town Hall, although this was never to happen. One picture, however, does adorn the walls of the Town Hall, and that is *Life* (Plate 297). When the Nazis threw it out of the Dresden art gallery, it was rescued and taken back to Norway where, by a lucky coincidence, it finally came to rest in the very building where the Oslo-bred Munch should have been given the room that he had hoped for and dreamed of. The painting was done in 1910 and had originally been intended as the backdrop for his decoration of the university assembly hall. The subject is a familiar one: the Tree of Life stretching its branches over the people. The heavy, dark shapes of the men act as a frame for the light-coloured figures of the women; there is no didactic symbolism, just simplicity, strength and a feeling of monumental intensity.

Neither these new subjects nor the new sense of vitality in his art signified any kind of hiatus in his development: they were an extension, a continuation of his old work. Throughout his life Munch was 'on the move', and

... *Norwegian landscapes in all their Spring glory, with figur[e] free men and people with their hands tied behind their backs b[e] set free—in fact, a scene of unfettered power. You should take [a] trip one day and come and visit the hermit of Skrubben.*
Munch to Jens Thiis

Now I am living a completely sound and healthy life—just lik[e a] monk (or a non-smoking, non-drinking Munch) ... I do not ov[er] estimate my capabilities and I realize that I am not immune t[o] things that may happen in the future ...
Munch to Dr. Jacobson

The following quotations are concerned with the portraits [on] pages 224–32, which Munch called 'The lifeguards of my a[rt].

A painter who is incapable of painting a landscape without injecting his own essential being into it, and can instil it with s[o] a depth of psychological feeling, must make a first-rate portra[it] painter. Franz Servaes[9]

When I meet people, I am very wary. I build up a wall of talk. Then I throw a rope over the wall, and if anyone tugs at it, I ha[ul] it in. Munch to Felix Hatz[10]

I must aim at a target. If I hit it, I always score a bull's-eye.
Munch[11]

Edvard Munch would never have been allowed to paint me as [he] wanted to so badly. He is a dangerous man. He sees right thro[ugh] us, and turns us inside out. Then he hangs us up on a nail, and there we hang for all time. Henrik Sørensen[12]

Even so I am still going to reproduce it, not because I admire it [or] recognize myself in its haughty expression, but because I think that it will amuse him to see it in the book, something he can hardly have expected.
Jens Thiis on the subject of his portrait in Munch's biography (Plate 289).[13]

Strangely enough, of all the portraits made of me Munch's is reckoned to be the best. Of course I would dispute that whole-heartedly, but everyone, even my close family, my sister and brother-in-law, say that I am mistaken. They think that he ha[s] captured me perfectly. I felt very unhappy one day when a girl, who I am very fond of, said that it looked exactly like she saw [me] —that really made me stop and think.
Jappe Nilssen on the subject of his portrait (Plate 292).[14]

Helge Rode should really be on show in the Zoo, with strange African animals, ostriches and giraffes, in the background. Th[at] would suit his eccentric appearance. H. P. Rohde[15]

Aha, he may say, that will be good when it has stood and had some time to collect itself ... Just wait until it has been rained [on] a bit, had a few scratches from nails and things like that, and been dragged round the world in all sorts of wretched cases ... Yes indeed, that could be good in time! It only needs a few flaw[s] to make it really perfect ... Munch to Christian Gierløff[16]

An example of how Munch 'talked' to his pictures: *I also m[ust] have some friends on the wall.*
Munch's reply to Ingse Vibe's husband when he wanted to buy a portrait for 50,000 kroner.[17]

Like all nervous people, I talk a lot. When I talk, I confide in th[e] person that I am with and prevent them from attacking me. So[me] people use speech like poison gas to silence their victims and thwart their intentions. They use talk as a weapon for attack. I use it as a means of self-defence. Munch[18]

222

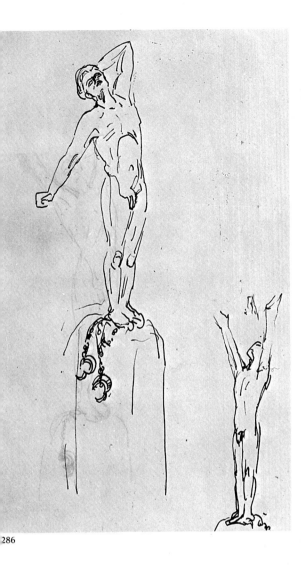

although he sometimes fell back on the past, he would at the same time be looking to the future, so that each period was like another step on the ladder of his development. He never, for example, abandoned his *Frieze of Life* or the ideas contained in it. He returned to these themes again, just as he had done when doing his two friezes for Linde and Reinhardt, and we shall discuss later his awareness of the connection between the *Frieze of Life* and his murals in Oslo University. Had not his whole life been a continuous struggle with the problems of realizing the *Frieze*, it is not absolutely certain that he would have been able to cope with the problems posed by the University murals.

Once back in Norway, his days of working in boarding houses and seedy hotel bedrooms were over, and he began to accumulate a number of studios. In his various properties he erected one open-air studio after another, as he found he needed more and more space. At 'Skrubben' he painted the landscape for *History*, a simple yet impressive panorama of cliffs and outcrops of stone, small islands and stretches of open sea, but for *Alma Mater* he needed a less harsh, inland setting, and so he bought Ramme farmstead, situated in a sheltered creek near Hvitsen. He became master not only of the farm and its land, but also a variety of dogs, horses, hens, turkeys and geese, and yet he still found time to paint *The Explorers* out in his open-air studio, with the sky as a roof, the sun as an overhead light, and a board fence for walls. However, he soon found that the rooms at Ramme were not big enough for use in the winter, and so, in 1913, he rented the imposing 24-room manor house of Grimsrød[315] on the island of Jeløy. One of the rooms was made habitable,

287

285 **Kneeling Female Nude**, 1920/30
Oil on canvas, 66 x 44 cm.
Rolf E. Stenersen Collection, RES A88

286 **Design for a Monument**,
Indian ink drawing, 26 x 40 cm.
Oslo Kommunes Kunstsamlinger, OKK 138

287 **Mother Norway**, 1909
Crayon, 38.1 x 30.7 cm.
Oslo Kommunes Kunstsamlinger, OKK 2463

isten Sandberg, 1901   289 Jens Thiis, 1909   290 The Frenchman, 1901   225
on canvas, 215 x 147 cm.   Oil on canvas, 203 x 102 cm.   Oil on canvas, 185 x 70 cm.
Kommunes Kunstsamlinger, OKK 3   Oslo Kommunes Kunstsamlinger, OKK 390   Nasjonalgalleriet, Oslo

291

292

294

295

alther Rathenau, 1907
on canvas, 220 x 110 cm.
smus Meyers Samlinger, Bergen

ppe Nilssen, 1909
on canvas, 194 x 95 cm.
lo Kommunes Kunstsamlinger, OKK 8

elge Rode, 1908/9
on canvas, 196 x 86 cm.
ationalmuseum, Stockholm

ristian Gierloff, 1910
on canvas, 207 x 100 cm.
teborgs Museum

dvig Karsten, 1905
on canvas, 194 x 91 cm.
ielska Galleriet, Stockholm

while the remainder became filled with a random mixture of canvases and prints, and the floors strewn with tubes of paint and palettes. In 1916, when his University murals were finally unveiled, he bought Ekely, his small estate outside Oslo, and people began talking of 'Munch the landowner'. He defended himself as best he could, explaining both to the tax authorities and to people in general that he was certainly not a rich man, but what use was it, when friends like Jappe Nilssen spoke of the twenty-four rooms at 'Skrubben', and Christian Gierløff stated that Munch at one time had owned forty-three studios in four different properties?

We should remember that Munch needed a lot of space. He used all available rooms as studios, and he felt no need for any of the conventional creature comforts. He had no use for the small things that we normally consider vital to life. But he became more and more reluctant to sell his 'children'. They were what made his life worth living. We have already heard how the big sale of works to Rasmus Meyer's collection[316] (Rasmus Meyers Samlinger) filled him with 'a silent and resigned melancholy . . . at the thought of losing so many of my beloved children'. He really did love his 'children': 'I have nobody else,' he once said. He talked to them, and he had a very definite belief that they should live their own lives, in rain and in storm, in snow and in cold. They had to be toughened up. Apart from calling his pictures his 'children', he also called them his 'soldiers', his 'warriors', his 'battalions', whom he sent out to fight for him whenever necessary.

He also spoke of 'the lifeguards of his art', by which he meant the portraits of those friends who had not deserted him. When Munch died, leaving all his works to the city of Oslo, a surprising number of full-length paintings of his friends and patrons were discovered. Perhaps he had intended to assemble this 'bodyguard' in its own room in some projected museum. We cannot be sure, but we do know that he was very unwilling to sell them, and that he deterred prospective buyers with the remark, 'I also must have some friends on the wall.'[317]

That Munch 'was incapable of painting a landscape without injecting his own personality into it', as his friend Servaes put it, has already been stated. We have also seen how he portrayed the details of a landscape with such precision that we really feel that we are standing amongst the boulders of the shore at Åsgårdstrand, for example. But, even more strikingly, his pictures have become deeply engraved on our consciousness so that a person now-adays, looking over the Oslo fjord at sunset, and seeing the dark outline of Ormøy island or the huddled mass of the city from Mosseveien, can easily be struck by the feeling that he is looking at 'a landscape that is just like Munch's'. It is for that reason alone, apart from the many others, that Munch was such an outstandingly effective painter.

In the first chapter we saw many examples of his highly revealing self-portraits, which were never flattering but almost always extremely probing. We saw also how he began by portraying his close family, then widened his range of subjects to include his bohemian friends and other non-professional models in Norway, Paris, and Berlin. We can see elements in these very early portraits that were to recur in the full-length ones painted at the start of the new century. There is an underlying link between the Jensen-Hjell portrait of 1885 (Plate 61), that of his sister Inger, completed in 1892 (Plate 67), and his painting of Dagny Juell from 1893 (Plate 101); each work marks a step forward in Munch's search for a feeling of the monumental in his portraiture. Some of his portraits have a quality that almost borders on solemnity and ceremonial, something that becomes even more marked in the large, repre-sentative portraits of his later years.

On the whole, it was his portraits which drew most praise from both the public and the critics, even though people thought that some of them were more like caricatures. Munch himself was fully aware of the great gift that he had for delving deep into peoples' inner selves: he once wrote: 'I can see behind everyone's masks.' And the technique he used for peering behind their 'masks' was simply the one that so many shy people use—talking. 'Why do you talk so much while you're painting?'[318] asked Elisabeth Förster-Nietzsche, as Munch worked on her portrait. 'Self-defence,' replied Munch to his sitter, who, incidentally, was not one of his favourite people. 'I build a kind of wall round myself, so that I can paint in peace.' Of one particularly difficult sitter, a Norwegian, he wrote: 'He only functions on short wave, and he refused to succumb to my long wave anaesthetic. I must have people in a receptive frame of mind if I am to paint them, and while I'm chattering away I can relax.' Later in life, he sometimes provided a bottle of champagne to help his sitters feel more at ease, although he himself never touched a drop of it.

The first decade of this century was the period in which Munch did most of his portraits, using basically the same compositional technique that he had used for the portrait of his sister Inger in 1892. He normally kept to a pale background, which often included the suggestion of a door, a carpet or some-thing similar. He began to place more and more emphasis on full-face portraiture, in order to reveal more of the character of his sitters, as, for example, in his painting of Aase and Harald Nørregaard (Plate 298), which dates from 1899. In this work, Munch's main interest lies in the person of Fru Nørregaard, who, as the painter Aase Carlsen, had been a very close friend in the early part of his life. Unlike her husband, who is in profile, she stares straight out at us, as she does in several other paintings: she is the woman, for example, who breaks away from the main group and comes towards us in Ladies on the Jetty (Plate 296), painted in 1903.

The same full-face technique is used in the portraits of his self-satisfied friend, the caricaturist Schlittgen, and the relaxed and thoughtful French-

297

Swiss writer Archinard. His desire to portray individual character is paralleled by that equally strong desire to endow his portraits with a feeling of the monumental, and this dual ambition resulted in pictures such as the two just mentioned. It is no coincidence that Munch nearly always calls the portraits not by the names of the sitters, but by the more general names of *The German* and *The Frenchman* (Plates 123 and 290).

He repeats the technique once again in his splendid portrait of the jovial and temperamental Consul Sandberg (Plate 288), a painting that is as full of life as it is imposing. The sitter was a personal friend of Munch's and had shown him a great deal of understanding when he was going through his difficult patch. While work was in progress he found that the canvas was too small for his subject's ample figure, and the first time that the picture was shown, the canvas had to be folded over, but he later added to it so as to make space for the left foot. A strictly frontal portrait would have done little to convey the reality of the subject's portly figure, as he stands silhouetted against the white door. The whole composition is given a sense of unity by the way in which the yellowish green of the wallpaper is repeated, in varying shades, in both the floor and the central figure.

The portraits that he did on commission have the same character as those he did of his friends, but the most interesting aspect is that the friends are treated in exactly the same representational way as the other subjects. All the pictures show the same combination of universality and individualism—whether Munch is portraying the intellectual industrialist Walther Rathenau (Plate 291), later to become a very important politician, or the critic Jappe Nilssen (Plate 292), his friend from the summer days at Åsgårdstrand, who looks out at us casually yet warily, or the self-opinionated Jens Thiis, who appears in the rough draft of a large portrait (Plate 289). Amongst the 'life-

298

Every time I paint people, I always find that the sitter's enemies think it is a good likeness. The subject himself says that all my pictures are good, except the one of himself. Munch[19]

I have been given a very large room, 10m x 15m. It is the biggest room in the exhibition. The main part will be devoted to van Gogh, Gauguin and Cézanne . . . I feel almost ashamed at having been given so much space . . . I hope that they are not going to regret their decision. As was to be expected, there is a lot of Matisse-ism and Cézanne-ism, just as in Norway. But I was happy to see that on this occasion there were hardly any apples . . . I asked a little Hungarian about it. He looked at me quizzically, enigmatically, but whispered: 'Our apples are at home—we have left them back in Hungary.'
Munch to Jappe Nilssen on the Sonderbund Exhibition in Cologne[20]

There is a collection here of all the wildest paintings in Europe— I am just a pure and faded classicist. Cologne Cathedral is shaking to its very foundations. Munch to Jappe Nilssen[21]

At the exhibition van Gogh definitely looks like a clear, Classical painter. Gauguin seems like an already rather passé romanticist, while Cézanne's pictures are as soft and gentle as milk and honey, when compared to the hot, spicy art that is being offered here to the hungry modernist. Believe it or not, but the section devoted to Edvard Munch's thirty-five works, along with the van Goghs, is the highlight of the exhibition. It really seems soothing, clear, tranquil and old-fashioned after all the shocks to which one's nervous system has been subjected, in the rooms leading to it. Jens Thiis on the Sonderbund Exhibiton in Cologne, 1912[22]

296 **Ladies on the Jetty,** 1903
Oil on canvas, 184 x 205 cm.
Bergen Billedgalleri

297 **Life,** 1910
Oil on canvas, 194 x 369 cm.
Oslo Town Hall

298 **Aase and Harald Norregaard,** 1899
Oil on cardboard, 50 x 126 cm.
Nasjonalgalleriet, Oslo

299 **Self-portrait with Hat,** 1905
Oil on canvas, 80 x 64 cm.
Oslo Kommunes Kunstsamlinger, OKK 507

300 **Ingse Vibe Müller,** 1903
Oil on canvas, 161 x 70 cm.
Oslo Kommunes Kunstsamlinger, OKK 272

guards of his art' he also placed the white-suited painter Ludvig Karsten (Plate 295), who, by virtue of the fact that he was Munch's only Norwegian pupil, probably merited the title more than anyone else. Certainly they both shared the same temperament: like Munch, Karsten's main ambition in life was to use his art as a means of relieving his own inner tensions. The blue shades of his highly evocative evening scenes have many similarities with Munch's paintings, but it was as a portrait painter that Karsten showed the clearest traces of the influence of his friend, thirteen years his senior.

In 1912 Munch was invited to take part in the great Sonderbund Exhibition at Cologne, where, as has been mentioned before, he and Picasso were the only two living artists to be given their own rooms. Munch himself wrote to Thiel: 'The intention is to create a comprehensive exhibition, that embraces the whole of modern European art. I have been awarded the most prominent place, next to Liebermann—after Cézanne, van Gogh and Gauguin.'[319]

The Cologne exhibition further strengthened Munch's international reputation. His most important contribution was the three main subjects of his planned decoration for the University Hall, which he had completed at a quarter of their projected size. And yet Oslo University was still hesitating to accept them.

301 Jens Thiis, 1913
Lithograph, 29.5 x 23.5 cm.
Oslo Kommunes Kunstsamlinger, OKK 371
Ref. G. Schiefler No. 410

4 : The Oslo University Murals

The Frieze of Life should be viewed in relation to the University decorations, for which in many respects it is the forerunner, and without which the latter would probably have been impossible to produce. It served to develop my decorative sense. They should also be viewed together with regard to the ideas that they contain. The Frieze of Life deals with the individual's joys and sorrows seen from close quarters—the University murals portray the powerful forces of eternity. Both the Frieze of Life and the University murals come together in the large Frieze of Life picture of Man and Woman in a Wood with the golden city in the background.   Munch[1]

302 **New Rays** (Side section from Oslo University murals)
Oil on canvas, 455 x 225 cm.

303 **Mother and children in the Sun**, 1910
Black crayon, 69.7 x 53.2 cm.
Oslo Kommunes Kunstsamlinger, OKK 1787

303

Two weeks after Munch left the psychiatric clinic in Copenhagen, he announced that he was going to participate in the competition for the decoration of the assembly hall of Oslo University.[320] Seven years later, on 19 September 1916, his work was unveiled.[321] In between, there was a great deal of controversy.[322]

In December 1908 the University authorities and the initiating committee decided that there should be a restricted competition for the work. In the following April, Lorentz Dietrichson,[323] the professor of art history, Jens Thiis, director of Nasjonalgalleriet, and the painter Erik Werenskiold were all asked to take part in the meetings of the building committee in an advisory capacity. When the entries were closed on 15 May 1909, the jury were faced with work by three sculptors and twenty-two painters, one of whom was Munch. Between April and December 1909 no fewer than eighteen meetings took place in connection with the projected work, but all of them ended in deadlock. Werenskiold and Thiis maintained that six artists should submit designs: Munch, Gerhard Munthe,[324] Eilif Peterssen,[325] Emanuel Vigeland,[326] Oluf Wold-Torne, and Thorvald Erichsen. But the artists all signed a statement[327] that they did not wish to take part under these conditions. There then followed a number of proposals and counterproposals from the committee and the artists, and the situation became more and more chaotic.

A series of fresh meetings was held, in which Munch's name was not mentioned, but at Werenskiold's suggestion[328] it was decided that Thiis should try and urge Munch to send in his preliminary sketches. Munch replied that he had suspended all work on the project, but nevertheless a telegram was sent to him, begging him to reconsider. Munch replied: 'Drafts not ready.' The final outcome was that four artists were asked to submit designs for the work: Munthe, Emanuel Vigeland, Peterssen, and Munch.

On 8 March 1910, a jury was convened, this time with the addition of the Danish painter Joachim Skovgaard.[329] Munch had submitted two proposed works: *History* and *The Mountain of Mankind*.[330] The three members of the jury were unanimous in their rejection of the latter work, but they decided that Munch should produce a full-scale draft of *History* for the side wall and Vigeland his *Fight with the Dragon* for the end wall.[331] They were both to provide further sketches for the whole hall. And a new deadline of 1 August 1911 was set.

Munch threw himself wholeheartedly into his work, completing draft after draft. He abandoned his plans for *The Mountain of Mankind* and re-designed *History*, now it had been decided that it should adorn one of the side walls, rather than the wall at the far end of the hall. He then began to concentrate on the problem of the end wall, and after a number of attempted solutions he finally decided on *The Sun* rising over the fjord.[332]

In August 1911, Munch presented a total of thirty works,[333] amongst which were four large draft versions of *History*, one of *The Researchers* (later to be known as *Alma Mater*) and one of *The Sun*, six large works in all. He also provided the committee with rough sketches for the smaller areas, along with fourteen other preliminary sketches and drafts. This large body of work, the vast majority of which had been completed in less than a year, was put on display in August 1911, partly in the University itself and partly in Dioramalokalet[334] on Karl Johan Street.

All three members of the jury rejected Vigeland's offerings,[335] but Professor Dietrichsen, although admitting the undoubted merits of Munch's work, said that he dared not pass judgement on the finished product.

Skovgaard had serious doubts, but finally recommended that Munch should go ahead with the pictures, and that they should stay on the walls 'until a final verdict is reached'.[336] The only person who supported Munch unreservedly was Thiis.

The University authorities and the members of the central committee, however, voted unanimously that 'none of the works under consideration should be accepted'. Munch and Vigeland were each given 5,000 kroner for their troubles and the whole matter remained unresolved.

Throughout this period, a fierce controversy had been raging in the press.[337] Not only members of the public, but important figures such as Christian Krohg and Andreas Aubert had written rather wild attacks on both Munch and the selection committee. Werenskiold, however, had shown a great deal more understanding, while Harriet Backer had come out strongly in Munch's favour. The experts soon found themselves divided into two rival camps.

In 1911 a fund-raising committee was formed with a view to buying Munch's works and presenting them to the University, and in 1914 this committee sent an appeal to the University authorities, urging them to acquire the pictures. It was pointed out to them that Munch's drafts had been exhibited in several towns abroad, 'where he has been widely admired'.[338] Eventually, in May 1914, the University declared that they regarded it as highly desirable that Munch's paintings should be acquired for the new assembly hall.

At last Munch was given the go-ahead to carry out preparatory work in the Hall itself; by the summer of 1916 the completed paintings were in place, and on 11 September 1916 they were formally presented to the University. Munch himself said that he was paid 40,000 kroner (plus the money that he had received for the two competitions).[339] The work had cost him seven years of mental and physical exertion.

We have already seen how Munch's life-long dream had been to have the chance of decorating a whole room—to realize the ideas of his *Frieze of Life*. The work that he had done for Linde had been rejected, his work for Reinhardt had been dispersed. Now he had finally fulfilled his ambition. But it is doubtful whether he would have been capable of such a major undertaking had it not been for the years of planning how best to realize his *Frieze of Life*. It had sharpened his decorative sense, and his poem 'of mankind's joys and sorrows' had developed his perception to a point where he was able to portray 'the powerful forces of eternity'. This he achieved without resorting to the device used by artists through the ages when faced with such a massive task, that of using allegories or tales from mythology. Munch had no use for such devices, and his work contains no elements borrowed from antiquity. The architecture of the hall is Neo-Classical, but Munch is Classical. P. A. Munch's nephew not only had respect for tradition; he treated it with great reverence. This becomes particularly evident in a work like *History*, which tells in all simplicity how the events of the past are handed down by word of mouth. The scene in which the grandfather is telling stories to the young boy makes one think of Munch and his brilliant uncle. We know from what Munch himself said, as well as from countless sketches and drawings, that the landscape behind the two figures is the one he saw every day at Kragerø. And yet he has succeeded in changing an ordinary Norwegian landscape into a scene of Classical simplicity. The old sailor Børre seems to remind us of Homer, and there is a suggestion that the oak tree will one day take root in the young boy's memory as the Tree of Life. The majestic goes hand in hand with the mundane, and the past and the present melt into one.

History having been initially intended to adorn the end wall, which is much shorter than the side walls, the composition had to be re-worked. Originally, the left side of the painting was taken up by the tree, with Børre and the boy occupying the right side, but in the final version Munch added a splendid, ice-blue landscape, whose primeval quality is enhanced by the sheer mountainside that catches our eye on the right and leads our gaze beyond the blue hills to the open sea in the distance. Suddenly we are no longer looking at the countryside around Kragerø—the whole scene has

I wanted the decorations to represent a complete and self-contained world of ideas, artistically expressed in a way that wa at the same time both essentially Norwegian and also universal.
      Munch[2]

Spring *was the longing of the mortally ill for light and warmth for life. The* Sun *in the University Hall is the sunshine through the window of* Spring.   Munch to Jens Thiis, 1933[3]

History *would never have come about, had I not seen Børre, the model.* Munch[4]

People are always talking about the central figure in History *being blind. I have really not given it much thought. When I painted that marvellous model Børre, the man who inspired the work, I saw how the eyes of the old sailor of the Seven Seas glinte whenever some memory of days gone by passed through his mind*
      Munch[5]

History *cannot be told by a fisherman, he said. Apart from anything else, the old man sitting there is a sailor, who had been on many a voyage across the sea. And anyway, were the Gospels not told by fishermen? He thought that the man's feet were too large But that was done on purpose . . . it is because of the size of his feet and legs that the man looks so tall and imposing.* Munch[6]

304 **Two Boys** (Preparatory sketch for *History*)
     Blue crayon, 36.6 x 27.2 cm.
     Oslo Kommunes Kunstsamlinger, OKK 153

305 Photograph of Børre, the model for *History*, c.1910

306 **History** in the open air studio at Skrubben. In the foreground is Munch himself and the portraits of Thiis, Sandberg and Fru Roede together with that of a male standing nude.

307 **Borre**, 1910/11
     Oil on canvas, 104 x 128 cm.
     Oslo Kommunes Kunstsamlinger, OKK 425

304

308

There are no oak trees on the coast, he said!!! What it is to be a know-all. The old tree that I used as a model has now rotted away, but it used to stand right down at the water's edge. And I always used to walk along the beach at Kragerø during the summer through a forest of thousands of oak trees.

    Then he began to find fault with the colours. Blue stones. Those I could never find, he said. I have seen a lot of blue stones—and, anyway, a horse can be red, yellow, white, and blue, depending on how the light strikes it.   Munch[7]

History shows a distant and historically emotive landscape, in which an old man from the fjords, who has spent a life of hard toil, now sits sharing his rich storehouse of memories with an eagerly listening young boy.   Munch[8]

308 **History** (Main section of left wall in Oslo University Hall)
Oil on canvas, 455 x 1160 cm.

309

History is a symbolic portrayal of experience, the supreme source of knowledge. Experience, which is brought alive by the memory and transmitted from generation to generation. But the artist has not searched for his symbolism in distant and antiquated ideas. He has found inspiration on his own doorstep — in a Norwegian fjord landscape at dawn. It is a simple and straightforward scene, taken from everyday life, and yet, by means of his own emotional intensity, he has raised it from the mundane to the monumental and achieved a feeling of timeless universality . . .

The old man in his tattered peasant's garb has a regal grandeur

and a Homeric serenity which transports the hall and its neo-Greek decoration back into the epic realms of Classical antiquity.
Jens Thiis[9]

I bought Nedre Ramme when I left Kragerø because I had to have a place for my open air studio and because I had to complete the Aula [assembly hall] pictures. It was there that I found inspiration for the scene in Alma Mater and was able to instil it with the same earthy quality that History gained at Kragerø . . . Alma Mater did not quite turn out as I wanted. It was for that reason that I kept Nedre Ramme on. Munch to Jens Thiis[10]

309 **Alma Mater** (Main section of right wall in Oslo University Hall)
Oil on canvas, 455 x 1160 cm.

310

311

How I have been attacked for having kept Nedre Ramme in orde[r] to do studies for the Aula pictures! People want it as a public bathing place. What is more important, I ask, that your childre[n] should bathe or that Alma Mater's children should? I have got another place some distance away which I use for ordinary, run-of-the-mill pictures. Munch to Jens Thiis[11]

I have never been completely satisfied with Alma Mater. The whole of the right hand side has too much movement. The other version is better . . . Munch to K. E. Schreiner[12]

The picture has been popularly called History, *but it really has more to do with learning—its crucial element is that aspect of knowledge which reaches into the past and into man's innermost consciousness . . .* History *is not just concerned with history. It deals with wisdom and learning in its fullest sense.* Munch[13]

It will interest you to hear that I still have the drawing that I di[d] as an eighteen-year-old up in Hedemark, the one of the peasant woman and children that gave me the idea for Alma Mater. Yet I still do not know whether to have it reproduced.
Munch to Jens Thiis[14]

The canvas [Alma Mater] was taken down again and removed t[o] Ekely. One day when I was sent for, I found it lying folded out in the garden in the snow. K. E. Schreiner[15]

The Researchers reflects a different [from History] side of the Norwegian landscape and spirit: the bountifulness of summer, the urge for discovery, the spirit of achievement and enquiry.
Munch[16]

Long after the University murals were finished, Munch continued working on *Alma Mater*. He was never completely satisfied with it, and was always in two minds as to how its theme should be developed. Right up to his death he remaine[d] uncertain as to whether that picture or the one called *The Researchers* should occupy the main place of honour in the Hall. In order to decide in his own mind whether he ought to make any alterations to the picture, he hand-coloured a number of lithographs, most probably after the paintings had already been installed in 1916. As late as 1933 he wrote to Thiis: *Alma Mater should have been the main picture. I would still like to do further work on the murals—but I doubt whether that would be feasible.*[17]

312

Despite the misgivings that I have expressed, I feel obliged to recommend that we take a gamble on giving Munch the commission; if people still feel unhappy at this idea, all I can say is that Norway stands to gain a great deal, and given the state of development in her decorative art, it would be greatly to her advantage to provide Munch with a place to work in and allow him to express himself artistically in whatever way he wishes. The best solution, however, would be for the paintings to be completed in the assembly hall anyway, and allowed to remain there for a few years until a clear verdict is possible. J. Skovgaard[18]

The sentiment behind History *is both noble and appealing. And yet, the old fisherman and the little boy create an effect that bears little relation to the picture's basically poetic concept. I wonder whether any fisherman has ever appeared before in such 'stylized' clothing in the midst of such a naturalistically evocative scene? The explanatory note's promise of an 'essentially Norwegian' portrayal is, in my opinion, not fulfilled by that figure, however solemn and worthy it may appear, and the feeling of 'gravitas' is notably lessened by its extraordinary garb.*

The boy standing at the man's side should at least display some of that spark of intelligence that can light up a child's eyes when he is listening to tales of his ancestors' exploits, but that little chap . . . looks anything but intelligent. If I were to be frivolous, I would say that whereas University professors would like to have some of the gravity that radiates from the old man's face, our students, on the other hand, would not ask to be represented by that engaging little figure . . . Lorentz Dietrichson[19]

I would conclude by saying that Munch's proposals for the decoration of the assembly hall should be adopted in all their essentials, and that his picture History *should be acquired and put on display (or, if preferred, executed as a fresco).*

The assembly hall demands the best pictures in the land. Without any form of artistic adornment it is just a large functional room, but with the right paintings it could be one of the most beautiful places in our country. Jens Thiis[20]

Munch rarely abandoned a particular subject. During the 1920s he returned to the idea of a 'Mountain of Mankind', placing an enigmatically androgynous figure, with his own features, as the central element in the foreground (Plate 314). He gave the idea different names: *Towards the Light, Mountain of Mankind,* or *Pillar of Mankind.*[21]

310 **History**, 1914
Hand-coloured lithograph, 39.5 x 77 cm.
Oslo Kommunes Kunstsamlinger, OKK 378
Ref. G. Schiefler No. 426

311 **Alma Mater**, 1914
Hand-coloured lithograph, 37 x 84 cm.
Oslo Kommunes Kunstsamlinger, OKK 379
Ref. G. Schiefler No. 427

*312 **The Researchers** (Once considered for use as the main section of the right wall)
Oil on canvas, 480 x 1160 cm.
Oslo Kommunes Kunstsamlinger, OKK 962

313 Drawing for **Alma Mater**, 1936
Ink on paper, 12.4 x 21.5 cm.
Private Collection

313

assumed universal significance. The oak tree has become even more dominant; its branches reach out to give a sense of unity and cohesion to the whole composition. Børre in his patched clothes radiates an aura of quiet dignity which is enhanced by the expressive movement of his hands, while the colours in his clothing are taken up in the roots and branches of the tree. The inclusion of the little boy listening was a brilliant stroke, almost certainly inspired by a scene that Munch had witnessed in real life; in the earliest versions he portrayed Stina Krafft's two grandsons standing there, but later reduced the figures to one. He had also aroused considerable criticism by originally showing the boy with one of his hands in his pocket, but he bowed to the critics' pressure and the boy now stands listening intently.

In contrast with the old man, who represents the past, Munch portrayed on the other wall a mature woman and her children, symbols of the years to come. The stark, ice-blue landscape of the coast has been changed to a rich and fertile inland scene. The final version was called *Alma Mater*, but the original picture, which now hangs in Munch-museet in Oslo, was entitled *The Researchers* (Plate 312). The inquisitiveness of the young children symbolizes man's innate need for discovery, which can only be satisfied by personal experience, and they are shown examining everything around them: flowers, stones, even strange insects. The mother sits enthroned at the centre of the picture with one small child at her breast and others by her side. The final picture,[340] however, shows a much simplified version of the scene, in which the enquiring children have disappeared, replaced by a peaceful bay, whose gently swelling shoreline we recognize from earlier pictures. Its sweeping lines lead our eye into the distance, while the tree trunk to the right acts as a kind of visual brake.

Munch said in his explanatory notes that the three main wall areas were intended to be bright splashes of colour, while the other areas were to be lighter and less demanding, but he made a number of changes in his original ideas for the Hall's decoration. In 1911 he had plans for a 'Sower'[341] and a man picking his way through a wood, with 'both of them moving towards the light', and he declared that he was willing to paint them in fresco.

At one stage he also thought of making *The Fountain* part of the *Sun* wall, whereas it now occupies the first space in the *Alma Mater* section. The waterfall rushes headlong down from the Fountain of Wisdom (or perhaps of Life), and in front of it we see the silhouettes of two people drinking from its life-giving waters. In *Alma Mater* the curving shoreline wends its way through the lush landscape, while the blue line of the hills reappears in the adjoining painting of the two women reaching up to pick apples (Plate 318), symbols of the countryside's rich autumn harvest. This theme of women gathering apples is one that we can also see in other works, particularly in pictures from the Reinhardt frieze (Plate 255).

When Munch exhibited some of his 'University pictures' he included *Man and Woman in a Wood*, also known as *Metabolism* (Plate 144), the work that he maintained was as important to *The Frieze of Life* as a buckle is to a belt. Even though that picture itself, completed at the turn of the century, was dropped from the final series in the hall, the two paintings flanking the central work, *New Rays*, also depict a man and a woman—'heart to heart,

314

316

315

314 **Sphinx** (Self-portrait for *Mountain of Mankind*), 1926
Oil on canvas, 141 x 102 cm.
Oslo Kommunes Kunstsamlinger, OKK 441

315 **Mountain of Mankind**, 1926
Oil on canvas, 300 x 420 cm.
Oslo Kommunes Kunstsamlinger, OKK 978

316 **Mountain of Mankind**, 1909
Tempera on canvas, 52.2 x 32.5 cm.
Oslo Kommunes Kunstsamlinger, OKK 714

317 **Neutrality**, 1916
Lithograph, 54.3 x 49 cm.
Oslo Kommunes Kunstsamlinger, OKK 395
Ref. G. Schiefler No. 459
(Poster for Nordic Exhibition)

318 **Women Picking Apples** (Side section of the
left hand wall)
Oil on canvas, 455 x 225 cm.

DEN NORSKE KUNST-
≈UDSTILLING≈
CHARLOTTENBORG
NOV.—DEC.

*o drafts for the Aula competition—History, which
vas   nd Towards the Light, also known as Mountain
of M   Pillar of Mankind, which depicted a number of
iake   riving towards the light, and rising up towards
he s   llar.*

*Th   nded to be the picture on the end wall—the side
valls   rtray mankind in struggle and movement. One
vas t   rm, showing people fleeing in the face of a natural
atast   , and the other of a rainbow, with people at rest, a
ymbol of peace and hope in a bright future.*

*I am working on that series of works out at Skøyen—I will now
se them as a sort of extension of the* Frieze of Life.   Munch[22]

*Whereas the three main pictures—*The Sun, The Researchers,
nd History—*are intended to create an impression of imposing
randeur in the room, the other (eight) works will be lighter and
ess demanding and will act as a bridge between the Hall's
rchitecture and the main paintings, rather in the manner of a
rame.*   Munch[23]

318

319

illuminated by the rays of a new sun' (Plate 302) or 'musing thoughtfully over the chemist's flask'. In the first painting the colourful rays of the rising sun herald the dawning of a new day, and in the second, the children in the steam from the flasks of Chemistry bear witness to coming generations in the age of research. It is the only place where Munch has chosen unrealistic symbols to portray the idea of experimentation and life. The pictures of sun-worshippers on each side of *The Sun* (Plates 320–21) have their roots in the large painting of bathers which Munch did at Warnemünde, but here they are taken out of the central composition so that they stand on either side of the sun, as it rises in all its splendour, giving life to the world.

Nobody had ever managed to portray the sun with such brilliant simplicity: not even van Gogh, the sun painter par excellence, had succeeded in achieving such a feeling of majestic grandeur. If we compare Munch's preparatory versions of the sun with the final result, we can see how he became more and more daring in its portrayal. The little sun with its geometrically aligned rays that appears in the version he submitted for the competition, had already become much larger in the completed draft (Plate 319), and in the final painting the sun sheds its life-giving rays over the whole scene with extraordinary intensity. Its golden orb has become white-hot. And what is more, Munch has painted the whole scene with such certainty and such creative pleasure that not only the people who look at it, but the

319 **The Sun** (preliminary version), 1912/13
Oil on canvas, 163 x 207 cm.
Oslo Kommunes Kunstsamlinger, OKK 362

320 **Women Stretching out to the Sun** (Left hand side section of far wall)
Oil on canvas, 455 x 165 cm.

321 **Men stretching out to the Sun** (Right hand side section of far wall)
Oil on canvas, 455 x 165 cm.

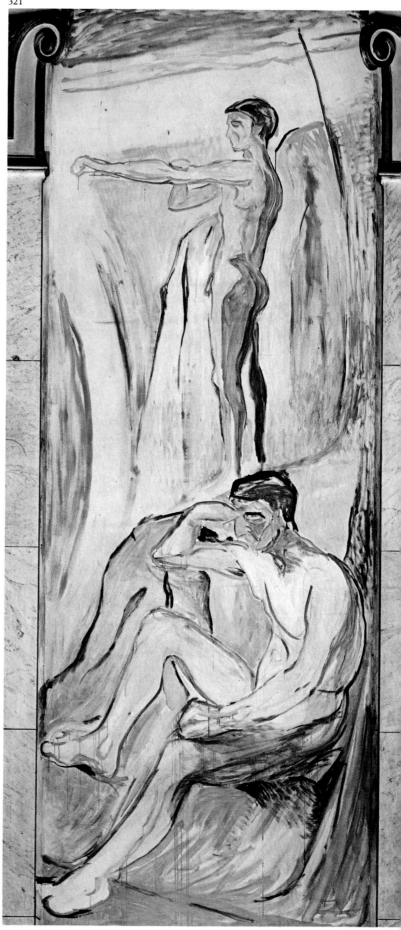

whole room as well, are filled with an overwhelming awe.

We must count ourselves fortunate that the far wall of the Hall is adorned by Edvard Munch's sun and not by Emanuel Vigeland's[342] dragon-slaying knight, and that we have the unpretentious portrayal of *History* on the left wall, rather than 'a Greek sage addressing Youth'. It is also a matter for considerable relief that on the right wall we have *Alma Mater*, instead of the different faculties 'represented by a selection of famous men'.[343] If Vigeland had had his way, all the greyish-white marble[344] would have been overpainted 'in warm colours', and Eilif Peterssen[345] would have included a painting of Pallas Athene holding a laurel wreath, with young men reaching out to grasp it. Another alternative, fortunately rejected, was Munthe's projected painting,[346] a typical example of the art of the time, showing large white-winged women and toga-clad men, and even the most Norwegian of the planned works, that of Werenskiold,[347] had a strong symbolic content: 'The guardian spirit of light holding out a torch' to three naked youths.

But we should also feel glad that Munch's plan to use *The Mountain of Mankind* (Plate 315) on the far wall was rejected. The jury were harsh in their condemnation of the preparatory work that he showed them, and it was deemed to be 'unusable'. It must have been a great blow for Munch, as he had already done work on the subject: for example, in his lithograph entitled *Funeral March*,[348] which dates from 1897. Several other contemporary artists treated similar subjects, amongst them the sculptor Gustav Vigeland, in his many studies which found their final form in the monolith in Oslo's Frogner Park.[349] Munch's inspiration was almost certainly Nietzsche's *Zarathustra*, which he had studied during his time at Weimar. When he found himself entrusted with the task of decorating Oslo University, both a major commission, and a great honour, he obviously felt that he should choose a theme of universal significance—and what better than a portrayal of mankind's striving towards ever greater heights. He had spent some time in Nietzsche's homeland and had been very influenced by German philosophy. Had he been given the chance to carry out his *Mountain of Mankind* as intended, there would have been a very real danger that the criticism of his being a literary painter, which was often unfairly levelled at him, would this time have been justified. Fortunately, however, he managed to shake off his philosophical tendencies, or, as the Swedish art historian Svenaeus put it, 'he burnt his boats', and Munch the painter overcame Munch the philosopher.[350] All his life he had painted what he saw; behind every picture there lies a true visual experience. And the same applies to his University murals.

While the controversy over the paintings was raging, Munch held a number of exhibitions, both in Norway and abroad. His major exhibition of the thirty preparatory works in Dioramalokalet in 1911 was followed by success in Cologne in 1912, while a further show, in Berlin in 1913, included twelve draft versions of his projected murals, completed at a quarter of their eventual size. The favourable reaction that his works elicited abroad did much to erode opposition to them in Norway—the university in Jena[351] had even let it be known that they were very keen on acquiring them in the event of their rejection by Oslo.

The murals differed radically from much of the decorative art of the time, but it is this modernity, combined with their highly individual character, both of which excited such extreme hostility amongst their detractors, that give them their impact today. As with all his work, it is Munch's own deep feeling of involvement that finally wins the day. He himself said: 'One must put one's whole soul into a large work to prevent it from being merely decorative.'

In his engraved self-portrait[352] from 1915 we no longer see a Munch tortured by the anxieties of youth. He was now fifty years old, and he could dance his macabre *Dance of Death* with the leering skeleton and still feel secure.

323

324

322 **The Sun** (Main section of end wall)
 Oil on canvas, 455 x 780 cm.

323 Munch in front of the rays of **The Sun**

324 **The Dance of Death**, 1915
 Lithograph, 48 x 29 cm.
 Oslo Kommunes Kunstsamlinger, OKK 381
 Ref. G. Schiefler No. 432

250

15 : A New Monumentality

Now it is the turn of the workers

One almost has to go back as far as Giotto and Piero della Francesca to find a similarly unaffected feeling of the monumental.   Arne Törnquist, 1977[1]

My two major works are the Frieze of Life *and the University murals. After I had completed the latter, I felt that I was ready to embark on other large-scale commissions, but my country had nothing similar to ask of me. However, when the plans for the Town Hall came up, I saw my chance. They have seen my rough drafts and I was deeply involved in the idea, but the possibility that I might be given the chance of doing the work has struck terror in the hearts of the local artistic clique. People came to me and suggested that I should have one room to decorate. It must have come as rather a set-back to them when I rejected their plans. I absolutely refused to have anything to do with it.*
Munch to K. E. Schreiner[2]

A painter's work ought not to just disappear like a scrap of paper into some private house where only a couple of people see it.
Munch[3]

I wonder if small-scale paintings will soon be pushed out. With their large frames, they are merely a bourgeois art form designed for sitting rooms. It is art dealer's art, that gained strength after the victory of the bourgeoisie in the revolution in France. Now it is the turn of the workers. Do you suppose that art will again become the property of everyone, and once more resume its rightful place on the spacious walls of public buildings?
Munch to Ragnar Hoppe, February, 1929[4]

325 **Galloping Horse,** 1912
Oil on canvas, 148 x 120 cm.
Oslo Kommunes Kunstsamlinger, OKK 541

In 1916, the year of the unveiling of the University murals, Munch had bought his estate at Ekely,[353] just outside the city limits of Oslo. The main house was a large old wooden villa, standing in eight or ten acres of grounds, with a stable for Rousseau, his horse, kennels for his dogs Bamse and Fips, a kitchen garden, an orchard, a gardener's cottage, and, most important of all, enough space for several new open air studios. In 1929 Munch designed and built a winter studio, where his *Frieze of Life*, like a 'crippled ship with half its rigging missing',[354] could find shelter. Although he retained his other properties, Ekely was to be Munch's home for the next twenty-eight years, but, even so, the house contained only two rooms with any sort of proper furniture, namely, a bed, a table, and a few chairs. Portraits of his family were hung on the walls, and one of the rooms also contained the 'conference sofa', on which he used to curl up and sleep like a child in an embryo position[355] when he could not get to sleep in his bed. At one stage he even acquired a grand piano, but there are no reports of anyone ever having heard him play it. From his large veranda he could see out to the blue waters of the fjord and beyond to the city that he disliked so much and never wanted to visit again, and yet somehow, when viewed from such a distance, it seemed less daunting. Although his life at Ekely may seem idyllic to us, perhaps his friend Gierløff, who often visited him there, was right in saying that Munch's years in Kragerø were the happiest ones of his life.

He waited hopefully for other large commissions from his fellow countrymen, 'but my country had nothing similar to ask of me'.[356] He still carried on working with his *Frieze of Life*, and in 1918, having suddenly felt the urge to see these 'storm tossed' pictures assembled together in one place once more, he exhibited them all in Blomqvists Lokale. He also published a small explanatory booklet,[357] from which a number of the quotations in this book are taken.

At Ekely Munch returned to many of his old themes. Although he always remained true to his inner vision, his art now reveals another whole new attitude to both Life and Nature. People who particularly admire his earlier work often maintain that he no longer achieved the same depth of psychological insight, but as a painter Munch had developed in both intensity and scale, while his colours have a more youthful quality than ever before.

While he was doing the final preparatory work for his University murals, Munch also completed several large canvases of themes from working life, which were taken up within a few years by a new generation of Norwegian artists. His decoration of the assembly hall had turned him into a monumental painter, and it was clearly with future decorative commissions in mind that he began experimenting with this new theme, first in Kragerø and later at Ekely. Working men began to appear more and more frequently in his paintings, but they were never depicted with any overt attempt at social comment.[358] Rather, they were portrayed simply as a result of Munch's admiration for the feeling of strength and power that they projected, and the respect that he had for ordinary working people. As early as 1910 he had painted his monumental *Workers in the Snow*, which now hangs in Tokyo Museum. The dark, imposing figure of the work crew's leader strides out towards us, his hand clenched over the handle of the spade that he is carrying on his shoulder, while the black shapes of his three companions stand out powerfully against the white snow. Behind this main group we can see another band of men, who give a great sense of depth to the background, which otherwise is brilliantly suggested by means of a few well-chosen brush strokes. During the winters at Kragerø he would almost certainly have

326

seen men like these shovelling away the snow in the narrow lanes, but the picture is by no means a realistic representation. He has developed the basic visual concept and simplified the composition so that the men become not just casually encountered road clearers, but representatives of a specific group of workers. He reworked the scene in another painting (Plate 328), in which the vertical structure of the original composition has given way to a much broader format that increases the vastness of the scene, while the rounded hilltop in the background imbues it with a sense of unity. Munch has succeeded in achieving a highly sculptural quality, and it is no co-incidence that we meet two of the figures again in one of Munch's few sculptures (Plate 331). Despite the small size of this work, the group still manages to convey the same feeling of vastness.

A similarly overwhelming sense of power is apparent in *Workmen Digging* (Plate 327), in which the men can be seen bending over their shovels in the snow round a cauldron of bubbling tar.

While Munch was working on these subjects, he undoubtedly had in mind the forthcoming decoration of Oslo Town Hall. Gerd Woll, in her work on Munch's *Working Man's Frieze*,[359] has pointed to the fact that in 1927 the *Dagbladet* journalist 'Hast' (Haldis Stenhamar) had had several interviews with Munch concerning the possibility of his being given a whole room to decorate. And in the autumn of 1928 Hieronymus Heyerdahl[360] proposed that the Town Hall committee should seek Munch's co-operation. That Munch himself was eager to participate is made clear by the fact that his 1929 exhibition at Blomqvists Lokale[361] included a number of sketches and pre-paratory drawings for the Town Hall interiors. At that time he had visualized the building itself in the background as a large, imposing block.[362]

As we now know, Munch never received any official invitation to carry out the work, and we have no idea of which room or rooms he had thought of working on. A subsequent design (Plate 326) shows that he had contem-plated a composite picture, containing elements from *Workers in the Snow* in the centre, *Snow Shovellers* to the right, and *Workmen Digging* to the left, the whole scene contained within a large arc. Munch often worked in that way, pasting and tacking several pictures and overpainted patches together, so that he was ultimately able to choose between several alternative com-positions.

The foundation stone of the Town Hall was finally laid in 1931, when Munch was nearly seventy. An eye complaint had impaired the sight of his

I am very interested in the idea of doing a frieze on working life in Oslo, says Munch. But how is one to design decorations for a castle in the air?—I cannot express my ideas on a commission that I have not been given . . . It would interest me to paint work-men about their daily tasks, masons working on a new building, ditch-diggers in the street, etc. . . . Perhaps it would be a good idea to paint them all in the snow, as one could achieve a feeling of continuity in that way.
    From an interview with Munch in *Dagbladet*, 1928[5]

Now they are flocking round me. I am to be given somewhere to decorate. Now, when I am old and sick. I have not got enough energy. When I did have enough, they had no use for me.
    Munch to Felix Hatz[6]

326 Sketch of decorations for Oslo Town Hall, 1929
     Crayon drawing, 27.3 x 58.5 cm.
     Oslo Kommunes Kunstsamlinger, OKK 2351

327 **Workmen Digging**, 1920
     Oil on canvas, 105 x 151 cm.
     Private Collection

328 **Workers in the Snow**, 1913/14
     Oil on canvas, 163 x 200 cm.
     Oslo Kommunes Kunstsamlinger, OKK 371

329

right eye, and that misfortune may well have been one of the reasons why his plans for the building were never realized. The architects, nevertheless, were very keen that he should obtain the commission.

There is one of Munch's pictures of workers that stands out particularly as more than just a straightforward representation of people about their daily work. He must somehow have sensed the inexorable progress of a class on the march, when in 1914–15 he painted *Workers Returning Home*[363] (Plate 329), a subject whose possibilities, judging by the many preliminary sketches and drawings, he had been exploring for a long time. But it was in the painting which now hangs in Munch-Museet in Oslo that Munch first succeeded in revealing the underlying significance of the dark mass of workmen who stream relentlessly out towards us. The figures nearest us have been dramatically foreshortened: they are seen from above, so that the lower part of their bodies seems much smaller, while their faces, either ruddy or pallid, take on an almost frightening prominence. He succeeds in endowing the men with a great feeling of power, while at the same time drawing our eye far into the distance by means of an irresistible perspective. We shall never know if this work was inspired by an instinctive reaction to the sight of workers leaving a factory, or whether Munch the Expressionist was making a statement of solidarity with the struggles of the working class. It is possible that the sound of the 'march of the millions' was ringing in his ears. His close friend Jappe Nilssen[364] wrote of the picture in 1918: 'It would take very little imagination to see this picture as an illustration of the latest happenings in Russia.'

I believe in what the Russians are trying to do, they have got the chance now. During the French Revolution it was the bourgeoisie who were fighting for their rights, now it is the workers, which is just as it should be.   Munch to his model Birgit Prestøe[7]

329 **Workers returning Home,** 1913/15
Oil on canvas, 201 x 227 cm.
Oslo Kommunes Kunstsamlinger 365

330 **Workers Returning Home,** after 1916
Watercolour, crayon and charcoal, 57 x 77.9 cm.
Oslo Kommunes Kunstsamlinger 1854

*331 **Two Workers,** 1920
Bronze sculpture, 70 x 57 x 45 cm.
Oslo Kommunes Kunstsamlinger 331

256

330

331

We do not know for certain what Munch's politics were. His remark to Ragnar Hoppe in 1929—'Now it is the turn of the workers'—could mean that he was at least interested in the working class movement. Munch was always very aware of contemporary events, and we have already seen in his paintings that, as the son of a doctor in some of the most deprived areas of Oslo, he had developed a strong social conscience. We also know that he felt alienated from the narrow-minded attitudes of the middle class and that he bitterly resented the criticisms which were levelled at him, particularly by the right wing press. His loyal aunt Karen[365] gave up *Aftenposten* when it started attacking her nephew, and she mentions that his brother took *Verdens Gang* and *Dagbladet*—'As a family we only have radical newspapers now'.[366] We have already seen how the ideas of the Oslo bohemians affected his philosophy of life, and by 1905[367] he had developed a considerable interest in politics, and made it quite clear that he was a republican.[368] Both in Paris and Berlin the majority of the people he consorted with were Radicals; Walther Rathenau[369] was a close friend, and his murder made a deep impression on Munch. Many of his pictures of workers were completed during the first world war, and in August 1916 he expressed dismay at the fact that while all his friends were German,[370] France was the country he was really most fond of. The horrors of war are reflected in his art, and he attacked Norway and Denmark for staying neutral and growing rich at the cost of countless sailors' lives (Plate 317). He even considered a monument for the League of Nations, depicting Europe rising from the ashes. Despite his almost hermit-like existence at Ekely, Munch took a keen interest in contemporary events and was an avid, if somewhat erratic reader of newspapers. He

332

assisted many of his German colleagues[371] who found themselves in need during the post-war years, and in the next chapter we shall examine his attitude towards the German occupying forces and German emigrés during the second world war. Judging by the remarks and writings of several of his friends, it would seem that if one were forced to include Munch in a particular political category, it would have to be that of Socialism.

As we have already established, for one reason or another, plans for Munch to decorate the Town Hall never came to anything. But in 1922 he received an informal invitation[372] to paint some murals for the canteen of the Freia chocolate factory, and there are several small sketches still in existence which show that he had plans to decorate not just one, but two canteens. The one frieze which was completed still hangs in its original place, while the other one, which would have portrayed scenes from workers' everyday life, was never realized. The completed one is based partially on themes taken from the *Frieze of Life*, but painted in a much lighter, brighter range of colours. He himself said that 'it is the *Frieze of Life* transferred to another location.[373] It is the life of a fisherman in a coastal town untroubled by tourists.' The mood is that of midsummer, with small children wandering in the woods, and once more we see the little girls from Åsgårdstrand and the fruit being gathered from the trees. A feeling of idyllic peace permeates the whole scene; even the tragic *Dance of Life* has become a happy Midsummer Night's party on the beach. The old technique of letting the gentle swell of the Åsgårdstrand shoreline wend its way through the picture is still used,

The true sign of a productive genius is that he is able to undergo a continual process of renewal, and that new and fresh sources of inspiration are constantly welling up from deep within him. He is able to draw on these with complete naturalness and almost somnambulant certainty, in itself a sign of true genius.
Ragnar Hoppe[8]

My breakthrough came very late in life, really only starting when I was fifty years old. But at that time [1922] I felt as though I had the strength for new deeds and new ideas.
Munch to J. P. Hodin, 1939[9]

258

333

332 **The Man in the Cabbage Field**, 1916
Oil on canvas, 136 x 181 cm.
Nasjonalgalleriet, Oslo

333 **Horses Ploughing**, 1919
Oil on canvas, 111 x 146 cm.
Nasjonalgalleriet, Oslo

but now it has lost all its sinister undertones.

In Munch-Museet there is a similar interpretation of *The Dance of Life*, painted in 1921 (Plate 351), at the request of the twenty-two-year-old stockbroker Rolf E. Stenersen,[374] who became a sort of 'Jack of all trades' to the ageing artist, helping him in all kinds of practical ways. The painting includes the old theme of the three stages of woman, combined with *The Dance of Life*, but here again the old melancholy is lacking.

By far the greatest feeling of monumental simplicity was achieved by Munch in his impressive painting of *The Man in the Cabbage Field* (Plate 332). Laden down with produce, the farmer strides through the rich cabbage field, which is depicted in every imaginable shade of green, and the triangular composition is made doubly impressive by its sheer simplicity. The broad, rolling countryside round Ekely reappears in several other pictures that Munch made of horses ploughing deep furrows in the rich Spring earth. He was extremely fond of horses, and one of his last thoughts was of how much he missed his beloved Rousseau, the horse he had used as a model for many years. As he himself remarked, one horse can reveal an infinite range of colouring, depending on how the light strikes it, something that is brilliantly illustrated in his picture of the two yellow and blue horses ploughing.

It is as if the rolling landscape of Eastern Norway had enabled Munch himself to experience a new feeling of space. We have seen how he had earlier begun to develop a greater sense of spatial awareness, but in his two very similar paintings of a *Starry Night*[375] (Plate 334) it is as if, standing on the

259

veranda, he has managed to take in the whole landscape at a single glance. His vantage point is defined by the perspective of the steps and the mysterious shadows in the foreground, from which point our eye is led into the distance by one gently swelling plane after another: over the blue-white snow, flecked with pink, beyond the domed trees and the brightly lit house, until finally we come to the glittering strip of the city, broken only by the vertical line of a group of trees that lead us from the crest of a hill up into the starry realms of the sky. The lonely, depopulated landscape creates a dramatically eerie atmosphere and the biting cold can be felt. Munch himself is reputed to have said that Ibsen's *John Gabriel Borkman* was the best winter landscape in Norwegian art, and it is tempting to think that it was in surroundings such as these that the lonely Borkman died.[376] We remember his dying words as he lay in the snow and looked out over his kingdom: 'Can you see the chain of hills there—far in the distance? One behind the other. They rise up. They tower. That is my deep, endless, inexhaustible kingdom.' Once again there is a connection between the work of Ibsen and Munch.[377] Quite possibly the lonely inhabitant of Ekely had felt a certain kinship with Borkman, as he wandered broodingly through the large, empty rooms.

Munch quite consciously isolated himself at Ekely. He had to keep to his chosen life-style in order to serve his art, and he gradually began to withdraw even further into this private realm, shielded from the world outside by his dogs and a tall board fence. Apart from long telephone conversations, his only links with the outside world were taxis, which he used to drive up into the mountains for a lonely walk to escape from the Oslo basin, or perhaps to go to some art exhibition before the official opening. Occasionally he would despatch his regular taxi driver to deliver letters or invitations, either to friends or his beloved sister, and sometimes, when he was feeling old and tired, he would take a taxi down to the main railway station in Oslo and buy a great bundle of foreign newspapers, which gave him the illusion that he was abroad once more.[378] At times when he was plagued by insomnia, he simply booked a sleeper to Stockholm, because he knew that he always slept well on trains. For most of the time he had a housekeeper, who had access to two of the rooms, but there were periods when he was quite alone, and during which he managed to survive with the minimum of domestic work, buying a cod, for example, cooking the tail part, and throwing away the rest. Apart from the one in which he ate and slept, all the rooms were used for working and were filled with easels and paintings, so he could wander through the house and work on those pictures he considered to be incomplete and in need of improvement. Towards the end of his life he developed the habit of painting the same subject on several canvases simultaneously. He would use two of them to experiment on, while the third he would complete, drawing his inspiration from the first ones. The floors at Ekely were strewn with his graphic works, which Munch neglected dreadfully, considering the careful way in which he looked after his other 'children', his paintings.

Just as in his other properties, a number of open air studios sprang up at Ekely. In these he spent his time working on large canvases or rearranging old pictures in different sequences to get ideas for new, monumental compositions. Despite his bronchial troubles, Munch often painted in deep snow, and his pictures were left exposed to the element; sometimes he even hung new oil paintings out to dry on the branches of apple trees. With a view to expanding his *Frieze of Life*, and also with an eye on the possibility of the Town Hall commission, he built his spacious winter studio.[379] This is now used as a sort of combined community centre and exhibition hall for members of the artists' colony founded by the council on Munch's estate at Ekely. The old wooden villa has unfortunately been torn down.

Munch's lonely life at Ekely, naturally enough, did little to lessen his introvertive tendencies. In fact, with the passing of the years, his capacity for ruthless self-analysis became more and more pronounced, until finally it became a major ingredient of his art. In *Self-portrait during Spanish 'flu'* (Plate 19), completed in 1919, he painted himself with ice-cold objectivity shortly after leaving his bed of sickness, whose crumpled duvet bears witness to his feverish tossings and turnings. He had painted many 'fever pictures' already, but in those the shapes of his imagination appear on the wall—now it is the 'duvet' that expresses his fevered fantasies. He sits slumped in the chair, his

As a painter Munch must be ranked amongst the greatest of the day: his art is a convincing expression of our times' sensitivity and feeling for form, and his significance for modern German art has been no less than that of Cézanne and van Gogh. In fact, his influence will be, if anything, even more permanent and lasting than theirs. Ludwig Justi[10]

A work of art is like a crystal—and just as a crystal has its own inner life and its own will, a work of art must possess the same qualities. It is not enough that it has the correct outward appearance and design. If you throw a stone at a group of boys, they will scatter and then re-group. The action of their dispersal is a physical happening. The function of art is to express that movement by means of colour, line and space. It need not necessarily be 'literary', that term of abuse which many people use to describe paintings that do not show apples on a tablecloth or a broken violin. Munch[11]

334 **Starry Night**, 1923/24
Oil on canvas, 121 x 100 cm.
Oslo Kommunes Kunstsamlinger, OKK 9

335

336

These storm tossed pictures, which after 30 years of the buccaneering life have finally found a harbour out at Skøyen, like a crippled ship with half its rigging missing, are not suitable for showing as a complete frieze.   Munch, 1918[12]

One must also reflect on the origins of these pictures over the past thirty years—one in an attic in Nice—another in a dark room in Paris—another in Berlin—or in Norway; always travelling under the most difficult conditions, being subjected to continual persecution, and never receiving the slightest encouragement. The room that they were supposed to adorn was little more than a castle in the air.   Munch, 1918[13]

I am exhibiting the frieze once more, mainly because I feel that it is too good to be forgotten, but also because it has had such a deep artistic significance for me over all these years. This gives me a personal desire to see it brought together again.   Munch, 1918[14]

In another small booklet, probably from 1929, he wrote: *I have only collected the remnants together now so that I would have something that roughly resembled what I had twenty years ago.*
Munch[15]

My health is getting better and better, and I find myself increasingly able to enjoy the company of my fellow men. But strangely enough that does not help my art. In fact, my earlier invalid's mentality had a very favourable effect on my work.   Munch[16]

We don't live in Italy at the time of the Renaissance. When someone has had the chance to work on something as large as the University Hall, then here in Norway he will never get any more major commissions.   Munch to 'Hast' in *Dagbladet*, 1927[17]

335 **On the Veranda**, 1925/26
    Oil on canvas, 89 x 76 cm.
    Oslo Kommunes Kunstsamlinger, OKK 454

336 **Dr. Lucien Dedichen and Jappe Nilssen**, 1925/26
    Oil on canvas, 160 x 136 cm.
    Oslo Kommunes Kunstsamlinger, OKK 370

337 **Self-portrait**, 1930
    Lithograph, 21 x 19 cm.
    Oslo Kommunes Kunstsamlinger, OKK 456

frail, skinny body covered by a brown dressing gown and a green rug, while his hands rest feebly on his lap. And yet his alert and defiant gaze tells us that 'the artist, Munch' is not one to let a bout of 'flu' stand in his way. He will carry on his work. And, indeed, in a portrait that he painted of himself at the age of sixty-three[380] (Plate 23), the man whom we see screwing up his eyes against the harsh sunlight, which brings the whole scene alive with shimmering flecks of green and blue, is both active and alert.

During this period Munch painted a number of works which reveal the sensual pleasure that he found in the mysteries of the female form. In the symbolic pictures of *Morning, Midday, Afternoon* and *Night*, he tells the story of his model's life. Now it is the qualities of his painting that are his main concern, as they also are in *Nude by the Wicker Chair* (Plate 338). In this painting, the light penetrates every corner of the scene, flickering in and out of the brightly-coloured rug on the chair, and modelling the rounded contours of the woman's body in pale, almost opalescent shades, which seem to combine feelings both of warmth and coolness. The restrained use of colour in her figure achieves an effect almost reminiscent of Renoir. The model's whole mood is characterized by her shyly downcast head, which, despite the beauty of her body, makes her seem withdrawn and isolated in a room whose yellow walls are contrasted with the blue of the neighbouring room that we see framed in the square opening.

The eye of a painter can sometimes be caught by a single, fleeting vision, which he captures and recreates exactly. This is true of *Model on the Sofa* (Plate 341). The painting's composition is based on the cross formed by the two diagonals of the woman's body and the bed, while the vertical strokes of the background enhance the natural feminine softness of his model. It is not hard to understand why Birgit Prestøe was such a favourite subject of his.

By this time Munch's fame had spread far and wide, and people clamoured for him to paint their portraits, although few of them succeeded. He now often painted his subjects in the open air, as he did the portrait of the golden-haired Else Mustad, painted in the shimmering light of the sun. Possibly his best portraits were those that he did of people he liked, when he felt that he was painting for himself rather than anyone else. One day, when two old friends from his bohemian days came to visit him at Ekely—Lucien Dedichen, who was also his doctor, and the critic Jappe Nilssen—Munch painted them[381] with extraordinary insight (Plate 336). He clearly took great delight in portraying two such contrasted characters: the tall, quiet and mild-mannered doctor, and the small, dark and bitter patient. It is as if they are frozen in mid-conversation, as though a moment of deep reflection has stilled both them and the room in which they find themselves. Munch has intuitively captured the doctor-patient relationship with uncanny accuracy.

A NEW GRAPHIC ERA

During 1915 and 1916, the last years of his career as an etcher, Munch turned several of his paintings into etchings, amongst them *Galloping Horse*. Even Åsgårdstrand and the dramatic conflicts of the distant past were still so fresh in his mind that he one day made an etching destined to tell the story of the fight he had had with his painter friend Ludvig Karsten.

Whilst engraving techniques can vary according to the needs of the subject, Munch's graphic work underwent no radical stylistic change, except where his lithographs and, most especially, his woodcuts, were concerned. It is possible that Munch abandoned etching because that technique did not suit his new aims as a graphic artist. We have already noticed how his oil paintings became more sketchy and more painterly around 1906–7, and it was during this period that space and form began to play more important roles in his lithographs and woodcuts. It was as if Munch's graphic work had freed him from the strictures of conventional art. In a totally new way, lithography and woodcuts had become art forms in their own right.

The majority of his lithographs after his time in the clinic in Copenhagen were produced between 1912 and 1920, and in the 1930s he also worked on old wood and stone blocks, experimenting with new colour combinations or simply hand-colouring earlier prints. Naturally enough, he also took up subjects from his paintings; scenes from everyday life in Kragerø, such as

337

338

Snow Shovellers, for example. It was inevitable, too, that his lithography should reflect all the hard work that he had done on the University murals; as late as the 1930s he was still making variations of both *History* and *Alma Mater*, as well as experimenting with their colouring. He had already used *Women Picking Apples* as a poster (Plate 317), and for one of his own exhibitions he even used the marvellous *Towards the Light*, in which we can trace the progress of the man's figure from the beach at Warnemünde, via the University Hall to the poster.

His etching of *The Dance of Death*, showed how he had managed to overcome his own 'angst'. We can still see anguish in his woodcuts of the subject, but now it is the anguish of mankind, and there is good reason to believe that it was the war which made him lift the anguish from a personal to a collective level. At the age of fifty his own problems lay behind him.

Ekely increasingly became a place for reminiscing, and in the mid-1920s he began to resurrect the memories of his bohemian days both in paintings and in lithographs. In 1930, however, Munch's great creative period as a lithographer came to an end, albeit on a high note, with the portraits of his friend and physician, Professor Schreiner. The anatomist stands like Hamlet, a skull in his hands (Plate 355), while in another print Munch shows himself lying on the dissecting table, an image that reminds us irresistibly of *The Death of Marat*.

It is likely that the eye trouble, which struck him down in 1930, put an end to his lithographic work. From now on, he was to be restricted to adapting and colouring earlier prints.

It was, above all, in his woodcuts that Munch made such dramatic advances, achieving results that were to provide inspiration for countless other

341

338 **Nude by the Wicker Chair,** 1929
    Oil on canvas, 123 x 100 cm.
    Oslo Kommunes Kunstsamlinger, OKK 499

339 **The Gothic Maiden** (Birgit Prestøe), 1930
    Woodcut, 60 x 32.2 cm.
    Oslo Kommunes Kunstsamlinger, OKK 703

340 **Girl Weeping,** 1912/15
    Charcoal drawing, 40 x 25.5 cm.
    Private Collection

341 **Model on the Sofa,** 1924/28
    Oil on canvas, 137 x 116 cm.
    Oslo Kommunes Kunstsamlinger, OKK 429

graphic artists. It is perhaps more than mere coincidence that in 1918, the last year of the war, he reprinted his old woodcut *Stormy Night* (Plate 278), in which the expressive force of the medium, and the contrasting effects of black and white, are both exploited to the full in the shining windows of the empty house, the whiteness of the fence, and the white highlights in the landscape and the figures of the women. The terror of anxiety lives in every line, just as it continued to live in Munch's mind. It also lives on in the picture entitled *Angst*, in which nameless, mindless people advance towards us, or jostle us in the narrow 'sunken road'. The collective anxiety of a whole generation is brilliantly expressed in *Panic Fear* (Plate 350), which dates from 1920. The nervous spontaneity of its execution makes the houses lean inwards as though in an earthquake, while the people in the foreground seem just like approaching masks, pushed on by the strength of the struggling masses behind.

Munch's own personal experiences, and the rooms in which he had seen people dying, reappear in new objective portrayals, as, for example, in the strange woodcut of the priest arriving with *The Sacrament* (Plate 348). Both the figures and their surroundings are brilliantly captured, and the people's anxieties and uncertainties are reflected in the nervous and restless black and white of the walls. But the past is not completely forgotten—just as in *Death in the Sickroom* we can see the figure of the brother leaving the room.

It was but a short step to another of his woodcuts of the same period, *The Final Hour* (Plate 349), in which Munch has succeeded, to an unparalleled degree, in isolating the feeling of solitude, rejection and doom. The dark, self-contained groups of people serve to underline the isolation of the lonely woman, while the two running figures behind her head and the shifting white lines of the flagstones against the strong Gothic arches are the only signs of movement that break the deathly stillness. These arches remind us

265

of the illustrations for Ibsen's *The Pretenders*, and the model that he used for Inga reappears in a number of brilliant portraits, such as *Gothic Maiden* (Plate 339).

We have often noted how loyal Munch remained, both to himself and to his art. When, in about 1920, he began to experiment with the possibilities of reproducing *Girls on the Jetty* as a combined woodcut and lithograph, we can see how he remained faithful to one of the subjects that had occupied him most since the end of the 1890s. In the final work (Plate 342) he has perhaps achieved an even more monumental quality than in his twelve oil paintings based on the same theme (e.g. Plates 218, 219, 347). This effect is achieved mainly by Munch's use of the grain of the wood, by the greatly simplified treatment of the dome-shaped trees and by the strong sense of perspective that he imparts to the jetty and the road that leads from it. The simplicity of the woodcut gives the white wall, which we recognize from so many paintings, a new strength of contrast against the dark waters. The fact that the scene is a mirror image of his painted versions shows that he had used the earlier works as a model, but the nature of the material with which he was working has produced a totally new effect.

342 **Girls on the Jetty**, 1920
Woodcut and lithograph, 49.6 x 42.9 cm.
Oslo Kommunes Kunstsamlinger, OKK 647
Ref. G. Schiefler No. 488

342 >

343 **The Red House,** 1926
Oil on canvas, 110 x 130 cm.
Private Collection

16 : The Final Years

I have now drafted a plan, in connection with the projected expansion of Nasjonalgalleriet, by which Munch-museet would be a separate building on the southern side of Tullinløkken . . . Please, dear Edvard Munch, do not raise too many objections; please give your consent to the outline plan . . . We must start work now . . . Neither of us are going to be buried or cremated before we have seen Munch-Museet completed . . . Only then will I be able to lay myself peacefully down to die, but not before.   Jens Thiis to Munch, 19/5/1937[1]

When you get my letter in a couple of days, you will understand that your plans for a museum for me are not suitable for my large and varied works. And besides, I already lost interest in such a museum a few years back. I abandoned the idea after objections had been launched from a number of quarters.
Munch to Jens Thiis, 27/5/1937[2]

344 **Two Women on the Shore,** 1935
Oil on canvas, 80 x 83 cm.
Oslo Kommunes Kunstsamlinger, OKK 866

345 **Self-portrait with damaged eye,** 1932
Charcoal and oil on canvas, 90 x 72 cm.
Oslo Kommunes Kunstsamlinger, OKK 207

345

Munch's activities were drastically curbed by the misfortune that struck him in 1930, when a blood vessel burst in his right eye. Despite the fact that he made light of it, saying that he could still see perfectly well[382] with his left eye, he was virtually incapable of painting for nearly a whole year. Nonetheless, he managed to complete a number of very fine lithographs, as well as a splendid woodcut of Birgit Prestøe, entitled *The Gothic Maiden* (Plate 339). But, accustomed as he was to working twelve hours a day (and also through the night, if he felt like it), he had to adapt to a slower tempo and take better care of himself, making sure that he did not read or write too much. Bronchitis, insomnia and nervous tension were also things that he had to try and combat, but worst of all was the fear that he might never be able to work again.

As he neared his seventieth birthday he was making plans to write his autobiography, and although that ambition was never realized, there still exist a number of notes that he made during this time. He still dreamed of decorating the interior of the Town Hall, but he felt that he was meeting opposition from all quarters, and so gave that idea up in 1930. With a certain amount of envy he saw how his home town gave every opportunity to Gustav Vigeland, who came from Mandal,[383] while he himself was forced to engage in endless battles with the tax authorities in an effort to convince them that he had to have his 'children' around him, and persuade them that they should not be made liable for tax. It should, however, be said that the authorities were not as heartless as he tried to make out, and that there were many people who wanted to help him. The architects of the Town Hall[384] wanted nothing better than for Munch to pay them the honour of adorning their building. The city architect Aars wanted to reserve a whole floor in the Town Hall for his art, and Thiis begged him[385] not to frustrate his plans for erecting a Munch museum at Tullinløkken. But Munch in his old age was not the easiest person to deal with.

Nevertheless, his seventieth birthday was a great experience for him. Greetings streamed in from the whole of Scandinavia and from Germany; the newspapers were all full of articles about him, and the two biographies, by Pola Gauguin and Jens Thiis, were both published. The Knight of the Order of St. Olav, who, twenty-four years earlier had felt rather ashamed at having accepted 'the pretty brooch', made no effort to hide his pleasure at being given the Grand Cross.[386] But, shy as he was, he joked about the fact that such a 'suit of armour',[387] such a 'coat of mail' could keep people at a distance. He managed to have cancelled plans for a torchlight procession in his honour, and he spent the whole of his birthday driving round in a taxi so that nobody should be able to get hold of him. The result of this manoeuvre was that he caught a very bad cold.

After the eye trouble had interrupted his work for a whole year, he took up his brushes once more and, in the mid-1930s, he painted a series of pictures whose subjects were familiar, but whose colours were more vivid than ever before. It is hard to say whether these strong colours were the result of his weakened eyesight, or whether they came from his desire to conform with the 'Fauve' movement. Is it possible that Munch was influenced by Matisse,[388] for example? He certainly knew the French artist's work, as they had both taken part in the great international exhibition at Dresden in 1926, and in 1924 Matisse had held a large exhibition in Oslo, which had had a great influence on Norwegian artists. It is inconceivable that Munch could have failed to notice Matisse's work.

During this period he again took up two of the best loved themes of his earlier years. In *Two Women on the Shore* (Plate 344) he was most probably trying to convince a geology professor, who had objected to *History*, that there were such things as blue stones. The group containing the heavy, dark shape of the mother makes the other colours seem even more garish by comparison, and give the individual blocks of colour even greater strength. The blackness of the mother's clothing makes the daughter's white dress even whiter. 'The moon's golden pillar' is there, moving in the water, but the eerie mood of the still summer's night has gone. Nor do we find the sinuous curve of the shoreline that occurs in earlier versions, both in oil and woodcut (Plate 165ff); now it has been changed into two almost horizontal lines, while the strict verticality of the girl's figure, echoed in the upright reflection of the moon, gives the whole scene a much more rigid quality.

Two other old subjects, *The Lonely Ones* and *Ladies on the Jetty*, were also painted in his electrifying new colours (Plates 346, 347). The latter achieves a Cubist effect in the white triangular group of women, which is painted in large, interconnected planes that give the picture a decorative quality. That Cubist tendency, combined with an extremely expressive use of colour, can be found in other pictures of the period. It was not just a question of the young Expressionist artists having studied Munch. During his extensive

Me? A torchlight procession? For heaven's sake, Thiis, am I supposed to stand up on a balcony and acknowledge it, then? Is that what you have in mind? In that case, I would have to make a drawing of it. Munch to Jens Thiis[3]

Four years ago I sustained damage to my right eye, the one that I have always used, since my left one was weak. My left eye can only be used as an aid. It will never be good.
Munch to Jens Thiis, 1934[4]

I am now staying at Åsgårdstrand, far away from that loathsome dump Ekely. Munch to Johs. Roede[5]

My pictures are the only children I have, and in order to be able to work I must have them round me. Often when I am working on a picture I get stuck, but by looking at my other pictures I am able to start work again. If I were separated from them I would only produce sketches. Munch[6]

346 **The Lonely Ones,** 1935?
Oil on canvas, 100 x 130 cm.
Oslo Kommunes Kunstsamlinger, OKK 29

347 **Ladies on the Jetty,** 1935?
Oil on canvas, 110 x 130 cm.
Oslo Kommunes Kunstsamlinger, OKK 30

346

travels, he, too, had seen examples of German Expressionism and French Cubism, and they had both left their mark on his art. We know, for example, that the exhibition of contemporary German art,[389] held at the Kunstnernes Hus in Oslo in 1932, had made a deep impression on him. This is, in itself, hardly surprising, as during their years of privation and financial hardship he had bought prints by many of those exhibiting, and in the difficult years to come he would offer assistance to those same artists, when they struggled under the heavy yoke of Nazism.

We have already seen how, at regular ten year intervals, he had painted new versions of *The Sick Child*,[390] and in 1926 he painted it for the fifth time, completing his sixth and final version in 1927, in order to include it in his 'continually plundered *Frieze of Life*'. The composition is the same as before, but the colours are new, and far stronger. Although some of the emotional element is missing, his later pictures still have a great deal of power. He was not painting merely to replace works that he had sold, nor to provide carbon copies of earlier versions, but rather to make sure that he did not stray from his original intentions. Perhaps he also wanted to provide some justification for not having followed contemporary fashion and painted 'apples on a tablecloth, or a broken violin'.[391]

347

348

349

I think that the picture has a simple and primitive power, when compared to all that colourless and slick Classicism that has emerged after Picasso. The picture is also given prominence in the Press. People complain loudly that I have painted it on several occasions, but a subject that I have struggled with for a whole year cannot be dismissed in one picture. Why should I not be allowed to paint such an important subject five times, when other painters produce an endless succession of apples, palm trees, church spires and haystacks?

Munch to Jens Thiis on the fifth version of *The Sick Child*[7]

At the beginning of this century Munch was the decisive factor in the artistic life of Scandinavia and the German-speaking countries, the places from which his worldwide fame developed. Without Munch, Expressionism, Central Europe's most important artistic movement, would be unthinkable. For Austria, the country that produced Klimt, Schiele and Kokoschka, Munch was already a considerable influence. Otto Benesch[8]

It will not be a local or national association; we will strive to gain contact with struggling young artists everywhere, and organize small and exclusive exhibitions.

Emil Nolde to Munch in 1909. He suggested thirteen German and ten non-German artists as members of the association, amongst them Munch, Vigeland, and Matisse.[9]

350

348 **The Sacrament,** 1919/20
Woodcut, 49.7 x 71.9 cm.
Oslo Kommunes Kunstsamlinger, OKK 672

349 **The Final Hour,** 1920
Woodcut, 43.2 x 58 cm.
Oslo Kommunes Kunstsamlinger, OKK 650
Ref. G. Schiefler No. 491

350 **Panic Fear,** 1920
Woodcut, 38.9 x 53.5 cm.
Oslo Kommunes Kunstsamlinger, OKK 648
Ref. G. Schiefler No. 489

The fifth version was painted in the year that the director of the Berlin Nationalgalerie, Ludvig Justi, held a vast exhibition of Munch's work in the Kronprinzen Palais, establishing him conclusively as an artist of international stature. The critics all saw his work through different eyes and from different intellectual standpoints, but they were unanimous in their acknowledgement of the part he had played in influencing contemporary German art. Some of them even stated that he would have a decisive influence on the art of future generations. The same exhibition, supplemented by six additional paintings,[392] was also shown that year in Oslo, at Nasjonalgalleriet. The public flocked[393] to see it, and the press were loud in their praise.

Munch has not had the overwhelming influence on Norwegian art that one would have expected. This results partly from the fact that for a long time he was a prophet without honour in his own land, and by the time that Norwegian artists had finally opened their eyes to his true greatness, other influences, primarily those of Matisse and the French Fauves, were sweeping across Norway.[394] Munch's friend Ludvig Karsten was the exception. Karsten had fallen under Munch's spell early on, and the time that he spent with him at Åsgårdstrand, which on occasion had resulted in dramatic and near-lethal confrontations, had far-reaching effects on his art. He worshipped Munch, as is illustrated by the story of how, when Dr. Jacobson showed him the portrait that Munch had made of him as evidence of his patient's insanity, Karsten fell to his knees and exclaimed that it was a work of sheer genius (see page 210). Another story tells of how, in Paris, he kissed the pavement in front of an embarrassed Munch's feet. The major Karsten exhibition at Nasjonalgalleriet in 1976 proved conclusively that, if one were to name a Norwegian pupil of Munch's, it would have to be Ludvig Karsten or perhaps, conceivably, Rudolf Thygesen.[395]

Munch's artistic standing on the Continent, however, was quite different. It was inevitable that his never-ending stream of exhibitions abroad, broken only by the two world wars, would have a profound effect on the young artists of the day. For example, following his sensational exhibition in Vienna in 1904, we can see traces of his influence on the work of the young Richard Gerstl.[396] Oskar Kokoschka[397] was too young at that time, being only eighteen, but he subsequently became a great admirer of Munch's.

We saw how Munch was hailed by the young bohemian artists in Prague (see page 187) when the 'Manes' group of artists invited him to hold an exhibition in their new pavilion in 1905. His German friends had warned him both against holding the exhibition and against travelling to Czechoslovakia: 'the Czechs are a sanguine people, and it is so easy to become nervous in Prague,'[398] wrote Kollmann. But his exhibition in that city and his brief stay

351

there were among the high spots of Munch's life, particularly in view of his deep depression at the time. His art had an immediate and catalytic effect on the young artists, and several of them subsequently described what Munch had come to mean for them.[399] They did not forget him when he lay in the clinic in 1909, but made him an honorary member of their association, and when the spectre of Nazism branded both them and Munch as 'degenerate', they again honoured him in 1933. The painter Emil Filla describes 'how the most terrible feeling of apathy had settled on the younger members of the academy' and how 'nobody helped them out of their lethargy—until suddenly Munch burst on the scene. His art hit us like an explosion'. His fellow painter Vaclav Spala also relates how Munch provided a much-needed intellectual stimulus for the younger generation, and how the debate that he stirred up resulted in the artists splitting into two camps: 'forward looking radicals and academics of the old school'. The famous Czech art critic Franticek Salda wrote: 'It is always a mystery, albeit an important one, how artists such as Munch fit into the pattern of artistic progress, and how the validity of their work changes. There are always isolated artists who swim against the mainstream, which they find hard to follow. They often herald the dawning of a new era.'

Salda also makes an important observation about artists who go their own way, when he warns Munch's admirers: 'Those who feel deep down in their hearts that it is their destiny, should by all means follow Munch; but they should remember that the road which he has chosen to travel is a dramatic and fateful one.'

During the period of the first world war, the term 'Expressionism'[400] began

After due consideration, my closest artist friends and I are firmly convinced of the true merits of your art. It must give you a great deal of pleasure that many of the youngest and most progressive artists here treat your work with great reverence. At the moment there is considerable discord amongst us, but we are all united in our acknowledgement of your greatness.
August Macke to Munch, 1913[10]

Movements? For a painter to admit that he is part of a movement is the same as nailing himself to the wall. There are no such things as 'movements'. That is the wrong word. There are duties.
Munch to Christian Gierløff[11]

Equally, it would be nice to have found a place for the life frieze on which I have worked for forty-five years, but which has not progressed beyond being just an ordinary frieze. It was exhibited for five years when Vigeland embarked on his life frieze, which he has managed to make large enough.
Munch to Jens Thiis, 1938[12]

351 **The Dance of Life**, 1921
Oil on canvas, 96 x 321 cm.
Rolf E. Stenersen Collection, RES A304

352 **The Dance of Life**, 1922
Oil on canvas, 134 x 387 cm.
Freia Chocolate Factory, Oslo

352

353

353 Edvard Munch in the 1930's.

354 **Self-portrait**, 1933
Produced by means of a hectograph, 25.0 x 21.0 cm.
Oslo Kommunes Kunstsamlinger, OKK 732

354

to be used to describe a new direction in art. Naturally, there had always existed expressive art, the kind of art that endeavours, to the point of exaggeration, to express the emotions that an artist feels when confronted by his subject, and in that sense, Munch the post-Impressionist was an Expressionist painter. His painting of *The Scream* (Plate 107), completed in 1893, which has been called 'der geballte Schrei des Expressionismus' ('the concentrated scream of Expressionism') could easily be classified as a dramatic example of Expressionist art.

The pictures of the *Frieze of Life*, together with all the graphic works connected with them and their themes, are expressionistic in the deepest meaning of the word. The essential qualities are brought out and accentuated, unnecessary and extraneous detail vanishes, the expressive force is enhanced, and the whole message is conveyed in the simplest possible form. Several of Munch's paintings from the beginning of the century—for example, *The Fisherman and his Daughter* (Plate 263), in which he uses colour superbly to achieve the desired emotional effect, or strongly-defined contours to simplify the composition—often remind us of the works of German Expressionists such as Emil Nolde and Ludwig Kirchner. Perhaps, however, the most obvious way in which Munch influenced his fellow artists was through his graphic work.

In 1905, the year of his Prague exhibition, he completed his woodcut of *Primeval Man*, and that same year, in Dresden, a number of artists banded together to form a group known as 'Die Brücke',[401] whose name became synonymous with German Expressionism. The following year, when they held their first exhibition of graphic art in Dresden, Munch also staged an exhibition of his paintings in the city. We should bear in mind that virtually all the young German artists, as well as those of the older generation, had had the chance to visit exhibitions of Munch's controversial art. If, for example, we follow the progress of the 'rediscovered' German 'pre-Expressionist' Wilhelm Laage,[402] whose graphic work was also catalogued by Schiefler from year to year, we see that the German painter, five years Munch's junior, not only stayed in the same places as the Norwegian, but also exhibited in the same places. However, whereas Laage had begun to experiment with new woodcut techniques at the same time as Munch, the position of the younger artists was different, and in later years some of them were reluctant to admit the possibility of their having been influenced by the Norwegian. There are even instances of certain of them deliberately predating their pictures.

The founders of 'Die Brücke' were all very young (between twenty-one and twenty-five years old), and they stayed together as a group for a relatively short time. In 1908 they held exhibitions in both Oslo and Copenhagen, but by 1913 they had disbanded. The names of those who founded the group, however, still live on: men such as Ludwig Kirchner, Fritz Bleyl, Erich Heckel, and Karl Schmidt-Rottluff. In a way, one could say that their programme had much in common with that of the Fauves, but the German Expressionists were less concerned with the problems of form than their French counterparts, and they demanded that the artist's personality should be given free rein. When 'Die Brücke' was dissolved, some of the members joined a new group, which had been formed round Herwarth Walden and was called 'Der Sturm'. The North German artist Emil Nolde had been one of the earliest to break away from 'Die Brücke', when, in 1909, he approached Munch[403] and invited him to join a group of artists that he was trying to set up. But Munch, who had already turned down 'Die Brücke', also refused Nolde's offer on the grounds that he was unwell, sending his reply through their mutual friend Schiefler.

In 1913 Munch received yet another invitation, this time from August Macke,[404] who asked him to exhibit alongside Henry Rousseau ('Le Douanier') in a new group called 'Der Blaue Reiter'.

It was a time of great change and upheaval, in which the declaring of group loyalties and artistic manifestos played an important role. But Munch had too much freedom of spirit to allow himself to be restricted by adherence to any particular group: it is 'like nailing oneself to the wall.' Subsequently, a number of these German Expressionists denied what several art historians maintain: namely that Munch was the father of 'Die Brücke'.[405] When

355

355 **Professor Schreiner as Hamlet**, 1930
Lithograph, 93.5 x 72 cm.
Oslo Kommunes Kunstsamlinger, OKK 550

356 **Hans Jaeger**, 1943/44
Lithograph, 53.7 x 42.5 cm.
Oslo Kommunes Kunstsamlinger, OKK 548

357 **Self-portrait with Stick of Pastel**, 1943
Pastel, 80 x 60 cm.
Oslo Kommunes Kunstsamlinger, OKK 749

356

Schmidt-Rottluff was asked in 1946 what influence Munch had had on the
group, he denied that he had had any. In his reply he wrote: 'Naturally we
appreciated Munch's work, but at the time when Munch exhibited in public,
the members of "Die Brücke" had already developed their own style.'[406]
And yet it is a fact that Munch had been holding exhibitions in Germany
several times each year since 1892. Schmidt-Rottluff, however, is perfectly
correct when he goes on to say that 'it is hard, from an art historian's point
of view, to assess Munch's importance, because he is such a unique
phenomenon.'

His friend Erich Heckel also states that 'the continually repeated sup-
position that Munch influenced and inspired "Die Brücke" really does not
hold water.' He does, however, admit that a similarity to Munch exists in
their treatment of human experience and their attitude towards people,
which is lacking in Kandinsky and Marc. 'In graphics the similarities are
purely those of a common craft.'

For his part, Munch viewed the young rebels with a certain degree of
scepticism, as shown by a story that Schiefler tells of the time in 1907 when
he showed Munch a work by Schmidt-Rottluff. Munch shook his head and
remarked, 'God help us, we really are heading for gloomy times.'[407] And
when his friend Professor Griesebach[408] asked him his impressions of Franz
Marc's exhibition in Frankfurt, Munch's ironic reply was: 'Remarkable and
amusing to look at. Cows in paintings always used to go nice and tidily to
church. Now they leap about and dance, which is a new departure. The
colours are fun, but I cannot understand where it is all leading to.'

357 >

358 Munch at Ekely in his old age

Munch's exhibiting activities reached a high point in 1922 with a series of exhibitions in Zürich and other Swiss towns, in which he showed seventy-three paintings and nearly four hundred graphic works. Switzerland has always been a great centre for art dealers, and this visit not only established him firmly as an international artist, but also assured him of ever-higher prices for his work. The way was now open for his massive exhibitions in Berlin and Oslo in 1927.

East of the Rhine, Munch held an unassailable position; one could even say that he had had the same influence on German art as Cézanne had had on French art, a statement that, in itself, reveals much about the difference between German and French art. Munch's indefatigable propagandist J. P. Hodin[409] was one of the Czechs to whom Munch opened his house in 1937, and he gives a pathetic description of his meeting with the old master. It was he who stated quite rightly that up to the middle of this century Munch was practically unknown in America, England, and France. One of the few Englishmen to recognize Munch's significance was Herbert Read, who wrote that he was, 'without doubt, one of the richest sources of inspiration during the last half century.'

In 1960 the exhibition entitled 'Les sources du XX siècle' was held in Paris, and revealed quite clearly that Munch had played a much more significant part in twentieth-century art than had previously been realized in that part of Europe.

In 1970 any lingering doubts as to his true significance were finally dispelled by the great Expressionist exhibition[410] in Munich and Paris, in which Munch was confirmed in his role as one of the founders of Expressionism, along with such men as Gauguin, van Gogh, Ensor, and Kandinsky.

In 1937 Munch had shared with Europe's finest painters the 'honour' of being included in the Nazis' exhibition of 'degenerate' ('entartet') art in Munich. Eighty-two of his paintings were thrown out of German museums and subsequently sold to gain precious foreign currency for the Third Reich. Now his art was so valuable that it could even contribute to a nation's economy![411]

It would seem that Munch accepted this betrayal of his art by the country to which he owed so much with remarkable calm. He was aware that his fellow artists in Germany were suffering the same fate, and the men whom he had supported and whose works he had bought during the difficult years of the 1920s were the very ones who fell foul of the Nazis during the 1930s.[412] Having felt alone and isolated throughout his own life, he doubtless found consolation in sharing his misfortune with other artists—particularly such fine ones. Naturally enough, he was anxious about the possibility of having to evacuate his whole life's work from Ekely, should the Germans carry out their threats to requisition his home there (see page 28). He had good cause for anxiety: there were already Panzers in the neighbouring farm and the Germans had set up an anti-aircraft battery nearby. He had been given fourteen days' notice to quit, but when Pola Gauguin came to visit him in 1940, he noted with surprise that a strange calm had fallen on the normally agitated Munch. When he expressed his surprise, Munch pointed up to the sky, where two large Junkers were passing overhead, and said, 'Can't you understand that all the old ghosts have now retreated into their mouse-holes in the face of that one great spectre.'[413]

Fortunately, the Germans never took over Ekely, and Munch carried on working, with the Junkers roaring past overhead. Professor Schreiner had said that he thought it was a pity that Munch's lithograph of Hans Jaeger (Plate 54) was no longer obtainable, and he asked him to do another one. And so Munch, surrounded by thousands of old letters and notes, all of which stirred up many memories for him, settled down, more than fifty years later, and completed a lithograph of his old friend and teacher (Plate 356).

He also painted a very striking portrait of himself during the Occupation (Plate 29). His attitude is unyielding, and his expression is closed and defiant, with the corners of his mouth firmly turned down. There is a warm, ruddy glow in his face, but the symbolic landscape through the window is dead and barren. In the last self-portrait that he ever did, which dates from 1943, his hand still grasps a stick of pastel, but as he looks searchingly at us he seems

As I have already said, most of my graphic work, probably nearly all of it, will be burnt. It is highly unlikely that I will be able to gain more from them than I already have. They have served their purpose.   Munch to Johs. Roede[17]

. . But I must soon return home to my easel. It is not that I have to sit, brush in hand, waiting for inspiration. That very rarely happens. It is just that I work continually on my paintings—I generally wander about waiting for the urge to paint to strike me. I cannot bear to be too far away from my charcoal stick and my pastels. I have to know that, should a wave of inspiration come over me, I have my brushes and drawing instruments to hand.
Munch to Ragnar Hoppe[18]

Munch's place in the development of modern painting will remain unchanged, even after people's tastes have veered away from the nervously sensitive Naturalism and Symbolism of his day. Munch will always remain the most important and most penetrating representative of expressive greatness, a position he has achieved by virtue of his impressive and invaluable artistic qualities.
Josef Čapek, 1924[19]

The neglect of Edvard Munch in Great Britain, comparable only to the neglect, until recently, of Oskar Kokoschka, can only be explained by someone thoroughly familiar with our cultural prejudices, prejudices that have no parallel in the rest of Europe. They are the product of our social and educational system, and constitute an intellectual snobbery often admired by foreigners.
Herbert Read, 1963

Worringer calls it the 'uncanny pathos' (unheimliche Pathos) of the North. It is the quality that returned to European art after several centuries of increasing enervation in the pictorial art of our time through Munch, and no one, not even Van Gogh, felt it so strongly or conveyed it so clearly as Munch.
Herbert Read, 1963[20]

Edvard Munch, a painter whose artistic legacy must be included amongst the most valuable and original contributions to modern culture both in Europe and throughout the world.
Jiri Kotalik, 1971[21]

This exhibition is as near perfection as one could hope to find this side of Paradise. People sit for hours, soaking up the colours and emotions and the underlying feeling of empathy with human frailty and greatness that shines through the Norwegian's life-work.   Review in *The Herald Tribune*, 1974[22]

It will be really interesting when the time comes that everything can be seen in context. And it will be possible to compare everything—all the studies and all the sketches with the more finished works, at every stage of their development.   Munch[23]

His painting reaches right into our nervous system: it is completely intoxicating and bewitching. And for this very reason he represents a definite danger to young painters . . . If one analyses Munch's paintings correctly, I believe that he can be of great help —despite the fact that he is dangerous and precisely because he is 'dangerous'.   Peter Dahl, 1977[24]

I believe that his pictures will continue to be relevant for as long as painting relies on any feeling of immediacy for its expressive force. What he portrayed as a painter we are able to experience in our lives.   Nisse Zetterberg, 1977[25]

tired and resigned. The most remarkable portrait, however, of Munch in his old age, the *Self portrait between the Clock and the Bed* (Plate 30), shows him coming out of a bright, sunlit room. He has stopped and stands rigidly to attention. The vacant clock-face by his side has told him that the hour has struck, while the bed awaits him like a coffin, covered with the embroidered rug from his childhood home. And above the bed there hangs the painting (Plate 359) of the slender model, painted in soft, luminous colours.

He lived to see his eightieth birthday, which took place on 12 December 1943, with greetings flooding in to him from all directions. But he was destined never to realize his dream of seeing the war's end and the destruction of Nazism fulfilled. A week later Ekely was shaken by the explosion of a nearby munitions dump, and although he himself was not injured, all the windows in the house were blown in, and as a result he contracted a severe bout of bronchitis that finally proved fatal. In his will he left all his works unconditionally to Oslo, the city of his childhood.[414]

On 23 January 1944 Edvard Munch departed peacefully for what he himself called 'The Land of Crystals'.

359 **Krotkaja, model study,** 1926/7
Oil on canvas, 117 x 58 cm.
Oslo Kommunes Kunstsamlinger, OKK 752

ABBREVIATIONS

OKK:	Oslo Kommunes Kunstsamlinger, (Oslo Municipal Art Collections)
Vennene:	*Edvard Munch son vi kjente ham. Vennene forteller*, (Edvard Munch as we knew him. Told by his friends). Oslo, 1946.
K & K:	*Kunst og Kultur*, (Norwegian art historical journal)
Tegn. Kat:	*Tegn. Katalog*, (Catalogue of drawings)
Fam. brev:	*Edvard Munch's brev. Familien*, (Edvard Munch's family letters). Oslo, 1949.
Livs. tilbl:	*Livsfrisens tilblivelse*, (Origin of the 'Frieze of Life')
Livs:	*Livsfrisen*, (The Frieze of Life)
Sch:	Gustav Schiefler. Schiefler numbers refer to his catalogue of Munch's prints, published by Cassirer, Berlin, 1907. New edition Cappelens, Oslo, 1974.
Lindebrevene:	*Edvard Munchs brev. fra Dr. Med. Max Linde*, (Edvard Munch's letters from Dr. Max Linde), Oslo, 1954.
Schiefler/Schack:	*Gustav Schiefler, Meine Graphiksammlung: Ergänzt und herausgegeben von Gerhard Schack*, (Hamburg, 1974)

NAMES

CG:	Christian Gierløff
EG:	Emanuel Goldstein
RH:	Ragnar Hoppe
SH:	Sigurd Høst
CK:	Christian Krohg
JN:	Jappe Nilssen
ET:	Ernest Thiel
JT:	Jens Thiis

BOOKS   Books which occur often are referred to simply by author and date, e.g. Thiis (1933). Full details are in the Bibliography. (Main titles here are Thiis, Hoppe and Schiefler.)

Notes

Page 11: **Chapter 1: SELF-PORTRAITS**

Text   1 Note OKK N 16. A similar note T.2748c.

2 Nabi—an old testament word for prophet. *Les Nabis*, a group of French painters founded 1888–9. They met in the editorial offices of *La Revue Blanche*, a journal with which Munch had connections. Both Cézanne and van Gogh were of significance to the group, but Gauguin was the most important figure. Some of the members can be said to have influenced Munch, e.g. Denis, Vuillard, Valloton. The group was dissolved c. 1900.

3 Unless otherwise stated, Munch's notes and memoranda are to be found at Munch-Museet, Oslo Kommunes Kunstsamlinger (Oslo Municipal Art Collection).

Quotations *1 OKK T. 2748*

2 Munch to K. E. Schreiner, Vennene, p. 21.
Professor Schreiner (1874–1957) was Munch's doctor and close friend from the middle of the twenties until Munch's death in 1944. Munch left him his writings and literary effects. These have since been left to OKK.

3 Livs. Tilbl. p. 2. (Warnemünde, 1907) Munch had several small booklets printed with comments on his art, and a great many of the quotations in this book are taken from them. Unfortunately the booklets are not clearly dated. We cannot here discuss their dating in detail, but refer the reader to Reinhold Heller's Doctoral thesis: Edvard Munch's Frieze of Life: its beginnings and origins. (Indiana University, 1960, pp. 42–61. There is a typewritten copy at Munch-Museet. Heller's work is the most important to date on the genesis of the Frieze of Life. He dates Livs. 1918 and Livs. Tilbl. 1929. With regard to the Frieze of Life see also Pål Hougen, Edvard Munch og den tsjekkiske kunst (1971). Also Munch-Museet catalogue no. 6 (1971); p. 41 of Roy Boe's dissertation: Edvard Munch: His Life and Work from 1880–1920, Vols I and II (New York University, 1971). (Boe has Munch's texts in English in appendices B, C, D, E and F) Trygve Nergaard, 'Edvard Munchs visjon' A contribution to the story of the Frieze of Life, K & K (1967), H. 2, pp. 69–92. He developed the theme in greater depth later in Refleksjon og Visjon, Naturalismens dilemma i Edvard Munchs kunst 1889–1894 (1968). Typewritten copy at Munch-Museet. Arne Eggum, in his detailed catalogue text for Munch exhibitions in Stockholm 1977, Edvard Munch Kulturhuset og Liljevalchs, p. 19, has written about Munch's late Frieze of Life. It is probable that Livs. was published in connection with his Blomkvist exhibition in 1918. At this time the University murals had already been in place for two years and he was dreaming of an opportunity to carry out his master work, the Frieze of Life (see Chp. VII) on a grand scale. Livs. tilbl. was probably published in 1929, again in connection with a Blomkvist exhibition. There is at Munch-Museet a personal copy of this booklet with corrections and additions. In the catalogue of the Blomkvist exhibition he held in the year, Munch included 1889–1929 Brief Selections from my Diary (Små utdrag av min dagbok). See Chp. V, p. 74. In Feb. 1929 Munch wrote to R.H.: 'But I am also thinking of gathering together all the personal observations which deal with other matters, what I call my spiritual diary, into a whole, but it takes time—I am trying to get some order into it now, but I have no idea how it will turn out. A couple of small pamphlets are already printed, few copies, but I am not showing them to anyone so far.' In this letter he discusses his pamphlet with an entry from 1889 in Paris and quotes his Manifesto. See note 5 below. Munch has also described his Aula decorations in Munch's competition entries for the main hall of the university *(Munchs konkuranceutkast til universitets festsal). Exhibited in Dioramalokalet, August 1911.*

4 Munch to his relative—the painter Ludvig Ravensberg (1871–1958), Vennene, p. 189. R's grandmother was the sister of Munch's father. Vennene has contributions to make about Munch—in addition to Schreiner and Ravensberg—there are also Munch's legal adviser Johs. Roede, Ingeborg Motzfeldt Løchen, Titus Vibe Müller, Birgit Prestøe, David Bergendahl, Christian Gierløff and Pola Gauguin, together with a collection of letters from Munch to Sigurd Høst in 1909.

5 Munch to the senior civil servant Ragnar Hoppe in a letter of 5/3/29. RH arranged a large exhibition of Munch's graphics at the National-museum, Stockholm, in 1929. RH wrote an article 'At Ekely with Edvard Munch' ('Hos Edvard Munch på Ekely', Nutida Konst, 1939, pp. 8–19), in which some Munch letters of 1929 are included.

Plate   1 Signed bottom right: 'E. Munch' was bought 1938 for the Olaf Schou foundation. Earlier it belonged to Munch's friend, the distinguished barrister, Harald Nørregaard and his wife. Nørregaard also owned one version of *The Sick Child*, pl. 74, which is today in Nasjonalgalleriet, Oslo. Günter Busch *Hinweis zur Kunst, Aufsätze und Reden* (1977), has compared this portrait of Munch with Paula Modersohn Becker's self-portrait of 1898–9, in the Kunsthalle Bremen. For early self-portraits by Munch see pl. 39, which is probably as early as 1880, and pl. 3 from 1881–2. In co-operation with photographer Ragnvald Vaering, Johan H. Langaard published *Edvard Munch's self-portrait* (Edvard Munchs selvportretter, Gyldendal, 1947) with a foreword of 7 pages and 72 photographs. An exhibition of 61 self-portraits was held at Munch-Museet in 1963–4. Leif Østby has written about other artists' portraits of E. Munch in 'Edvard Munch as seen by his contemporaries' ('E.M. stik samtiden så ham'), *K & K*, 1963, pp. 243–56. For other *self-portraits* in this book see illustrations: 39, 65, 168, 191, 207, 216, 217, 231, 299, 314, 324, 337, 345, 354, 357. In addition Munch's features occur in a number of his *Frieze of Life* pictures. See also Pål Hougen, 'The Artist as a Representative Figure', *The Peaks of Norwegian Art: Year Book of the Swedish National Museum* ('Kunstneren som stedfortreder', Höjdpunkter i Norsk Konst 1968, pp. 123–40). In the catalogue which Pål Hougen wrote for the exhibition of Munch's drawings in Munch-Museet, 1973, pp. 12–13, there are references to a number of self-portrait drawings. In his catalogue of the *Exhibition of drawings in Bremen*, 1973, the self-portrait drawings can be found under numbers 229–49.

Page 12:

Quotations 6 OKK T. 2758b.

7 OKK T. 2547. Tree of Knowledge (Kunnskapens tre). *See also OKK T. 2782bb.*

8 OKK T. 2760, Violet Book, p. 11.

Plates   4 Painted in Berlin and dated by most authorities 1892–93, but probably painted later in the nineties. This sinister woman's mask indicated that Munch was influenced by Przybyszewski's and Strindberg's attitude to women.

5 Signed bottom left 1895; bought for Nasjonalgalleriet in the year it was painted.

Page 15:

Quotations *9 Livs. tilbl., p. 1*

10 Munch to Schreiner, Vennene, p. 20.

11 Munch note from Elgersburg, 1905. See Tegn. Kat., p. 5.

12 Munch note from Warnemünde, 1907–8. Livs. tilbl., p. 2.

13 Munch to JN, 13/1/1904. Bang (1963), p. 19. Jappe (Jacob) Nilssen (1870–1931) was Munch's close friend from youth. Munch used this author, seven years younger than himself, many times as a model, pl. 114 and portrait p. 292. From 1908 JN was the art critic for Dagbladet.

14 Tegn. kat., p. 5.

Plates   **6** See Otto von Fisenne on 'Munch in Travemünde', *Schleswig-Holstein Monatsschrift H.2* Neumünster, (1976), pp. 35-6. The author states that his father, the painter Adolf Hölterhoff, inspired Munch to paint this portrait.

    7 Ingrid Langaard points out in *Edvard Munch—the Maturing Years* (Edvard Munchs Medningsår, Gyldendal, 1960, p. 259), that it is not improbable that the Swiss artist Felix Vallotton two years younger than Munch was the inspiration of this lithograph. Vallotton did a number of graphic works in which the head is sharply portrayed against a black background, e.g. woodcut of Dostoievsky 1895, and there are marked similarities between the two artists. See also Chp. VIII.

Page 16:
Quotations **15** *OKK T. 2761 E.M.1.*

    16 *Munch in a letter of 1907 to Jens Thiis (1870-1942), director of Nasjonalgalleriet, Oslo (1909-40). He was a friend of Munch's youth and a champion of his art throughout a long life. Munch-Museet has a number of unpublished letters and drafts of letters to and from JT and Munch. JT's comprehensive biography,* Edvard Munch and his Time *(Edvard Munch og hans samtid, Gyldendal, 1933) is an important source for any study of Munch's life and art. JT also wrote many articles about Munch in magazines and the daily press. There is an abridged edition in German of his book with a postscript by Erich Büttner (Berlin, 1934).*

    17 *Munch in 1905 from Bad Elgersburg to the Danish poet Emanuel Goldstein (1862-1921). Munch was with Goldstein in Paris in 1889-90 (see Chp. V). Goldstein played an important part in developing Munch's writing. The friendship lasted for many years and Goldstein often visited Munch at the psychiatric clinic in Copenhagen in 1908-9. Munch-Museet has a large collection of letters from both, to be published. Trygve Nergaard has written on Emanuel Goldstein and Edvard Munch in the* Louisiana Revy *(Oct. 1975), pp. 16-18.*

    18 *Munch to ET, June 1906 from Weimar, quoted in Gierløff* Selected Letters *(Enkelte brev, 1953, pp. 276-95). ET was a Swedish banker who supported Munch (and also Gustav Vigeland) in difficult years. Thielska Galleriet in Stockholm owns 12 paintings and 96 graphic works by Munch.*

    19 *OKK 2800.*

Page 17:
Quotations **20** *Munch to EG. Undated letter at Munch-Museet.*

    21 *Tegn. Kat., p. 10.*

    22 *Munch to SH, 4/4/1909.* Vennene, *p. 146. The school-teacher Sigurd Høst (1866-1939) was also among Munch's closest friends. He was chairman of the Kunstforening (Art Society) in Bergen and asked Munch to hold an exhibition there in 1909 while Munch was under treatment at the Copenhagen clinic. SH also arranged sales to Rasmus Meyer's collection. See Chp. XIII.*

    23 *Munch to EG. Undated letter at Munch-Museet.*

Plates   **11** The drawing is a sketch for the cover of the journal *Quickborn* (1897) in which Munch illustrated Strindberg's text. This self-portrait illustrates Munch's own philosophy: the artist's life must be laid bare. His heart's blood fertilizes art, which is symbolized by the growing flower. A year later he depicted the same theme as a woodcut (OKK 586). It is a mirror image and the blood flows therefore from the man's right side. As Gösta Svenæus has pointed out, in *Im männlichen Gehirn* (1973) p. 204, the motif of the heart's blood of the artist occurs in the works of a number of contemporary artists including Strindberg and Ola Hansson. Remember that Jaeger also in his defence speech before the High Court proclaimed with regard to naturalistic literature: 'It is written with warm human blood. Those beings which rise to meet you from their works, they live, live with the breath of reality . . . they are fashioned of living flesh. Listen! You will hear the throbbing of their hearts!' Munch, as we shall see, uses this motif several times. We must, however, assume that this drawing also refers to the name of the journal: *Quickborn*—a low German word which means a spring of gushing, life-giving water. We shall see how Munch throughout his life used the motif of the artist who helps others to understand the meaning of life by laying bare his own bleeding heart. With regard to 'The artist as a representative figure' see Hougen (1968), pp. 123-40.

    12 This self-portrait must have been painted in 1904. Munch writes from Lübeck 14.12.1904: 'I have painted a large self-portrait.' See *Fam. brev.* no. 230. The Munch-Museet documents include 425 family letters from the period 1860-1943. Selection by Inger Munch. Munch bequeathed to her his correspondence and diaries and she presented them in toto to OKK.

    13 This drawing dates from about the same time as the various versions of *The Blossom of Pain* to which it is ideologically related. The artist embraces his instrument, the lyre, as if it were a woman.

Page 18:
Quotations **24** *Munch to SH, 1909, from the clinic.* Vennene, *p. 145.*

    25 *Munch to JN, 9/3/1909. Erna Bang,* Edvard Munch's Years of Crisis *(Edvard Munchs kriseår, Oslo, 1963, p. 58).*

    26 *Munch to JN, 28/12/1908. Bang (1963), p. 33.*

Plates   **14** The self-portrait was painted in a very difficult period of Munch's life. Lonely and miserable, he sat alone in empty restaurants. The wine bottle shows that he was in the grip of alcohol. Both the mood and the colours reveal that the crisis is approaching.

    15 On the other hand, the self-portrait from the clinic shows Munch fit again and ready to take up his life's work. The two contrasting styles and the strikingly different colouring make it clear that a new phase of his life is beginning.

Page 19:
Quotations **27** *Munch to K. E. Schreiner,* Vennene, *p. 26.*

    28 *Munch to SH, 14/9/1909, after the big sale in Bergen.* Vennene, *p. 175.*

Page 20:
Quotations **29** *Rolf E. Stenersen, Naerbilde av et geni (Gyldendal, Oslo, 1946), p. 125. English version:* Close-up of a Genius *(Oslo 1969).*

    30 *The Tree of Knowledge, OKK T. 2547 A. 33.*

    31 *Munch to RH, Feb. 1929. Hoppe (1939), p. 16.*

Page 22:
Quotations **32** *Munch to RH, Feb. 1929. Ibid., p. 17.*

    33 *T. 2748b. A similar quote from Schreiner,* Vennene, *p. 21.*

Plates   **21** In the nineteen-twenties Munch took up several themes from his bohemian period.

Page 24:
Quotations **34** The Tree of Knowledge, 2547 a/31.

    35 *Munch to RH, 1/7/1929. Hoppe (1939), p. 19.*

    36 *Munch to RH, 29/1/1929. Ibid., p. 15.*

    37 *Munch to JT, 5/2/1934.*

Page 26:
Quotations **38** *Munch to CG, 14/2/1943. The journalist and author Christian Gierløff (1879-1962) was also one of Munch's close friends. Apart from his contribution to* Vennene *('Years of Strife', pp. 113-40), he wrote* Edvard Munch Himself *(Edvard Munch selv, Gyldendal, 1953), from which comes the following, p. 43: 'In the Grimsrød years, when he was approaching fifty, he suddenly decided that he must tidy up his letters and other writings. He had his old* Opptegnelser *(Notes) and* Erindringer *(Reminiscences)—and I still have a little notebook with black covers which is only partly filled in his handwriting and in mine from those years.' Gierløff quotes a number of these 'Notes', p. 44, and also quotes pp. 276-95 from* Selected Letters, *which contains Munch's correspondence with Ernest Thiel and with Gierløff himself. Munch portrayed Gierløff on several occasions, e.g. illus. 294.*

    39 *Munch to CG, 14/2/1943. Gierløff (1953), p. 293.*

    40 *Munch to K. E. Schreiner,* Vennene, *p. 22.*

    41 *Munch—see Gierløff (1953), p. 44.*

    42 *Tree of Knowledge, OKK T. 2547.*

    43 *Ibid.*

Page 28:
Quotation **44** *Munch to CG, 1943. Gierløff (1953), p. 294.*

Page 31: **Chapter 2: THE HOME**

Text   **4** P. Hougen: OKK Kat. A3, 1973. *Tegn. Kat.*, p. 5.

    5 Munch to Thiis, undated letter but probably 1933.

    6 The author who has written in most detail about Munch's childhood and young manhood is his friend Jens Thiis. His biography (1933) is based on information provided, *inter alia* by Munch himself, and by his sister Inger. Another friend, Gierløff (1953), uses material from conversations as well as Munch's notebooks and letters. Roy Boe (1970) obtained much information from Inger Munch for his detailed chapter on the family. Biographical details on Christian Munch (1817-89) are to be found in Thiis (1933) 'Slekten' (The Family), pp. 3-42. Also Gierløff (1953), p. 25 and Boe (1971), p. 20. Indispensable for any student of Munch is Johan H. Langaard and Reidar Revold's *Edvard Munch from Year to Year* (Edvard Munch fra år til år. Aschehoug, 1961). It also has an English text. A good deal of information can be found here including the following family dates:

Christian Munch   m. Laura Cathrine Bjølstad
(Regimental Doctor)
(1817-89)   (1838-68)
Five children of the marriage:
Edvard Munch (1863-1944)
Johanne Sophie (1862-77)
Peter Andreas (1865-95)

Laura Cathrine (1867–1926)
Inger Marie (1868–1952)
Munch's aunt, Karen Bjølstad (1839–1931)

7 The Christiania Theatre controversy.
In 1837 the new Christiania Theatre was opened. From the beginning it was a bone of contention between two opposing factions in the intellectual life of the capital; the so-called Norwegian Party, led by Henrik Wergeland, and the Intelligence Party, led by J. S. C. Welhaven. Wergeland urged a replacement of the traditional Danish-style theatre by rapid 'Norwegianization', including the training of specifically Norwegian actors. Welhaven, on the other hand, favoured a more gradual building-up of a Norwegian dramatic tradition based on Danish expertise. The first production in the new Christiania theatre was Andreas Munch's *The Youth of King Sverre*, the winner in a competition for original Norwegian plays. Following this, in January 1838, Wergeland's own play *Campbellerne* was produced. This became the cause of violent scenes in the theatre between the two factions, out of which the Wergeland party emerged victorious.

8 Munch's relative, the painter Ravensberg, gives a lively account of the cultured home in 'Edvard Munch in Close-up' (Edvard Munch på nært hold, *Vennene*, p. 183 ff.).

Quotation 1 *Schreiner*, Vennene, *p. 17. A similar note is to be found in* Tegn. Kat, *E.M. III p. 15.*

Plate 35 This drawing is reproduced in Hougen (1973), p. 2, and in *Edvard Munch Handzeichnungen: herausgegeben von Pål Hougen*, Ernest Rathenau, (New York, 1976), no. 88. In the accompanying text on p. 21, Hougen quotes in detail Munch's own observations on his childhood illness.

Page 32:
Quotation 2 *Laura Munch in a letter to her children,* Fam. brev *No. 12.*
Page 33:
Text 9 See p. 155, quotation 2. Munch to JT—draft letter 1933.
10 See Thiis (1933), p. 63 for portrayal of Julius Middelthun and the school.
11 Ravensberg, *Vennene*, p. 184.
12 Munch in unpublished letter to Thiis. See also p. 60, quotation 11.
13 *Livs. tilbl.*, p. 1.

Quotations 3 Tegn. Kat., *p. 10.*
4 *The four quotations from the diary are taken from* Fam brev., *pp. 47, 51.*

Plate 40 This drawing shows that Munch was interested at an early age in Norwegian history.

Page 34:
Quotations 5 Livs. tilbl., *p. 1.*
6 Livs. tilbl., *p. 13.*
7 Fam brev *No. 82. The observation was probably written in the 1890s.*
8 Fam. brev *No. 39.*

Plates 41 This chalk drawing was probably done at the time when Munch was making his great lithographs, pl. 173 & 174.
42 Painting is discussed in *Fam. brev* No. 39, 1881.
43–44 *The dead mother and the child* is another of the themes on which Munch often worked. There is a picture with this motif in the Kunsthalle Bremen. See Günter Busch, *Über Gegenwart und Tot—Edvard Munch Probleme*, (1973). See also paintings in OKK 516 and 756 which are strongly reminiscent of Max Klinger's treatment of the same theme. In 1901 Munch made an etching with the same motif. OKK G-r 54.

Page 36:
Text 14 See p. 31 quotation 1.
15 Compare p. 107 quotation 15.
16 The resources of the household do not seem to have been so bad when the mother was alive. Mrs. Laura Munch writes in letter no. 13 to Oliana Oline Hansen (Edvard's nanny): '. . . and also my sister is here and has taken over the running of the house. We have three maidservants.' (Nedre Slottsgate no. 9 14.4.1868.)
17 There are at Munch-Museet a few sheets of paper; sketchbook VI in a loose cover 122 'Views of various rooms in Christiania where Doctor Munch and his family have lived. Drawn by Edvard Munch.'
18 Ravensberg relates (*Vennene*, p. 187) that Munch's old father received anonymous Christian tracts and admonished biblical texts, and had to withstand much bourgeois sarcasm because his son wanted to become a painter. 'I am inclined to believe that these incidents of his early youth are the cause of Munch's fear of bourgeois families, and of the isolated life he led all his days remote from social contacts.'

Plate 47 *Morgenbladet*, 28.10.1886. The only comment of the Norwegian newspaper on this superb portrait was to mention 'the frighteningly ugly portrait of a lady dressed in black'.

Page 38:
Plate 49 There are a number of related pictures of Old Aker and Telthusbakken as well as of the surroundings of the city. See letter 40, from which it emerges that in February 1882 Munch failed to place his drawings in the *Ny Illustreret Tidende* but that he 'will draw a few smaller scenes of the Kristiania district'. See also Harald Hals, *E.M. and the City* (Edvard Munch og byen, Oslo Bymuseum, 1955) with many reproductions of these early pictures. See also Karl Haugholt, *Omkring E.M.'s tegninger fra Maridalen*, St Halvard 5, (1959). See also Masaaki Suzuki, *Edvard Munch 1977, foto og maleri av Telthusbakken og Gamle Aker kirke*, which shows how exactly Munch rendered this theme.

Page 40:
Plate 51 This motif is found in many variations. The best known is the version in Nasjonalgalleriet, thought to date from 1892. Presented by Olaf Schou in 1910. Here, and in OKK's versions, Munch employs very consciously a technique which he often uses to heighten impact: frontality. Werner Hofmann has pointed this out in 'Zu einem Bildmittel Edvard Munchs Alte und neue Kunst' *Wiener kunstwissenschaftliche Blätter III* 1 (1954), pp. 20–40.

Page 45: **Chapter 3: THE BOHEMIAN**

Text 19 Draft of a letter from Munch to Broby Johansen, Berlin 11.12.1926. BJ had written an article ('Edvard Munch', *Samlerer*, No. 10, 1926), in which he put forward the view that the bohemian period had meant a great deal for Munch, and wrote to Munch asking if he was right in this. The quotation is from Munch's reply. He says something similar in a letter (Feb. 1929) to RH: '*The Frieze of Life* and my spiritual art had its origin in the bohemian days.' Hoppe (1939), p. 16.
20 Picture referred to is in Munch-Museet.
21 'I am sitting at "the Grand" (Hotel) now with Hans Jæger who will be shoved into a cell tomorrow.' Munch to Arne Garborg, Aug. 1888. Collection of letters, University Library 32, Oslo.
22 Arne Brenna in *Hans Jæger's Prison Frieze* (Hans Jægers fengelsfrise, St. Halvard, 1972, pp. 238–66).
23 See, for instance, A. H. Winsnes, *Norges literaturhistorie V*, (Oslo, 1961), p. 156. Olav Storstein, Hans Jæger, (The Norwegian Students' Association's historical documents 18, 1935). Jens Bjørneboe has also written an interesting article about Hans Jæger (*Horisont I*, 1955, pp. 23–8), in which he draws parallels with our time. See also Odd Eidem's introduction to *From The Christiania Bohemians* (Fra Kristiania Bohemen, Dreyers Publishing House) which was released from censorship only in 1950—sixty-five years after it was first confiscated.
24 See p. 52, quotation 20.
25 See Leif Østby 'Fra naturalisme til nyromantik' (*K & K*, Gyldendal 1934).

Quotations 1 *Munch to Broby Johansen, 1926. See page 45, text note 19.*
2 *See page 45, text note 22. This must, as Arne Brenna points out, refer to another prison sentence: Brenna, 'Hans Jæger og Edvard Munch: Vennskapet', (Nordisk Tidskrift 52nd year, 1976, pp. 89–115). Brenna wrote another article in the same journal: 'Hans Jæger og Edvard Munch', pp. 188–215, II.*
3 *Andreas Aubert in his article in* Dagbladet, *19/5/1889, printed after Munch's one-man exhibition was closed.*

Plate 53 Jæger's portrait was bought for Nasjonalgalleriet in 1897.
Page 46:
Text 26 This foreword was printed before the book was published and was probably the reason for the confiscation of *From The Christiania Bohemians* a mere hour after it appeared. Superintendent of police, Aimar Sørensen sent a telegram to all police superintendents in the country: 'Stop the sale!' That was 11th Dec. 1885. Fifty years later —in 1935—Olav Storstein tried in vain to persuade the authorities to release it. A gathering of six hundred people at the Oslo Arbeidersamfunn (Oslo Labour Association) sent a request to the authorities to lift the ban.
27 Reduced from eighty days by the Supreme Court. Jæger was dismissed from his post as parliamentary shorthand writer. It is interesting to note that the Danish critic, J. J. Ipsen, received a sentence of one month on prison diet for his review in the Danish paper *Sosialdemokraten* of Jæger's Sick Love.
28 Oscar Thue has discussed the controversy regarding *Albertine* in *Samtiden* (Annual Issue 65, Oslo, 1956), pp. 662–70. The controversy attracted a great deal of attention and was the subject of a

number of newspaper articles. Public prostitution was abolished in 1887—an event to which Krohg's campaign surely contributed.

29 Munch insisted that he had painted one of the figures, but CK denied this. The figure in dispute is seated by the door. Thiis (1933), p. 80. See Oscar Thue 'Edvard Munch og Christian Krohg', *K & K* (1973), pp. 237-56.

30 *The Impressionist* edited by Krohg and a committee, (Christiania, 1886-9).

31 B. H. Schubothes Boghandels forlag, Copenhagen, 1888. The studio described belonged to the sculptor, Rolf Schefte. It was so named (Kjaerka) because it was directly above the Catholic church in Akersgata. The scene is set in 1884-5. Munch appears here under the name of Nansen, a name which he uses of himself in his novel fragment. Another pseudonym in the book is Moen-Wentzel, a contemporary naturalistic painter. See Oscar Thue, 'Gustav Wentzel: The Day After . . . 1883' ('Gustav Wentzel: Dager Derpå . . . 1883) *Year Book of the Trondheim Art Association* (Trondheims Kunstforenings årbok 1962, pp. 6-13).

Quotations 4 *OKK N. 12. Another of Munch's observations can be found here: 'I could not understand Jæger. I could love him—but also hate him. The business with Jæger was the worst part of it for my father.' See also R. Heller,* Edvard Munch's Frieze of Life; its beginnings and origins, *p. 76. He states that this note of Munch's can very probably be dated as early as Dec. 1889 or early 1890. See also Brenna (1976), pp. 99-100.*

5 *JN in his review in* Dagbladet, *1/4/1911. See Holmboe-Bang,* Edvard Munch and JN: Posthumous letters and reviews *(Edvard Munch og JN: Etterlatte brev og kritiker, Oslo, 1946, p. 74).*

Plates 55 We do not know who the two men are. Possibly Jæger and Jappe Nilssen.

56 Munch made several portraits of Heiberg. They were close friends for a time but the relationship later turned sour. Munch became increasingly suspicious and this resulted in a number of vicious cartoons of his former friend (see, e.g. pl. 272). Heiberg was throughout his life a warm admirer of Munch. Jan Groos Helmer, Heiberg's nephew, relates how GH approached Munch at the exhibition in Nasjonalgalleriet in 1927 to express his admiration. 'I had to do it' Heiberg said. Munch was a little reserved in his response and said among other things 'I have always thought of you as on the outer fringe of my enemies so it must be possible to exchange a few words'. In the conversation which followed GH said, 'I have never quite realized before that you were so great an artist.'

58 This picture can be seen as an illustration of the milieu which Herman Colditz describes in his novel.

Page 48:
Text 32 In his *Violet Book,* OKK 2760, Munch also notes, with regard to Jæger: 'I looked at him—Do you know what,—I think you'll end by dancing the cancan on the graves of all your friends—those who drank themselves to death—those you persuaded to do just that. Jaeger laughed.' See Brenna, (1976, I), p. 98.

Quotations 6 *Munch to JN, on learning that Jæger was very ill; Bang, (1963) p. 78. JN replied: 'HJ was very moved by your greetings. He had obviously not expected the gesture. In fact he probably had the idea you were among his enemies. He asked me to tell you how grateful he was.' (Ibid., p. 80) HJ died on 8/2/1910.*

7 *Gustav Vigeland note from the nineteen thirties. The relationship between Munch and Gustav Vigeland was probably tinged with mutual scepticism, but in their younger years they had more to do with each other than is generally thought; e.g. GV modelled a portrait of Munch in Berlin in 1895. It is true, however, that he smashed the bust into pieces. See also p. 96.*

8 *See pl. 68. Gunnar Heiberg was one of the very first to review Munch. See* Dagbladet, *22/12/1883, when Munch had this picture in Høstutstilling. (Autumn Exhibition) Jæger made an almost identical remark three years later about* The Sick Child. *See Brenna (1976) II, pp. 188-9.*

9 *Kitty Wentzel in her book on Gustav Wentzel has elucidated several of the pseudonyms in the Colditz book. (Oslo 1956, p. 36.)*

10 *Munch to JT, in a letter of 1933.*

11 *Hans Jæger in* Impressionisten, *No. 1, (1886).*

12 Aftenposten, *23/3/1909.*

Plate 59 The first version was at the Christiania gilders' workshop and was burned in December 1890 together with four other pictures. These were: *En fransk kneipe* (A French Tavern), *Kanalen i Paris, Dame i landskap,* and *Strandbilde.* Munch received 750 kr in insurance for the five pictures, and remarked, 'That fire was a stroke of luck'. *Fam. Brev. No. 92.*

Page 51:
Quotations 13 *JT in* Verdens Gang, *31/3/1909.*

14 *Hans Dedekam in* Morgenbladet, *27/3/1909. The museum director, HD, was a great admirer of Munch.*

15 *'SS' in* Aftenposten, *1885. No less than ten citizens of Christiania were concealed behind the pseudonym SS. See Thiis (1933), p. 154.*

16 *Henning Gran has written about Werenskiold's ambivalent attitude in 'Munch through Werenskiold's Eyes',* Art Today, *(Kunsten idag, 1951). A similar statement on W's reaction: Munch wrote to Thiis in an undated letter that W said: 'It should never have been assumed.'*

17 *Sigbjørn Obstfelder, 'Edvard Munch—an Experiment' (Edvard Munch—et forsøg,* Samtiden, *1896, pp. 17-22). Written 1893.*

18 *Ibid., p. 19. Sigbjørn Obstfelder (1866-1900). The relationship between his and Munch's art has often been pointed out, e.g. by Hans Dedekam in* E. M. Kristiania *(1909), p. 4 ff. He draws attention to the fact that it was the lyric poet, three years younger than Munch, who first used the expression 'sjaelemaleri' (soul painting) in his article in* Samtiden *written as early as 1893 but not printed until 1896. Munch's 'angstbilder' (fear pictures) in particular bring Obstfelder's poetry to mind. There was a proposal that Munch should illustrate SO's volume of poetry. See letter to his brother, 25/7/92, p. 144: 'As I've said, I had a letter yesterday from Vilhelm Krag. His publisher (John Grieg) wants to bring out my poems for the Christmas season—the painter Edvard Munch will do one or more of the vignettes,' JT writes in a letter to Anders Stilloff, 1928, from Paris: 'He [Obstfelder] sent me as a greeting a small volume of the poems he had written at that time. On the cover he had written "Tannhäuser Marschen". Unhappily the manuscript was borrowed and never returned. I had it with me on my long journey abroad and in Berlin I showed it to Chr. Sinding, Munch and Gunnar Heiberg. At that time Munch was probably the one who understood him best.' See Solveig Tunold,* Letters to his Brother *(Brev til hans Bror, p. 256). See also JT's further account of Obstfelder in Berlin, ibid. p. 264. In notes in an article on Munch and SO, Louisiana Revy, Oct. 1975, pp. 33-6) Øyvind Hjørt states that Nergaard drew his attention to the fact that there were SO's poems among Munch's papers. It is possible that these are the poems which JT showed to Munch.*

Page 52:
Quotations 19 *Note T 2800. In 1903 Munch wrote to Dr Linde from Paris in an undated letter: 'My syphilitic art was hung in a chambre particulier and achieved a splendid succés de rire. The room was always full of people who shrieked and laughed. (Mein Syphiliskunst wurde in ein Chambre Particulier aufgehängt und errichtete eine Succés de rire. Es war in dem Zimmer immer voll von Menschen welche geschrien und gelacht haben.) Gustav Lindtke,* Edvard Munch—Dr Max Linde, Briefwechsel 1902-28 *(Lübeck). In letter No. 8, Carl Nordenfalk quotes a statement of J. Leclerc in 1898: What fascinated him in the first instance was the delicate nature of the theme and then the effect of the red on the child's sick flesh against the mother's clothes. (Apropos the Munch exhibition,* Konstperspektiv, *Annual Issue 3, 1947, pp. 3-*

20 *Cf. Pola Gauguin, (Aschehoug, 1933) p. 15; and J. P. Hodin,* Edvard Munch, *(London, 1972) pp. 34-5.*

21 *Regarding 'fru Heiberg', see Trygve Nergaard,* Refleksjon og visjon *(1968) No. 163. See also p. 77. The material is to be found in E.M. 1. OKK 2761 and 2781—d. Nergaard has identified the pseudonym 'fru Heiberg', who plays a large part in Munch's notes about this early period, as Milly (Emilie) Ihlen (1865-1936), who married Dr Carl Thaulow, brother of the painter, as early as 1881. She divorced him in 1891 and in the same year married the actor Ludvig Bergh.*

22 *See Nergaard, p. 78.*

23 *Undated note by Munch at Munch-Museet, written on the back of a letter with the designation L'art Cosmopolite, Paris.*

Page 55: **Chapter 4: THE NATURALIST**

Text 33 According to Thiis, (1933), p. 78, the six others were: Halfdan Strøm, Jørgen Sørensen, Thorvald Torgersen, Harald Bertrand (Hansen), Lorentz Norberg, Andreas Singdahlsen. Boe (1970) p. 67, mentions also Kalle Løchen and Oscar Thue (1962) mentions in addition Schjefte, Colditz and Macody Lund.

34 The studio was on the fourth floor of the building, 'Pultosten', directly opposite the Storting (Parliament).

35 Thiis (1933), p. 78.

36 Undated letter, Munch to Thiis OKK. These letters were written in 1933 when Thiis was writing the biography. See Thiis, (1933) pp. 80-1.

37 See text p. 46, text note 29.

38 *Fam. brev.* No. 43.

39 *Verdens Gang,* 27.4.1889.

40 *Verdens Gang,* 27.4.1889.

41 *Verdens Gang,* 27.11.1891.

42 *Verdens Gang,* 27.11.1891.

43 *Fam. brev.,* No. 53, 18.7.1889, from Inger to Karen Bjølstad.

44 'Last year the same painter entertained us with an interior showing, a seamstress sitting half-dressed on an unmade bed and pulling on

her stockings.' SS in *Aftenposten* (5.11.1885). The picture was painted at Thaulow's Friluftsakademi (Open Air Academy) at Modum.

Quotations   1 Livs, p. 2. Warnemünde 1907–8.
2 Thaulow, I Kamp og Fest *(1908), p. 146.*
3 *Munch to JT, undated letter, probably 1933.*

Page 57:
Text   45 *Morgenbladet*, 4.11.1884.
46 Thaulow's mother, Nina, was the daughter of Jacob Munch and Emerenze Barcley. See Boe (1970) p. 50.
47 Håkon Kongsrud *Modum in our Pictorial Art* (Modum i malerkunsten vår, Drammen, 1954). Off-print of *Drammen Museum's Year Book 1948–53),* p. 110. Kongsrud names the young painters who visited the open air academy. Among them are several of the group who rented the studio opposite the Storting. It is obvious from *Fam. brev.* No. 45 that he worked and was happy and contented with the Dedichen family. That Gunnar Heiberg, too, was happy there emerges from an article in *Dagbladet* (3.12.1883) by H from Modum: 'We spend the evenings either at home or with a hospitable local family, a broad-minded and charming family. Broad-minded even when the children are downstairs.' Jensen-Hjell has painted a picture of this charming home: *Doktorgården på Modum (1887).* Privately owned. Plate 76 of Line Dedichen was also drawn here at Modum in 1884.
48 Among others Gustav Wentzel—*Fam. brev.* No. 40: 'Thaulow has provided him with the money for it.' (1882)
49 Gauguin's wife, Mette Gad, was the sister of Thaulow's first wife, Ingeborg.
50 *Fam. brev.* No. 44, 5.3.1884.
51 Thiis (1933), p. 104.
52 *Aftenposten*, 5.11.1885.

Quotations   4 *Munch to JT, undated letter, probably 1933.*
5 *CK, Verdens Gang, 27/11/1891.*
6 *Munch to JT, draft letter, probably 1933.*
7 The Struggle for Existence *(Kampen for Tilvæ relsen, B.I. 1920, pp. 9–19).*
8 *Andreas Aubert in* Morgenbladet, *9/11/1886. Aubert (1851–1913) was art critic of* Morgenbladet *and* Aftenposten—*later of* Dagbladet. *He belonged very much to the older generation and had little understanding of the young Munch.*

Plate   69 Recently acquired by OKK in exchange for Munch graphic works. OKK 1111.

Page 59:
Text   53 There is only one letter from this stay in Paris (No. 46, 5.5.1885) which is not particularly informative.
54 At the Autumn Exhibition in Christiania in 1884. Two of them *Mette Gauguin* and *Basket of Flowers* are now in Nasjonalgalleriet.
55 *Morgenbladet* 16.10.1890. 'In Paris he has fallen for a new style which is represented at our exhibition by the French painter Bizarro (sic).' [Pissarro].

Quotations   9 *Fritz Thaulow to his relative Christian Munch. See* Fam. brev. *No. 44, 5/3/1884.*
10 *Fritz Thaulow in a controversy with Bjørnstjerne Bjørnson,* Dagbladet, *17/12/1891.*

Page 60:
Text   56 Bought by the German critic Julius Elias in 1892. The models for *Tête à tête* are probably Munch's sister Inger and the painter Jensen-Hjell.
57 This is the version which is today in Nasjonalgalleriet (pl. 74). Munch gave it to CK. From him it passed to the barrister, Harald Nørregaard and thence in 1931 to Nasjonalgalleriet.
58 The fire at Axel Thoresen's lodgings occurred between 1889 and 1893, although by 1929 he could not remember exactly when. See Ida Sherman, 'Edvard Munch og Felicien Rops', *K & K* (1976) pp. 243–58.
59 Nasjonalgalleriet 1885–6.
2. Göteborgs Museum, signed 'E.M.—1896'.
3. Thielska Galleriet, Stockholm, 1907.
4. Tate Gallery, London, 1907 (?). Removed from the Dresden Gallery during the Nazi period.
5. OKK 52. signed upper right: 'Edv. Munch 1926'.
6. OKK 51. signed upper right: 'E. Munch', but no date. Probably 1927.
60 See p. 63, quotation 16.
61 In *Norges Billedkunst*, (Gyldendal, Oslo, 1951), pp. 374–6.
62 *Morgenbladet*, 28.10.1886.
63 *Morgenbladet*, 28.10.1886.
64 The problems regarding the date of this painting are discussed *inter alia* by Ida Sherman, *K & K* (1976).

Quotations   11 *Munch to JT, probably 1933.*
12 *Livs. tilbl., p. 9.*
13 *Livs. tilbl., p. 9.*
14 *HJ in* Dagen, *20/10/1886.*
15 *Andreas Aubert in* Morgenbladet, *9/11/1886.*

Page 63:
Text   65 K & K (1963) reproduces a photograph from the Munch exhibition in the Equitable Palace 1892. It is not easy to see from the photograph what Munch's repeat version looked like, but it is not identical with the painting in Nasjonalgalleriet, which, according to JT, was done in 1894–5. (Catalogue so dated.)
66 In *Impressionisten* No. 1, (1886).
67 Munch to Thiis, 1933. See pp. 48–9, quotation 10.
68 Thiis (1933), p. 137. Gierløff (1953). p. 56. Also: Axel Romdal 'Edvard Munch som expressionist', *Tidskrift för Konstvetenskap* (Journal of Art Studies). (1947) p. 169. Swedish.
69 Jan Thurmann Moe has drawn the attention to the fact that this picture is painted over another. There was a figure in front of Laura and another on the steps. But Nergaard is quite right when he says that the omission of the two figures creates a greater tension. *Refleksjoner*, (1968), p. 22.
70 C. Krohg, *Kunstnere*, Series 1892, p. 24.
71 Ingrid Langaard (1960), p. 18 ff. discusses in greater detail what Munch might have seen in 1885.
72 His protest in *Dagbladet* 16.12.1892. Thaulow answers him, 17.12.1891. Munch responds, 4.1.1897. See also *Fam. brev.* No. 119, 'B's article was disgusting'.

Quotations   16 *See* Colour in Print *(Farge på trykk, Cat. No. 5, 1968, No. 88).*
17 *Munch to Ingeborg Motzfeldt Løchen, 3/1/1937.* Vennene*, p. 68.*

Page 64:
Text   73 CK took the first version of *The Sick Child.* Werenskiold bought *Inger on the Beach* and Thaulow bought *Morning.* We might add that Ludvig Meyer bought *Girl Kindling the Stove.* In the summer of 1891 Krohg painted Munch in grisaille (now in Nasjonalgalleriet) for use together with an interview which appeared in 1892 in *Norsk kunstnere.* Oscar Thue dealt with the relationship in 'E.M. og Christian Krohg', *K & K* (1973), pp. 237–56. He also discusses the very difficult relations between Munch and CK at a later stage in their lives.
74 Trygve Tveteraas discusses public attitudes of the eighties. 'Publikum i åttiårene' *Santider*, (1932) pp. 1–15.

Page 67: **Chapter 5: 1899– A YEAR OF DECISION**

Text   75 These included Heyerdahl, Krohg, Amaldus Nielsen and C. Skredsvig.
76 He received 1.500 kr.
77 In the Studentersamfunnet's (Student Assoc.) small hall in Universitetsgaten, 20th April–12th May.
78 These literary and artistic movements are discussed in Chapter VI.
79 *Morgenbladet* 20.10.1889.
80 *Aftenposten* 15.10.1889. See also p. 73, quotation 4.

Quotations   1 *OKK 2770 4/2/1890.*
2 *Livs. tilbl., p. 10.*
3 *The full text with deletions is to be found in Heller (1969), p. 75. Because of the type of paper, he dates this note December 1889.*

Plates   79 The best known version of *Night in St Cloud* is in Nasjonalgalleriet and dates from 1890. A third version is privately owned. There is also an etching, OKK G/r 12. At the Munch-Museet there is a draft letter in which Munch writes to his friend Aase Carlsen Nørregaard (probably in February): 'I did not like Paris at all . . . so I moved down here to St. Cloud—where it is so beautiful.' Later he writes of how he 'sits by the window and admires the scene outside in the moonlight and of how in the semi-darkness of the room the moon throws a clear bluish rectangle on the floor'.
80 Léon Bonnat's studio in March 1890—according to Håkon Kongsrud *Modrum in malerkunsten vår*, 1954, p. 85. At that time Munch had left Bonnat. Kongsrud gives the following names: (foreground from the left) Gudmund Stenersen, Joyeaux, Jørgen Sørensen, (standing from the left) Sverre Ihle, Anders Kongsrud, Valentin Kielland, Bouvet (with cap). Karl Konow refers to Bonnat's school in 'The Artist's Life in Paris', (Kunstnerliv i Paris *Aftenposten*, 16.10.1926): 'We Norwegians were most interested in Edvard Munch. At that time he was already a genius from whom we expected great things. Everything he produced we admired.'

Page 70:
Text   81 *Edvard Munch*, (Oslo, 1933), p. 74.
82 'On the Occasion of E.M.'s Exhibition', (I anledning av Edvard Munchs utstilling, *Dagbladet*, 19.5.1889).
83 The State Scholarship for pictorial artists—1.500 kr. He was granted

the same sum in 1890, and on the third occasion when he was awarded the scholarship, he received 1.000 kr. In making the award to Munch the majority found 'nothing to prevent it in an exceptional case and with regard to an exceptional talent'. See Bjørnson's protest, p. 82, quotation 6.

84 See e.g. *Fam. brev.*, Nos. 51 and 53.

85 Munch himself relates that he painted this picture for a shoemaker in exchange for a pair of boots. See the 'journal of the Grand Hotel waiters'. Tankard (*Kruset*, 1928, p. 13.)

86 Kalle Løchen and Valentin Kielland. See *Fam. brev.* No. 54, 9.10.1889. 'Presumably we start tomorrow at Bonnat's studio'.

87 Léon Bonnat (1833–1922) taught several Norwegian painters. I. Langaard (1960), p. 96, names *inter alia*: Harriet Backer, Heyerdahl, Asta Nørregaard and Skredsvig. At a later stage: Kalle Lochen, Wentzel and Werenskiold. Bonnat was a much sought after portrait painter.

Page 72:
Text 88 Puvis de Chavannes (1824–98). This great French painter was not unknown in Norway. This is clear from a painting by Jensen-Hjell which depicts Kalle Løchen sitting under a large copy (tapestry?) of Chavannes' *Sacred Forest*. Jensen-Hjell's picture was painted in 1886 and is now in Nasjonalgalleriet.

89 *Fam. brev.*, No. 67, 7.12.1889. But by 2.1.1890 he had already moved to St. Cloud outside Paris, *Fam. brev.*, No. 73.

90 Emanuel Goldstein (1862–1921) Danish poet who wrote a few volumes of verse under the pseudonyms Alexander Hertz and Hugo Falck. His collection of poems *Alruner* ('alrune' means mandrake) was published in 1892, as 'Psychological Poems. Second Edition', under his own name. EG wrote to Munch, (12.12.1891) 'Do you think you could be bothered to draw me a vignette for the cover?' Munch took on the job. That Munch admired EG emerges from many statements and he wrote to EG, 20.2.1892, in connection with the vignette: 'I cannot be other than happy and proud that my name should be associated with a book which is one of the very few I have been able to enjoy—one of the few books that I added at once to my little library, which consists of your book, the Bible, Hans Jæger and Raskolnikow.' EG wrote, 15.7.1892: 'There are so many things on the tip of my tongue which I would love to talk to you about . . . When I hear from you I know once again that there are fellow beings in the world and that living is worthwhile.' The correspondence between Munch and EG is at Munch-Museet.

Page 73:
Text 91 See note 93 below. Munch writes 20.2.1902: 'If we made up our minds to publish together a volume of our thoughts and moods— with drawings—it might be the beginning of a literary monthly!' EG published some of his aphorisms in Ove Rode's paper, *København*, (Feb. 8th and 20th 1892). See EG to Munch when he suggests that Munch should do the same: 'He (Ove Rode) will pay at least 10 kr a letter. That is a higher rate than he usually pays. If you could put together ten pieces that would be a hundred kroner which is after all worth having.' Nergaard (1975), p. 18, has given some of G's aphorisms which are clearly related to Munch's concept of art.

92 Munch to Hoppe, 5.3.1929. See Hoppe (1939), p. 18.

93 Munch to Goldstein, 8.2.1892. 'All those splendid realistic notions we both had in Paris then . . . All the phonographic reproductions of scenes . . . which were so well thought out, will they ever be used? You must have quite a big pile of them, you too. I suppose it is the same for you as for me and my painting. The possibility of getting rid of realism altogether is not in our power . . .' In a later, undated, letter Munch writes: 'Have you given up thinking of our plan—to produce a small literature-art publication?'

94 Jæger not only inspired Munch in his writings but also in his peculiarities of spelling.

95 See p. 74, quotation 10. Extract from Munch's *Manifesto*, 1889.

Quotations 4 *Aftenposten*, 5/10/1889.
5 *CK in* Verdens Gang, *27/11/1891. See continuation of quotation 32 p. 96: 'Out in the still water . . .'.*
6 See also Dagbladet, *27/11/1891.*
7 Verdens Gang, *27/11/1891.*
8 Livs. tilbl., *p. 8.*
9 *EG to Munch, 15/7/1892.*

Page 74:
Quotations 10 *This comment was written on the back of pl 85 and was probably made in 1889–90. When Munch published* Livs. tilbl. *in 1929, he used this old drawing and made the related 'A portrayal of the Origin of the* Frieze of Life *(Avbildet Livsfrisens tilbl., p. 5, OKK T. 363). See chp 1 quotation note 3, which gives the most important literature on the dating of this comment. The 'manifesto' should more correctly be referred to as 'thoughts' from 1889 recalled later in life.*
11 *Hamsun,* Samtiden, *(1890) p. 333.*

12 *Franz Servaes was one of the four authors who published* Das Werk des Edvard Munch *(1894). See Przybyszewski (1894). This quotation is from p. 53. Servaes also wrote an autobiographical novel,* Gährungen. *He used pseudonyms—to some extent Norwegian names. Servaes himself stands for Herbrand; Munch stands for Sigurd Björn; Przybyszewski stands for Dr Spiridon.*

Plate 88 Munch made several portraits of Emanuel Goldstein. OKK 271—273 —273 and 732.

Page 76:
Text 96 James Abbott McNeill Whistler (1834–1903). According to Ingrid Langaard (1960) p. 52, Whistler had two portraits in the Salon of 1885 which Munch visited. He was also represented at the Paris World's Fair of 1889. With regard to Whistler's influence on Norwegian art, see Østby (1934) p. 52 ff.

97 Vilhelm Krag: 'The river flows so slowly . . .' VK also wrote a poem to another of Munch's pictures, *Sunset Mood. Dagbladet* 19.9.1892.

Quotation 13 Livs. tilbl., *p. 12. See also pp. 70–1, 1.43.*

Page 79: **Chapter 6: FACE TO FACE WITH A NEW ERA**

Text 98 G. Lafenestre in 'Les Peintres étrangers à l'Exposition Universelle de 1889. *Artistes et Amateurs*, (Paris).

99 See I. Langaard (1960), p. 419, note 14. She quotes several critics who wrote about the Norwegian painters.

100 Charles Baudelaire (1821–67). His volume of poems *Les Fleurs du Mal* was published in 1857 and CB was prosecuted on account of the impropriety of some of the poems. CB meant a great deal to the Symbolists and is regarded as their first theorist. There is an obvious affinity between CB and Munch and it was no accident that the painter of *angst* was commissioned by M. Piat, chairman of the association Les Cents Bibliophiles, in 1867 to illustrate *Les Fleurs du Mal*. He died, however, in the same year and Munch's work came to a standstill. There are few drawings at Munch-Museet which are associated with Baudelaire's poems. See Johan H. Langaard, *OKK Year Book 1952-59*, pp. 13–18, where two of B's poems are reproduced with Munch's drawings.

101 Stéphane Mallarmé (1842–98) also belonged to the Symbolist group. His aesthetic theories greatly influenced their conception of art. Two years before Mallarmé died Munch made a lithograph (Pl. 93) and an etching (OKK G/r 164) of him. See quotation 4, p. 82 and note 4. Munch's association with these two poets shows how closely he was involved with the artistic problems of the Paris of the time.

102 Paul Verlaine (1844–96) was the pioneer of Symbolism. His poems, like those of Mallarmé, have a distinctive melodious quality.

103 On the other hand the works of Maurice Maeterlinck (1862–1949) who was of the same age as Munch were closer to the perceptions of a visual artist. Contemporary critics were aware of the affinity between Munch and the Belgian poet. For instance, Edouard Gérard wrote an article in *La Presse* (May, 1897) by which Munch set great store. Gérard says: 'I am bound to put these two names together. To me the similarities between them are strikingly obvious.' Munch's friend, Walter Leistikow, writing in *Freie Bühne* (1893) said of Maeterlinck: 'I know of nobody who paints better than this poet'. Munch's friend, Hans Dedekam, wrote an excellent little article in which he also pointed out the likenesses between the poet and the painter 'Edvard Munch', *K & K* (*Studies and Monographs*, 1909). See also Nergaard (1968) p. 37 ff. A letter from the Danish translator Anna Mohr (3.1.1894) shows that Munch had considered illustrating Maeterlinck's *Pélleas et Mélisande*: 'If you do get down to the illustrations will you please let me see as soon as you have worked something out.' Nothing came of these illustrations either. Milly Bergh who was a friend of Munch's youth and the model for Fru Heiberg in Munch's novel fragment, translated the play into Norwegian in 1909.

Quotations 1 Violet Book, *OKK 1760, Nice, Jan. 1892.*
2 Violet Book, *OKK 1760, Nice, Jan. 1892.*

Plate 91 See *Fam. brev.*, no. 113, postmark 25.4.1891. 'I am living in a beautiful little room with a balcony. Address: Rue Lafayette 49.' In his next letter he writes that he is wandering round the galleries. Here he may have seen, as Heller points out, the Van Gogh memorial exhibition. See Heller, *The Scream*, (London, 1973) p. 62. Heller also draws attention to the similar perspectives in *Rue Lafayette* and *The Scream*.

Page 80:
Text 104 Jean Moréas (1856–1910) published the Symbolists' *Manifesto*, 18th Sept. 1886.

105 Gauguin. It is not certain whether Munch knew Gauguin as early as 1889. Henri Dorra, however, has pointed to several facts which indicate that this is probable. See HD's article 'Munch, Gauguin and

the Norwegian Painters in Paris' *Gazette des Beaux Arts*, (Nov. 1976), pp. 175–9. As mentioned on p. 59, Munch had certainly seen pictures by G in Norway in 1884. (The reference here is to *Paul Gauguin, not Pola, his son*.)

106 Nabi . . . See text note 2. The *Nabis Manifesto, 1890*. Werner Haftmann, *Malerei im 20 Jahr.* (Munich, 1952), p. 56 ff.

107 Gustave Moreau (1826–98) was from 1892 a professor at the École des Beaux Arts and as a teacher he had a great influence upon Fauve painters such as Matisse and Rouault. It is worth noting that when Gustav Vigeland visited Moreau's gallery in January 1901 he was deeply moved. See letter No. 23 to Larpent in Ragna Stang's *Gustav Vigeland: Om Kunst og Kunstner*, (Oslo, 1955), p. 22.

108 The ancient Rosicrucian Society was revived by Joséphin Peladan, an eccentric gentleman who practised occultism and opened a new salon in Durand-Ruel's gallery. The artist members of the Nabis gathered here. We must bear in mind that Munch had an introduction from Fritz Thaulow to the Belgian artist Fernand Khnopff who belonged to the Peladan Circle. Thaulow had met FK at Les Vingt exhibition in 1885. We do not know if Munch called on FK.

109 The programme was published in *La Plume* 15.3.1892.

Page 81:
Text
110 Frederick Deknatel, *Edvard Munch*, (New York, 1950), p. 19.

Page 82:
Text
111 *Violet Book*. OKK 2760.

112 Bought at Autumn Exhibition, 1891. Cat. No. 118.

113 Christian Skredsvig (1854–1924) wrote about his associations with Munch in *Days and Nights among Artists* (Dage og Nætter blandt Kunstnere, Oslo, 1943, pp. 147–54).

114 There are two versions of this theme, *Gaming Tables at Monte Carlo* in OKK nos. 50 and 266. A third version is privately owned.

115 See Ole Sarvig, 'Edvard Munchs grafik'. *Stranden. Louisiana Revy*, (16th Year of Issue, no. 1, Oct. 1975) p. 12.

116 Skredsvig (1943) p. 152.

117 See Jan Askeland 'Angstmotivet i Edvard Munchs kunst', *Kunsten idag*, No. 4 (Oslo, 1966), pp. 5–57, with an English translation.

Quotations 3 *Violet Book, 30/8/1891*.

4 *Letter from Mallarmé to Munch, 15/6/1896. See chp. 6 text note 101.*

5 *Munch to EG, 22/1/1891.*

6 *Bjørnstjerne Bjørnson in* Dagbladet, *16/12/1891.*

7 *Fritz Thaulow in* Dagbladet, *17/12/1891. Munch put his case 4/1/1892.*

8 *Violet Book 2760, 8/1/1892.*

9 *Ibid.*

Page 84:
Text
118 *The Exhibition at Tostrup's Building*, 14th Sept.–4th Oct. 1892. Fifty paintings; ten studies and drawings.

Quotation 10 *Julius Meier-Graefe, quoted from Erich Büttner*, Postscript to Thiis (Etterord til Jens Thiis) 1934 (Der leibhaftige Munch) *p. 88. Cf. also Julius Meier-Graefe*, Geschichte neben der Kunst, *(Berlin, 1933) pp. 146–56. This book contains a section on Ducha's husband Stachu, pp. 136–45.*

Page 86:
Text
119 P. 174, quotation 6.

120 See p. 73. Also Brenna (1976) II, p. 201.

121 See p. 73, text notes 93 and 94.

122 See Heller 'Affaeren Munch', *K & K* (1969) pp. 175–91. See also 'Der Bruch innerhalb der Künstlerschaft Berlins', *Freisinnige Zeitung VIII*, no. 270, (30.11.1892).

123 *Aftenposten*, 14.9.1892.

124 *Aftenposten*, 14.9.1892, p. 95, quotation 28.

125 *Morgenbladet*, 14.9.1892.

126 *Verdens Gang*, 15.9.1892.

127 See, e.g. *Aftenposten* 9.10.1892. 'The two champions who set us all rocking with laughter.'

128 Johan Rohde (1856–1935). See Henning Gran 'Two Letters from Munch to a Danish Painter' (To brev fra E.M. til en dansk maler, *Verdens Gang* 26.8.1950). The first letter was written 8.2.1893, just after the exhibition in Berlin and before the Munch exhibition in Copenhagen with which Rohde was going to help him. In the next letter, undated but written at roughly the same time, Munch wrote: 'At the moment I am working on some studies for a series of pictures. As they are now they are something of a puzzle . . . I think when they are all put together they will be more easily understood . . . it is going to be about love and death.'

129 Adelsteen Normann's letter is dated 24.9.1892. In his article 'Affaeren Munch', *K & K* (1969) pp. 175–91, Reinhold Heller has written both lucidly and informatively. Here the reader will find references to contemporary newspapers and journals. The account here is based on Heller's article.

Page 86:
Quotations 11 *Munch in* Kristiania Dagsavis *(25/6/1901) on the occasion of Dagny Przybyszewska's death. For further details on the couple see chp. 6 text note 146.*

12 *Undated draft letter to a lawyer. Munch-Museet. Copy in sister Inger's own hand. See pl. 168 in which the woman's face is reminiscent of Dagny Juell. This letter to a lawyer could be connected with a letter which district medical officer H. Juell addressed to Munch on 10/10/1895. Munch had portrayed the features of the two Juell sisters in a number of his works and Dr Juell wrote: 'It was with great interest, but I must admit with mixed feelings, that I recently made the round of your exhibition at Blomkvist's. The place was full of people but what an ignorant crowd they were! . . . If I have in fact correctly interpreted the series, A Woman who Loves, then quite frankly I do not understand what possessed you to put it on public display in Christiania . . . Could it perhaps be that there is a quite different interpretation of these pictures of women surrounded by "fœtuses"?! Forgive me . . . that I ask you to do us the great favour of removing our daughter Ragnhild's picture from the exhibition! I appreciate that you yourself and others with you find a meaning in this picture quite different from the one I see. For me it was nothing other than a painful experience to see my daughter's features reproduced in such a context.' See Fam. brev. No. 159. It is not clear to which picture Dr Juell is referring.*

13 *Przybyszewski*, Underveis *(On the Way, p. 65).*

Page 88:
Text
130 See *Kunstchronik* N.F. IV, (1892/3), p. 76.

Plate
105 There is a related picture in the Museum of Fine Arts, Boston. *The Voice* was originally titled *A Summer Night's Dream*. Franz Servaes has described it, certainly after consulting Munch, in *Das Werk des Edvard Munch*, (Berlin, 1894), p. 47. This book was the first monograph on Munch and it contains four contributions from his friends Przybyszewski, who wrote the foreword, Willy Pastor, Franz Servaes and Julius Meier-Graefe. In this picture, too, Munch uses the frontal pose in order to make an impact on the viewer. The young girl is addressing us directly. See Johan H. Langaard, 'Edv. Munchs formler', *Samtiden*, (Oslo, 1948).

Page 89:
Text
131 Quoted in *Kunstchronik*, N.F. IV (1892/3) p. 74.

Page 90:
Text
132 Anton von Werner (1843–1915). Chairman of the Art Assoc. 1887–95. Among Munch's supporters he was known as 'der Uniformt und Stiefelmaler' (Uniform and Boots Painter).

133 *National-Zeitung*. (6.11.1892) See *Beiblatt*. (Supplement).

134 Rosenberg. *Kunstchronik*, pp. 74–5.

135 Theodor Wolff 'Bitte ums Wort'. *Berliner Tageblatt* XXI, 12.11.1892 and 16.11.1892. The friendship between Munch and TW endured for thirty years. He died in a concentration camp during the war.

136 Walter Leistikow, *Freie Bühne*, 15.12.1892 under the pseudonym of Walter Selber, (printed as 'Edvard Munch i Berlin', *Samtiden* 1893, pp. 38–43). WL belonged to an opposition group of artists, 'Die Elf', who wanted to rejuvenate the conventional art of Berlin. Munch became his friend and at home with WL and his Danish wife, Munch met people such as Liebermann and Corinth, as well as a number of authors. The painter Ludvig von Hofmann was also a member of 'Die Elf' and his friendship with Munch lasted until the thirties. Hofmann visited Munch at Ekely in 1927. For Leistikow see Julius Elias, *W.L. Die Kunst* (1902–3) VII, p. 345. 'Die Elf' held their exhibitions at E. Schulte's salon. Schulte was a champion of the young artists and Munch also exhibited there.

137 See *Aftenposten*, 12.11.1892, and also a number of minor articles in November including 'Edvard Munch og Berlinerkunstnerne', *Verdens Gang*, 14.11.1892, and *Dagbladet*, 16th, 21st and 30th Nov. and 4th Dec. 1892.

138 Max Kruse's description is given in the postscript by E. Büttner to the abridged German edition of Thiis: *Edvard Munch og haus Samtid* (1934) pp. 83 ff.

Quotations 14 *Adolf Paul. Quoted from Büttner: Thiis (1934) op. cit., p. 87. Also catalogue, Basel, 1965. Munch treated the theme of* Puberty *a number of times as a painting, lithograph and etching:*
1. The first version from 1886 is lost. It was destroyed in a fire at student Axel Thoresen's lodgings between 1889 and 1893. We do not know precisely what this picture looked like, but according to Thoresen's memory of it in 1929 (letter at Munch-Museet) it must have resembled the version in Nasjonalgalleriet. The first version was shown at the Munch exhibition April–May 1889.
2. Painted in Berlin probably January–March 1894 (Paul refers to the dazzling rays of the spring sun as Munch painted), now in Nasjonalgalleriet. Przybyszewski does not mention Puberty *in his article* Freie Bühne, February 1894, *while Meier-Graefe uses the title* Pubertät *(Das Werk, 1894, note p. 90).*

3. *Lithograph 1894 Sch. 8—OKK G/1 189. This is the first lithograph Munch made—i.e. at about the same time as the painting. See pl. 150.*
4. *Painting OKK. M 281. This is a later version and is unlikely to have been painted in 1893 as is often stated e.g. in Munch-Museet's latest catalogue, Stockholm 1977, No. 20.*
5. *Etching 1902 Sch. 164—OKK. 74. At Night.*
6. *Painting OKK. M 450 c. 1914.*
7. *Painting c. 1914. Privately owned. Not really a depiction of puberty, but a naked girl in the same pose on the edge of a bed. See also Ida Sherman 1976, pp. 243-58. With regard to whether Munch had seen Félicien Rops' etching* Le plus bel amour de Don Juan, *made in 1886, it is believed that Munch was not acquainted with it when he made his first version. On the other hand we must assume that he knew Rops well in 1894 because he was a popular figure. It would be very strange if Przybyszewski, a great admirer of Rops, had not shown Munch the etchings in his possession. See Svenæus* Das Universum der Melancholie, *(Lund, 1968) p. 55 and note p. 231.*

15 *Munch in* Tree of Knowledge, *OKK 2547. See also 2782 ah. In* Pan *(April–May 1895), there is a closely related drawing by F. Khnopff.*
16 *Munch and the Finnish artist Akseli Gallen-Kallela (Axel Galleé, 1865-1931) held an exhibition together in March 1895 at Baroccio's in Berlin. Information from Aune Lindström. See Ingrid Langaard (1960), p. 423, note 73.*
17 *T 2748. See also Schreiner,* Vennene, *p. 21, and p. 24, quotation 1.*
18 *Mikita's reply in Przybyszewski's* Over bord, *p. 17. The Mikita of the book has certain resemblances to Munch, but Dagny Juell did not agree: 'I find it quite incomprehensible that a book by Stachu should upset you. Perhaps the reason is that there is a character in the book* Over Bord *who is a painter. The person concerned is about as different from you as it is possible for two human beings to be even if we all are created in the image of God—but the evil of this world is great beyond measure.'* Fam. brev., *No. 153.*
19 *Munch c. 1905. See* Tegn. Kat., *p. 10. In the swirling art nouveau sky of the painting* The Scream *in Nasjonalgalleriet pl. 107 there is an inscription: 'Can only have been painted by a madman.' See text note 172.*
20 *C. Skredsvig (1943), p. 152.*
21 *Heller has written a whole book about this picture:* The Scream *(London, 1973). In the appendix, pp. 103-9, he gives all the versions, in Norwegian (8), English and German of the text which Munch attached to this picture. The version given here is taken from* Livs. tilbl., *p. 12. See also versions T 2760 and 2547. Heller also refers to Søren Kierkegaard,* The Concept of Angst *(Begrepet Angst).*
22 *This note by Munch is taken from I. Langaard (1960), p. 286. It was given in* La Revue Blanche *(1st Dec. 1895) with a drawing of the lithograph* The Scream.
23 *Vilhelm Krag in* Dagbladet.

Plate **107** *The Scream*: version at the Nasjongalleriet. Signed lower left 'E. Munch 1893'. Other versions: Versions OKK M122b: coloured chalk on cardboard, with a picture of the *Vampire* on the verso. This cardboard has now been split. Version OKK M 514: oil on cardboard. Also a version in pastel. Signed lower left 'E. Munch 1895'. Now privately owned in Norway. Version OKK G/L 193: (Sch. 32) 1895, pl. 112. With regard to the inscription on Nasjonalgalleriet version, . . . painted by a madman', see pp. 106-7, note 11.

Page 93:
Text 139 *Berliner Tageblatt.* See p. 98, quotation 41.
140 Quoted in *Kunstchronik,* 'Münchener Neueste Nachrichten' XLV no. 522 (15.11.1892) and XLV no. 534 (22.11.1892). See also *Freisinnige Zeitung* VII no. 276 (13.11.1892).
141 The Munch exhibition was not the cause of the conflict in the art world. Rather it was the last straw. The three professors Franz Skarbina, Hugo Vogel and August von Heyden resigned from the Academy in protest. See *Kunstchronik*, N.F. IV (1892-3), p. 363.
142 See for instance *Das Atelier* (Jan. 1893): 'Munch has woven a martyr's halo for his young head and he uses this fortunate chance to appear at the exhibition and parade before the public in all his glory'.
143 Walther Rathenau bought the picture for 100 marks. He wrote to Munch (25.7.1893) to ask if he might acquire more later. He had seen Munch's pictures at the 'Freie Berliner Kunstausstellung' and would very much like to meet him. Munch painted two portraits of R in 1907, see pl. 291. Several letters from R to Munch are in existence. Shortly before he was murdered in 1922, he invited Munch to visit him. On 27.6.1922 Munch attended a large protest demonstration in Frankfurt against the murder of Rathenau. See Count Harry Kessler, *Walther Rathenau,* (New York, 1930), pp. 356 and 368.
144 *Die Post* No. 153. (7.6.1893) carried a review by AR of Strindberg's and Munch's pictures at the 'Freie Berliner Kunstausstellung' or 'Salon des Zurückgewiesenen' (Salon of the Rejected): '. . . die öden

völlig unverständlichen Schmierereien des Herrn Munch . . . darf auch der Norweger (!) August Strindberg nicht fehlen, der leider nicht bloss dichtet, sondern sich auch als "hoffnungsvoller junger Maler" das Malen angewöhnt hat . . . Als malerische Kunstwerk betrachtet stehen sie doch etwas tiefer als die Farbenflecke Munchs, bei dem Herr Strindberg gelernt zu haben scheint . . .' (. . . the barrer and totally incomprehensible smudges of Herr Munch . . . are not lacking with the Norwegian (!) August Strindberg who unfortunately is not only a poet, but has taken up painting as "a promising young artist" . . . As works of pictorial art they are somewhat more meaningful than the smears of colour of Munch from whom Herr Strindberg appears to have learnt his craft . . .) See also Franz Servaes 'Von der "freien" Kunstausstellung' in *Die Gegenwart*, 43B no. 25. (1893), p. 398. FS writes extremely negatively about Strindberg and is somewhat disparaging on Munch: 'I know now what Munch can do and perhaps also what he cannot do. Now I would very much like to see what else he has learnt.' A year later FS was much more favourable to Munch in *Das Werk*. Jaro Springer (1856-1915), who later became famous as an art historian, was at that time an assistant in the printroom of the Berlin Museum. Under the signature 'Dr Relling' he wrote: '. . . as a painter the brilliant creator of Miss Julie is undoubtedly a dilettante'. *Kunst für Alle*, (1892-3), p. 314. Springer raised the question whether it was 'polite' to reject Strindberg's pictures, and referred to Goethe's many drawings, which were greatly prized in Weimar but not elsewhere. In no way did this diminish the fame of Goethe. Of Munch, Springer wrote: 'He has sent in two pastels, two good mannered pictures which are very different from the violent colour fantasies which offended the old gentlemen when they were put on exhibition.' FS thought that one of them, *Night in St. Cloud*, was a fine study in light and that to reject this picture was a 'wounding injustice'. FS praised Ludwig von Hofmann's poster, which incidentally, was banned for some time on moral grounds. It portrayed a youthful figure.

Page 94:
Text 145 Käthe Kollwitz (1867-1945). 'I was one of them,' she said when speaking of those whose rejected paintings were exhibited at the 'Salon der Zurückgewiesenen' in 1893. Dr Julius Elias—the translator of Ibsen—wrote of KK's pictures at this exhibition: 'Nearly everyone who has visited this exhibition has failed to notice a feminine talent. She can easily survive the ignominy of being rejected because success will surely come in the future.' Elias also pointed out that she had been influenced by Munch, *Die Nation* X 673, (1893). Isa Lohmann-Siems says in her catalogue of the exhibition in Hamburg, *Käthe Kollwitz in Ihrer Zeit*, 1967 that KK's etching *Junges Paar* of 1893 'in der Empfindung von Munch inspiriert ist' (is influenced by Munch in its sensitivity). Independently of I.L-S, Werner Schmidt said the same thing in a lecture to a conference at the Humboldt University 23.11.1967. He mentions it also in his article 'Zur Künstlerischen Herkunft von K.K.' *Year Book of the Staatl. Kunstsamml.,* (Dresden, 1968), pp. 83-90. We are reminded of Munch by the entry in KK's diary: 'I have never been able to carry out any work coolly. On the contrary it is done, so to speak, with my own blood. Anyone who looks at my works must be able to sense that.' *Tagebücher und Briefe*, (1948) p. 137.

Quotations 24 *Gustav Schiefler in 1893.*
25 *Obstfelder in* Samtiden, *1896. In Jæger's book* Sick Love, *there is a description related to* The Scream *(Pax edition) p. 90.*
26 *This quotation is given in French by Sch. to the woodcut* Angst, *pl. 110. See Schiefler,* Verzeichnis des graphischen Werkes E.M.'s bis 1906, *(Oslo, 1974) p. 65, No. 62.*
27 *Munch to RH, 5/3/1929. Hoppe (1939). In the same letter Munch refers to Strindberg's article in* La Revue Blanche *(1896): You will find here poems in prose to the pictures* The Scream, Vampire, The Kiss, Woman in Extasy *and* Jealousy. *Heller (1973) p. 68, points out that Munch's copy of* Begrepet Angst *(Kierkegaard) of 1920 has its pages carefully cut.*

Page 95:
Text 146 Dagny Juell (1867-1901). Daughter of District Medical Officer Juell at Kongsvinger. She came to know Munch when she arrived in Berlin in the spring of 1893 to study music. She married, as early as September the same year, the Polish author Stanislaw Przybyszewski (1868-1928). They had a son, Zenon, and a daughter, Iwa, who are still living. The married couple became close friends of Munch. Several people have hinted that there was an affair between Dagny Juell and Edvard Munch. It is true that she had affairs with both August Strindberg and the young Bengt Lidfors early in her stay in Berlin. There is, however, no proof either in writing, or by word of mouth, of any intimate relationship with Munch. The letters they exchanged give no hint of it either. The most recent writer to deal with this subject is Knut Heber: 'Dagny Juell—the woman who

released the artist in Munch during the years of struggle.' ('Dagny Juell. Utløseren av Edvard Munchs kunst i kampårene 1890–1908'. *K & K* 1977, pp. 1–15.) It seems to me that Heber (quite regardless of any affair) greatly exaggerates her influence on Munch as an artist in those eighteen years. Munch never made any secret of the fact that he was captivated by her charm and that he set store by her friendship. He acknowledges as we know, p. 86, quotation 12, that *Madonna* has a certain resemblance to 'fru Dagny'. There is no doubt at all that her features occur in several of his graphic works and the fact that he gave her husband the first coloured version of the lithograph, pl. 162 would surely indicate that he was friendly with them both. Munch is on the whole quite frank about his intimate relationships in his autobiographical notes. It is obvious however, from his portrait of Dagny, pl. 101 that he was aware of her erotic charm. He kept it all his life. There were certainly several members of the group who were attracted to her and possibly Gustav Vigeland was among them. There is not much we know about it. Vigeland smashed the bust he had made of her in Berlin in the spring of 1895. He had also made a bust of Munch. They lived in adjacent rooms in the same hotel and the fact that he smashed the two busts at the same time might indicate that there was an element of jealousy involved. On the other hand, Vigeland was by no means satisfied with the busts he made in Berlin and he destroyed several of them. 'The busts, I've destroyed them, both the one of Munch and the one of fru P.' Letter, 16.3.1895, to Larpent, No. 1137, Vigeland Museum. In another letter 7.9.1897, No. 1191 he says that he would make a new bust of Munch. Unhappily this was never done. When the news of Dagny's tragic death in Odessa reached Munch, he was profoundly moved and wrote a superb obituary for her, in *Kristiania Dagsavis* (25.6.1901). The article which Gierløff wrote in *Arbeiderbladet* as long afterwards as 10.3.1956 was surely based on the facts in Munch's article and suffused with Munch's warm affection and respect for this girl of his younger years. Gierløff's article is reproduced in the book by Dagny's and Stanislaw's son, Zenon P. Westrup, *Jag har varit in Arkadien, Natur och Kultur*, (Stockholm, 1975) reacted violently against all the gossip which was bandied about in the newspapers at the time of her death. The sister, Ragnhild Bäckström, wrote thanking Munch: 'You are the only one who has said anything good about her.' See *Fam. brev.*, No. 199, dated Djursholm 3.7.1901.

We cannot do more here than touch upon the considerable literature which has accumulated round the name of Dagny Juell Przybyszewska. It extends from Strindberg's slanderous attacks (reproduced in Erik Vendelfelt's study of Bengt Lidfors, Lund, 1962) to Martin Nag's many articles in the press and in *Samtiden* (1975 and 1976), where he deals very fully with her literary achievements and calls her 'a Norwegian Chekhov'. Even if the comparison is somewhat exaggerated, Nag is quite right in saying that she was an extremely gifted woman and in many ways a pioneer. Also worthy of mention is Sonja Hagemann's informative article 'Genienes inspiratrise', *Samtiden* (1963) pp. 655 ff. Munch's close friend, Przybyszewski edited, and wrote a section in, the first biography of Munch, *Das Werk des Edvard Munch* (1894) from which we have frequently quoted. He also wrote a book about Gustav Vigeland, *Auf den Wegen der Seele* (Berlin, 1897: dated Nov. 1895), and as well as a number of articles on both Munch and GV, he also wrote about them in *Erinnerungen an das literarische Berlin* (1965). In Poland there is much literature about S.P. In Norway, works about him include Stanislaw Sawichi, 'S.P. und Norvegen', *Edda*, year 21 B XXXIV (1934), and Ole Michael Selberg's study in *Samtiden* (1970) H. 2. Munch wrote about S.P. at his death, 'Min venn P'. *Oslo Aftenavis* no. 25, (30.1.1929); see quotation 38 pp. 98–9. This was published in *Pologne Litteraire* (15.12.1928). The Polish-Norwegian film *Dagny* produced by Haakon Sandøy portrays Ducha's and Stachu's dramatic marriage and the milieu in which they lived. Lise Fjeldstad conveyed beautifully Dagny's charm, but the film role gave her no opportunity of portraying Dagny as a significant personality and a serious author. The film made by the English director Peter Watkins is an interesting work of art, but it would be a mistake to believe that it gives an accurate picture of Munch. The doleful young man who played Munch undoubtedly looked like him, but what became of his charm, his self-irony and his witty repartee? The film also gave a totally false picture of the childhood home and family he was so proud of and to which he was closely attached. It is unthinkable that the rough-and-ready old father we saw in the film was the brother of that great genius P. A. Munch. But Mr. Watkins has certainly done his bit to stir up interest in Munch!

Quotation   *28* Aftenposten, *14/9/1892.*

Plate   **114** Nasjonalgalleriet version was a gift from Charlotte and Christian

Mustad 1970. Signed lower left 'E.M.', probably 1892. Other versions: Version OKK 58: signed upper right 'E. Munch 1891'. See pl. 83. Version OKK 33: an oil. Another oil, now privately owned, Norway. Version in Rasmus Meyers Samlinger, datable 1894–5. Signed lower left 'E. Munch'. Version OKK G/T 571: datable 1896. See pl. 179 and detail of variant pl. 180. Version OKK G/T 606: datable 1901.

Page 96:
Text
147 Ola Hansson (1860–1925), the Swedish poet who moved in the same circle, asserted in the women's journal *Framåt* as early as 1886 that 'a voyage of discovery should be made into the hidden and inaccessible regions of the human soul'. A year later he published his *Sensitiva amorosa* which was admired by the circle of friends. *An Essay on Love, Death and the Life Everlasting* (Uppsats om Kärleken, Döden och Det eviga Livet) by Bengt Lidfors was probably also one of the publications which inspired Munch at that time.

148 Richard Dehmel (1863–1920) symbolist author and poet. He wrote about Munch in *Pan* II (1895).

149 Akseli Gallen-Kallela (Axel Gallén) (1865–1931). Finnish painter who exhibited with Munch at Ugo Barocci's in Berlin 3rd–14th March, 1895. He painted a portrait of Munch which is now at the Ateneum in Helsinki.

150 Gustav Vigeland and Munch lived in adjacent rooms at the Stadt Köln Hotel, Mittelstrasse, during the winter and spring of 1895. Pål Hougen has pointed out to Dr Stang that there is a drawing among Munch's papers (OKK Tg 328) which portrays two men relaxed and smoking. One of them must be Obstfelder. The two clay models show that this must have been Vigeland's room. GV made in addition a mask-like portrait of Przybyszewski whose book was an extreme tribute to GV – 'the portrayer of the soul' . . . 'I will speak to one who is in a state of grace, one who has looked into the soul and found unspeakable secrets' . . . He wrote of the 'naked and until now undiscovered life of the inner mind which will now find full expression'. GV took the tribute with a grain of salt and wrote to Larpent, 8.7.1896 from Florence (1169): 'I knew well enough that if P should do a picture of me it would look more like a huge sexual organ than a complete human being. But the article has given me pleasure just the same. It probes into several matters and I think it is done with great ardour. As I read it I kept saying to myself "Damn it! This is the best thing I've read on art" and sitting here I still think that is true . . .' GV received recognition, however, from others in Berlin. His relief *Hell* was reproduced in *Pan*, see the amusing description in *Thiis* (1933), p. 221. Max Klinger was willing to pay 500 marks to have the work cast (Vigeland never received the money!) and Count Harry Kessler bought the group *Dans*. If GV had followed up his international success at that time, there is little doubt that he would have achieved fame earlier than Munch. See, for instance, Gallén-Kallela — *Vigeland is a great artist; Munch is not one yet*. It is well known however that he exhibited only reluctantly and he wrote later (an undated note on the back of a drawing of *The Fountain*): 'Ach, I nearly went down that slippery slope in 1895. Everything was set for me to do it although I was not even trying to put my things on show. The Polish author Przybyszewski wrote a book about me. Count Kessler bought one of my bronzes. Meier-Graefe was of the same mind and Liebermann was omnipotent. The first issue of *Pan* came out, etc., etc. But I withdrew (he went to Florence) and since 1895 I have kept my distance more so that now I scarcely know a single person even here in Kristiania.'

151 Hermann Schlittgen (1859–1930) he was a caricaturist in *Fliegende Blätter*. In his memoirs he wrote about Munch at the Hotel zum Elefanten in Weimar. See Büttner in *Thiis*, (1934) p. 92 ff. See pl. 123 and quotation 43, p. 100.

152 Count Harry Kessler. See p. 187 and pl. 242.

153 Thiis (1933), p. 324.

154 Strindberg arrived in Berlin on 1st October 1892. He was there for the Munch exhibition which created such a scandal. The two of them formed a wary kind of friendship which in fact lasted until they both moved to Paris. It was in these years that their European reputation was founded. We have already seen that they were both ruthlessly criticised for their pictures at the 'Salon der Zurückgewiesenen' in 1893. Munch painted his greatest Strindberg portrait for the re-opening of his exhibition this time in the Equitable Palace where the portrait was given the place of honour. In 1934 Munch presented the portrait to Nationalmuseum in Stockholm. The Austrian journalist Frida Uhl met both Munch and Strindberg at the home of the critic Julius Elias. She married Strindberg in the spring of 1893. After his marriage with Frida Uhl had broken up, Strindberg moved to Paris in the summer of 1894. Here he found a milieu which resembled that of the Zum Schwarzen Ferkel in Berlin, and he became drawn into the mental crisis described in his book *Inferno*. Munch arrived in Paris in the beginning of 1896 and

Strindberg wrote about his exhibition at the Galérie de l'Art Nouveau in the Nabi's journal *La Revue Blanche*. This extraordinary prose poem on Munch's paintings is not easy to make sense of. He addresses Munch as 'le peintre ésoterique de l'amour, de la jalousie, de la mort et de la tristesse'. Munch made his famous lithograph of Strindberg and wrote home in June: 'I have finished a lithograph of S.' *Fam. brev.* No. 182. At this time Strindberg's nerves were at breaking point and he heard voices in the next room: he imagined it was 'Popoffsky' (i.e. Przybyszewski) threatening his life. In January 1899, the fourth volume of the German journal *Quickborn* was published with a contribution by Strindberg and illustrations by Munch. After this they had little contact with each other. Munch wrote a short prose poem to Strindberg on his death in 1912. Among Munch's papers there was a manuscript in French of Strindberg's profoundly personal description of his relationship with Siri von Essen, *Defence plea of a Simpleton* (En dåres forsvarstale). This is a clear indication of how close the two artists were. See also, John Boulton Smith, 'August Strindbergs billedfantasi', *K & K*, (Oslo, 1970), and 'Strindberg's Visual imagination', *Apollo*. (London, Oct., 1970.)

155 Munch is the model for 'vakre Henrik' a Danish painter in *Inferno*. The friendship between Munch and Strindberg began in 1892 and lasted in Paris until 1897. See Göran Lundström, 'Edvard Munch i Strindbergs Inferno' *Ord och Bild* (1955). See also John H. Langaard, 'Om Edvard Munchs bekjentskap med August Strindberg', *Vinduet* no. 8, (1948). Also: Gösta Svenæus on Strindberg and Munch in 'Inferno' *K & K* (1969).

156 Frederick Delius (1862–1934). Delius and Munch probably first met at the beginning of the 1890s in Paris, where the composer knew many Norwegians. They maintained a lifelong friendship, keeping in contact in the worlds of Paris, Germany and Norway through which they both moved, and their last correspondence comes from the year of the composer's death. For an account of their relationship see John Boulton Smith, 'Edvard Munch og Frederick Delius' *K & K* (Oslo, 1965), and 'Portrait of a Friendship: Edvard Munch and Frederick Delius', *Apollo* (London, Jan. 1966). For an account of Munch, Delius and Strindberg in Paris, see Frederick Delius, 'Recollections of Strindberg', *The Sackbut*, (London, Dec. 1920), I No. 8. This article is reprinted in Peter Warlock, *Frederick Delius*, (revised ed., London, 1952), pp. 49–52. Delius recounts a visit to Strindberg which he made with Munch after which the dramatist sent Munch a postcard (July 1896) accusing the artist of attempting to kill him. A copy of the postcard is in Munch-Museet. Its text was published in *Strindbergs brev. XI, May 1895–November 1896*, (Bonniers, Stockholm 1969), p. 277, and in English translation in Lionel Carley (see below), p. 31. For Delius's connections with Norway and Norwegians, see Lionel Carley and Robert Threlfall—*Delius. A Life in Pictures*, (Oxford, 1977).

Quotations 29 *OKK 59.*
30 *OKK T 2782 r. See also similar entry 2782 bw.*
31 *See Nergaard (1968), p. 110, n. 44.*
32 *CK in* Verdens Gang, *27/11/1891. Continuation of quotation 5, p. 73.*
33 *Thiis (1933), pp. 182–3.*

Plate 115 There are five versions of the *Madonna* painting: Nasjonalgalleriet, Kunsthalle Hamburg, OKK M 68, and two privately owned versions. Also lithographs: OKK G-L 194 and 442. Etching: OKK G/r 15, see p. 136, pls. 161–4. In December 1893 the picture was called *Das Madonna Gesicht* (and is labelled d. in group 4: *Studie zu einer Serie* 'Die Liebe'). The title *Loving Woman* crops up in 1894. Two pictures were exhibited in the Berlin exhibition of 1895: no. 6 *Das liebende Weib* and no. 7 *Madonna*. Identification is uncertain and we have to reckon with at least one lost version. In *Das Werk*, p. 19, Przybyszewski describes the picture as 'eine Madonna im Hemde auf zerknitterten Laken mit dem Glorienschein des kommenden Geburtsmartyriums' ('a Madonna in an under-garment lying on crumpled sheets wearing the halo of the coming martyrdom of birth'). Servaes also discusses the picture in the same book, pp. 47–8. In *Aftenposten* (1895) H. Grosch compares Munch's pictures, especially the *Madonna*, with Hans Jaeger's *Sick Love*. The *Madonna* title is used by several contemporary artists both painters and writers: Baudelaire, Heiberg, Obstfelder, Bödtker, Jaeger and Krohg.

Page 98:
Text 157 This story is told, for instance, in Hodin 'Et møte med Edvard Munch', in *Konstrevy*, (1939).
158 *Quickborn* . . . See the cover design pp. 16–17, pl. 11. Torsten Svedfelt has written about *Quickborn* in *Bokvännen*, (1969), no. 3.
159 This story is told by Erich Büttner, among others in Thiis, (1934), p. 94.
160 Adolf Paul, *Min Strindbergsbok*, (Stockholm, 1930), p. 52.

161 Holger Drachmann (1846–1908) was brother-in-law to both Krohg and Thaulow and was closely associated with this Norwegian milieu. His *Berlinerbrev* (Berlin Letter) was printed in *Politiken* (24.5.1894). In addition to the lithograph, pl. 120, there is an oil painting, OKK 985.

Quotations 34 Samtiden *(1896)*.
35 *Tree of Knowledge, OKK T.*
36 *Przybyszewski in the foreword to* Das Werk des Edvard Munch *(1894)*.
37 *W. Leistikow in* Freie Bühne *(1892), pp. 1296–1300. This is quoted from the article in* Samtiden *(1893), p. 41.*
38 *Munch in* Oslo Aftenavis, *30/1/1929, My Friend Przybyszewski (Min venn Przybyszewski). Note Munch's use of the word 'malerier' (paintings) of Przybyszewski's great countryman Chopin.*
39 *Fam. brev., No. 126, undated.*
40 *Fam. brev., Nos. 128–9.*
41 *E.M. og Berlinerne,* Dagbladet, *15/11/1892, quoted from* Berliner Tageblatt.

Page 100:
Quotations 42 *Adolf Paul in* Min Strindbergsbok *(1910).*
43 *Herman Schlittgen memoires.*

Plate 123 See p. 96 note 151, for Schlittgen. His portrait is signed bottom right 'E. Munch 1904'. The last figure is not wholly clear.

Page 103: **Chapter 7: THE FRIEZE OF LIFE**

Text 162 The Copenhagen exhibition at Georg Kleis's 24th Feb.–14th Mar. Fifty-four paintings. For critical reactions see Arne Eggum 'Edvard Munch i Danmark', *Louisiana Revy* (Oct. 1975), pp. 23–7. Emil Hanover especially (he was later director of Kunstindustrimuseet) wrote a perceptive review in *Politiken* (23rd February).
163 For the five important exhibitions, (1892–3) he rented premises on Unter den Linden. See Pål Hougen (1971), p. 41.
164 See pp. 10–11, note to quotation 3.
165 See pp. 62–3, quotation 16.
166 See pp. 262–3, quotation 12.
167 Munch mentioned Klinger in a letter to Rohde: see Gran (1950). CK and Klinger were close friends since their 'Hungerthurm' time together.

Quotations 1 *Livs. p. 2.*
2 *Livs. p. 2.*
3 *OKK N. 46.*
4 *Livs. p. 3.*
5 *Munch to Johan Rohde. See Henning Gran (1950).*
6 *Livs. tilbl., p. 17.*
7 *Draft of a letter to JT c. 1933. Munch obviously felt more and more strongly the need to emphasise to both RH and JT that he had completed his most important work before his stay in Berlin. But his statement that the* Frieze of Life *had been finished long before is scarcely accurate!*
8 *Livs. p. 3.*

Page 104:
Text 168 OKK T 2782 ah.
169 See p. 136, quotation 16.
170 Pl. 114; p. 96, quotation 32.
171 See Nergaard, (1975), p. 17.

Page 106:
Text 172 For instance Heller, (1969), p. 207 and p. 222, note 96. He repeats this in *The Scream*, p. 87.
173 See chapter XVI, pp. 276–7.

Page 107:
Text 174 See p. 90, quotation 20.
175 Pål Hougen showed me these railings some years ago. It is possible that they have been removed by now.
176 Stockholm exhibition October 1894 in Konstföreningen. Przybyszewski's description of *The Scream* was included in translation. He describes the person on the bridge as a mythical beast.
177 *Sick Mood* is today titled *Despair*, see pl. 111.
178 Ugo Baroccio 16th–24th March with Akseli Gallen-Kallela and Blomqvist, Christiania, October 1895.
179 Salon des Indépendants. See p. 106, quotation 9.
180 Max Liebermann (1847–1935) was strongly influenced by French Impressionism. In 1898 he was a professor in Berlin and he played a part in founding the Berlin Secession. With regard to the invitation see Munch's letter to Aubert, 18.3.1902, Oslo University Library, collection 32.
181 Leistikow and von Hofmann. See p. 90.
182 Munch to Hoppe, Feb. 1929. Hoppe (1939), p. 16.

Quotations   *9 Livs., p. 6.*
    10 Edvard Munch II from St. Cloud.
    11 Edvard Munch I from St. Cloud.
    12 The Tree of Knowledge, 2547.
    13 Obstfelder, Collected Works I, (1950) p. 8.
    14 OKK. N. 45.
    15 OKK T 2748.
    16 Adolf Paul, Berliner Tageblatt (15th April, 1927). Also in the Basel catalogue, Beyler Gallerie 1965.
    17 Munch to JT, c. 1933. See also quotation note 7, ch. VII.

Page 108:
Text   183 The Struggle for Existence (Kampen for tilværelsen 1952, p. 179). 'He takes his place as our fourth greatest poet,' by C. Krohg.
    184 Hoppe, (1939), p. 16.

Quotations   *18 Paul Scheerbart in Adels- und Salongblatt in connection with. Munch's exhibition in Berlin 1895.*
    19 Munch to RH, 1929. Hoppe (1939).
    20 Büttner in Thiis (1934), p. 91.

Page 109:
Plates   130 *Vampire* exists in six versions in oil in OKK M 122, 169, 192, 533, 679 and 706. There is one version in Göteborgs (Gothenburg) Konstmuseum, two privately owned in the USA and one in Oslo. It caused a great stir when Nini Roll and Johan Anker bought it at a Blomkvist exhibition for 2.000 kroner. Gierløff, (1953) makes an entertaining story out of it and dates the event 1903. Jappe Nilssen, however, wrote in March 1909 to Munch about the happy occasion.
    131 Munch sometimes produced prints that combined several techniques. Some prints of *Vampire*, for example, are done in a combination of lithography and woodcut. He used two lithographic stones and one wooden block sawn into three pieces. On the first stone he drew the scene in greyish green or black. On the second one he drew the woman's red hair tumbling over the man's head. With the first section of the wooden block he printed the woman's body and the man's yellow face, with the second, the man's blue jacket and the blue shadows behind and with the third, the dark green background. The first stone dates from 1895, while the second one, together with the sawn-up wooden block, is from 1902.

Page 110:
Text   185 See Thiis, (1933), p. 218: 'a symbolic frame with human sperm and embryos which were also repeated later in the first colour lithograph. This offensive frame was afterwards removed'. Heller is of the opinion (1969, p. 22, note 79) that Thiis influenced Munch to remove the frame, but JT makes no mention of it.

Page 111:
Text   186 See p. 116, quotation 37.
    187 This can be seen in an old photograph. Eggum (1977) thinks that the foetus was painted out before the Blomqvist exhibition in Oct. 1918.
    188 Otto Benesch wrote about 'The Beliefs of Edvard Munch' ('Edvard Munchs tro', OKK Year Book, 1963, pp. 9–23). A number of the quotations in this book are to be found in Benesch's article, but he interprets them extremely subjectively as when, for instance, he writes: 'Thus we come to realize that Munch the artist was also a believer'. Munch was certainly no 'believer' in the accepted sense, although he was a deeply religious man. Benesch repeats the story that Munch in conversation with Gierløff talked of an entry he had made in one of his notebooks: 'God is in everything. I have never doubted that.' Gierløff (1953), p. 224. But the preceding sentence (which OB does not quote) has an ironic undertone: 'I think it is quite crazy to believe that there isn't a God, but I cannot help thinking at the same time how odd it is that there is a God.' A true believer would scarcely use the expression: 'how odd it is that there is a God'. If speculation of this kind is necessary, it cannot be on the basis of what people think they recall of Munch's talk of boyhood memories, but rather on what Munch himself has put on record. The only possible conclusion we can reach is that he held a pantheistic belief that 'nothing is ever lost'. Dr Stang's conviction is that the three quotations on p. 120 provide a truer answer to the complex question of Munch's belief: in one of them he clearly states he is a doubter who never denies or mocks religion.

Quotations   *21 Przybyszewski in The Vigil (Vigilien, Berlin, 1895. Dated 16th Nov. 1893).*
    22 Dedekam (1909), p. 24.
    23 Notes of a madman (Den gales opptegnelser) 2743.
    24 OKK T 2800.
    25 OKK T 2800.
    26 Willy Pastor, Das Werk, p. 71.
    27 OKK T 2760. Cf. a similar statement OKK T 2781 aq.

Page 112:
Text   189 *Pan*—Munch and Vigeland were deeply involved with this highly topical journal. They were both represented in the first number which appeared in April–May 1895. The editors had a bias toward France, but they also used a good deal of Scandinavian material. Munch was closely associated with the *Pan* circle and it appeared in three extremely interesting editions. Editorial control, however, was then taken over by a group which maintained that '*Pan* must become a German art journal' (*Pan muss ein deutsches Kunstblatt werden*). After a while it lost its relevance and ceased to be a window on the world. Munch's friends Bierbaum and Meier-Graefe had to resign from the editorial staff.
    190 Sudermann (1857–1928) stated: 'A light has come to us from the North'. See A. Paul, *Min Strindbergsbok*, p. 75.

Plate   135 The painting is signed lower left 'E. Munch 99' and upper right 'E. Munch 1900'. Other versions: OKK M 179, 777 and 1031.

Page 115:
Quotations   *28 Aftenposten, 23/3/1909.*
    29 Livs. tilbl., p. 1.
    30 Livs. tilbl., p. 3.
    31 Livs., p. 2.
    32 Heilberg, Love's Tragedy (Kjaerlighetens tragedie, 1904).
    33 Livs. tilbl., p. 5.

Page 116:
Quotations   *34 See Colour in Print (Farge på trykk, catalogue No. 5 Munch-Museet, 1968, p. 12.*
    35 Gunnar Heilberg, Balkonen (1894) Munch used this quotation as an epigraph for The Sphinx, No. 62, catalogue of the Stockholm exhibition of 1894. Other authors have used similar expressions, e.g. Jæger, Sick Love (Pax edition) p. 83: 'The fact is you have more than a hundred faces.' Jæger also writes of the 'Madonna smile' in p. 115.
    36 Livs. tilbl., pp. 13–17.
    37 Livs. tilbl., p. 2.

Page 120:
Text   191 See R. Heller, 'The Riddle of Edward Munch's Sphinx', papers from the *X Aica Congress* at the Munch-Museet (Oslo, 1969), which deals very thoroughly with *Woman in three stages*. Published in *Art Forum*, 'The Iconography of Edward Munch's The Sphinx', Vol. IX, 2. (*New York, October 1970*) There is in *Samtiden* (1893), pp. 51–2, a poem by Johannes Jørgensen entitled *The Three Women* (De tre kvinner).
    192 Pål Hougen, *Edvard Munch og Henrik Ibsen*. Catalogue to the Vestlandske Kunstindustrimuseum (Vestland Museum of Applied Art) May–June 1975.
    193 For Obstfelder, see pp. 50–1, quotation 18.
    194 For Maeterlinck, see p. 79, with note 103.
    195 See pp. 106–7, quotation 12.

Quotations   *38 Violet Book 2760, 8th Jan. 1892.*
    39 OKK T 2347. A number of Munch's works express similar thoughts.
    40 'The mad poet's diary', listed OKK 2734 with entries largely from 1908–9, and some from 1929.

Page 121:
Text   196 See pp. 14–15, quotation 9.
    197 *Tegn. kat.*, p. 3.
    198 Johan Scharffenberg. In a letter to Pål Hougen, Scharffenberg said that he regretted using the expression, but Munch was deeply hurt. See *Tegn. kat.*, p. 3.

Page 123:
Text   199 OKK T 2794, *Yellow Book.*

Page 124:
Plate   146 In his catalogue to the Sigvald Bergesen (II) collection, Johan H. Langaard dated this picture 1902. Dr Stang was inclined to make it earlier; perhaps in the same year as the woodcut on the same theme which Schiefler dates 1898. The version at Munch-Museet OKK M 280 is possibly from 1902.

Page 127: **Chapter 8: THE GRAPHIC ARTIST**

Text   200 Richard Mengelberg had written a favourable article, 'Aus dem frankfurter Kunstleben', *Frankfurter Zeitung* (6th April 1894). See *Fam. brev.*, No. 156, 'from Stachu (Przybyszewski) to Edzin (Munch)' 16/4/1894: 'die kritik ist sehr gut'.
    201 See, e.g., Werner Timm, *Edvard Munch, Graphik* (Berlin, 1969), p. 23. English edition of the same year, *The Graphic Art of Edvard Munch*, pp. 23–6.
    202 Letter to Johan Rhode, see Gran (1950).
    203 Julius Elias. See p. 94, and text note 145.
    204 Karl Köpping. Both Ole Sarvig (1975) p. 16, and Werner Timm (1969) p. 16, mention Professor Köpping as one of those who might have persuaded Munch to try etching.

205 Hermann Struck, *The Art of Etching* (Die Kunst des Radierens, Berlin, 1908).
206 To Hoppe, see p. 133, quotation 13.
207 Thiel, Kollmann and Linde. See chapter XI, on friends and patrons.
208 Gustav Schiefler (1857–1935). A lawyer and magistrate whose hobby was making useful catalogues of the works of a number of graphic artists. His catalogue of Munch was published in 1907. That of Emil Nolde followed in 1910 and then Wilhelm Laage (1912) and Ernst Ludwig Kirschner (1924), among others. Schiefler had a large collection of graphic works by older as well as contemporary artists. See Gerhard Schack. Gustav Schiefler: *Verzeichnis des graphischen Werks Edvard Munch*, (Berlin, Cassirer, 1907. Norwegian edition: 1974, Cappelens, Oslo). This publication in two parts is indispensable for all students of Munch.
209 See p. 130—quotation 6 from the article about Edvard Munch in Schiefler/Schack (1974), p. 30.

Quotations 1 *OKK N. 39 c. 1890.*
2 *Thor Hedberg, in Dagens Nyheter 3/2/1929 on the exhibition of Munch's graphic works in the Nationalmuseum (Stockholm). Included in* Essay and reviews in D.N. 1921–31 *(Uppsatser och kritiker in Dagens Nyheter 1921–31, Stockholm, 1939).*
3 *Schiefler/Schack, (Hamburg, 1974) p. 38.*

Plates 147 This is an excellent print and a good example of Munch's mastery of the 'colour mezzotint'. It is a mezzotint and dry point on zinc. It was printed by Lemercier in Paris and very few copies are in existence. Sch. 42.
148 Several prints are framed with faint drawings of foetuses. There is an OKK painting with the same motif. In his brief but informative introduction to his magnificent study of Munch's etchings, Sigurd Willoch discusses several individual prints and makes this comment on *Death and the Maiden*: 'After a couple of experimental prints comes the splendid *Death and the Maiden* in which the drypoint technique is applied in such a masterly fashion. The interaction between the gentle lines making up the girl's body and the darker and deeper cuts elsewhere allows the concept of the picture to emerge in all its subtlety.' Willoch, *E.M's Etchings* (Edvard Munchs raderinger, OKK Munch-Museet Skrifter II, Tanum, Oslo, 1950, p. 8). This book contains Munch's etchings, with a precise and detailed commentary on 198 of them. Willoch, at that time director of Nasjonalgalleriet, made the inventory of Munch's estate at Ekely. He makes frequent ref. to Schiefler, *Verzeichnis*, I and II. Apart from Schiefler's and Willoch's great studies, the most important books on Munch's graphic works are: Pola Gauguin *Edvard Munch's Graphic Art, Woodcuts and Etchings*. (Grafikeren Edvard Munch, tresmitt og raderinger, Trondheim, 1946.) Ole Sarvig *Edvard Munchs grafik*, Copenhagen 1959. Eli Greve *Life and Work in the Light of the Woodcuts* (Liv og verk i lys av tresnittene Oslo 1963) Werner Timm *Edvard Munch, Graphik*, East Berlin, 1969. (English Edition, London 1969). Among articles concerned with this aspect of Munch are: Rudolf Mayer 'Edvard Munch: Pioneer in Graphic Art,' *Art Today*, ('Edvard Munch: Fornyoer i grafikken', *Kunsten idag*, 1972, No. 1) W. Wartmann 'Der Graphiker', *Graphis*, (Zürich, 1945). Pål Hougen has written the introduction to the catalogues of many of Munch-Museet exhibitions. See Stavanger *Kunstforening* (Art Association), April 1967.

Page 128:
Text 210 *Tegn. kat.*, OKK 1973, p. 5.
211 See p. 138, quotation 17.

Plates 149 In his earlier engravings from 1894 and 1895 Munch takes up the central themes of the *Frieze of Life*, such as *Death and the Maiden*, pl. 148, *The Day After*, *The Lonely Ones*, pl. 156 and *The Three Stages of Woman*, pl. 149. There is also a variation of the latter work, in which the old woman on the right holds a man's head in her folded hands, in the manner of Salome. In 1899 he returned to the theme of the three stages in a lithograph, pl. 177. He painted *The Sick Child* as early as 1885, pl. 74, and he regarded it as one of his major works. It is therefore natural that he should have returned to the subject very early on, portraying it in an etching, pl. 151 on two occasions. In 1896 his large lithograph of the work was published in France.
150 Munch's first lithograph, pl. 150 was completed in 1894, and here too the subject was taken from a painting, that of *Puberty*, pl. 103. The first version of that picture, from 1886, had been lost by that time, but he painted the subject again in 1894.

Page 130:
Text 212 In 1895, Meier-Graefe, pl. 99 published a portfolio with eight of Munch's first engravings, amongst which were *The Sick Child*, pl. 151 and *The Lonely Ones* pl. 156. This collection, which was offered for sale in Germany, France and Scandinavia, was not a great success. But, even so, by the following year Munch had already

started planning *The Mirror* see note to pl. 188. The eight etchings with titles provided by Meier-Graefe were:
1. *Girl at the Window*, Sch. 5 OKK 5.
2. *The Sick Child*, (with landscape), Sch. 7 OKK 7, pl. 151.
3. *The Christiania Bohemians*, Sch. 10 OKK 9.
4. *Tête à tête*, Sch. 12 OKK 11.
5. *Moonlight, Night in St. Cloud*, Sch. 13 OKK 12.
6. *The Day After*, Sch. 15 OKK 14.
7. *Two People*, Sch. 20 OKK 19.
7 *The Lonely Ones*, pl. 156, alternatively titled.
8. *Portrait*, Sch. 27 OKK 26. Dr Asch.
All printed by Angerer in Berlin.
According to Willoch (1950), p. 9, Munch did up to thirty etchings in the period 1894–5, but by 1916 his output declined. 'That was the last year in which he put his mind to the delicate art of etching.'
213 Max Linde's portfolio appeared in 1902: *Aus dem Hause Max Linde*, Sch. 176–91 OKK 79. This includes both etchings (printed by Felsing) and lithographs (printed by Lasally).

Quotations 4 *Lindebrevene No. 488, 23/11/1905. OKK Munch-Museet documents 3 (Oslo, 1954).*
5 *OKK N. 59.*
6 *Sch., foreword to* Verzeichnis *(1974).*
7 *Sch., Edvard Munchs graphische Kunst (Dresden, 1923).*
8 *Sch., Verzeichnis, (1907) p. 20.*

Plate 153 The lithograph *Harpy* appeared on p. 7 in volume IV of *Quickborn* which Munch and Strindberg published Jan. 1899. Perhaps Munch in this lithograph aimed to illustrate Strindberg's words: 'the enchanting wisdom of married love or the delightful insanity of sensual love.'

Page 133:
Quotations 9 *Sch., Edvard Munchs graphische Kunst, p. 5.*
10 *Ibid., p. 2.*
11 *Harald Hals,* Tidssignaler *(23/11/1895) p. 659, in reply to an article by Holger Sinding Larsen in No. 36 of the same journal.*
12 *Munch to RH, Feb. 1929. Hoppe (1939). A number of these observations are quoted in this book.*
13 *Munch to RH, Feb. 1929. Hoppe (1939).*

Page 134:
Quotations 14 *Note by Munch 1902 OKK.*
15 *Schiefler/Schack (1974) p. 30. This refers to pl. 127.*

Page 136:
Quotation 16 *Munch's comment on this lithograph.* The Tree of Knowledge, *in which Munch used several of his graphic prints. OKK T 2547.*

Page 138:
Quotations 17 *Büttner in* Thiis *(1934), p. 100.*
18 *OKK 2782.*
19 *Edvard Munch III 2759.*

Page 141:
Quotations 20 *Munch OKK 2782 ah.*
21 *Colour with Prints (Farge på trykk, 1968, p. 11).*
22 *Edvard Munch, Nærbilde av et geni (1946), pp. 16–17. See also English edition* Edward Munch—Close-up of a Genius *(Oslo, 1969), quotation pp. 10–11. The memory of that incident was so deeply impressed on Munch's imagination that at the age of forty he did a monumental and highly moving woodcut of the scene, pl. 172.*

Page 142:
Quotation 23 *Paul Hermann wanted to have his own work printed by Clot in Paris. When he arrived there he saw Munch's lithographic stones. Quoted from Büttner in* Thiis *(1934), p. 92.*

Page 144:
Quotations 24 *Quoted from Przybyszewski's novel* Over board *(1896).*
25 *Quoted from Przybyszewski's* The Vigil, *p. 19, which was published in 1895 with a vignette by Munch. See pl. 102.*
26 *Schiefler/Schack (1974), p. 40.*
27 *Munch to RH, 1929. Hoppe (1939).*
28 *Munch to RH, 1929. Hoppe (1939).*

Page 146:
Quotation 29 *Quotation by RH.*

Plates 179 Munch had thought that his woodcut of *Evening* (also known as
&   *Melancholy* or *On the Beach*) should be included in the 'Mirror'
180 series. We have already seen the subject in a mixed technique of crayon, oil and pencil, and also in pure oil. See pl. 83 and 114. Even in the early days it must have had a special significance for him, as he painted it four times, and we should also remember that he returned to it once more when he had to do a vignette for Goldstein's collection of poems. In 1901 he also did a new woodcut of the scene, in which the picture is reversed so that the man is looking to the left, as in the painted versions.

Page 148:
Quotation   30 OKK T 2782c.
Page 152:
Quotations   31 *Obstfelder in 'Fragment', Collected Works 3 (Samlede verker 3, p. 64).*
             32 *Max Linde,* Edvard Munch und die Kunst der Zukunft, *(1902) p. 7.*

Plate   188 *Man's Head in Woman's Hair* is printed in grey, blue and red, by means of two wooden blocks, one of which is divided into four pieces. The man bears a slight resemblance to Przybyszewski, and the subject could mean that Munch did indeed have his Polish friend in mind. We have already noted that Munch often uses women's hair to symbolize the way in which men become tied to women, e.g. *Attraction* and *Separation*, pl. 169–71. The same kind of symbolism can also be found in the works of Baudelaire and Maeterlinck. Munch designed illustrations of the former, and planned to do the same for the latter.

In 1896 Munch had plans to assemble the main themes of his graphic work into a definite and meaningful sequence. This is also verified by Schiefler's reference to 'a sort of graphic life-frieze'. He wanted to call it *The Mirror* (Speitletr: See Hougen in the Czech catalogue, 1971, p. 42) and his woodcut of *Man's Head in Woman's Hair*, pl. 188, was to provide the cover illustration. When he held his exhibition at Dioramalokalet in Oslo's Karl Johan Street in 1897, he announced his plans publicly, but the series, which was to comprise twenty prints, each with their own explanatory text, was never published. Several of these texts are quoted in this book.

In April 1896 Munch received a letter from Axel Heiberg, informing him that he was commissioning twelve engravings by Norwegian artists, suggesting, amongst others, Werenskiold, Thaulow, Munthe, and Krohg. He later went on to say that he wanted Munch to participate, and: 'Harriet Backer and Kitty Kielland really go together with these men, perhaps we should include them too'. But although this project was soon abandoned in July Munch painted a decorative panel for Axel Heiberg.

Page 155: **Chapter 9: THE DRAUGHTSMAN**

Text   214 See *inter alia* Hals II (1955).
            215 Thiis (1933), p. 64.
            216 *Fam. brev.*, Nos. 25–31 & 39, extracts from Edvard Munch's diary.
            217 See Nergaard (1968), p. 71. He believes it is a farewell with 'fru Heiberg'.

Quotations   1 *Ravensberg,* Vennene, *p. 185.*
              2 *Undated letter to JT, probably 1933.*
              3 *Munch note from 1898, quoted from Hougen (1975), p. 6.*

Page 156:
Text   218 See p. 164. Hougen dealt with the Ibsen–Munch relationship in his little catalogue to the Vestlandske Kunstindustrimuseum, May-June 1975. In her book, *Edward Munch, Life and Work in the Light of the Woodcuts (Edvard Munch, Liv og Verk i lys av tresnittene,* Oslo, 1963) Eli Greve has a fine little essay on Munch and Ibsen, pp. 32–48. As we saw p. 116, quotation 36 Munch himself felt that his work *The Three Stages of Woman* influenced Ibsen's *When we Dead Awaken.*

Page 157:
Plate   191 This drawing is similar in content to the painting *Golgotha*, made in 1900, OKK M. 36. Hougen, (1968), p. 124, discussed both the painting and the four drawings of *The Empty Cross*. He points to a Munch quotation which is obviously relevant to these interesting drawings. 'The bohemian period came with its free love—God—and everything were overturned—the whole world rushed into a wild, insane dance of Life—a blood-red sun hung in the sky—the cross was atoned for—But I could not rid myself of the dread of Life (the Life angst) and the thought of eternal life.' There are four drawings that bear a definite relationship to each other. It is likely that Munch did a lot of work on their subject matter and that they had a special significance for him. We are shown a bleak coastal landscape, with two trees and an empty cross on the cliff's edge. People are rushing down the steep cliffside into the sea or into the swamp-like water, where they drown. One of the drowning heads bears a resemblance to Munch himself, and the same applies to the man pressed against the fat prostitute's breast, pl. 65 and also, to a certain extent, to the monk-like figure in the foreground. Munch often made this pun on his own name and the Norwegian word for 'monk' ('munk'), both of which are pronounced in the same way. In other drawings this figure looks somewhat like Przybyszewski. In one variation of the subject the black-garbed figure wanders away from the cross and towards us, led by the monk-like man, while at the side the loving couples desport themselves in joyless revelry. Almost certainly, these drawings reflect the conflict between Munch's pious back-

ground and his relationship with the bohemians. It was roughly at the same time that he painted *Golgotha* with a figure nailed to the cross that could be thought to resemble himself.

Page 159:
Text   219 The expert who has concerned himself most with Munch's drawings is P. Hougen. He supervised the selection and wrote the catalogue for the large Munch exhibition which opened in Bremen in 1970. It visited thereafter a number of cities, including Oslo in 1973. A selection of Munch's *Drawings* (Handzeichnungen) were published by Ernst Rathenau, (N.Y. 1976).
                 Journals *Kunsten Idag*, No. 4 (1957) and No. 1 (1958), Johan H. Langaard and Reidar Revold published a series of Munch's drawings with a short introductory text. In 1958 they published jointly *Edward Munch from Year to Year (Edvard Munch fra år til år).*

Page 160:
Quotations   4 *See Hougen (1975), p. 6.*
              5 *Arthur Kahane. See Lothar Lang in* Weltbühne, *11/1/1972, on the occasion of the Munch exhibition in East Berlin. There are a number of interesting letters from Hermann Bahr to Munch, 3/12/1906, 9/1/1907, 25/1/1907 in which Bahr asks Munch to get together chairs, furnishings and the like for a production of* Hedda Gabler.

Plate   202 Max Dauthendey (1867–1918) was a poet with strong Scandinavian connections. In 1893, together with the Swede C. G. Uddgren, he published a little brochure in Copenhagen, called *The Universe, The new sublime in art.* In it, he spoke admiringly and evocatively of Munch's art, describing in graphic terms such things as his 'thunder-blue evening sea' or his 'melodious, jewel-like colours, green, pink, and silver'.

Page 166:
Plate   217 Munch-Museet in Oslo possesses roughly 4,500 drawings of very varying quality. Some of them are swiftly-executed little sketches and impressions on the pages of pads, while others are small, insignificant drawings in letters, which almost seem to merge into his rapid, nervous handwriting. There are tongue-in-cheek and malicious caricatures of friends and enemies, self-mocking observations, and serious attempts at new treatments of old themes. Years could pass between the first rough sketch and the finished picture: Munch said, for example, that the basis for his *Alma Mater* at Oslo University was a drawing that he did between eighteen and nineteen of a peasant woman up in Hedmark breastfeeding a child. However, there are also large-size, completed, coloured drawings and water-colours, pictures of the finest quality, which are works of art in their own right. All in all, the Museum's collection of drawings is invaluable to a deeper understanding of Munch's work. They were rarely displayed during his lifetime, and the first major exhibition of Munch's drawings and watercolours was opened in 1970. It started at the Kunsthalle in Bremen, then travelled to Switzerland and Poland, finally returning to Germany (both East and West). It aroused such interest that three years later Munch's fellow Norwegians were given their first opportunity to see the exhibition, which was increased to 550 works for the occasion, that is to say, approximately a tenth of the Museum's collection.

Page 169: **Chapter 10: A DECADE OF MISFORTUNE AND PROGRESS**

Text   220 This is according to Schiefler, *Verzeichnis* (1974).
            221 Laura died of cancer in 1926.
            222 Svenæus (1968) p. 205 ff, points out an interesting parallel in the colour lithograph which Edouard Vuillard exhibited in 1899 at Vollard's gallery. Svenæus quite correctly observes that the pattern on the table cloth in Vuillard's picture *Interieur à la suspension* has a disturbing but powerful effect similar to that of the pattern in Munch's picture. This is scarcely an accident. There is a picture with the same motif in the Rolf E. Stenersen bequest. Munch took up the theme again in 1925 (the year before Laura's death) in two lithographs—494 in which the figure faces the same way as in the picture and 495 in which she faces the other way.
            223 See p. 52, quotation 19.
            224 This was Hammer's guest-house, which exists today as an old people's home. Leif Østby discussed this group of pictures, 'Et Edvard Munch motif', *K & K* (1966), pp. 151-8. He includes also a poem of Reiss-Anderssen to Munch.

Quotations   1 *Stenersen (1946), p. 87. The Japanese author Masaaki Suzuki (1977) took photographs of several of Munch's settings in Åsgårdstrand. These photographs show how Munch reproduced the smallest details without becoming what he called 'en spiker og kvistmaler' ('twigs and nails painter'). To this day we can recognise every stone in the painting of* Inger on the Beach, *for instance. In the period when Munch lived abroad he returned practically every summer to Åsgårdstrand.*

2 *Munch to Andreas Aubert, 7/2/1902. Letter in Oslo University Library collection 32.*

3 *Discussed by Reidar Revold, 'Omkring en motivgruppe av Edvard Munch' (OKK Year Book 1952–9, 1960, pp. 38–50).*

Page 170:
Text 225 One version privately owned in USA.
226 See p. 169, quotation 3.

Page 172:
Text 227 See p. 96, quotation 32.
228 Undated letter to JT, probably 1933: 'All the same those years from 1902 until the Copenhagen clinic were the unhappiest, the most difficult and yet the most fateful and productive years of my life.
229 Kornhaug. Munch painted *Golgotha* here. OKK 36, with his self-portrait in the foreground.
230 Mathilde (Tulla) Larsen, born 1869—six years younger than Munch. Daughter of wine merchant P. A. Larsen. Munch met her at the end of the nineties and their stormy relationship lasted until 1902. Beyond doubt she played a powerful role in Munch's life, both while they were on good terms and certainly later when the memory of her dramatic departure loomed disproportionately large in Munch's over-sensitive mind and found violent expression in his art. For a long time they lived at odds with each other. 'You believe in the gospel of pleasure,' he wrote, 'I believe in the gospel of pain.' In September 1902 that memorable pistol shot deprived Munch of two joints of the middle finger of his left hand. Arne Eggum (1977), p. 62, has published some notes written by Munch which were possibly the 'draft of a novel'. From these it emerges that she declared she would go far away and leave him for ever. Munch sat in anguish with a revolver in his right hand: 'What are you thinking of doing with that revolver? Is it loaded?' There was a shot and the room was filled with smoke. According to Munch's notes he then went on his own to the State Hospital (Rikshospitalet), 1902. He asked to be given a local anaesthetic so that he could watch the operation, which he later depicted in a violently dramatic form. In 1903 Tulla Larsen married the painter Arne Kavli. Munch could never forgive his old friends for taking her side. There were many of them, apart from the 'bohemian friends', who thought that Munch had treated her harshly. There are, e.g., some letters from the author Max Dauthendey, 14/12/1900 to Munch in which she is referred to as his 'Bride' (Braut). Dauthendey pleads with Munch to return to her. He calls her 'the most beautiful lady of Norway' (die hübschste Dame Norwegens). There is another letter from Dauthendey, 17/9/01 in which he asks if she might 'be given a chance to talk to Munch or receive from him some sign of life'. A little exhibition was held at Munch-Museet in 1976 which showed that Tulla Larsen was an able graphic artist.

Page 174:
Text 231 Eva Mudocci (1883?–1953). Her real name was Evangeline Hope Muddock. Like a number of British musicians of the time she felt that a continental sounding name would be a professional advantage. Waldemar Stabell has written an informative article: 'Edvard Munch og Eva Mudocci', *K & K*, (1973) pp. 209–36. Together with her pianist friend Bella Edwards, she toured a number of Norwegian towns in 1902, 1904, 1907 and 1909. Munch met her in Paris in March 1903 and the relationship lasted for several years. The two friends visited Munch in his little summer home in Åsgårdstrand. He tried repeatedly to paint her but gave up. On the other hand he did complete three lithographs: a large one which (according to Schiefler) he himself called *Madonna* pl. 232; its counterpart *Salome* pl. 231 and *The Violin Concert* pl. 229 which shows the two musicians together. Christian Krohg painted Bella Edwards in Paris during 1902–3 and Olaf Gulbransson made some drawings of Eva Mudocci. There is also an uncompleted painting by Munch probably 1903–4 which is reproduced in Stabell's article, p. 226. Stabell also reveals that her portrait was painted on four occasions by Matisse. The same article gives a number of letters from Matisse to Edvard Munch dated 1903–8. They appear to have met for the last time in the summer of 1909 in Åsgårdstrand or Kragerø. He sent her a note of thanks for her message of congratulations on his seventieth birthday in 1933. See also L. Carley and R. Threlfall, *Delius. A Life in Pictures* (Oxford, 1977), p. 49.
232 See p. 178, quotation 9. 'It was that title [Salome] which caused our only row.'
233 See pp. 214–16, the fable *Alpha and Omega*.
234 *Death and the Maiden* pl. 148 and OKK M. 49. Svenæus (1973) has drawn attention to an interesting picture in which death is a woman, Abb. 256. I am however unable to follow Svenæus when he sees a death's head in Eva Mudocci's violin.

Quotations 4 *Munch to RH.*
5 *Munch to JT, c. 1920. See Thiis (1933), p. 276.*

6 *Quoted from the facsimile in Inger Alver Gløersen, Lykkehuset, p. 1*
7 OKK 2782 ba.

Page 177:
Text 235 Munch was given this advice by Linde.
236 Eli Greve (1963), p. 23.
237 Page 187, quotation 7.
238 This reference here is not to the bohemian circle around Jæger, bu to Christiania society at the turn of the century.
239 See p. 46, quotation 4.

Page 178:
Text 240 His father, aunt and two sisters. We know only a little about Munch's relations with his brother Andreas, but it indicates that they understood each other well. He died young—at the age of thirty.
241 See Benesch, *Edward Munch's Beliefs* (Edvard Munchs tro, pp. 110 11, note to line 30).
242 See for instance Aunt Karen's letter, *Fam. brev.*, No. 218.

Quotations 8 *Munch to SH.*
9 *Stabell (1973), p. 217.*
10 *Munch note T 2782 a. This quotation is not directly linked with the lithograph or to Eva Mudocci, but it does illustrate Munch's capacity offer himself in devotion. According to Schiefler, Munch himself calle the picture* Madonna.

Page 183: Chapter 11: FRIENDS AND PATRONS

243 Munch to EG, 1905, from Bad Elgersburg.
244 This is today a small Munch museum.
245 *La Revue Blanche*. The editor was the well known critic Thadée Natanson whose reviews of Munch were not merely favourable. He wrote of 'a barbaric taste' but also 'a clear attempt to express an exhalted lyric mood in terms of a picture'.

Quotation 1 *The article appeared in La Presse (May 1897).*

Plates 234 Ludvig Meyer was one of those who appreciated Munch's art at an early stage. We have already noted his reaction to *The Sick Child*— see p. 60, quotation 13. He bought *Girl stoking the Stove* from 1883. Munch painted Meyer in 1882, the year after he had joined the Social Democrats. There is however something comic about his appearance—the radical looks embarrassed standing with a top hat in his hand. In *A Game of Memories* (Lek med minner, Oslo, 1966, p. 19) Meyer's daughter, Eli Krog, tells an amusing story of how she as a young girl was so furious about the picture, which was on shov at Blomkvist's, that she bought a knife with the firm intention of going to the exhibition to slash it to pieces. Munch's picture of the Meyer children was the cause of a legal dispute. Ludvig Meyer did not like the picture and refused to accept it. Munch took the matter to court and Meyer was ordered to pay the 500 kroner fee, (Eli Krog, ibid. pp. 14–19).
235 The painter Ivo Hauptmann has written very entertainingly about the way this successful picture of the Esche children came about in 'Memories of Edvard Munch', ('Minner om Edvard Munch', *OKK Year Book* 1963, p. 62). Reinhold Heller has told the story perhaps more accurately in 'The Stocking Manufacturer van de Velde and E. Munch' ('Strømpefabrikanten van de Velde og Edvard Munch', *K & K*, 1968, pp. 89–104). He also reproduces a photograph, p. 92 which Munch obviously made use of when he painted the children.

Page 184:
Text 246 Albert Kollmann (1837–1915). Son of a dean in Mecklenberg with ten children. He wanted to study painting but became a business-man. Art became his mission in life, and he championed the German Impressionists Max Liebermann and Fritz von Uhde as well as Gauguin and Ernst Barlach. From 1892 and especially after 1900 Munch was his primary concern. Both Barlach and Munch made a number of portraits of Kollmann. An entertaining little publication appeared in 1921, *Ein Leben für die Kunst*, published by H. V. Flotow in which several German personalities well known in the world of the arts, wrote about this extraordinary art lover. The quotations which follow in the text—Liebermann, Th. Däubler and Curt Glaser—are taken from this publication. Munch also wrote a contribution.
247 Munch to JT, 10/11/1904. See p. 187, quotation 7.

Quotations 2 *Albert Kollmann to Munch, 31/10/1902.*
3 *Undated letter Munch to JT, probably c. 1933. See also quotation belou from 1904, p. 187, quotation 7.*
4 *Munch to EG. Unposted card from Ilmenau where Munch was in 1906*

Page 185:
Quotations 5 *Munch to JT, 6/8/1907.*
6 *Munch to ET, 21/6/1908.*

Page 186:
Text 248 Ivo Hauptmann (1963), p. 64.
249 *Edvard Munch and the Art of the Future* (Edvard Munch und die Kunst der Zukunft, Berlin, 1902). The new edition (1905) had a promising title and, as Munch said himself, a *bold* title, but it is a very slim volume of fifteen pages.
250 The painting referred to is *Fertility*, pl. 146.
251 Kollmann to Munch, 5/10/1902.
252 The house in the Ratzburger Allée is today a Registrar's Office for civil marriages. This beautiful home contained at one time superb works of art by Böcklin, Leibl, Manet, Degas, Whistler, Liebermann and, first and foremost, Rodin. Emil Heilbut wrote about 'Sammlung Max Linde', in *Kunst und Kunstler* (Oct. 1903 and May 1904).
253 Max Linde's letters to Munch have been published by OKK, *Edvard Munchs brev fra Dr. Med. Max Linde*, (Munch-Museet documents no. 3, 1954). The book includes 113 letters, Nos. 426–538. At a later date (year unknown) Gustav Lindtke wrote, *Edvard Munch—Dr Max Linde, Briefwechsel 1902–28*, Publication VII by the Senate of the City (Hansestadt) of Lübeck. This publication includes not only Munch's letters but also Linde's replies. With regard to Munch's connections in Lübeck, see Carl George Heise, *Edvard Munchs Beziehungen zu Lübeck* (Der Wagen, Lübeck, 1927).
254 Herbert Esche. See above-mentioned articles by Hauptmann (1963) and Heller (1968). See note to pl. 235.
255 Van de Velde to Frau Esche. Letters from Munch to the Esche family are now in the possession of Ivo Hauptmann. The architect and designer van de Velde was one of those responsible for the development of the Art Nouveau or Jugendstil. Munch wrote to Thiis, then Director of the Applied Art Museum (Nordenfjellske Kunstindustrimuseum) in Trondheim: 'I am on my way from Chemnitz . . . van de Velde was there too and asked me to send his regards. He told me that Trondheim was the first place where a museum had ordered any of his things.' Thiis equipped a very modern van de Velde room in the museum.

Plate 241 Photograph. The painter Jan Preisler (left) who prepared the poster for the Munch exhibition and (right) the painter Milos Jiránek. These two were responsible for the exhibition which was such an important event for Czech artists. In 1971 the Munch-Museet reconstructed the Prague exhibition of 1905 and included the works of a number of Czech painters influenced by Munch. Dr Jiri Kotalik, the Director of the Narodni Gallery in Prague, organised this additional part of the exhibition and wrote the foreword to the Czech section of the catalogue. The Norwegian section of the catalogue was prepared by Bente Torjusen among others and contains a good deal of useful information.

Page 187:
Text 256 Quoted in Heller (1968) p. 95.
257 See e.g., the detail pl. 260, p. 201.
258 Esche replied that he had seen a Van Gogh exhibition and 'A picture with gaps was on show but nowhere had the tube been squeezed directly on to the canvas.' ('Ein Bild mit Löchern war dabei, jedoch war nirgends die Tube direkt auf die Leinwand ausgedrückt.')
259 'The family picture is still not dry.' ('Das Ahnenbild ist immer noch nicht trocken') 15th Nov. When Munch finally settled down to a frenzy of painting in the last week of October 1905, he first painted the portraits of the children and then six other portraits of the family in the course of four days.
260 For instance, Frau Esche wrote to Munch in 1905: 'You gave us the impression of a poor desolate being, hounded from house and home with no place to lay his head . . . Now the important thing is to master the demon alcohol and work hard at your painting.'
261 Ernest Thiel (1859–1947). See Brita Linde, *Ernest Thiel and his Art Gallery* (Ernest Thiel och hans konstgallerie, Stockholm, 1969).
262 Munch to JT, 23/8/1905 and 7/2/1908: 'Thiel is buying on a large scale.'
263 See Ragna Stang, 'Mecenen Ernest Thiel og Gustav Vigeland', 'Life's Faces' ('Livets ansikter'), *exhibition catalogue* (Stockholm, 1975), pp. 76–9. There is also an English text.
264 Munch to ET, 25/7/1905.

Quotations 7 *Munch to JT, 10/11/1904, when Thiis was preparing a lecture on Munch.*
8 *Munch to the barrister Nørregaard.*
9 *Munch to JN, 13/1/1904.*
10 *Munch to JT, dated Berlin 1905.*
11 *The painter Emil Filla in K & K (1939). It was J. P. Hodin who made the Norwegian public aware of the importance of Munch's art in Prague in 1905. On his initiative several articles by Czech painters were published in K & K (1939 and 1969).*
12 *Vaclav Spala 'Et minne om Edvard Munch' in* Volne Smery *(1938–49).*
13 *Munch to Karen Bjølstad. Fam. brev. No. 248.*
14 *Munch to JN, Bang (1963), p. 14.*

Page 188:
Text 265 Munch to ET, 2/9/1905.
266 Munch used this expression himself in an undated letter to ET.
267 For the relationship between Munch and Nietzsche, see Gösta Svenæus, 'Trädet på berget', *OKK Year Book* (1963), pp. 24–46. On 25/7/1905, Munch wrote to ET that he would be delighted to undertake the commission. Letter at Thielska Galleriet.
268 There is in Munch-Museet picture store a sketch entitled *Ibsen and Nietzsche surrounded by Genius*, M 917. This might have been conceived as a part of the portrait series. Two portraits of Nietzsche exist, one in OKK, pl. 237, and a related one in Thielska Galleriet in Stockholm. Thor Hedberg writes of *three* portraits in *Svenska Dagbladet* (8/2/1907). There is one portrait of Nietzsche's sister, Elizabeth Föster Nietzsche, in Thielska Galleriet and another in OKK. Drawings of both brother and sister also exist. Her portrait shows clearly that Munch used a photograph when he painted it, as he often did. See *Malerei nach Fotographie*, catalogue from an exhibition in Munich by Professor Schmoll (Eisenwerth).

Page 189:
Text 269 See the portrait of Anker Kirkeby's little girl.
270 Munch wrote to Kollmann, 9/12/1904 that the frieze had been put up temporarily. He acknowledges, however, that the effect is too violent for the white Empire furniture and is willing to paint it again in a more subdued manner. But Linde would not accept the frieze and we do not know whether this was because it was too massive for the room, or whether Munch had not followed Linde's request: '. . . in other words, no kissing or loving couples' (also bitte keine Küsse oder Liebenden). See p. 194, quotation 16.
271 See Hougen (1975) p. 5, on Munch and Ibsen. Also Midboe 'Max Reinhardt's production of Ibsen's *Ghosts*' ('Max Reinhards iscenesettelse av Ibsens *Gespenster*', *Kammerspiele des deutschen Theaters*, Berlin, 1906). Decor by Edvard Munch. This is in the papers of Kgl. N. Videnskabers Selskabs Skrifter (Royal Norwegian Society of the Sciences), 1969, no. 4.

Page 190:
Quotation 15 *Max Linde to Munch, autumn 1904.*

Page 192:
Text 272 Arthur Kahane, *Berliner Tageblatt*, 28/10/1926. See also Heinz Kindermann, *History of the European Theatre* (Theatergeschichte Europas, VIII, pp. 340–1).
273 In Munch-Museet catalogue of 1971 the following Nos. are on exhibition and designated as sketches for the *Reinhardt Frieze*: OKK 869, 720, 981, 696, 721, 840, 180 and 53. They are painted in tempera. The curator of the museum, Arne Eggum, put together this series of pictures and has in preparation an article about it and also about the *Linde Frieze*. The following Nos. 54, 19, 13, 695, 14, 719 and 35 designated the *Linde Frieze*, and were exhibited in 1971. These are oil paintings. The themes are closely related. There is a picture in the Kunsthalle in Hamburg, *Girls on the Shore*, which was once owned by Carl Georg Heise and in letters to Munch dated 9/9/1925 and 3/9/1932, is referred to as belonging to the *Reinhardt Frieze*. By a regrettable mistake it is reproduced in *Lindebrevene*, p. 81, as belonging to the *Linde Frieze*.
274 See also p. 194, quotation 17.
275 Quoted from Lothar Lang, *Die Weltbühne*, 11/1/1972.
276 Given in the Berlin gallery's catalogue as Nos. 242–9.

Plate 248 See Carl George Heise, *Die vier Söhne des Dr Max Linde*, Reclam Bd. 7, (Stuttgart, 1956).

Page 194:
Quotations 16 *Munch wrote on the drawing,* Deutsche Zeitung*: 'The Norwegian painter goes home in the summer to rest.' ('Im Sommer fährt der norwegische Maler in seine Heimat um sich auszuruhen.') Norwegian news sheets (Norske Intelligenssedler): 'The painter Munch once again was the cause of a disturbance in the street yesterday. Five ruffians, all with previous records, attacked him while he was painting in the Studenterlunden in the light summer night.'*
17 *Undated letter to Thiis.*

Page 195:
Text 277 See quotations and notes to pp. 186–7.
278 Count Harry Kessler (1868–1937). Author, politician and art lover in Weimar. There are sixteen letters at Munch-Museet written by Kessler to Munch, most of them concerned with fixing an appointment for a portrait sitting. The first is dated as early as 18/4/1895, that is at the time when Kessler bought Vigeland's *Vals*. The last is as late as 25/6/1928. By 1895 Munch had already done Kessler's portrait as a lithograph, Sch. 30 OKK 191. In the Nationalgalerie, Berlin, there is a full-length portrait from 1906. Kessler wrote a full biography of his friend Rathenau. He was called 'Der rote Graf'— e.g. in *Der Spiegel* (Hamburg, 1961). See *Fam. brev.* No. 217. Munch to Karen Bjølstad, 18/3/1904.

279 Weimar is often called 'The Athens of the Ilm'. The river Ilm flows through the city.
280 Sch. 246, OKK 262.
281 Ludvig von Hofmann was a member of *die Elf*. The friendship endured and in 1927 Hofmann and his wife visited Munch at Ekely. In a letter of 1934, Munch writes that after seeing von Hofmann's woodcuts he was inspired to take up woodcuts again himself.
282 He wrote in an undated letter from Bad Kösen to Karen Bjølstad: 'It was high time that my friends in Weimar took me up, otherwise the same would have happened to me as to Laura.' *Fam. brev.* No. 256.
283 *Fam. brev.* No. 263.

Page 197:
Text 284 It is a pity that the various parts of this work are scattered; another version of *Men Bathing* is in Helsinki (Ateneum) and of *Youth* in Bergen (Rasmus Meyers Samlingen). It is an important example of Munch's output showing a new vitality even before his breakdown. In the painting it is possible to detect the influence of Matisse and the 'Vitalists', but it should not be overlooked that the young Max Beckmann (born 1884) had in 1905 painted his great related picture *Young men by the Sea*. That Munch had met Beckmann in Weimar is clear from the book by Benno Reifenberg and Wilhelm Hausenstein, *Max Beckmann* (Munich, 1949), p. 41: 'When Beckmann had exhibited this picture to much acclaim, an unknown painter took him to one side and advised him not to continue with that type of figure composition. . . . That painter was Edvard Munch. The other Beckmann picture, which Munch regarded as better, was the *Great Death Scene*, 1906. Beckmann did not follow the advice.' The authors consider that Ensor, Munch and Beckmann will come to be regarded as the great 'visionaries' . . . 'Therefore there is something momentous about this quiet conversation between the aging Munch and the young Beckmann'. Munch's painting was made on the nudist beach at Warnemünde, and it was refused as an exhibit by Commeter, in Hamburg, November 1907. Schiefler wrote to tell Munch, 3/11/1907 that his efforts to get the picture accepted by Commeter had failed. See Erik Kruskopf, *Edvard Munch och Finnland*, M.M. documents No. 4, (1968) p. 324. Off-print of *Svenska Litteratursällskapets Studier* No. 43. (Swedish Literary Society Studies.)

Page 198:
Quotation 18 *Schiefler, Edvard Munchs graphische Kunst (1923) pp. 1–3.*
Page 199:
Text 285 In contrast to these pictures expressing the joy of life, he made at the same time a group of paintings which can be seen as an attempt to break out of 'the circle of the Self'. They have not to date been exhibited together as a group, but Arne Eggum gathered together a number of strongly expressionist paintings in the *catalogue for the Stockholm exhibition* (p. 62 ff) in the spring of 1977. They were designated 'The Green Room' ('det grønne rom'), an expression Munch himself used. They were painted in Warnemünde and their common theme is destructive love between two human beings. The titles make this clear enough: *Hate, Jealousy, Desire, The Murderess*. They have also been made as lithographs and Munch-Museet possesses hand-coloured prints. Both these themes and the technique of these pictures betray a nervous restlessness which is an omen of the breakdown to come. The Stockholm exhibition in spring 1977 mentioned above took place at Liljevalchs og Kulturhuset.

Page 200:
Plate 259 The details of this picture, pl. 260 shows how Munch experimented with leaving parts of the canvas untouched, and how he squeezed the contents of the tube directly on to the canvas—for which (as we have seen) Esche reproached him.

Page 202:
Quotation 19 *Munch sent JT the following letter, undated but written in connection with the seventieth birthday biographies by JT and Pola Gauguin:*
'*Dear Thiis, I have sent Gauguin the following amendments which you could make use of in your book too. It is not correct to say that I used something of pointillism in Amor and Psyche. This merely introduces an element of confusion into a rather important period. At the start of the century I felt compelled to break up the flat areas and line, I felt that they were becoming mere mannerisms. I tried three approaches to the problem: I painted some realistic pictures such as those of the children in Warnemünde; then I tried again some of the techniques of The Sick Child. On one occasion I copied this picture for Olaf Schou. This was subsequently acquired by our gallery and went from there to Gothenburg. As you can see from The Sick Child in the gallery, it is constructed on horizontal and vertical lines as well as converging, diagonal strokes. Subsequently I painted a number of pictures with broad, distinct lines, sometimes a metre long, or with brush strokes that went vertically, horizontally or diagonally. The surface was broken up and a kind of pre-Cubism took form.*
The sequence was: Amor and Psyche, Consolation and Murder.

Then there was the self-portrait *from Jacobsen's clinic and the two red-haired girls in Rasmus Meyer's collection*
I sought another solution in pictures as Ladies on the Jetty *which is as you say, a kind of* Cubism*. It was in the air then. I called it crystallization. (The Land of Crystals—lithograph) Murder was exhibited at l'Indépendant (sic) in Paris in 1907. The picture is known today as* Death of Marat.'

Plate 262 *Amor and Psyche* is a very clear example of Munch's technique at that time with its long broad strokes. See also pl. 266.
Page 206:
Quotation 20 *Munch to CG, 19/3/1908.*

Page 209: Chapter 12: ILLNESS AND BREAKDOWN

Text 286 This painting exists in a number of versions. OKK M 4, pl. 266 and a larger version from 1905—OKK M 351. There are also many related pictures.
287 See p. 202, quotation 19.
288 Addressed to ET in a draft letter never sent. Munch writes: 'I hope you understood that I was ill. I had to struggle all the time with one thought—I must not go mad!—and if I had not always been a little mad I would have lost my senses altogether.'
289 Munch to ET from Hamburg, 1908.
290 This was Sigurd Mathiesen.
291 Munch to ET, 28/10/1908.

Quotations 1 *Munch to JT, undated draft letter.*
2 *Undated note but headed 'Looking back 1902–8'.*

Plate 267 The portrait in OKK was painted in 1909 and a similar one in Copenhagen in 1908. OKK has a portrait of the head only.
Page 210:
Text 292 Munch to JN, 4/2/1909. Bang (1963), p. 46.
293 For instance with Andreas Haukland in Copenhagen in the autumn of 1904. He also brawled with von Ditten and the painter Karsten. In February 1909 he described the whole business to Jappe Nilssen who replied in pacifying tones and tried to explain to Munch that: 'there cannot possibly be any question of your being the victim of a persecution campaign, nobody is planning to harm you in that way . . . All the same I will admit that you have some grounds for feeling yourself pursued, but that could only be by fate or, if you will, by blind chance'.
294 From the undated note at Munch-Museet. 'Looking Back'. A number of research students have investigated the problems of Munch's mental disorder and its relation to his art. Few of them fully mastered Norwegian and were therefore unable to study Munch's own written observations or the letters of his which deal with these problems. For this reason their analyses, some of which are psychoanalytical, are relatively superficial and subjective. The most exhaustive study in this field is that of the physician Dr Hans Burckhardt, 'Angst und Eros bei Edvard Munch', *German Medical Journal* (Deutsches Arzteblatt, 39/65, 25/9/1965, Cologne, pp. 2098–2102). Max Huggler has written on 'The Conquest of Angst in the Work of Edward Munch' ('Die überwindung der Lebensangst im Werk von Edvard Munch', *Confina Psychiatrica*, N.Y., Vol. I, pp. 1–16). This analysis is based on Munch's artistic works, and on Stenersen's and Hodin's books as well as on a personal visit to Ekely in 1932, but Huggler himself appreciates that this is no evidence. G. W. Digby's *Meaning and Symbol in these modern artists* is on Munch, Moore and Paul Nash. He has been unable to study all the available literature or Munch's own notes. Most of the authors who have written on this subject are not aware that the change in Munch's artistic style occurred *before* his breakdown. They regard his works after treatment at the Copenhagen clinic as 'new' in style and they therefore ascribe too great an importance to his stay there.
295 Gierløff (1953), p. 186 ff.
296 Ludvig Karsten. This story has been repeated many times, by, *inter alia*, H. P. Rohde, *K & K* (1963), p. 268.
297 Helge Rohde. See pl. 293. There is also a portrait OKK M 111, OKK G/r 50 and G/1274. The poem to Munch is to be found in *K & K* (1963), p. 198.
298 Svenæus (1973), p. 262, has put them together, with reproductions.
299 E.g., Pernille Anker Kirkeby.
300 See also p. 209, quotations 1 and 2.

Quotations 3 *Munch's diary entries from the clinic. Inger Munch copied them out.*
4 *Munch to JN, 17/10/1908, Bang (1963), p. 24.*
5 *Schiefler (1974), p. 17.*
6 *Munch to JN, 27/12/1908.*
Page 211:
Text 301 Munch to JN, 1/3/1909, Bang (1963), p. 24.

Page 212:
Quotations 7 *See also quotation 26, p. 18.*
8 *Munch to JN, 27/10/1908. Bang (1963), p. 27.*
9 *Munch to ET, 17/12/1908.*
10 *JN to Munch, March 1909, after the great success of the exhibition. Bang (1963), p. 69.*
11 *Max Linde to Munch, No. 503, 10/2/1908.*
12 *Munch to JN, 27/10/1908. Bang (1963), pp. 27–8.*
13 *Munch to SH, 12/4/1909. Vennene, p. 147.*

Page 213:
Text 302 JT to Munch, Sept. 1908.
303 Munch to Karen Bjølstad, *Fam. brev.*, No. 272. See also p. 276: 'I am not altogether in favour of that sort of decoration.'
304 Receipts totalled about 60,000 kroner. Jappe Nilssen to Munch, 15/3/1909. Bang (1963), p. 59.
305 See Ravensberg, *Vennene*, p. 208 and letter from Munch to JN, 13/3/1909.
306 See Gierløff (1953), pp. 198–212.
307 Munch to SH, 12/4/1909. *Vennene*, p. 147.
308 Gierløff (1953), p. 291.
309 In a rough draft (undated) to Linde. Also given in an account of an improvised speech of Munch in Gierløff (1963), p. 200.

Page 214:
Text 310 It is astonishing how many of these great portraits of his friends he kept. Was he perhaps thinking of creating for them their own exhibition room in some museum of the future? They are today in Munch-Museet.
311 See pl. 15.
312 The series is made up of eighteen lithographs together with the title page and vignettes.

Page 219: **Chapter 13: BACK HOME IN NORWAY**

Text 313 'That rather dreadful period in Copenhagen is over and I move on to face an uncertain future. The Norwegian mountains loom threateningly before me.' Munch to JN, 24/4/1909. Bang (1963), p. 77.
314 Odd Hølaas, *Eyes Which See* (Øynene som ser, 1964, p. 50).

Quotations 1 *Munch to ET, 24/5/1909. Gierløff (1953), p. 280.*
2 *Munch to SH, 14/4/1909. Vennene, p. 149.*
3 *K. A. Kleppe in Bergens Tidende 9/6/1909 Vennene, p. 169.*
4 *Munch to ET, 2/10/1909. Gierløff (1953) p. 280.*

Page 220:
Quotations 5 *Munch to ET, 2/10/1909. Gierløff (1953) p. 280.*
6 *Undated letter from Munch to JT. It appears that Munch at that time really could contemplate working together with Vigeland on an Eidsvoll monument project. Whether Vigeland would have considered working with Munch is another matter.*

Page 222:
Quotations 7 *Another letter to JT about the same project (see note 6 above).*
8 *Munch to Dr Daniel Jacobson, undated draft.*
9 *Franz Servaes in Das Werk, (1894) p. 54.*
10 *Munch to Felix Hatz. See catalogue of the Malmö exhibition (1975), p. 36 by Felix Hatz.*
11 *Birgit Prestøe, 'Some aspects of Munch' ('Småtrekk om Edvard Munch', K & K, 1946, p. 138).*
12 *Dyre Vaa, 'Om Munch', Farmand's Christmas supplement, 1968, p. 133. Sørensen's comments and several entertaining anecdotes.*
13 *Thiis (1933), p. 296.*
14 *JN to Munch, 1910. Bang (1963), p. 79.*
15 *Munch on Helge Rode. H. P. Rohde, K & K (1963), p. 267.*
16 *Munch to CG.*
17 *See Titus Vibe Müller, Vennene, p. 89.*
18 *This is a quotation of Munch. Compare text p. 228, note 318.*

Page 223:
Text 315 Gierløff (1963), p. 218, reckons that Munch at this time had forty-three studios scattered round his four houses at Kragerø, Ramme, Åsgårdstrand and at Grimsrød on Jeløy.

Page 227:
Text 316 For the R.M. Collection see Sonja Hagemann, 'When the R.M. Collections were formed', 'Da Rasmus Meyers samlinger ble til', K & K, 4, (1966).

Plates 291 There is a related Rathenau painting in the Märkisches Museum in East Berlin.
293 The picture was stolen from the Swedish National Museum in 1976, but has since been recovered.

Page 228:
Text 317 See p. 222, quotation 17.
318 See Gierløff (1963), p. 222.

Page 230:
Quotations 19 *See Büttner, Thiis (1934), p. 92.*
20 *Munch to JN. Spring of 1912, p. 87 ff.*
21 *Munch to JN, Spring of 1912, p. 87.*
22 *Thiis, K & K (1912).*

Page 232:
Text 319 Munch to Thiel, 1912.

Page 235: **Chapter 14: THE OSLO UNIVERSITY MURALS**

Text 320 Letter (13/5/1909) to the competition committee for the decoration of the university assembly hall.
321 See p. 235, quotation 1.
322 This account of the controversy is based primarily on Otto Lous Mohr, *Edvard Munch's university murals in the light of unknown preliminary sketches and the documents of the case* (Edvard Munchs Auladekorasjoner i lys av ukjente utkast og sakens akter, Gyldendal, Oslo, 1960). Mohr was in a position to amend earlier accounts because he had access to confidential documents previously unknown. He refutes Jens Thiis's account in the biography of 1933 and points out a number of slips of memory. At the same time he gives Thiis full credit for his vigorous support of Munch and calls him Munch's 'tireless and far-sighted champion'.
323 Lorentz Dietrichson (1834–1917), professor of art history, was seventy-five years old and admitted himself that his sight was failing. In his formal statement he wrote: 'Should my failing eyesight make it impossible for me to apprehend the interplay of colour, which is so totally the essence of a work that classic concepts, correct drawing and composition are irrelevant, then clearly I must suspend my judgement. This is a matter for others to judge—not me.'
324 Gerhard Munthe (1849–1929) studied in Düsseldorf and Munich. He painted some major Norwegian landscapes and carried out decorative works including Håkon's Hall in Bergen, 1910–16.
325 Eilif Peterssen (1852–1928) studied in Copenhagen, Karlsruhe and Munich. When he returned to Norway he painted beautiful landscapes. He made several altar-pieces and carried out decorations for private persons.
326 Emanuel Vigeland (1875–1958), brother of the sculptor Gustav Vigeland, had done the decorations for Vålerenga church and later for the Old Crematorium (1912) in Oslo. He made a number of stained glass paintings in Sweden, Denmark and Norway. His studio at Slemdal in Oslo with its large-scale decorations was opened to the public in 1949.
327 See Mohr (1960), p. 17.
328 Thiis wrote to Munch, 9/11/1909: 'Werenskiold will not stand in your way. Eilif Peterssen is a disaster. I do not have all that amount of faith in Emanuel Vigeland.'
329 Joachim Skovgaard (1856–1933). Danish artist who had done the large frescoes in Viborg Cathedral.
330 The submitted draft has been lost. It was reproduced in *Dagbladet*, 22/8/1931 in connection with an interview with Munch. Several variants however exist including some of a much later date. See pl. 315.
331 Vigeland's proposed design. The various drafts are described and some of them reproduced in Andreas Aubert, 'Universitetets nye festsal og den norske kunst og kultur', *K & K (1911)*, pp. 166–80. It is a violent attack on the whole conduct of the competition 'which more and more takes on the semblance of farce' (p. 168). He is strongly opposed to Vigeland's submission. 'Behind Munch stood Thiis with faith in his hero. Behind Vigeland stood Dietrichson. And behind Dietrichson were the two master builders of the auditorium with their faith in Vigeland . . . As we have seen Edward Munch is certainly covering the walls of Dioramalokalet with enormous canvasses at about the same rate as another artist would fill the pages of his sketch book.'
332 *Life, The Fountain, History, The Pathfinder* and *The Sower*.
333 Eleven drafts were shown at the large Munch exhibition at Liljevalch's and in Kulturhuset, Stockholm, in the spring of 1977. Catalogue Nos. 151–61.
334 See catalogue of August 1911 with Munch's own descriptions and three jury pronouncements. Dioramalokalet was originally a hall where the public could see paintings of well-known places and events painted by W. Peters. At the beginning of this century it was taken over by Blomkvist's, the art dealers.
335 Emanuel Vigeland's statement to accompany his submissions is reproduced in the booklet, *The Competition—Decoration of the new Assembly Hall of the University*, (Konkurransen om Den Kunstneriske utsmykning av universitetets nye festsal, 1911, p. 5). Included in the booklet is the architect's pronouncement on Munch's and Vigeland's submissions.

Quotation   1 See Livs., p. 3. Man and Woman in a Wood. *Munch is referring here to pl. 144.*

Page 236:
Text   336 This was Skovgaard's luke-warm 'judgement of Solomon'. See pp. 242–3, quotation 18.
337 See Mohr, *The Verdict of some other 'Experts'* 'Noen andre 'Sakkyndiges' dom), pp. 57–65. This gives a number of pronouncements. There are quotations from, *inter alia*, A. Krohg, Aubert, Werenskiold, and Harriet Backer. One contribution which Mohr does not mention is that of Fernanda Nissen, 'Munch's pictures in the University Assembly Hall', ('Munchs billeder i Universitetets festsal' in the paper *Socialdemocraten*, No. 153, 29/6/1912). This is an enthusiastic tribute.
338 The members of the fund raising committee were: Johan Anker (Chairman), the lawyer Fr. Stang-Lund, Professor Olaf Broch, Vilhelm Krag, and Fredrick Stang who was at the time a government minister. Mohr is of the opinion that JT's name was not included for 'tactical reasons'. Thiis was however—according to Mohr—the driving force behind it. See Mohr, p. 78. Letter from the committee submitted to the Senate of the University, 21/3/1914. With regard to Munch's success abroad at that time see chapter XIII on the Cologne exhibition in 1912, and *K & K*, (1913), pp. 125–8. In the *K & K* article, Einar Lexow reviews the press reaction to the Munch exhibition in Berlin: 'This is no more than a random selection of press reviews, but they establish beyond dispute that in the eyes of the world Edvard Munch is one of the very greatest figures of modern art. His is no longer a controversial name; only tributes come to him from all quarters. It may well be that not all the tributes are equally enthusiastic but the days of controversy are long since gone.'
339 See Mohr, (1960) p. 84.

Quotations   2 *Munch in the catalogue to the exhibition in Dioramalokalet (August 1911), p. 3.*
3 *Draft of letter probably to JT, 1933.*
4 *Munch entry in a little grey notebook OKK 204 p. 24.*
5 *Munch note after the pictures were in position. See Colour in Print, (Farge på trykk) cat. 1968, No. 121, by P. Hougen.*
6 *Munch note. Ibid.*

Page 238:
Quotations   7 *Ibid. The critic may well have been W. C. Brøgger.*
8 *Munch's explanation with the designs. Printed in* Competition for the Decoration of the University Assembly Hall *(Konkurransen om Den kunstneriske utsmykning av U's festsal, 1911, p. 4). Can also be found in Munch's catalogue to the exhibition in Dioramalokalet (Koukurranseutkast til Universitets festsal, August 1911), p. 3 ff.*

Page 240:
Quotations   9 *JT's written opinion as adviser to the jury. Ibid. pp. 22–3.*
10 *Munch to JT, 30/9/1933.*

Page 242:
Quotations   11 *Munch to JT, undated.*
12 *Munch to K. Schreiner, Vennene, p. 25.*
13 *Munch in* Colour in Print. *See commentary on no. 21 in that catalogue (Hougen).*
14 *Munch to JT, 8/11/1933. Thiis (1933).*
15 *Schreiner, Vennene, p. 25.*
16 *Munch's commentary for the committee of judges 1911, p. 4. Also given in* Dioramalokalet cat. *(Konkurranseutkast til Universitets Festsal, 1911).*
17 *Munch to JT, 1933, ending: 'Young boys' bodies are my field.'*

Page 243:
Text   340 See Ida Sherman's article in *K & K* (1975), pp. 137–53, for *Alma Mater* and the picture's long history. She points out that the old photograph and the old drawing (pl. 36 and 37 in this volume) could have been of importance to the conception of *Alma Mater*. She is probably right when she says that Munch, who became an orphan at such a young age, did turn back to these old pictures—cf. Munch's note to Thiis, 8/11/1933, p. 242, quotation 14. See also Munch entry in the little grey notebook which is a continuation of quotation 4, p. 236. '*Alma Mater* would not have taken the form it did, had I not as an eighteen-year-old near my birth place in Hedemark made a drawing of a peasant woman and her child with the same stance and style.'
341 See reproduction, p. 64, in Curt Glaser's excellent article 'Edvard Munchs Wandgemälde für die Universität in Kristiania' in *Zeitschrift für bildende Kunst* N.F. (1914), pp. 61–6.

Quotations   18 *Skovgaard's half-hearted support for Munch is given in* Konkurransen, *see* Dioramalokalet cat. *(Konkurranseutkast), p. 6. Skovgaard as an invited foreigner was in a very difficult position.*
19 *Dietrichson's assessment,* Konkurransen *pp. 12–18, (this statement, p. 13).* Dioramalokalet cat. *(Konkurranseutkast), p. 10.*

20 *The assessment by JT,* Konkurransen, *pp. 18–27 (this statement p. 26).* Dioramalokalet cat., *(Konkurranseutkast), p. 15.*
21 *See Svenæus, (1953) p. 106 and (1973) p. 305. The Madonna of the Mountain of Mankind (Die Madonna des Menschenberges).*

Plate   312 Munch continually debated whether to re-paint his pictures, and he kept on hanging *The Researchers* and *Alma Mater* alternately on the wall. During the Second World War the paintings were evacuated and in 1946 there was considerable controversy as to which one should be used as the main section of the right hand wall (OKK 962 Munch-Museet, Oslo). The final choice was on *Alma Mater*, mainly because *The Researchers* was in a bad state of preservation.

Page 245:
Quotations   22 *Munch in* Livs. tilbl.
23 *Munch* Dioramalokalet cat. *(Konkurranseutkast), p. 3.*

Page 250:
Text   342 See Emanuel Vigeland's statement on his proposals (1911), p. 7.
343 See Emanuel Vigeland's statement on his proposals (1911), p. 7.
344 '. . . it will be possible to achieve a truly festive effect only by painting the marble in a warmer tone.' Emanuel Vigeland's application, p. 6.
345 For E. Petersen's proposal, see Aubert's article (1911), p. 175.
346 See Aubert (1911), p. 177.
347 E. Werenskiold's proposal. See Aubert (1911), p. 169.
348 Munch had thought of including this lithograph in *The Mirror*. This shows that he regarded the theme as an important one.
349 Curator Wikborg dealt with this subject at a symposium at Munch-Museet, 1973. Typewritten copy in OKK.
350 Dr Otto H. Förster writes in 'Edward Munch in German Art Criticism' ('Edvard Munch i Tysk kunst-kritik', *K & K*, 1927, p. 120): 'It would appear to be an absurdity to renounce all the essential ingredients of monumental painting since Raphael's day, namely the shapely bodies, the elegant and harmonious lines, the calm surfaces and the subdued colours. Yet it so happens that *Mother suckling her Child* persists in the mind and that all the murals handed down to us through the decades seem empty and meaningless when in the mind's eye that massive figure appears beside them. The great revelations of life are not actresses who strut as Pallas Athene across the stage, they are closer to the child at its mother's breast.'
351 In a letter from Jena, 20/1/1914, Eberhard Grisebach tells Munch that he has seen his Christmas exhibition in Berlin before it went on to Frankfurt: 'The pictures are superb.' He asks: 1. Would it be possible to exhibit them in Jena? 2. Was there any chance of obtaining a draft version of for instance *The Sun* for the University of Jena? 3. Would Munch provide any draft painting or do something especially for Jena? See Lothar Grisebach, *Maler des Expressionismus im Briefwechsel mit Eberhard Grisebach*, (Hamburg, 1962) pp. 39–40. At that time Grisebach was lecturer in philosophy at Jena. Munch's tireless supporter Albert Kollmann wrote (1/9/1911): 'There is great interest about your university decorations here in the Secession circles.' Kollmann suggested an exhibition.
352 Compare plate 324 with for example plate 6 and 7.

Page 253: **Chapter 15: A NEW MONUMENTALITY**

Text   353 Gierløff (1953), pp. 228–75.
354 *Livs.*, in connection with the reviews, p. 1.
355 Schreiner, *Vennene*, p. 19.
356 See p. 253, quotation 2.
357 Part of the later *Frieze* was included in the Stockholm exhibition of 1977 and in the comprehensive catalogue, pp. 19–24; Arne Eggum has given an account of this. The catalogue includes (in Swedish and English) Munch's own account from his booklet.
358 Gerd Woll wrote on *Munch's Working Man's Frieze* in her Master's degree treatise, Oslo University (1972). She published some of this material in the catalogue to the exhibition held in Kulturhuset, Stockholm, 1977, pp. 137 ff, Swedish and English (Arbeiderfrise).

Quotations   1 *Arne Törnquist in* Dagens Nyheter, *5/4/1977.*
2 *Munch to K. Schreiner,* Vennene, *p. 24.*
3 *Quotation of Munch. Source not noted by Dr Strang.*
4 *Munch to RH, February 1929.* Nutida Konst *(Stockholm, 1939), p. 17.*

Page 254:
Text   359 Woll, (1972) p. 101.
360 Hieronymous Heyerdahl (1867–1959) launched the Town Hall project in 1915. Arneberg and Poulsson won the architect's competition in 1918. As early as 1916–17 Munch made portraits of Heyerdahl and Arneberg, see Woll (1972), p. 155, and it is not improbable that even at that time the possibility of Munch making the Town Hall decorations was discussed.

361 In the catalogue for 1929, Munch printed several diary entries from as far back as 1889: *Brief Excerpts from my Diary*. Most of them are reproduced in this volume.

362 See, e.g., the watercolour in OKK M 986, 1929 or earlier. Reproduced in the Stockholm catalogue 1977, p. 195.

Quotations 5 *On 15th Nov. 1928 ten well-known artists and art experts put a proposal to the Town Hall committee that Munch should decorate a room in the projected Town Hall. The proposal was published the same day in* Dagbladet *and on 17th Nov. the paper printed an interview by Gunnar Larsen: 'Edvard Munch tells us how he would portray Oslo' (Edvard Munch forteller hvorledes han vil skildre Oslo).*

6 *Munch to Felix Hatz: 'Memory of a Meeting with Edward Munch' ('Minnen av möten med Edv. Munch'),* Malmö cat., *1975, p. 35.*

Page 256:

Text 363 Pl. 329. There are a number of works on this theme. See Woll, 1977 *Stockholm catalogue* p. 177. Hoppe described this picture in *Ord och Bild*, 1917 when it was exhibited at Liljevachs. There is a related picture in Copenhagen. The version presented to Nasjonalgalleriet, in Oslo, by Charlotte and Christian Mustad dates from 1920.

364 *Dagbladet*, 19/2/1918.

Quotation 7 *Munch to his model Birgit Prestøe; she wrote 'Småtrekk om Edvard Munch', K & K (1946), pp. 205–16.*

Plate 331 This work in bronze is one of the few pieces of sculpture Munch made. Only two were cast in bronze. The other was ruined because the plaster was left out in the rain before it could be cast.

Page 257:

Text 365 *Fam. brev.*, No. 55.

366 *Fam. brev.*, No. 131.

367 In 1905 the union between Norway and Sweden was dissolved. Although there were some republican feeling, the majority of Norwegians decided by a plebiscite to invite Prince Carl of Denmark to be their King, which he became as Haakon VII.

368 *Fam. brev.*, No. 237. See Woll (1972), pp. 39–63, on Munch's political views. Pål Hougen, in 'Edvard Munch and 1st May' ('Edvard Munch og 1ste Mai', *Arbeiderbladet*, 30/4/1977) pointed out that *Social Demokraten* on its front page for 1st May 1898 used Munch's *The Scream* together with a flaming torch as an illustration to two verses of the poem by Nils Collett Vogt. It is not certain that Munch himself drew the hand with the flaming torch. *The Scream* would, however, have been used with Munch's permission.

369 Walther Rathenau was murdered on 24/6/1922 by nationalist terrorists.

370 Munch commented to his relative Johan Mellbye when they were standing reading the telegrams outside Morgenbladet in August 1914: 'Good heavens Johan, my world is falling apart! What shall I do? What shall I say? All my friends are German, but it is France I love.' Dyre Vaa, (1968), p. 138.

Page 258:

Text 371 Munch bought the works of younger German artists, both in the harsh years after the First World War and during the Nazi period. On 27/10/1947 Blomqvist held an auction of graphic works of other artists which had been in Munch's possession. The works of the younger German Expressionists are well represented in the catalogue, for instance: 10 by Heckel, 3 by Pechstein, 4 by Schmidt-Rottluff, 2 by Müller, 2 by Barlach and 1 by the Viennese, Kokoschka. All these artists were thrown out of German collections either before or at the same time as Munch. See, *inter alia*, Paul Ortwin Rave, *Kunstdiktatur im dritten Reich*. (Hamburg, 1949) This book contains lists of confiscated works including: Heckel 729, Pechstein 326, Schmidt-Rottluff 608, Müller 357, Barlach 381, Beckmann 509, Kokoschka 417 and Wilhelm Nay 10. Munch helped Nay come to Norway in 1937. Erik Blomberg, 'Munch returns home from Germany' ('Munch flytter hem fra Tyskland', *Konstrevy*, 1939, I, pp. 14–16), deals with the 14 paintings brought home by Holst Halvorsen. See chapter XVI for more details.

372 According to Woll (1972), p. 76, it was the chief chemist, Munch's friend, Georg M. Dedichen, who must share some of the honour for this initiative. He was the brother of Henrik Th. Dedichen and Lucien Dedichen who became Munch's medical adviser shortly afterwards. The brothers were Munch's friends from his young days, when he worked for a short time at Frits Thaulow's open air academy at Modum, where the Dedichen family lived.

373 Woll (1972), p. 83.

Quotations 8 *RH on Munch in the catalogue to the Stockholm exhibition Nationalmuseum (1929), p. 5.*

9 *Munch to J. P. Hodin, A Meeting with Edvard Munch, (et møte med Edvard Munch, 1939, Konstrevy, p. 12).*

Page 259:

Text 374 See Arne Eggum, *catalogue of Rolf E. Stenersen's bequest to the city of Oslo—Akersamlingen* (the Aker collection). OKK Kat. A6 (1974), p. 197.

375 The related picture is OKK M 32.

Page 260:

Text 376 See *John Gabriel Borkman*, Act IV.

377 See, *inter alia*, Pål Hougen, *Edvard Munch og Henrik Ibsen, Catalogue Vestlandske Kunstindustrimuseum* (1975), p. 10 in the text and Nos. 84–101 in the catalogue. Eli Greve (1963), pp. 32–48, has drawn a fine parallel between Munch and Ibsen.

378 Munch to Felix Hatz. *Catalogue to the Malmö exhibition*, 1975, p. 37: 'When I sit here at the station and listen to the bells ringing and watch people running with their luggage and I have these papers, then I am in Paris, or Berlin or Milan. I am on my travels again. But I cannot be a traveller any more . . . I am old and sick.'

379 Munch made a number of paintings on the theme of the winter studio under construction. See, e.g., OKK M 376. Several were shown in the Stockholm exhibition 1977. See Woll, *Stockholm catalogue*, p. 186 ff., 1977.

Quotations 10 *Museum Director Ludwig Justi, in the foreword to the exhibition he arranged at the Kronprinzen Palais in Berlin, 1927.*

11 *Munch 1929. This observation was printed again in* Brief Excerpts from my Diary (Små utdrag fra min dagbok) *in the catalogue of the Blomqvist exhibition (1929), p. 2.*

Page 262:

Quotations 12 *Livs., p. 1, responding to the critics.*

13 *Ibid., p. 3.*

14 *Ibid., p. 4.*

15 *Livs. tilbl., p. 17. In the 1920s, Munch painted new versions of the old themes, but the human figures are now set against a natural background. For the 1927 Berlin exhibition Justi selected 11 pictures from the* Frieze of Life, *4 from the* Linde Frieze, *3 from the* Reinhardt Frieze *and 8 from the preliminary paintings for the university murals.*

16 *Munch to Ebenhard Grisebach 17/2/1913. Briefwechsel, (Hamburg, 1962) p. 33.*

17 *Munch to 'Hast' in* Dagbladet, *(19/2/1927). 'Hast' was Haldis Stenhamar who, according to Gerd Woll, should be given the credit for suggesting, or at least making public, the idea that Munch should contribute to the decoration of the Town Hall.*

Page 263:

Text 380 Pl. 23. A similar self-portrait was in the Mannheim Gallery, but was sold from the museum. It was bought by H. Holst Halvorsen and brought back to Norway. Sold by auction 1947 (No. 34). Privately owned, USA.

381 *Dr. Lucien Dedichen and Jappe Nilssen*, pl. 336. There are two versions in the OKK. One of Dr. Dedichen alone is owned by the family.

Page 265:

Quotations 18 *Munch to Birgit Prestøe.*

19 Dagbladet, *22/1/1932.*

Page 271: **Chapter 16: THE FINAL YEARS**

Text 382 See p. 272, quotation 4.

383 See p. 276, quotation 12.

384 See p. 265, quotation 19.

385 A committee was formed, 12/12/1933 whose aim it was to build a Munch museum. It did not become a reality until 1963.

386 Knight Grand Cross of the Order of St. Olav. Munch also became a Commander of the Légion d' Honneur.

387 'No sir! One might have had such a suit of armour, such a one as Ibsen had—such a breast-plate of medals right across his chest which keeps people at a distance.' Munch to Odd Hølaas, *Eyes which see* (Oyne som ser, 1964, p. 58).

388 Munch exhibited with Matisse among others at Cassirer's in Berlin 1907-8, where Matisse had six works while Munch had thirty-four. At the Internationale Kunstausstellung in Dresden 1926, Munch exhibited eleven paintings and Matisse twelve. See Marit Werenskiold, *Norwegian pupils of Matisse. Apprenticeship and Achievement 1908-1914* (De norske Matisse-elevene. Laeretid og gjennombrudd, 1908-1914, Oslo, 1972).

Quotations 1 *JT to Munch, 19/5/1937.*

2 *Munch to JT, 27/6/1927. It is not very clear why Munch would not agree to JT's plan. According to a letter he wrote 25/8/1937 Munch's view was: . . . 'a Munch museum at Tullinløkken would not fulfil the conditions I require of a museum.' He is afraid that it will not be large enough. At the same time he has lost interest in many things. 'I have therefore abandoned the idea of a museum and after some reflection*

reached the conclusion that a museum would not be a happy outcome for me. Stenersen has been talking about incendiary bombs and I agree with him that it would be too great a hazard for me to have all my works gathered in one place.'

Page 272:
Quotations 3 Gierløff (1963), p. 140.
4 Munch to JT, 1934. Sven Larsson, 'The Eyes of the Artist' ('Konstnärens öga', Natur och Kultur, Stockholm). He discusses the effect of diseases of the eye on the artist's work. See p. 86 ff.
5 Johs. Roede, Vennene, p. 56. Excerpt from letter c. 1934.
6 J. P. Hodin, Edvard Munch (Stockholm 1948), pp. 99–100.

Page 273:
Text 389 The objective of the exhibition was to show what had been achieved in Germany since 1905. It was organized by Dr Ludwig Thormaehlen of the Nationalgalerie, Berlin.
390 See p. 275, quotation 7. In the same letter to JT, unfortunately undated, Munch writes: 'With regard to "The Sick Child", I have painted it (during my exhibition in Nasjonalgalleriet) for the fifth time. I had to have it for the "Frieze of Life" which is always being plundered. It was taken by Lerolle for the Carnegie exhibition and is reproduced in the catalogue . . . I think etc.' We venture to suggest that Munch's memory was at fault here, and that it was not for the fifth but the sixth time. In that case it is this last and undated version which is at Munch-Museet, OKK 51, and it can be given the date 1927.
391 Munch, Brief excerpts from my Diary, 1889–1929. Printed in the catalogue to the exhibition at Blomqvist's, 1929, p. 2: 'There is no need for a painting to be literary—that term of abuse which so many people use about paintings that do not portray apples on a tablecloth or a broken violin.'

Page 275:
Text 392 223 works in Berlin and 229 in Oslo.
393 20,000 paid to see it in Berlin and 30,000 in Oslo.
394 For the influence of Matisse in Norway, see M. Werenskiold (1972).
395 Rudolf Thygesen: '. . . in my callow youth I saw a Munch exhibition and it determined my destiny.' See Prestøe (1946), p. 137.
396 Richard Gerstl. see Hans Bisanz: Edvard Munch and the portrait painter's art in Vienna after 1900 ('Edvard Munch og portrettkunsten i Wien etter 1900', OKK Year Book, 1963, pp. 68–101). Summary in German, pp. 136–44. E. Rothers describes Gerstl as 'ein südlicher gegenspieler Munchs' (a southern counterpart of Munch), p. 76 of his detailed study of Europäische Expressionisten.
397 See Oskar Kokoschka, 'Edvard Munch expresjonisme', K & K, (1952), pp. 129–50, or Der Expressimismus Edvard Munchs, (Wien-Linz-München, 1953).
398 Kollmann to Munch, 8.1.1905.

Quotations 7 Munch to JT, undated letter.
8 Otto Benesch, Edvard Munch (Phaidon, London, 1960).
9 E. Nolde to Munch, 24/1/1909.

Page 276:
Text 399 K & K, (1939), pp. 65–75 and (1969), p. 37. Emil Filla, Tsjekkerne og Edvard Munch and V. Spala, Minner om Edvard Munch. In Munch-Museet catalogue prepared by Bente Torjusen and others for the exhibition on Edvard Munch and Czech Art of February–April 1971, there is a good deal of material on the significance of Munch for Czech art. See also Kunsten idag, (1971), no. 3, pp. 5–55, with a summary in English.
400 See, inter alia, E. Rothers (1971), pp. 7–8.

Quotations 10 Macke to Munch, 29/3/1913. He invites Munch to take part in their exhibition on 22nd Sept. in Berlin and lists some of the artists taking part: Picasso, Derain, Nolde, Heckel, Kirchner, Marc, Kandinsky and Henri Rousseau. The publisher of Sturm, H. Walden, was to organise the exhibition. Munch did not take part on this occasion.
11 See Gierløff (1953), p. 226.
12 Munch letter to JT, 1938.

Page 277:
Text 401 See Marit Werenskiold, 'Die Brücke und Edvard Munch', Zeitschrift des deutschen Vereins für Kunstwissenschaft B. XXVIII, Haft 1–4. (Berlin, 1974), pp. 140–52. See also her article, 'Tysk ekspressionsme i Norden: Die Brücke exhibitions in Copenhagen and Christiania 1908,' K & K, (1975), pp. 155–68.
402 See Alfred Hagenlocher, Wilhelm Laage (Munich, 1969). This is a first-rate review of 431 of his works. Schiefler regarded Laage as one of the 'vollwichtigen Vertreten der Epoche von 1890–1914' (most important representatives of the period 1890–1914). Schiefler catalogued Laage's work in 1912 in the same way as he did Munch's. The Schiefler quotation is taken from Meine Graphik-Sammlung (1974), pp. 43–5.

403 See p. 275, quotation 9.
404 August Macke. See p. 276, quotation 10.
405 See, inter alia, Donald E. Gordon 'Kirchner in Dresden', The Art Bulletin XLVIII, (1966), pp. 335–61. This article gives the whole background to the dating and pre-dating of the works of the artis who were members of 'Die Brücke' in particular those of Kirchner With regard to the influence of Munch, Gordon points out, p. 346 that Kirchner had an opportunity in 1908 to see four works by Munch at the Berlin Secession. He believes that Munch's Lübeck Harbour and the portrait of Walther Rathenau could have influenc Kirchner. He gives as an example Kirchner's Dodo and her Brother. The original painting is at Smith College, Northampton. Bernard S. Myers is one of the art historians who regards Munch as one of the founders of 'Die Brücke'. See his book Die Malerie des Expressionismus, (Cologne, 1957). Also Expressionism: a generation in revolt, (London, 1957), pp. 109–110, 119–20.

Page 278:
Text 406 Schmidt-Rottluff, to Gustav Vriesen, 1/7/1946, who had asked him how important Munch had been for 'Die Brücke'. See Die Schanze (Münster, 1951) pp. 5–6. Also Heckel's statement 8/7/1946 in the same journal, p. 6. At a later date (4/2/1973) Marit Werenskiold received a letter from Schmidt-Rottluff in which he took a differen view of the importance of Munch to the group. Here he writes of 'grosse Anregung' (great stimulus).
407 Schiefler described this reaction of Munch's; Schiefler/Schack (1974), p. 53.
408 Grisebach (1962), p. 44.

Quotations 13 Munch letter to JT, undated but probably 1937.
14 Munch to K. Schreiner, Vennene, p. 14.
15 Ibid., p. 13.
16 Munch to his legal adviser Johs Roede, Vennene, p. 59.

Page 282:
Text 409 J. P. Hodin. Czech art historian who has proclaimed Munch's inter national importance in books, articles and speeches. In 'Et møte med Edvard Munch', Konstrevy, (1939), p. 12, he gave an account o a meeting with Munch. In 1940 he wrote about August Strindberg and Edvard Munch in the same journal. Hodin made a start on his biography of Munch in 1938. The war prevented him from visiting Munch again, but his book was published in German in Stockholm 1948. His latest book on Munch appeared in London in 1972.
410 Haus der Kunst, Munich, March–May 1970.
411 On 23rd January 1939 an auction was held at Wang's the Oslo art dealers, of 14 paintings and 31 graphic works which Holst Halvorsen had bought up in Germany.
412 See pp. 257–8.
413 Munch to Pola Gauguin.

Page 283:
Text 414 See K & K, (1946), pp. 73–8.
415 As early as 1897 Munch made a lithograph with this title. It portray a group of people carrying with outstretched arms a lidless coffin. The figure in the coffin is seated upright and stares into a distant land where the sun is rising. It is clear that Munch valued this work because he wanted to include it in his portfolio The Mirror.

Quotations 17 Munch to Johs. Roede. Excerpt from undated letter. Vennene, p. 60.
18 Munch to RH.
19 Josef Čapek, in Lidové Noviny (4/7/1924). Čapek (1887–1945) was a Czech author and painter influenced by Cubism. Also a critic for the daily paper Lidové Noviny. Died in the concentration camp Bergen-Belsen.
20 Both quotations from a Munch centenary article by Herbert Read (1893–1968) on the significance of Munch to him personally. See OKK Year Book (1963) in Norwegian and English (pp. 126 and 130).
21 Museum Director Jiri Kotalik in the foreword to the catalogue of the Czech exhibition in Oslo, 1971.
22 Review in The Herald Tribune (27th Jan.) of the Munch exhibition in 1974.
23 The innumerable exhibitions of paintings, drawings and graphic works which the OKK has organized all over the world and in Munch-Museet since the artist's death have gone a long way towards fulfilling Munch's wish that his art should be seen in context.
24 Peter Dahl (b. Oslo 1934) now professor at Konsthögskolan (College of Art) in Stockholm. Quoted from the catalogue of the Munch exhibition in Stockholm (1977) p. 6.
25 Nisse Zetlerberg (b. 1910, Stockholm) painter and at one time senior lecturer at the Stockholm Konstfackskolan (State School of Arts and Design). Ibid., p. 10.

List of illustrations

Chapter 1

*1 **Self-portrait (age 23)**, 1886
Oil on canvas, 33 x 25 cm.
Nasjonalgalleriet, Oslo

2 **Sketch for No. 1**
Brown chalk on paper, 33 x 24.5 cm.
Rolf E. Stenersen Collection, RES A220

3 **Self-portrait**, 1881/2
Oil on canvas, 26 x 18 cm.
Oslo Kommunes Kunstsamlinger, OKK 1049

*4 **Self-portrait under Woman's Mask**, 1892/3
Oil on cardboard, 69 x 44 cm.
Oslo Kommunes Kunstsamlinger, OKK 229

*5 **Self-portrait with Cigarette**, 1895
Oil on canvas, 111 x 86 cm.
Nasjonalgalleriet, Oslo

*6 **Self-portrait in Hell**, 1895
Oil on canvas, 82 x 66 cm.
Oslo Kommunes Kunstsamlinger, OKK 591

*7 **Self-portrait with Skeleton Arm**, 1895
Lithograph, 45.5 x 31.7 cm.
Oslo Kommunes Kunstsamlinger, OKK 192
Ref. G. Schiefler No. 31—45.5 x 31.7 cm.

8 **Edvard Munch (age 27)**
Admission card for Christiania Theatre

9 **Edvard Munch (age 22)**
Admission card to Société Royale d'Encouragement des Beaux Arts

10 **Head to Head**, 1905
Woodcut, 40 x 54 cm.
Oslo Kommunes Kunstsamlinger, OKK 612
Ref. G. Schiefler No. 230

*11 **The Blossom of Pain**, 1897
Watercolour, pencil and crayon, 50 x 32.8 cm.
Oslo Kommunes Kunstsamlinger, OKK 2451

*12 **Self-portrait with brushes**, 1904
Oil on canvas, 197 x 91 cm.
Oslo Kommunes Kunstsamlinger, OKK 751

*13 **Self-portrait with Lyre**, 1896/7
Pencil, ink, watercolour and gouache,
68.8 x 53 cm.
Oslo Kommunes Kunstsamlinger, OKK 2460

*14 **Self-portrait with Wine Bottle**, 1906
Oil on canvas, 110 x 120 cm.
Oslo Kommunes Kunstsamlinger, OKK 543

*15 **Self-portrait at Clinic**, 1909
Oil on canvas, 100 x 110 cm.
Rasmus Meyers Samlinger, Bergen

16 **Self-portrait in Bergen**, 1916
Oil on canvas, 90 x 60 cm.
Oslo Kommunes Kunstsamlinger, OKK 263

17 **Self-portrait with Hand Under Chin**,
1911/12
Oil on canvas, 83 x 69 cm.
Oslo Kommunes Kunstsamlinger, OKK 117

18 **Self-portrait with Cigarette**, 1908
Lithograph, 56 x 45.5 cm.
Oslo Kommunes Kunstsamlinger, OKK 227
Ref. G. Schiefler No. 282

19 **Self-portrait during Spanish 'flu'**, 1919
Oil on canvas, 151 x 131 cm.
Nasjonalgalleriet, Oslo

20 **Self-portrait. Inner Turmoil**, 1919
Oil on canvas, 151 x 130 cm.
Oslo Kommunes Kunstsamlinger, OKK 76

*21 **The Bohemian's Wedding**, 1925
Oil on canvas, 65 x 80 cm.
Oslo Kommunes Kunstsamlinger, OKK 848

22 Sketch for *Self-portrait. Inner Turmoil* (No. 20)
Crayon drawing, 31 x 24 cm.
Oslo Kommunes Kunstsamlinger, OKK 246/2

23 **Self-portrait at Ekely**, 1926
Oil on canvas, 92 x 73 cm.
Oslo Kommunes Kunstsamlinger, OKK 318

24 **Self-portrait The Night Wanderer**, c.1930
Oil on canvas, 90 x 68 cm.
Oslo Kommunes Kunstsamlinger, OKK 589

25 **Self-portrait eating a 'truly magnificent
cod's head'**, 1940
Oil on panel, 46 x 34 cm.
Oslo Kommunes Kunstsamlinger, OKK 633

26 **Self-portrait as Seated Nude**, 1933/4
Pencil and watercolour, 70 x 86 cm.
Oslo Kommunes Kunstsamlinger, OKK 2462

27 **Self-portrait**, 1919
Oil on canvas, 100 x 95 cm.
Oslo Kommunes Kunstsamlinger, OKK 449

28 **Self-portrait (after the Spanish 'flu')**, 1919
Black crayon drawing, 43 x 61 cm.
Oslo Kommunes Kunstsamlinger, OKK 2766

29 **Self-portrait by the Window**, 1949/51
Oil on canvas, 84 x 107.5 cm.
Oslo Kommunes Kunstsamlinger, OKK 446

30 **Self-portrait between the Clock and the
Bed**, c.1940
Oil on canvas, 150 x 120 cm.
Oslo Kommunes Kunstsamlinger, OKK 23

31 The old artist in Ekely in 1943

32 Edvard Munch in 1938, age 75

Chapter 2

33 **At the deathbed**, c.1915
Oil on canvas, 140 x 183 cm.
Statens museum for Kunst, Copenhagen

34 **At the deathbed (also called Fever or
The Son)**, 1896
Lithograph and indian ink, 39.3 x 50
Oslo Kommunes Kunstsamlinger, OKK 214
Ref. G. Schiefler No. 72.

*35 Drawing for No. 34, 1892/3
Indian ink and crayon, 23 x 18 cm.
Oslo Kommunes Kunstsamlinger, OKK 286

36 **Dr. Munch with his wife and children**, c.1895
Charcoal drawing, 48 x 63 cm.
Oslo Kommunes Kunstsamlinger, OKK 2266

37 Laura Munch with her five children
(Left: Sophie and Andreas. Right: Edvard and
Laura. On her lap is Inger.)
Photograph

38 **Dr. Christian Munch**, 1885
Oil on canvas, 38 x 28 cm.
Oslo Kommunes Kunstsamlinger, OKK 1056

39 **Self-portrait**, 1880
Oil on panel, 43.6 x 35.4 cm.
Bymuseet, Oslo

*40 **The Death of Hakon Jarl**, 1877
Indian ink drawing made by Munch, age 14
Oslo Kommunes Kunstsamlinger, OKK 35

*41 **The Sick Child**, 1896
Chalk drawing, 42.1 x 40.9 cm.
Private Collection

*42 **The Aunt's Sitting Room**, 1881
Oil on canvas, 21 x 27 cm.
Oslo Kommunes Kunstsamlinger, OKK 1047

*43 **The Dead Mother and the Child**, 1894
Pencil and charcoal, 50 x 65 cm.
Oslo Kommunes Kunstsamlinger, OKK 301

*44 **The Dead Mother and the Child**, 1899
Tempera on canvas, 104 x 180 cm.
Oslo Kommunes Kunstsamlinger, OKK 420

45 **Sister Inger, age 14**, 1882
Charcoal drawing, 34.5 x 25.8 cm.
Oslo Kommunes Kunstsamlinger, OKK 2361

46 **Sister Laura, age 14**, 1881/2
Oil on panel, 23 x 18 cm.
Oslo Kommunes Kunstsamlinger, OKK 1046

*47 **Sister Inger, age 16**, 1884
Oil on canvas, 97 x 68 cm.
Nasjonalgalleriet, Oslo

48 **Siesta**, 1883
Oil on paper mounted on panel, 35 x 48 cm.
Oslo Kommunes Kunstsamlinger, OKK 1055

*49 **Old Aker Church**, 1881
Oil on cardboard, 21 x 15.5
Oslo Kommunes Kunstsamlinger, OKK 1043

50 **Aunt Karen in her Rocking Chair**, 1884
Oil on canvas, 47 x 41 cm.
Oslo Kommunes Kunstsamlinger, OKK 1108

*51 **Death in the Sickroom**, c.1893
Oil on canvas, 136 x 160 cm.
Oslo Kommunes Kunstsamlinger, OKK 418

52 **Brother Andreas studying Anatomy**, 1883
(He later became a doctor, but died in 1895,
thirty years old)
Oil on cardboard, 62 x 75 cm.
Oslo Kommunes Kunstsamlinger, OKK 202

Chapter 3

*53 **Hans Jaeger**, 1889
Oil on canvas, 110 x 84 cm.
Nasjonalgalleriet, Oslo

54 **Hans Jaeger**, 1896
Lithograph, 46 x 33 cm.
Oslo Kommunes Kunstsamlinger, OKK 218
Ref. G. Schiefler No. 76

*55 **Two Bohemian Friends**, c.1890
Pastel
Private Collection

*56 **Gunnar Heiberg**, c.1890
Crayon drawing, 73.5 x 59.5 cm.
Private Collection

57 **Tête-à-tête** (Jensen-Hjell and Inger), c.1884
Oil on canvas, 65.5 x 75.5 cm.
Oslo Kommunes Kunstsamlinger, OKK 340

*58 **A Fight In the Studio**, 1881/2
Oil on cardboard, 47 x 63.5 cm.
Oslo Kommunes Kunstsamlinger, OKK 628

*59 **The Day After**, 1894
Oil on canvas, 115 x 152 cm.
Nasjonalgalleriet, Oslo

60 Detail of No. 59
(The first version, from 1886, was destroyed in
a fire)

61 **The Painter Jensen-Hjell**, 1885
Oil on canvas, 190 x 100 cm.
Private Collection

62 **Sigbjørn Obstfelder**, 1896
Lithograph, 36 x 27.5 cm.
Oslo Kommunes Kunstsamlinger, OKK 818
Ref. G. Schiefler No. 78a

63 **The Hands**, 1895
Lithograph, 48 x 29 cm.
Oslo Kommunes Kunstsamlinger, OKK 196
Ref. G. Schiefler No. 35

64 **Inheritance**, 1897/99
Oil on canvas, 141 x 120 cm.
Oslo Kommunes Kunstsamlinger, OKK 11

65 **Young Man and Whore** (Edvard Munch and
Rose), c.1895
Watercolour and charcoal, 50 x 47.5 cm.
Oslo Kommunes Kunstsamlinger, OKK 2445

66 **The Hands**, 1893
Oil on canvas, 89 x 76.5 cm.
Oslo Kommunes Kunstsamlinger, OKK 192

Chapter 4
67 **Sister Inger**, 1892
Oil on canvas, 172 x 122.5 cm.
Nasjonalgalleriet, Oslo

68 **Girl Kindling the Stove**, 1883
Oil on canvas, 97 x 66 cm.
Private Collection

*69 **Country Road**, 1891–92
Oil on canvas, 85 x 91 cm.
Oslo Kommunes Kunstsamlinger, OKK 1111

70 **Evening**, 1888
Oil on canvas, 37 x 75 cm.
Private Collection

71 **Drawing for No. 69**
Indian ink, 17 x 24 cm.
Oslo Kommunes Kunstsamlinger, OKK 129

72 **Spring Day on Karl Johan Street**, 1891
Oil on canvas, 80 x 100 cm.
Bergen Billedgalleri

73 **Morning**, 1884
Oil on canvas, 96.5 x 103.5 cm.
Rasmus Meyers Samlinger, Bergen

74 **The Sick Child**, 1885/86
Oil on canvas, 119.5 x 118.5 cm.
Nasjonalgalleriet, Oslo

75 Detail of No. 74

76 **Line Dedichen**, 1884
Pencil drawing, 23 x 17 cm.
Private Collection

77 **Arrival of the Mailboat**, 1890
Oil on canvas, 98 x 130 cm.
Private Collection

78 **Evening at Vrengen**, 1888
Oil on canvas, 75 x 101 cm.
Private Collection

Chapter 5
*79 **Moonlight (Night in St. Cloud)**, c.1893
Pastel, 80 x 75 cm.
Private Collection

*80 **Léon Bonnat's Studio**

81 **Spring**, 1889
Oil on canvas, 169 x 263.5 cm.
Nasjonalgalleriet, Oslo

82 **Inger on the Beach**, 1889
Oil on canvas, 125 x 162 cm.
Rasmus Meyers Samlinger, Bergen

83 **Evening (Melancholy)**, 1891
Crayon, oil and pencil, 73 x 101 cm.
Oslo Kommunes Kunstsamlinger, OKK 58

84 **Landscape in St. Cloud**, 1890
Oil on canvas, 46 x 38 cm.
Oslo Kommunes Kunstsamlinger, OKK 1109

85 **Man and Woman**, c.1890
Ink drawing, 30.2 x 28.5 cm.
Oslo Kommunes Kunstsamlinger, OKK 365A
(On left hand side of the drawing and on the
back Munch wrote several important notes
dealing with, amongst other things, the forthcoming *Frieze of Life*)

86 **Dr. Munthe reading**, 1882
Pencil drawing, 26 x 20.6 cm.
Private Collection

87 **Karen Bjølstad knitting**, 1882
Pencil drawing, 19 x 13 cm.
Private Collection

*88 **Emanuel Goldstein**, 1908/9
Lithograph, 27.5 x 24.5 cm.
Oslo Kommunes Kunstsamlinger, OKK 272
Ref. G. Schiefler No. 276

89 **Death at the Helm**, 1893
Oil on canvas, 100 x 120 cm.
Oslo Kommunes Kunstsamlinger, OKK 880

90 **Military Band on Karl Johan Street**, 1889
Oil on canvas, 102 x 142 cm.
Kunsthaus, Zurich

Chapter 6
*91 **Rue Lafayette**, 1891
Oil on canvas, 92 x 73 cm.
Nasjonalgalleriet, Oslo

92 **Rue de Rivoli**, 1891
Oil on canvas, 80 x 63 cm.
Fogg Museum, Cambridge, U.S.A.

93 **Stéphane Mallarmé**, 1896
Lithograph, 51.2 x 28.9 cm.
Oslo Kommunes Kunstsamlinger, OKK 221
Ref. G. Schiefler No. 79b

94 Sketch for Charles Baudelaire's *Les Fleurs du
Mal*, 1896
Indian ink drawing, 28 x 20.5 cm.
Oslo Kommunes Kunstsamlinger, OKK 402

95 **In the Open Air**, 1891
Oil on canvas, 66 x 120 cm.
Oslo Kommunes Kunstsamlinger, OKK 495

96 **Night in Nice**, 1891
Oil on canvas, 48 x 54 cm.
Nasjonalgalleriet, Oslo

97 **Gaming Tables at Monte Carlo**, 1892
Oil on canvas, 75 x 116 cm.
Oslo Kommunes Kunstsamlinger, OKK 50

98 Dagny Juell, at the beginning of the 1890's

99 **Julius Meier-Graefe**, 1895
Oil on canvas, 100 x 75 cm.
Nasjonalgalleriet, Oslo

100 **Girl by the Window**, 1891
Oil on canvas, 96 x 65 cm.
Private Collection

101 **Dagny Juell Przybyszewska**, 1893
Oil on canvas, 148.5 x 99.5 cm.
Oslo Kommunes Kunstsamlinger, OKK 212

102 **Vignette** for Przybyszewski's collection of
poetry *The Vigil*, 1894
Charcoal drawing, 61.5 x 47.1 cm.
Oslo Kommunes Kunstsamlinger, OKK 2449

103 **Puberty**, 1894
Oil on canvas, 150 x 111 cm.
Nasjonalgalleriet, Oslo

104 **Mother and Daughter**, 1897
Oil on canvas, 135 x 163 cm.
Nasjonalgalleriet, Oslo

*105 **The Voice**, 1893
Oil on canvas, 90 x 119 cm.
Oslo Kommunes Kunstsamlinger, OKK 44

106 **Eyes**, 1894/95
Charcoal drawing, 41.5 x 50.3 cm.
Oslo Kommunes Kunstsamlinger, OKK 329

*107 **The Scream**, 1893
Oil, casein and pastel on cardboard, 91 x 74 cm.
Nasjonalgalleriet, Oslo

108 **Angst**, 1894
Oil on canvas, 94 x 74 cm.
Oslo Kommunes Kunstsamlinger, OKK 515

109 **Angst**, 1896
Watercolour and indian ink, 37.0 x 32.3 cm.
Oslo Kommunes Kunstsamlinger, OKK 259

110 **Angst**, 1896
Woodcut, 46 x 37.7 cm.
Oslo Kommunes Kunstsamlinger, OKK 568
Ref. G. Schiefler No. 62

111 **Despair**, 1892
Oil on canvas, 92 x 67 cm.
Thielska Galleriet, Stockholm

112 **The Scream**, 1895
Lithograph, 35 x 25.2 cm.
Oslo Kommunes Kunstsamlinger, OKK 193
Ref. G. Schiefler No. 32

113 **The Mystery of the Beach**, 1892
Oil on canvas, 100 x 140 cm.
Private Collection

*114 **Melancholy (The Yellow Boat)**, 1892/93
Oil on canvas, 65 x 96 cm.
Nasjonalgalleriet, Oslo

*115 **Madonna**, c.1894
Oil on canvas, 95 x 75 cm.
Private Collection

116 **Madonna**, 1894/95
Oil on canvas, 91 x 71 cm.
Nasjonalgalleriet, Oslo

117 **Walter Leistikow and his Wife**, 1902
Lithograph, 52.2 x 86.8 cm.
Oslo Kommunes Kunstsamlinger, OKK 243
Ref. G. Schiefler No. 170

118 **August Strindberg**, 1892
Oil on canvas, 120 x 90 cm.
Nationalmuseum, Stockholm

119 **Henrik Ibsen at the Grand Café**, 1906/10
Tempera on canvas, 116 x 181 cm.
Oslo Kommunes Kunstsamlinger, OKK 717

120 **Holger Drachmann**, 1901
Lithograph, 58.6 x 44.8 cm.
Oslo Kommunes Kunstsamlinger, OKK 240
Ref. G. Schiefler No. 141

121 **Knut Hamsun**, 1896
Drypoint, 27.9 x 18.3 cm.
Oslo Kommunes Kunstsamlinger, OKK 40
Ref. G. Schiefler No. 52

122 **Stanislaw Przybyszewski**, 1895
Pastel and oil, 62 x 55 cm.
Oslo Kommunes Kunstsamlinger, OKK 134

123 **The German** (Hermann Schlittgen), 1904
Oil on canvas, 200 x 120 cm.
Oslo Kommunes Kunstsamlinger, OKK 367

Chapter 7
124 **The Kiss**, 1892
Oil on canvas, 99 x 81 cm.
Oslo Kommunes Kunstsamlinger, OKK 59

125 **The Kiss**, 1892
Oil on canvas, 72 x 91 cm.
Nasjonalgalleriet, Oslo

126 **The Kiss**, 1894/95
Pencil drawing, 18.8 x 28.8 cm.
Oslo Kommunes Kunstsamlinger, OKK 362

127 **The Kiss**, 1895
Drypoint and aquatint, 32.9 x 26.3 cm.
Oslo Kommunes Kunstsamlinger, OKK 21
Ref. G. Schiefler No. 22

128 **Evening on Karl Johan Street**, 1893/94
Oil on canvas, 85 x 121 cm.
Rasmus Meyers Samlinger, Bergen

129 **Evening on Karl Johan Street**, 1896
Hand-coloured lithograph
Private Collection

*130 **Vampire**, c.1893
Oil on canvas, 78 x 98 cm.
Oslo Kommunes Kunstsamlinger, OKK 292

131 **Vampire**, 1895/96
Lithograph and woodcut, 38.2 x 54.5 cm.
Oslo Kommunes Kunstsamlinger, OKK 567
Ref. G. Schiefler No. 34

132 **Jealousy**, 1895
Oil on canvas, 67 x 100 cm.
Rasmus Meyers Samlinger, Bergen

133 **Jealousy**, 1896
Lithograph, 46.5 x 56.5 cm.
Oslo Kommunes Kunstsamlinger, OKK 202
Ref. G. Schiefler No. 58

134 **The Virginia Creeper**, 1898
Oil on canvas, 119 x 121 cm.
Oslo Kommunes Kunstsamlinger, OKK 503

*135 **The Dance of Life**, 1899/1900
Oil on canvas, 126 x 191 cm.
Nasjonalgalleriet, Oslo

136 Detail of No. 135

137 Detail of No. 135

138 Sketch for *The Dance of Life*, 1898
Indian ink, charcoal and (bluegreen) crayon,
35.9 x 45.8 cm.
Oslo Kommunes Kunstsamlinger, OKK 2392

139 **The Storm**, 1893
Oil on canvas, 98 x 127 cm.
Museum of Modern Art, New York

140 **Starry Night**, 1893
Oil on canvas, 135 x 140 cm.
Private Collection

141 **Ashes**, 1894
Oil on canvas, 121 x 141 cm.
Nasjonalgalleriet, Oslo

142 **The Three Stages of Woman**, 1894
Oil on canvas, 164 x 250 cm.
Rasmus Meyers Samlinger, Bergen

143 **Red and White**, c.1894
Oil on canvas, 93 x 130 cm.
Oslo Kommunes Kunstsamlinger, OKK 460

144 **Metabolism or The Transformation of
Matter, (Man and Woman in a Wood)** c.1898,
but overpainted later, c. 1918
Oil on canvas, 175 x 143 cm. (excluding
painted frame)
Oslo Kommunes Kunstsamlinger, OKK 419

145 **Eye to Eye**, 1893
Oil on canvas, 137 x 110 cm.
Oslo Kommunes Kunstsamlinger, OKK 502

*146 **Fertility**, 1898
Oil on canvas, 120 x 140 cm.
Private Collection

Chapter 8
*147 **The Lonely One**, 1896
Mezzotint and drypoint on zinc, 28.7 x
21.7 cm.
Olso Kommunes Kunstsamlinger, OKK 816
Ref. G. Schiefler No. 42

*148 **Death and the Maiden**, 1894
Drypoint, 29.3 x 20.8 cm.
Oslo Kommunes Kunstsamlinger, OKK 3
Ref. G. Schiefler No. 3

*149 **The Three Stages of Woman**, 1895
Drypoint, etching and aquatint, 28.5 x 33 cm.
Oslo Kommunes Kunstsamlinger, OKK 20
Ref. G. Schiefler No. 21

*150 **Puberty**, 1894
Lithograph, 40 x 27.5 cm.
Oslo Kommunes Kunstsamlinger, OKK 189
Ref. G. Schiefler No. 8

151 **The Sick Child**, 1894
Drypoint with roulette, 36.1 x 26.9 cm.
Oslo Kommunes Kunstsamlinger, OKK 7
Ref. G. Schiefler No. 7

152 **Gustav Schiefler**, 1905
Drypoint, 23.2 x 18.5 cm.
Oslo Kommunes Kunstsamlinger, OKK 112
Ref. G. Schiefler No. 238

*153 **Harpy**, 1900
Lithograph, 36.5 x 31.5 cm.
Oslo Kommunes Kunstsamlinger, OKK 239
Ref. G. Schiefler No. 137

154 **The Lonely Ones**, 1899
Woodcut, 39.5 x 53 cm.
Oslo Kommunes Kunstsamlinger, OKK 601
Ref. G. Schiefler No. 133

155 **The Lonely Ones**, 1899
Woodcut, 39.5 x 53 cm.
Oslo Kommunes Kunstsamlinger, OKK 601
Ref. G. Schiefler No. 133

156 **The Lonely Ones**, 1895
Drypoint, 15.5 x 21.4 cm.
Oslo Kommunes Kunstsamlinger, OKK 19
Ref. G. Schiefler No. 20

157 **Melancholy**, 1896
Woodcut, 33.3 x 42.2 cm.
Oslo Kommunes Kunstsamlinger, OKK 588
Ref. G. Schiefler No. 116

158 **The Insane Woman (Melancholy)**, 1908/9
Lithograph, 25 x 12 cm.
Oslo Kommunes Kunstsamlinger, OKK 281
Ref. G. Schiefler No. 286

159 a, b, c, **The Kiss**, 1897/98
Woodcut
Oslo Kommunes Kunstsamlinger, OKK 577–580
(Variations of the same subject)
Ref. G. Schiefler No. 102

160 **The Kiss**, 1895
Drypoint and aquatint, 32.9 x 26.3 cm.
Oslo Kommunes Kunstsamlinger, OKK 21
Ref. G. Schiefler No. 22

161 **Madonna**, 1895–1902
Lithograph, 55.5 x 35.3 cm.
Oslo Kommunes Kunstsamlinger, OKK 194
Ref. G. Schiefler No. 33

162 **Madonna**, 1895
Lithograph
Oslo Kommunes Kunstsamlinger, OKK 194
(This version is hand-coloured and is dedicated
to Przybyszewski)

163 **Madonna**, 1895
Drypoint, 36 x 26.5 cm.
Oslo Kommunes Kunstsamlinger, OKK 15
Ref. G. Schiefler No. 16

164 **Madonna**, 1895–1902
Lithograph, 60.4 x 44.5 cm.
Oslo Kommunes Kunstsamlinger, OKK 194
Ref. G. Schiefler No. 33

165 **Women on the Beach**, 1898
Woodcut, 45,4 x 50.8 cm.
Oslo Kommunes Kunstsamlinger, OKK 589
Ref. G. Scheifler No. 117

166 **Women on the Beach**, 1898
Woodcut (Block), 45.5 x 51.3 cm.
Oslo Kommunes Kunstsamlinger, OKK 589

167 **Women on the Beach**, 1898
Woodcut, 45.5 x 50.8 cm.
Oslo Kommunes Kunstsamlinger, OKK 589
Ref. G. Schiefler No. 117

168 **Lovers in the Waves**, 1896
Lithograph, 31 x 4.19 cm.
Oslo Kommunes Kunstsamling, OKK 213
Ref. G. Scheifler No. 71

169 **Attraction**, 1896
Lithograph, 39.5 x 62.5 cm.
Oslo Kommunes Kunstsamlinger, OKK 208
Ref. G. Schiefler No. 66

170 **Separation**, 1896
Lithograph, 41 x 62.5 cm.
Oslo Kommunes Kunstsamlinger, OKK 210
Ref. G. Schiefler No. 68

171 **Attraction**, 1896
Lithograph, 47.2 x 35.5 cm.
Oslo Kommunes Kunstsamlinger, OKK 207
Ref. G. Schiefler No. 65

172 **Old Man Praying**, 1902
Woodcut, 45.8 x 32.5 cm.
Oslo Kommunes Kunstsamlinger, OKK 607
Ref. G. Schiefler No. 173

173 **The Sick Child**, 1896
Lithograph, 42.1 x 56.5 cm.
Oslo Kommunes Kunstsamlinger, OKK 203
Ref. G. Schiefler No. 59

174 Detail of a different version of No. 173
Oslo Kommunes Kunstsamlinger, OKK 203–18

175 **Nude Girl**, 1896
Mezzotint and drypoint on zinc, 14.5 x 12.7 cm.
Oslo Kommunes Kunstsamlinger, OKK 29
Ref. G. Schiefler No. 39

176 **In Man's Brain**, 1897
Woodcut, 37.2 x 56.7 cm.
Oslo Kommunes Kunstsamlinger, OKK 573
Ref. G. Scheifler No. 98

177 **The Three Stages of Woman**, 1899
Lithograph, 46.2 x 59.2 cm.
Oslo Kommunes Kunstsamlinger, OKK 238
Ref. G. Schiefler No. 122

178 **The Voice**, 1896
Woodcut, 37.8 x 56 cm.
Oslo Kommunes Kunstsamlinger, OKK 572
Ref. G. Schiefler No. 83

*179 **Evening (Melancholy)**, 1896
Woodcut, 37.6 x 45.5 cm.
Oslo Kommunes Kunstsamlinger, OKK 571
Ref. G. Schiefler No. 82

*180 Detail of another version of Plate 179

181 **Moonlight**, 1896
Woodcut, 41.2 x 46.7 cm.
Oslo Kommunes Kunstsamlinger, OKK 570
Ref. G. Schiefler No. 81

182 **The Maiden and the Heart**, 1896
Etching and drypoint, 23.4 x 23.7 cm.
Oslo Kommunes Kunstsamlinger, OKK 37
Ref. G. Schiefler No. 47

183 **The Maiden and the Heart**, 1899
Woodcut, 25.2 x 18.4 cm.
Oslo Kommunes Kunstsamlinger, OKK 602
Ref. G. Schiefler No. 134

184 **Encounter in Space**, 1899
Woodcut, 18.1 x 25.1 cm.
Oslo Kommunes Kunstsamlinger, OKK 603
Ref. G. Scheifler No. 135

185 **To the Forest**, 1915
Woodcut, 51 x 64.6 cm.
Oslo Kommunes Kunstsamlinger, OKK 644
Ref. G. Scheifler No. 444

186 **Kiss on the Hair**, 1915
Woodcut, 15.5 x 16.8 cm.
Oslo Kommunes Kunstsamlinger, OKK 643
Ref. G. Scheifler No. 443

187 **Tingel-Tangel**, 1895
Lithograph, 41 x 62.8 cm.
Oslo Kommunes Kunstsamlinger, OKK 198
Ref. G. Scheifler No. 37
(This hand-coloured version is from a private collection)

*188 **Man's Head in Woman's Hair**, 1896
Woodcut, 54.6 x 38.1 cm.
Oslo Kommunes Kunstsamlinger, OKK 569
Ref. G. Scheifler No. 80

Chapter 9
189 **Seated Model**, 1896
Charcoal, pencil and watercolour, 62 x 47.7 cm.
Oslo Kommunes Kunstsamlinger, OKK 2459

190 **Madonna**, 1893
Charcoal and pencil, 73.7 x 59.7 cm.
Oslo Kommunes Kunstsamlinger, OKK 2430

*191 **The Empty Cross**, 1901
Indian ink and watercolour, 43.1 x 62.7 cm.
Oslo Kommunes Kunstsamlinger, OKK 2452

192 **Farewell** (The original inspiration for *The Kiss*), 1890(92?)
Pencil drawing, 27 x 20.5 cm.
Oslo Kommunes Kunstsamlinger, OKK 2356

193 **At the Window**, before 1889
Crayon drawing, 27.3 x 24.5 cm.
Oslo Kommunes Kunstsamlinger, OKK 2379

194 **An Evening with the Family**, 1884
Pencil drawing, 34.7 x 48.3 cm.
Oslo Kommunes Kunstsamlinger, OKK 2365

195 **Inger Munch**, 1882
Pencil drawing, 25.6 x 19.2 cm.
Oslo Kommunes Kunstsamlinger, OKK 2377

196 **Blue Standing Nude**, 1920's
Watercolour, 51 x 35 cm.
Oslo Kommunes Kunstsamlinger, OKK 1072

197 **Standing Nude**, c.1900
Tempera, coloured chalk and charcoal, 65.4 x 29 cm.
Oslo Kommunes Kunstsamlinger, OKK 1131

198 **Charwomen in the Corridor**, 1906
Gouache and coloured chalk on paper, 71.6 x 47.5 cm.
Oslo Kommunes Kunstsamlinger, OKK 534

199 **Girl with her hands in front of her Mouth**, after 1912
Charcoal drawing, 40.8 x 26.9 cm.
Oslo Kommunes Kunstsamlinger, OKK 519

200 **Girls Bathing**, c.1935
Watercolour and crayon, 59.8 x 57.4 cm.
Oslo Kommunes Kunstsamlinger, OKK 1570

201 **Girls on the Beach**, c.1920
Watercolour, 23.8 x 28.9 cm.
Oslo Kommunes Kunstsamlinger, OKK 310

*202 **Max Dauthendey**, 1897
Black crayon drawing, 40 x 60 cm.
Oslo Kommunes Kunstsamlinger, OKK 672

203 **Lady with a Blue Hat**, after 1920
Watercolour, 66.5 x 52 cm.
Oslo Kommunes Kunstsamlinger, OKK 699

204 **Kneeling Nude**, after 1910
Crayon drawing, 35.6 x 26.5 cm.
Oslo Kommunes Kunstsamlinger, OKK 897

205 **Portrait of a Man**, c.1912
Crayon drawing, 40 x 27 cm.
Oslo Kommunes Kunstsamlinger, OKK 733

206 **Ottilie Schiefler**, 1907/8
Watercolour and pastel, 49.4 x 38.5 cm.
Oslo Kommunes Kunstsamlinger, OKK 660

207 **Munch and the Woman in Green** (mirror image), 1920/30
Pencil drawing, 51.5 x 23.2 cm.
Oslo Kommunes Kunstsamlinger, OKK 1642

208 **Half-length Female Nude**, after 1910
Crayon drawing, 40 x 27 cm.
Oslo Kommunes Kunstsamlinger, OKK 910

209 **Stones at Åsgårdstrand**, after 1912
Crayon drawing, 29 x 42 cm.
Oslo Kommunes Kunstsamlinger, OKK 2382

210 Sketch for Ibsen's *Ghosts*, 1906
Drawing, oil and pencil on paper
Kunstmuseum, Basel

211 Oswald from Ibsen's *Ghosts*, 1920
Lithograph, 39 x 50 cm.
Oslo Kommunes Kunstsamlinger, OKK 421
Ref. G. Scheifler No. 487

212 Draft for Ibsen's *Ghosts*, 1906
Tempera on cardboard, oil and pencil on paper, 69 x 90 cm.
Rolf E. Stenersen Collection

213 **Ibsen and Jappe Nilssen**, late 1920's
Indian ink drawing, 17 x 20.8 cm.
Oslo Kommunes Kunstsamlinger, OKK 195/145

214 Sketch for Ibsen's *Ghosts*, 1906
Oil and pencil on paper
Location unknown

215 Sketch for Ibsen's *Hedda Gabler*, 1907
Watercolour and pencil, 57.5 x 45.5 cm.
Oslo Kommunes Kunstsamlinger, OKK 1584

216 **Anitra's Dance**, 1913
Crayon drawing, 35.5 x 26 cm.
Oslo Kommunes Kunstsamlinger, OKK 1645

*217 **Peer Gynt and the Button Moulder** (Edvard Munch and Albert Kollmann), 1929/30
Pencil drawing, 21.9 x 28.2 cm. (mirror image)
Oslo Kommunes Kunstsamlinger, OKK 1635

Chapter 10
218 **Girls on the Jetty**, 1899
Oil on canvas, 136 x 126 cm.
Nasjonalgalleriet, Oslo

219 **Girls on the Jetty**, 1900
Oil on canvas, 84 x 129 cm.
Private Collection

220 **Train Smoke**, 1900
Oil on canvas, 85 x 109 cm.
Oslo Kommunes Kunstsamlinger, OKK 1092

221 **The Island**, 1900
Painting
Private Collection

222 **White Night**, 1901
Oil on canvas, 116 x 111 cm.
Nasjonalgalleriet, Oslo

223 **Adam and Eve**, 1908
Oil on canvas, 130 x 202 cm.
Oslo Kommunes Kunstsamlinger, OKK 391

224 **Birch Tree in the Snow**, 1901
Oil on panel, 60 x 68 cm.
Private Collection

225 **Avenue in the Snow**, 1906
Oil on canvas, 80 x 100 cm.
Oslo Kommunes Kunstsamlinger, OKK 288

226 **Sin (Nude with Red Hair)**, 1901
Lithograph, 49.5 x 39.7 cm.
Oslo Kommunes Kunstsamlinger, OKK 241
Ref. G. Schiefler No. 142

227 **Mathilde (Tulla) Larsen**, c.1898
Oil on canvas, 119 x 61 cm.
Oslo Kommunes Kunstsamlinger, OKK 740

228 **Female Nude with Red Hair**, 1898/1902
Oil on canvas, 120 x 50 cm.
Oslo Kommunes Kunstsamlinger, OKK 469

229 **The Violin Concert**, 1903

Oslo Kommunes Kunstsamlinger, OKK 254
Ref. G. Schiefler No. 211—48.0 x 56.0 cm.

230 Photograph of Eva Mudocci

231 **Salome**, 1903
Lithograph, 40.5 x 30.5 cm.
Oslo Kommunes Kunstsamlinger, OKK 256
Ref. G. Schiefler No. 213

232 **Madonna (The Brooch)**, 1903
Lithograph, 60 x 46 cm.
Oslo Kommunes Kunstsamlinger, OKK 255
Ref. G. Schiefler No. 212

233 **Melancholy**, c.1899
Oil on canvas, 110 x 126 cm.
Oslo Kommunes Kunstsamlinger, OKK 12

Chapter 11
*234 **Ludvig Meyer's Son Karl**, 1895
Oil on canvas (Detail of No. 243)
Private Collection

*235 **Herbert Esches's children**, 1905
Oil on canvas, 147 x 153 cm.
Private Collection

236 **Albert Kollmann**, 1902
Drypoint, 18.8 x 14.1 cm.
Oslo Kommunes Kunstsamlinger, OKK 69
Ref. G. Schiefler No. 159

237 **Friedrich Nietzsche**, 1906
Oil on canvas, 201 x 160 cm.
Thielska Galleriet, Stockholm

238 **The Banker Ernest Thiel**, 1907
Oil on canvas, 191 x 101 cm.
Thielska Galleriet, Stockholm

239 **Max Linde's House**, 1902/3
Etching, aquatint and drypoint on zinc, 44 x 60.5 cm.
Oslo Kommunes Kunstsamlinger, OKK 88
Ref. G. Schiefler No. 189

240 **Dr. Max Linde**, 1904
Oil on canvas, 133 x 81 cm.
Rolf E. Stenersen Collection, RES A74

*241 Munch between Jan Preisler and Milos Jiránek, 1905

242 **Count Harry Kessler**, 1904
Oil on canvas, 86 x 75 cm.
Private Collection

243 **Ludvig Meyer's children, Eli, Hakon and Karl**, 1895
Oil on canvas
Private Collection

244 **Four Girls in Åsgårdstrand**, 1904-05
Oil on canvas, 87 x 110 cm.
Oslo Kommunes Kunstsamlinger, OKK 488

245 **The Bathers Triptych**, 1907/9, Youth, Manhood, Old Age
Oil on canvas, c.206 x 425 cm.
Oslo Kommunes Kunstsamlinger, OKK 704, 705, 706

246 Edvard Munch painting on the beach at Warnemunde. On the right is his large *Men Bathing* picture.

247 Detail of No. 244

*248 **Max Linde's Sons,** 1903
Oil on canvas, 144 x 179 cm.
Behnhaus, Lubeck

249 **Girls Watering Flowers,** 1903/4
Part of the Linde Frieze
Oil on canvas, 100 x 80 cm.
Oslo Kommunes Kunstsamlinger, OKK 54

250 **Munch being arrested in Palace Park,**
drawn in 1903, lithograph from 1911,
40 x 44 cm.
Oslo Kommunes Kunstsamlinger, OKK 334
Ref. G. Schiefler No. 343

251 **Loving Couple in the Park,** 1903/4
Part of the Linde Frieze
Oil on canvas, 92 x 171 cm.
Oslo Kommunes Kunstsamlinger, OKK 695

252 **Young People on the Beach,** 1903/4
Part of the Linde Frieze
Oil on canvas, 90 x 175 cm.
Oslo Kommunes Kunstsamlinger, OKK 35

253 **Trees on the Beach,** 1903/4
Part of the Linde Frieze
Oil on canvas, 93 x 167 cm.
Oslo Kommunes Kunstsamlinger, OKK 14

254 **Summer in the Park,** 1903/4
Part of the Linde Frieze
Oil on canvas, 92 x 171 cm.
Oslo Kommunes Kunstsamlinger, OKK 13

255 **Girls Picking Apples,** 1906/7
Part of the Reinhardt Frieze
Tempera on canvas, 87 x 159 cm.
Oslo Kommunes Kunstsamlinger, OKK 696

256 **Mothers and Children,** 1906
Oil on canvas, 96 x 101 cm.
Private Collection

257 **Mason and Mechanic,** 1908
Oil on canvas, 90 x 70 cm.
Oslo Kommunes Kunstsamlinger, OKK 574

258 **Weeping Woman,** 1906/7
Part of the Reinhardt Frieze
Tempera on canvas, 93 x 143 cm.
Oslo Kommunes Kunstsamlinger, OKK 53

*259 **Children in the Street,** c.1915
Oil on canvas, 92 x 100 cm.
Oslo Kommunes Kunstsamlinger, OKK 836

260 Detail of No. 259

261 **Man with Sledge,** c.1912
Oil on canvas, 65 x 116 cm.
Oslo Kommunes Kunstsamlinger, OKK 761

*262 **Amor and Psyche,** 1907
Oil on canvas, 120 x 99 cm.
Oslo Kommunes Kunstsamlinger, OKK 48

263 **The Fisherman and his Daughter,** c.1902
Oil on canvas, 49 x 67 cm.
Stadelsches Kunstinstitut, Frankfurt

264 **The Murderer,** 1910
Oil on canvas, 95 x 154 cm.
Oslo Kommunes Kunstsamlinger, OKK 793

265 **Village Street in Elgersburg,** 1905
Oil on canvas, 100 x 105 cm.
Oslo Kommunes Kunstsamlinger, OKK 548

266 **Death of Marat,** 1907
Oil on canvas, 152 x 149 cm.
Oslo Kommunes Kunstsamlinger, OKK 4

Chapter 12
*267 **Dr. Daniel Jacobson,** 1909
Oil on canvas, 204 x 112 cm.
Oslo Kommunes Kunstsamlinger, OKK 359

268 Photograph of the model, the portrait and the
artist

269 **The Poison Flower** (the first illustration of
the Alpha and Omega series), 1908
Lithograph, 30 x 18.5 cm.
Oslo Kommunes Kunstsamlinger, OKK 304
Ref. G. Schiefler No. 309

270 **The Sphinx,** 1909
Chalk, 43.3 x 63 cm.
Oslo Kommunes Kunstsamlinger, OKK 2453

271 **Caricature. Prof. Jackson passing electricity through the famous painter Munch,
charging his crazy brain with the positive
power of masculinity and the negative
power of femininity,** 1908/9
Pen and ink, 27.3 x 21.2 cm.
Oslo Kommunes Kunstsamlinger, OKK 1976

272 **Caricature of Heiberg and Bodtker,** 1907/8
Lithograph, 22.5 x 32.5 cm.
Oslo Kommunes Kunstsamlinger, OKK 252
Ref. G. Schiefler No. 208

273 **Omega and the Tiger,** 1908/9
Lithograph, 24.5 x 46 cm.
Oslo Kommunes Kunstsamlinger, OKK 311
Ref. G. Schiefler No. 317

274 **The Nurse,** 1908/9
Drypoint, 20.5 x 15.2 cm.
Oslo Kommunes Kunstsamlinger, OKK 128
Ref. G. Schiefler No. 269

275 **Mandrill,** 1909
Lithograph, 26 x 14.7 cm.
Oslo Kommunes Kunstsamlinger, OKK 286
Ref. G. Schiefler No. 291

276 **The Rag Picker,** 1908/9
Etching on zinc, 60 x 44 cm.
Oslo Kommunes Kunstsamlinger, OKK 131
Ref. G. Schiefler No. 272

277 **The Big Cod,** 1902
Etching, 11.8 x 17 cm.
Islo Kommunes Kunstsamlinger, OKK 75
Ref. G. Schiefler No. 165

278 **Stormy Night,** 1908/9
Woodcut, 21.7 x 32.5 cm.
Oslo Kommunes Kunstsamlinger, OKK 622
Ref. G. Schiefler No. 341

279 **Alpha Asleep,** 1908/9
Lithograph, 25 x 44 cm.
Oslo Kommunes Kunstsamlinger, OKK 305
Ref. G. Schiefler No. 310

280 **Omega and the Donkey,** 1908/9
Lithograph, 23.5 x 35 cm.
Oslo Kommunes Kunstsamlinger, OKK 315
Ref. G. Schiefler No. 320

281 **Omega's children,** 1908/9
Lithograph, 25.5 x 50 cm.
Oslo Kommunes Kunstsamlinger, OKK 319
Ref. G. Schiefler No. 324

Chapter 13
282 **Winter in Kragero,** 1912
Oil on canvas, 132 x 131 cm.
Oslo Kommunes Kunstsamlinger, OKK 319

283 **Winter Landscape from Kragero,** 1915
Oil on canvas, 103 x 128 cm.
Nasjonalgalleriet, Oslo

284 **The Cliff at Kragero,** 1910/14
Oil on canvas, 91 x 112 cm.
Oslo Kommunes Kunstsamlinger, OKK 579

285 **Kneeling Female Nude,** 1920/30
Oil on canvas, 66 x 44 cm.
Rolf E. Stenersen Collection, RES A88

286 **Design for a Monument,**
Indian ink drawing, 26 x 40 cm.
Oslo Kommunes Kunstsamlinger, OKK 138

287 **Mother Norway,** 1909
Crayon, 38.1 x 30.7 cm.
Oslo Kommunes Kunstsamlinger, OKK 2463

288 **Christen Sandberg,** 1901
Oil on canvas, 215 x 147 cm.
Oslo Kommunes Kunstsamlinger, OKK 3

289 **Jens Thiis,** 1909
Oil on canvas, 203 x 102 cm.
Oslo Kommunes Kunstsamlinger, OKK 390

290 **The Frenchman,** 1901
Oil on canvas, 185 x 70 cm.
Nasjonalgalleriet, Oslo

*291 **Walther Rathenau,** 1907
Oil on canvas, 220 x 110 cm.
Rasmus Meyers Samlinger, Bergen

292 **Jappe Nilssen,** 1909
Oil on canvas, 194 x 95 cm.
Oslo Kommunes Kunstsamlinger, OKK 8

*293 **Helge Rode,** 1908/9
Oil on canvas, 196 x 86 cm.
Nationalmuseum, Stockholm

294 **Christian Gierløff,** 1910
Oil on canvas, 207 x 100 cm.
Goteborgs Museum

295 **Ludvig Karsten,** 1905
Oil on canvas, 194 x 91 cm.
Thielska Galleriet, Stockholm

296 **Ladies on the Jetty,** 1903
Oil on canvas, 184 x 205 cm.
Bergen Billedgalleri

297 **Life,** 1910
Oil on canvas, 194 x 369 cm.
Oslo Town Hall

298 **Aase and Harald Norregaard,** 1899
Oil on cardboard, 50 x 126 cm.
Nasjonalgalleriet, Oslo

299 **Self-portrait with Hat,** 1905
Oil on canvas, 80 x 64 cm.
Oslo Kommunes Kunstsamlinger, OKK 507

300 **Ingse Vibe Müller,** 1903
Oil on canvas, 161 x 70 cm.
Oslo Kommunes Kunstsamlinger, OKK 272

301 **Jens Thiis,** 1913
Lithograph, 29.5 x 23.5 cm.
Oslo Kommunes Kunstsamlinger, OKK 371
Ref. G. Schiefler No. 410

Chapter 14
302 **New Rays** (Side section from Oslo University
murals)
Oil on canvas, 455 x 225 cm.

303 **Mother and children in the Sun,** 1910
Black crayon, 69.7 x 53.2 cm.
Oslo Kommunes Kunstsamlinger, OKK 1787

304 **Two Boys** (Preparatory sketch for *History*)
Blue crayon, 36.6 x 27.2 cm.
Oslo Kommunes Kunstsamlinger, OKK 153

305 Photograph of Børre, the model for **History,**
c.1910

306 **History** in the open air studio at Skrubben. In
the foreground is Munch himself and the
portraits of Thiis, Sandberg and Frue Roede
together with that of a male standing nude.

307 **Børre,** 1910/11
Oil on canvas, 104 x 128 cm.
Oslo Kommunes Kunstsamlinger, OKK 425

308 **History** (Main section of left wall in Oslo
University Hall)
Oil on canvas, 455 x 1160 cm.

309 **Alma Mater** (Main section of right wall in
Oslo University Hall)
Oil on canvas, 455 x 1160 cm.

310 **History**, 1914
Hand-coloured lithograph, 39.5 x 77 cm.
Oslo Kommunes Kunstsamlinger, OKK 378
Ref. G. Schiefler No. 426

311 **Alma Mater**, 1914
Hand-coloured lithograph, 37 x 84 cm.
Oslo Kommunes Kunstsamlinger, OKK 379
Ref. G. Schiefler No. 427

*312 **The Researchers** (Once considered for use as
the main section of the right wall)
Oil on canvas, 480 x 1160 cm.
Oslo Kommunes Kunstsamlinger, OKK 962

313 Drawing for **Alma Mater**, 1936
Ink on paper, 12.4 x 21.5 cm.
Private Collection

314 **Sphinx** (Self-portrait for *Mountain of Mankind*), 1926
Oil on canvas, 141 x 102 cm.
Oslo Kommunes Kunstsamlinger, OKK 441

315 **Mountain of Mankind**, 1926
Oil on canvas, 300 x 420 cm.
Oslo Kommunes Kunstsamlinger, OKK 978

316 **Mountain of Mankind**, 1909
Tempera on canvas, 52.2 x 32.5 cm.
Oslo Kommunes Kunstsamlinger, OKK 714

317 **Neutrality**, 1916
Lithograph, 54.3 x 49 cm.
Oslo Kommunes Kunstsamlinger, OKK 395
Ref. G. Schiefler No. 459
(Poster for Nordic Exhibition)

318 **Women Picking Apples** (Side section of the
left hand wall)
Oil on canvas, 455 x 225 cm.

319 **The Sun** (preliminary version), 1912/13
Oil on canvas, 163 x 207 cm.
Oslo Kommunes Kunstsamlinger, OKK 362

320 **Women Stretching out to the Sun** (Left hand
side section of far wall)
Oil on canvas, 455 x 165 cm.

321 **Men stretching out to the Sun** (Right hand
side section of far wall)
Oil on canvas, 455 x 165 cm.

322 **The Sun** (Main section of end wall)
Oil on canvas, 455 x 780 cm.

323 **Munch in front of the rays of The Sun**

324 **The Dance of Death**, 1915
Lithograph, 48 x 29 cm.
Oslo Kommunes Kunstsamlinger, OKK 381
Ref. G. Schiefler No. 432

Chapter 15
325 **Galloping Horse**, 1912
Oil on canvas, 148 x 120 cm.
Oslo Kommunes Kunstsamlinger, OKK 541

326 Sketch of decorations for Oslo Town Hall,
1929
Crayon drawing, 27.3 x 58.5 cm.
Oslo Kommunes Kunstsamlinger, OKK 2351

327 **Workmen Digging**, 1920
Oil on canvas, 105 x 151 cm.
Private Collection

328 **Workers in the Snow**, 1913/14
Oil on canvas, 163 x 200 cm.
Oslo Kommunes Kunstsamlinger, OKK 371

329 **Workers returning Home**, 1913/15
Oil on canvas, 201 x 227 cm.
Oslo Kommunes Kunstsamlinger 365

330 **Workers Returning Home**, after 1916
Watercolour, crayon and charcoal, 57.0 x 77.9
cm.
Oslo Kommunes Kunstsamlinger 1854

*331 **Two Workers**, 1920
Bronze sculpture, 70 x 57 x 45 cm.
Oslo Kommunes Kunstsamlinger

332 **The Man in the Cabbage Field**, 1916
Oil on canvas, 136 x 181 cm.
Nasjonalgalleriet, Oslo

333 **Horses Ploughing**, 1919
Oil on canvas, 111 x 146 cm.
Nasjonalgalleriet, Oslo

334 **Starry Night**, 1923/24
Oil on canvas, 121 x 100 cm.
Oslo Kommunes Kunstsamlinger, OKK 9

335 **On the Veranda**, 1925/26
Oil on canvas, 89 x 76 cm.
Oslo Kommunes Kunstsamlinger, OKK 454

336 **Dr. Lucien Dedichen and Jappe Nilssen**
1925/26
Oil on canvas, 160 x 136 cm.
Oslo Kommunes Kunstsamlinger, OKK 370

337 **Self-portrait**, 1930
Lithograph, 21 x 19 cm.
Oslo Kommunes Kunstsamlinger, OKK 456

338 **Nude by the Wicker Chair**, 1929
Oil on canvas, 123 x 100 cm.
Oslo Kommunes Kunstsamlinger, OKK 499

339 **The Gothic Maiden** (Birgit Prestøe), 1930
Woodcut, 60 x 32.2 cm.
Oslo Kommunes Kunstsamlinger, OKK 703

340 **Girl Weeping**, 1912/15
Charcoal drawing, 40 x 25.5 cm.
Private Collection

341 **Model on the Sofa**, 1924/28
Oil on canvas, 137 x 116 cm.
Oslo Kommunes Kunstsamlinger, OKK 429

342 **Girls on the Jetty**, 1920
Woodcut and lithograph, 49.6 x 42.9 cm.
Oslo Kommunes Kunstsamlinger, OKK 647
Ref. G. Schiefler No. 488

343 **The Red House**, 1926
Oil on canvas, 110 x 130 cm.
Private Collection

Chapter 16
344 **Two Women on the Shore**, 1935
Oil on canvas, 80 x 83 cm.
Oslo Kommunes Kunstsamlinger, OKK 866

345 **Self-portrait with damaged eye**, 1932
Charcoal and oil on canvas, 90 x 72 cm.
Oslo Kommunes Kunstsamlinger, OKK 207

346 **The Lonely Ones**, 1935?
Oil on canvas, 100 x 130 cm.
Oslo Kommunes Kunstsamlinger, OKK 29

347 **Ladies on the Jetty**, 1935?
Oil on canvas, 110 x 130 cm.
Oslo Kommunes Kunstsamlinger, OKK 30

348 **The Sacrament**, 1919/20
Woodcut, 49.7 x 71.9 cm.
Oslo Kommunes Kunstsamlinger, OKK 672

349 **The Final Hour**, 1920
Woodcut, 43.2 x 58 cm.
Oslo Kommunes Kunstsamlinger, OKK 650
Ref. G. Schiefler No. 491

350 **Panic Fear**, 1920
Woodcut, 38.9 x 53.5 cm.
Oslo Kommunes Kunstsamlinger, OKK 648
Ref. G. Schiefler No. 489

351 **The Dance of Life**, 1921
Oil on canvas, 96 x 321 cm.
Rolf E. Stenersen Collection, RES A304

352 **The Dance of Life**, 1922
Oil on canvas, 134 x 387 cm.
Freia Chocolate Factory, Oslo

353 **Edvard Munch in the 1930's.**

354 **Self-portrait**, 1933
Produced by means of a hectograph, 25.0 x 21.0
cm.
Oslo Kommunes Kunstsamlinger, OKK 732

355 **Professor Schreiner as Hamlet**, 1930
Lithograph, 93.5 x 72 cm.
Oslo Kommunes Kunstsamlinger, OKK 550

356 **Hans Jaeger**, 1943/44
Lithograph, 53.7 x 42.5 cm.
Oslo Kommunes Kunstsamlinger, OKK 548

357 **Self-portrait with Stick of Pastel**, 1943
Pastel, 80 x 60 cm.
Oslo Kommunes Kunstsamlinger, OKK 749

358 **Munch at Ekely in his old age**

359 **Krotkaja, model study**, 1926/7
Oil on canvas, 117 x 58 cm.
Oslo Kommunes Kunstsamlinger, OKK 752

Chronology

1863   Born 12 December at Engelhaug farm in Løten, Hedmark (about 100 kilometres north of Oslo).

1864   The family moves to Oslo.

1868   Mother dies of tuberculosis.

1877   Sister Sophie dies of tuberculosis at age of 15.

1880   Gives up engineering studies in order to become a painter.

1881   Pupil at Royal School of Drawing.

1882   Rents a studio on Stortings plass (Parliament Square) in Oslo with six colleagues. They receive technical advice from Christian Krohg.

1885   Three weeks' study visit to Paris.

1886   First painted versions of *The Sick Child*, *Puberty* and *The Day After*.

1889   First one-man exhibition in the Students Association in Oslo. Awarded State Scholarship. Father dies. Travels to Paris in autumn and studies under Léon Bonnat.

1890   Stays in St. Cloud with the Danish poet Emanuel Goldstein. Visits Norway during the summer.

1891   Goes to Paris and Nice. Applies for and is granted State Scholarship for third time.

1892   His exhibition at Verein Berliner Künstler is forcibly closed down.

1893   Lives in Berlin. His circle of friends includes Richard Dehmel, August Strindberg, Holger Drachmann, Adolf Paul and the contributors to the newly started *Pan* magazine. Exhibits his 'Ein Menschen-Leben' (Life of Man) series. Major works: *The Scream*, *Vampire*, *The Storm*, *Madonna*, *The Voice*. *The Frieze of Life* begins to take shape.

1894   First engravings and lithographs printed in Berlin. Exhibitions in Germany and Stockholm. Publication of the first biography: *Das Werk des Edvard Munch* by Przybyszewski, Servaes, Pastor and Meier-Graefe.

1895   His Berlin friends include a number of Scandinavians, amongst whom are the Norwegian sculptor Gustav Vigeland, who produces a bust of him (since destroyed) and the Finn Gallén-Kallela, with whom he exhibits. Meier-Graefe issues a portfolio of 8 engravings. His younger brother Andreas dies of pneumonia.

1896   Travels to Paris. His companions there include Frederick Delius, Vilhelm Krag, Meier-Graefe, Strindberg and Obstfelder. First coloured lithographs and woodcuts produced. Completes another version of *The Sick Child* for Olaf Schou and a number of graphic works.

1897   Exhibits at the Salon des Indépendants. Buys house at Åsgårdstrand. Exhibition at Dioramalokalet in Oslo.

1898   Illustrations commissioned by *Quickborn* magazine for an article by Strindberg. Meets Mathilde (Tulla) Larsen.

1899   Italy, Paris and Norway.

1900   Kornhaug Sanatorium. Travels to Florence and Rome via Berlin. Paints *The Dance of Life*.

1902   Winter and spring in Berlin. Introduced by Albert Kollmann to Dr. Max Linde in Lübeck. Threatened with the forced sale of his paintings. Breaks with Tulla Larsen. His left hand is injured by pistol shot during scuffle. Completes the *Linde portfolio*. Schiefler begins to catalogue his work. Successful exhibition at Berlin Secession

1903   Berlin and Paris. Friendship with the violinist Eva Mudocci. Starts work on the *Linde Frieze*.

1904   Stays at Weimar. The *Linde Frieze* is rejected. Series of exhibitions in Vienna, Paris, Copenhagen and Oslo.

1905   His nervous condition deteriorates. The success of his exhibition in Prague provides a much needed boost.

1906	Visits spas in Germany. Paints Nietzsche on commission for Thiel. Joins Count Harry Kessler and van der Velde at Weimar. Drafts scenery for Max Reinhardt's production of *Ghosts*.
1907	Decorates the foyer of Reinhardt's Kammerspeile theatre. Visits Warnemünde during summer.
1908	Nervous breakdown at Copenhagen. Enters himself in Dr. Jacobson's clinic. Awarded the Order of St. Olav.
1909	Completes the 'Alpha and Omega' series. Continues to paint (self-portrait and portraits of Jacobson and Rode). In March that year a number of his works are bought for Nasjonalgalleriet by Thiis. Returns to Norway in May and settles at Kragerø. A large number of his works are also bought for Rasmus Meyer's collection.
1910	Buys Nedre Ramme at Hvitsten. Works on Oslo University murals.
1911	Wins competition for the University murals in August, but the members of the Academy and the Committee agree that 'none of the works under consideration should be accepted'.
1912	The only living artist, besides Picasso, to be granted a room to himself at the Sonderbund Exhibition at Cologne. Jena University expresses interest in acquiring some of the drafts for the Oslo University murals.
1913	Rents Grimsrød manor on Jeløya. His 50th birthday is marked by universal tributes.
1914	The Oslo University authorities launch a strong plea for the acquisition of Munch's murals.
1916	Buys Ekely estate outside Oslo. In September the murals are unveiled.
1918	Publishes an explanatory booklet on the *Frieze of Life* in connection with an exhibition at Blomqvist's Lokale.
1919	Continues work on the *Frieze of Life*. Suffers from bout of Spanish 'flu.
1922	Paints murals for the canteen of the Freia Chocolate Factory. Large exhibitions in Switzerland. Buys seventy-three graphic works by German artists to help them.
1927	Important exhibitions in Berlin and Oslo.
1928	Works on designs for mural decorations for Oslo Town Hall.
1929	Builds winter studio at Ekely.
1930	An eye infection restricts his working capacity for several years.
1933	Awarded the Grand Cross of the Order of St. Olav on his 70th birthday. Biographies by Jens Thiis and Pola Gauguin.
1936	Continues work on decorations for Oslo Town Hall, but is unable to complete the task. First London exhibition at the London Gallery.
1937	Eighty-two works by Munch in German public collections are confiscated as 'degenerate'.
1942	Four paintings by Munch are included in an exhibition organized by the Norwegian Nazis and entitled 'Kunst og ukunst' (Art and non-art).
1943	Munch's 80th birthday. He is struck by bronchitis following the explosion of an ammunition dump that blows in the windows of his home.
1944	23 January, Munch dies at Ekely, leaving all his work unconditionally to the city of Oslo.
1963	Opening of Munch-Museet in Oslo.

Bibliography

ASKELAND, JAN. 'Angstmotivet i Edvard Munchs kunst'. *Kunsten idag*. Oslo. Nr. 4. 1966. Norwegian and English text.

AUBERT, ANDREAS. 'I anledning av Edvard Munch utstilling'. *Dagbladet* 19/5-89.

AUBERT, ANDREAS. 'Universitetets nye festsal og den norske Kunst og Kultur'. *Kunst og Kultur*. 1911. pp. 166-80.

BANG, ERNA HOLMBOE. '*Edvard Munchs Kriseår*'. Belyst i brever. Gyldendal. Oslo 1963.

BANG, ERNA HOLMBOE. '*Edvard Munch og Jappe Nilssen*'. Efterlatte brev og kritikker. Oslo 1946.

BENESCH, OTTO. 'Edvard Munchs tro'. *OKK. Årbok* 1963 pp. 9-23.

BENESCH, OTTO. *Edvard Munch*. Køln and London 1960.

BEYER, NILS. 'Strindberg och Bengt Lidfors'. *Bonniers literära Magasin*. 1962 nr. 10.

BISANZ, HANS. 'Edvard Munch og portrettkunsten i Wien'. *OKK. Årbok* 1963 pp. 68-101. Summary in German.

BJØRNEBOE, JENS. 'Hans Jæger'. *Horisont I*. 1955 pp. 23-8.

BLOMBERG, ERIK. 'Munch flyttar hem från Tyskland'. *Konstrevy 1*. 1939 pp. 14-16.

BOE, ROY A. '«Jealousy» an. important Painting by Edvard Munch'. *The Minneapolis Institute of Arts Bulletin* Jan.-Feb. 1956.

BOE, ROY. *Edvard Munch: His Life and Work from 1880 to 1920*. Vol. I and II. Dissertation, New York University 1970. MS in M.M.

BOULTON SMITH, JOHN. *Edvard Munch. 1863-1944*. Berlin 1962.

BOULTON SMITH, JOHN. *The Graphic Work of Edvard Munch*. Introduction to Arts Council Exhibition, Folkestone. 1964.

BOULTON SMITH, JOHN. Edvard Munch og Frederick Delius. *Kunst og Kultur*, Oslo 1965. Portrait of a Friendship; Edvard Munch. *Apollo*, London, Jan. 1966.

BOULTON SMITH, JOHN. August Strindbergs billedfantasi. *Kunst og Kultur*, Oslo 1970. Strindberg's Visual Imagination. *Apollo*, London, Oct. 1970.

BOULTON SMITH, JOHN. Edvard Munch; European and Norwegian. *Apollo*, London, Jan. 1974.

BOULTON SMITH, JOHN. *Munch*. Oxford and New York, 1977.

BRENNA, ARNE. *Hans Jægers fengselsfrise*. St. Hallvard. 1972 pp. 238-66.

BRENNA, ARNE. 'Hans Jæger og Edvard Munch' I and II. *Nordisk Tidskrift*. 52: 89-115 and 188-215, 1976.

BRYNILDSEN, AASMUND. *Giganten og tiden, en Munchstudie*. Janus 1939.

BURCKHARDT, HANS. 'Angst und Eros bei Edvard Munch'. *Deutsches Ärzteblatt* 1965 pp. 2098-2101.

BUSCH, GÜNTER. Über Gegenwart und Tod-E. M. und Paula Modersohn Becker i *Edvard Munch—Probleme*, 1973 pp. 161-76.

BUSCH, GÜNTER. 'Edvard Munch und Paula Modersohn Becker'. 1977. *Hinweis zur Kunst*. Aufsätze und Reden.

BÜTTNER, ERICH. «Der leibhaftige Munch». Etterord til Jens Thiis: *Edvard Munch*, Berlin 1934.

CAPEK, JOSEF. 'Edvard Munch'. *Lidové Noviny*. 1924.

CARLEY, LIONEL and THRELFALL, ROBERT. *Delius. A Life in Pictures*. Oxford 1977.

CASSOU, JEAN. 'Munch i Frankrike'. *OKK Årbok* 1963 pp. 1-14 also French text.

COLDITZ, HERMAN. *Kjærka, Et atelier-Interiør*. Shubothe, København 1888.

DAUTHENDEY, MAX. *Aus meinem Leben*, München 1930.

DEDEKAM, HANS. *Edvard Munch*, Kristiania 1909. 25 pages.

DEHMEL, RICHARD. Article on Munch in *Pan* II, 1895.

DEKNATEL, FREDERICK B. *Edvard Munch*. 120 pp. ill. New York, Chanticleer Press 1950.

DELIUS, FREDERICK. 'Recollections of Strindberg'. In *The Sackbut*, London Dec. 1920, I, No. 8. See also WARLOCK, PETER. *Frederick Delius*.

DIGBY, GEORGE WINGFIELD. *Meaning and symbol in three modern Artists*. Faber & Faber, London 1955.

DORRA, HENRI. Munch, 'Gauguin and Norwegian Painters in Paris'. *Gazette des Beaux Arts*. Nov. 1976.

EGGUM, ARNE. 'E. M. i Danmark'. *Louisiana revy*, Oct. 1975 pp. 23-7.

EGGUM, ARNE. 'Edvard Munchs första utställning i Sverige'. *Katalog. Malmö Konsthall*, March-May 1975 pp. 19-24, also English text.

EGGUM, ARNE. In *Edvard Munch*. Catalogue of exhibition at Liljevalchs and Kulturhuset, Stockholm 1977, p. 19 about Munch's late Frieze of Life (also in English, p. 33).

EGGUM, ARNE. 'Rolf E. Stenersens gave til Oslo by'. *Katalog OKK* A 6 1974 p. 197.

EIDEM, ODD. New edition of *Fra Kristiania-Bohemen*. 1950. Dreyers Forlag, Oslo, with an informative foreword.

EKELÖF, GUNNAR. 'Edvard Munch, refleksjoner i anledning utstilling i Kunstakademin i Stockholm ill'. *Konstrevy 13* pp. 79-83 1937.

ESSWEIN, HERMAN. *Edvard Munch*. München 1905.

FILLA, EMIL. 'Tsjekkerne og Edvard Munch', *Kunst og Kultur* (Oslo) 25 pp. 65-71, 1939.

FISENNE, OTTO VON. 'E. M. in Travemünde, Neu-Münster', 1976. *Monatsschrift* H. 2. pp. 35-6.

FLOTOW, H. V. *Ein Leben für die Kunst*, Berlin 1921, with contributions from a number of German cultural personalities around Albert Kollmann. Includes a contribution by Munch.

FÖRSTER, OTTO H. 'Edvard Munch i tysk kunstkritikk'. *Kunst og Kultur*, 1927 p. 120.

GAUGUIN, POLA. *Grafikeren Edvard Munch, tresnitt og raderinger*. Trondheim 1946.

GAUGUIN, POLA. *Edvard Munch*, Aschehoug 1933, new edition 1946.

GÉRARD, EDOUARD. On Munch's exhibition at the Salon des Indépandants. *La Presse*, Paris, May 1897.

GIERLØFF, CHRISTIAN. *Edvard Munch selv*. Gyldendal, Oslo 1953.

GLASER, CURT. 'Edvard Munchs Wandgemälde für die Universität in Kristiania'. *Zeitschrift für Bildende Kunst* (Leipzig) neue Folge 25: 61-6, 1914.

GLASER, CURT. *Edvard Munch*. Berlin 1917.

GLOERSEN, INGER ALVER. *Lykkehuset*. Oslo 1970.

GOLDSTEIN, EMANUEL. *Alruner*. København 1892.

GORDON, DONALD. 'E. Kirchner in Dresden'. *The Art Bulletin* XLVIII, 1966 pp. 335-61.

GRAN, HENNING. 'Munch gjennom Werenskiolds briller'. *Kunsten Idag*. Oslo nr. 1 1951. Norwegian and English text.

GRAN, HENNING. *Billedhuggeren Julius Middelthun*, Oslo 1946.

GRAN, HENNING. 'To brev fra Edvard Munch til en dansk maler'. *Verdens Gang*, Oslo Aug. 26, 1950.

GREVE, ELI. *Liv og verk i lys av tresnittene*, Oslo 1963.

GRISEBACH, EBERHARD. *Maler des Expressionismus in Briefwechsel mit E. G. herausgegeben von Lothar G*. Hamburg 1962

HAFTMANN, WERNER. *Malerei im 20 Jahrh*. München 1952 p. 56 ff.

HAGEMANN, SONJA. *Genienes inspiratrise*. Samtiden 1963.

HAGEMANN, SONJA. 'Da Rasmus Meyers Samlinger ble til'. *Kunst og Kultur* 1966.

HAGENLOCHER, ALFRED. *Wilhelm Laage*. München 1969.

HALS, HARALD II. *Edvard Munch og byen*. Oslo Bymuseum 1955. Includes list of illustrations and brief summary in English.

HALS, HARALD I. 'Edvard Munch'. *Tidssignaler* 23/11-95. Also English text. *Katalog til utstilling i Malmö Konsthall*, March-May 1975.

HAUGHOLT, KARL. *Omkring Edvard Munchs tegninger fra Maridalen*. St. Hallvard 5. 1959.

HAUPTMANN, IVO. 'Minner om Edvard Munch'. *OKK Årbok* 1963. p. 62 ff.

HEBER, KNUT. Dagny Juell. 'Utløseren av Edvard Munchs Kunst i kamp—årene 1890-1908'. *Kunst og Kultur*, 1977 pp. 1-15.

HEDBERG, THOR. M's grafikutställning i Nationalmuseums gravyrsal 3/2-29.

Konst och litteraturuppsatser i Dagens Nyheter, åren 1921–31, *Konst och Litteratur*, Stockholm 1939 pp. 95–8.

HEILBUT, EMIL. 'Sammlung Max Linde'. «*Kunst und Kunstler*», Oct. 1903 and May 1904.

HEISE, CARL GEORG. Edvard Munchs Beziehungen zu Lübeck. *Der Wagen*, Lübeck 1927.

HEISE, CARL GEORG. *Die vier Söhne des Dr. Max Linde.* Stuttgart 1956.

HELLER, REINHOLD. 'Strømpefabrikanten, v. d. Velde og Edvard Munch'. *Kunst og Kultur*, 1968 pp. 89–104.

HELLER, REINHOLD. *Edvard Munchs 'Life Frieze': Its Beginnings and Origins.* Doctor Degree, Indiana University, June 1969. MS in M. M.

HELLER, REINHOLD. 'Affæren Munch'. *Kunst og Kultur*, 1969 pp. 175–91.

HELLER, REINHOLD. 'The riddle of Edvard Munchs Sfinx'. *Papers from the X Aica Congress* at M. M. Oslo 1969 (on 'Woman in three stages').

HELLER, REINHOLD. 'The Iconography of E. M's. «The Sphinx»'. *Art Forum* Vol. IX, 2. New York, Oct. 1970.

HELLER, REINHOLD. *The Scream*, London 1973.

HJORT, ØYSTEIN. 'Munch og Obstfelder. En norsk halvfemserparallel'. *Louisiana revy. 16 årg.*, Oct. 1975 pp. 33–6.

HODIN, J. P. 'Et møte med E. M.' *Konstrevy*, Stockholm 1939, 15: pp. 9–13.

HODIN, J. P. 'August Strindberg om Edvard Munch'. *Konstrevy*, Stockholm 1940, 16: pp. 199–202.

HODIN, J. P. *Edvard Munch, der Genius Nordens*, Stockholm 1948.

HODIN, J. P. 'Edvard Munch and depth Psychology'. *The Norseman* 1. 1956.

HODIN, J. P. *Edvard Munch*, London 1972.

HOFMANN, WERNER. 'Zu einem Bildmittel Edvard Munchs. Alte und Neue Kunst'. *Wiener Kunstwissenschaftliche Blätter* III, 1954 pp. 20–40

HOPPE, RAGNAR. 'Hos Edvard Munch på Ekely'. In *Nutida Konst* 1, pp. 8–19, 1939. Includes some of the letters from M. til H.

HOUGEN, PÅL. 'Farge på trykk'. *Katalog M. M.* nr 5, 1968.

HOUGEN, PÅL. 'Kunstneren som stedfortreder'. *Nationalmusei årsbok. Höjdpunkter i Norsk Konst*, 1968 pp. 123–40.

HOUGEN, PÅL. 'Edvard Munch. Das zeichnerische Werk'. *Ausstellung Kunsthalle*. Bremen, May–June 1970.

HOUGEN, PÅL. In catalogue *E. M. og den tsjekkiske Kunst*. M.M. 1971. See Bente Torjusen. Prepared by B.T. with section on Frieze of Life by P.H. pp. 41–5.

HOUGEN, PÅL. 'Edvard Munch. Tegninger, skisser og studier'. *OKK Kat.* A 3, 1973 v. P.H. Here referred to as Tegn. kat.

HOUGEN, PÅL. 'Edvard Munch og Henrik Ibsen'. *Katalog til utstilling i Vestlandske Kunstindustrimuseum*, May–June 1975.

HOUGEN, PÅL. *Edvard Munch. Handzeichnungen*, edited by P. H. Ernest Rathenau, New York 1976.

HUGGLER, MAX. 'Die Überwindung der Lebensangst im Werk von Edvard Munch'. *Confinia Psychiatrica*, Bern nr. 1. 1958 pp. 3–16.

HØLAAS, ODD. *Øyne som ser*, Oslo 1946 pp. 50–60.

HØST, SIGURD. In *Edvard Munch som vi kjente ham. Vennene forteller.* Oslo 1946.

JOHANSEN, BROBY R. 'Edvard Munch'. *Samleren*, København, 3, pp. 173–8, 1926.

JUSTI, LUDVIG. Catalogue of exhibition in Nationalgalerie, Berlin 1927.

KOKOSCHKA, OSKAR. 'Edvard Munchs ekspresjionisme'. *Kunst og Kultur*, Oslo nr. 3, 1952.

KOLLMANN, ALBERT. 'Ein Leben für die Kunst'. *Kroepelinscher Buchhandlung*, Berlin, 1921.

KOLLMANN, ALBERT. See Flotow H. V.

KONGSRUD, HÅKON. *Modum i Malerkunsten vår.* 1954. Offprint from *Drammens Museums Årbok*, 1948–53.

KONOW, KARL. «Kunstnerliv i Paris». *Aftenposten* 16/10–26.

KROG, ELI. *Lek med minner*, Oslo 1966.

KROHG, CHRISTIAN. *Kunstnere 2. serie.* Abel, Christiania 1892.

KROHG, CHRISTIAN. *Kampen for tilværelsen*, I, pp. 186–205 ill. København. Gyldendalske Boghandel, Nordisk Forlag 1920.

KRUSKOPE, ERIK. 'Edvard Munch on Finland'. *M. M. Skrifter nr. 4.* OKK. Oslo 1968. Offprint from *Svenska litteratursällskapets studier*, Helsingfors 1968.

Kunst og Kultur. Special numbers on Edvard Munch, 1913–33–46–63.

LANG, LOTHAR. Edvard Munch in Berlin. *Weltbühne*, 11/1–72.

LANGAARD, INGRID. *Edvard Munchs modningsår.* Gyldendal, Oslo 1960. Summary in English.

LANGAARD, JOHAN H. *Calcografie, litografie, solografie, scette e annotate da Johan H. Langaard.* Firenze 1970.

LANGAARD, JOHAN H. *Edvard Munchs selvportretter*, 161 pp. ill. Oslo, Gyldendal Norsk Forlag, 1947.

LANGAARD, JOHAN H. 'Edvard Munchs formler, et lite forsøk på en formalanalyse'. *Samtiden*, Oslo, p. 50 ff, 1948.

LANGAARD, JOHAN H. 'Om Edvard Munchs bekjentskap med August Strindberg'. *Vinduet*, Oslo nr. 8, 1948.

LANGAARD, JOHAN H. and VÆRING, RAGNVALD. *E. M's selvportretter.* Gyldendal, Oslo 1947.

LANGAARD, JOHAN H. and REVOLD, REIDAR. '*Edvard Munch', Universitets-dekorasionene.* Forlaget Norsk Kunstreproduksjon, Oslo 1960. *Edvard Munch. Th University Murals.* Oslo 1960.

LANGAARD, JOHAN H. and REVOLD, REIDAR. *Mesterverker i Munch-museet*, Oslo 1963. Edvard Munch. *Masterpieces from the Artist's Collection in the Munch Museum in Oslo.* Oslo 1964.

LANGAARD, JOHAN H. and REVOLD, REIDAR. *Munch som tegner*, Oslo 1958. *The Drawings of Edvard Munch.* Oslo 1958.

LANGAARD, JOHAN H. and REVOLD, REIDAR. '*Edvard Munch. Fra år til år'.* En håndbok ('A year by year record of Edvard Munch's life'. A handbook), 1961. Text in Norwegian and English.

LARSSON, SVEN. *Konstnärens öga.* Natur och Kultur, Stockholm 1965.

LEISTIKOW, WALTER (pseudonym Walter Selber). 'Die Affare Munch', *Freie Bühne*, Berlin, 3. pp. 1296–1300, 1892.

LEISTIKOW, WALTER (Walter Selber). 'Edvard Munch i Berlin'. *Samtiden*, Bergen 1, 1893.

LEXOW, EINAR. 'Edvard Munch og Tyskland. *Kunst og Kultur*, 1913, pp. 125–8.

LINDE, BRITA. *Ernest Thiel och hans Konstgalleri*, Stockholm 1969.

LINDE, MAX. *Edvard Munch und die Kunst der Zukunft.* 15 pp. Berlin, Gottheiner, 1902.

LINDE, MAX. '*Edvard Munchs brev. Fra dr. med. Max Linde'* (Munch-Museets skrifter 3), Dreyer, Oslo 1954 95 pp.

LUNDSTRÖM, GÖRAN. 'Edvard Munch i Strindbergs «Inferno»'. *Ord och Bild*, 1955.

LINDTKE, GUSTAV. 'Edvard Munch—Dr. Max Linde'. *Briefwechsel 1902–1928*, Lübeck, no date.

LOHMANN-SIEMS, ISA. *Käthe Kollwitz in ihrer Zeit*, Hamburg 1967. Catalogue.

MAYER, RUDOLF. 'Fornyeren i grafikken'. *Kunsten idag*, 1972 pp. 4–23.

MEIER-GRAEFE, JULIUS. *Introduksjon til mappe med 8 raderinger av Munch*, Berlin 1895.

MEIER-GRAEFE, JULIUS. *Geschichte neben der Kunst*, Berlin 1933.

MESSER, THOMAS M. *Edvard Munch.* NY 1973.

MIDBØE, HANS. *Max Reinhardts iscenesettelse av Ibsens «Gespenster» i Kammer-spiele des Deutschen Theaters. Berlin 1906. Dekor: Edvard Munch.* Trondheim 1969. Det Kgl. N. Vid. Selskabs skrift nr. 4.

MOEN, ARVE. *Edvard Munch. Samtid og miljø.* Norsk Kunstproduksjon, Oslo 1956. *Edvard Munch. Age and Milieu.* Oslo 1956.

MOEN, ARVE. *Kvinnen og Eros*, Oslo 1957. *Edvard Munch. Woman and Eros.* Oslo 1957.

MOEN, ARVE. *Landskap og dyr*, Oslo 1958. *Edvard Munch. Nature and Animals.* Oslo 1958.

MOHR, OTTO LOUS. *Edvard Munchs Auladekorasjoner i lys av ukjente utkast og sakens arter*, Gyldendal, Oslo 1960.

MULLER, HANNAH B. 'Edvard Munch. A Bibliography'. *Oslo Kommunes Kunstsamlinger Årbok 1946–1951*, Oslo 1951. Supplement in *Oslo Kommunes Kunstsamlinger Årbok 1952–1959*, Oslo 1960.

Edvard Munchs brev. Familien. Et utvalg ag Inger Munch. Forord av Johan H. Langaard, Oslo Kommunes kunstsamlinger, Munch-Museets skrifter 1, 309 pp. Oslo, Johan Grundt Tanum, 1949.

Edvard Munch som vi kjente ham. Vennene forteller. 221 pp. Oslo, Dreyers Forlag, 1946. Contributions from K. E. Schreiner, Johs. Roede, Ingeborg Motzfeldt Løchen, Titus Vibe Müller, Birgit Prestøe, David Bergendahl, Christian Gierløff, Pola Gauguin (on Munch exhibition in Bergen, 1909; with correspondence from EM to Sigurd Høst), L. O. Ravensberg.

MUNCH, EDVARD. 'Dagny Przybyszewska', *Kristiania Dagsavis*, 25/6–01. *Munchs Konkurranceutkast til Universitetes festsal.* Utstillet i Dioramlokalet, august 1911. Includes catalogue of over 30 works; Munch's own description; statements by Joachim Skovgaard, Lorentz Dietrichson and Jens Thiis.

MUNCH, EDVARD. *Livsfrisen*, pamphlet, 18 pp., n.d. probably published in 1918. Contents: *Livsfrisen* pp. 1–4. I anledning Kritikken pp. 1–7. Edouard Gerards anmeldelse i «*La Presse*», May 1897 pp. 1–7. Vi gjør Strike. Innlegg i *Aftenposten* og *Verdens Gang* fra 1902 samt nye arbeider av Edvard Munch. Anmeldelse i *Aftenposten*, 4/10–1895 av—h (= Grosch).

MUNCH, EDVARD. *Livsfrisen tilblivelse*, pamphlet, 19 pp. n.d. probably published 1929 in connection with the Blomqvist exhibition.

MUNCH, EDVARD. *Katalog til utstilling hos Blomqvist*, Oslo 1929. «Små utdrag av min dagbok».

MUNCH, EDVARD. Mein Freund Przybyszewski. *Pologne Litteraire*, Warszawa, 3 no. 27, December 15, 1928. Også i Oslo Aftenavis nr. 25, 1929.

MYERS, BERNHARD. S. *Die Malerei des Expressionismus*, Köln 1957. *Expressionism; a generation in revolt*, London 1957.

NAG, MARTIN. *Norsk Iyrikks Camilla Collett.* Samtiden, 1975 p. 512 ff.

NAG, MARTIN. *En norsk Tsjekhov.* Samtiden, 1976 p. 55 ff.

NATANSON, THADÉE. Correspondance de Kristiania. *La Revue Blanche*, Paris 59–1895.

NERGAARD, TRYGVE. 'Edvard Munchs visjon. Et bidrag til Livsfrisens historie'. *Kunst og Kultur*, 1967, No. 2 pp. 69–92.

NERGAARD, TRYGVE. *Refleksjon og visjon. Naturalismens dilemma i E. M's Kunst, 1889–94*, 1968. MS in M. M.

NERGAARD, TRYGVE. 'Emanuel Goldstein og Edvard Munch' in *Louisiana revy*, 1975, Oct.

NILSSEN, JAPPE. Edvard Munch. *A/s Freia Chokoladefabriks Spisesalsdekorasjoner*. Kristiania 1922.

NISSEN, FERNANDA. 'Munchs billeder i Universitetets festsal'. *Sosialdemokraten*, 29/6–1912.

NORDENFALK, CARL. 'Apropos Munch utställningen'. *Konstperspektiv*, Stockholm, 3 no. 1 pp. 3–7, 1947.

OBSTFELDER, SIGBJØRN. 'Edvard Munch. Et forsøg'. *Samtiden*, Bergen, 7: 17–22, 1896.

OBSTFELDER, SIGBJØRN. *Breve til hans Bror*, by Solveig Tunold, Stavanger 1949.

ØSTBY, LEIF. *Norges Billedkunst*, Gyldendal, Oslo 1951 Vols. I and II.

ØSTBY, LEIF. Edvard Munch slik Samtiden så ham. *Kunst og Kultur*, 1963 pp. 243–56.

ØSTBY, LEIF. Fra naturalisme til nyromantikk. *Kunst og Kulturs serie*, Gyldendal, Oslo 1934.

ØSTBY, LEIF. Et Edvard Munch motiv. *Kunst og Kultur*, 1966 pp. 151–8.

PASTOR, WILLY. See Przybyszewski. *Das Werk*, Berlin 1894.

PAUL, ADOLF. *Berliner Tageblatt*, 15/4–1927.

PAUL, ADOLF. *Min Strindbergsbok*. Norstedt, Stockholm 1930.

PRESTØE, BIRGIT. See Edvard Munch som vi kjente ham, 1946.

PRESTØE, BIRGIT. 'Småtrekk om Edvard Munch'. *Kunst og Kultur*, 1946 pp. 205–16.

PRZYBYSZEWSKI, STANISLAW. Das Werk des Edvard Munch. (Four contributors). 95 pp., Berlin, Fischer, 1894.

PRZYBYSZEWSKI, STANISLAW. *Vigilien*, Berlin 1895.

PRZYBYSZEWSKI, STANISLAW. *Over Bord* (The book's 'Mikita' is supposed to be Edvard Munch), Copenhagen 1896.

PRZYBYSZEWSKI, STANISLAW. *Erinnerungen an das literarische Berlin* 1965. Introduction by Willy Haas.

Quickborn, Berlin, No. 4. Jan. 1897, 24 pp. Text Strindberg, illustrations by Munch.

RAVE, PAUL ORTWIN. *Kunstdiktatur im dritten Reich*, Hamburg 1949.

RAVENSBERG, L. O. See Edvard Munch som vi kjente ham, 1946.

READ, HERBERT. 'Edvard Munch'. *OKK Årbok* 1963 pp. 56–61. Also in English, pp. 126–30.

REIFENBERG, BENNO and HAUSENSTEIN, WILHELM. *Max Beckmann*, München 1949.

REISS-ANDERSEN, GUNNAR. 'Edvard Munch (dikt)'. *Konstrevy*, Stockholm, 1–2, 1944.

REVOLD, REIDAR. Omkring en motivgruppe hos Edvard Munch. *OKK Årbok* 1952–9, Oslo 1960 pp. 38–50.

REVOLD, REIDAR. See Langaard og Revold, 1958, 1960, 1961, and 1964.

RODE, HELGE. 'Til Edvard Munch'. *Kunst og Kultur* 1963, p. 198.

ROHDE, H. P. 'Edvard Munch på klinikk i København'. *Kunst og Kultur*, 1963 pp. 259–70.

ROMDAHL, AXEL. 'Edvard Munch som expressionist'. *Tidskrift för Konstvetenskap*, 1947 p. 168 ff.

ROTHERS, E. *Europäische Expressionisten*, Berlin 1971.

SARVIG, OLE. *Edvard Munchs Grafikk*. 303 pp., København, J. H. Schultz, 1948.

SARVIG, OLE. 'Edvard Munchs grafik. Stranden'. *Louisiana revy*. 16 Vol. no. 1, Oct. 1975 p. 12.

SAWICKI, STANISLAW. 'Stanislaw Przybyszewski und Norwegen'. *Edda*, Oslo, 1, 1934.

SCHACK, GERHARD. Gustav Schiefler. *Meine Graphiksammlung*. Completed and edited by Gerhard Schack, Hamburg 1974, 338 pp.

SHERMAN, IDA. 'Edvard Munchs «Alma Mater». Tretti år i kamp med et motiv'. *Kunst og Kultur*, 1975 pp. 137–53.

SHERMAN, IDA. Edvard Munch og Felicien Rops. *Kunst og Kultur*, 1976 pp. 243–58.

SCHIEFLER, GUSTAV. *Verzeichnis des graphischen Werks Edvard Munch*, Berlin, Cassirer 1907. New edition, Cappelen, Oslo 1974. I and II.

SCHIEFLER, GUSTAV. *Edvard Munchs graphische Kunst*, Dresden 1923.

SCHIEFLER, GUSTAV. *Meine Graphik-Sammlung*. Completed and edited by Gerhard Schack, Hamburg 1974.

SCHMIDT, WERNER. Zur 'künstlerischen Herkunft von Käthe Kollwitz'. *Jahrb. d. Staatl. Kunstsaml.*, Dresden 1968 pp. 83–90.

SCHMOLL, J. A. gen. Eisenwerth. *Malerei nach Fotografie*, München 1970.

SELBERG, OLE MICHAEL. Stanislaw Przybyszewski. *Samtiden*, 1970 No. 2.

SERVAES, FRANZ. 'Von der «freien» Kunstausstellung' in *Die Gegenwart* 43 B, nr. 25, 1893 p. 398 ff.

SERVAES, FRANZ. See Przybyszewski Das Werk, 1894.

SKREDSVIG, CHRISTIAN. *Dage og nætter blandt Kunstnere*, Oslo 1943.

SPALA, VACLAV. 'Et minne om Edvard Munch'. *Kunst og Kultur*, 1939 pp. 72–5. (Volne Smery 1938).

SPRINGER, JARO. 'Die Freie Berliner Kunstausstellung'. *Kunst für Alle*, München 8: 314–15, May 15, 1893.

STABELL, WALDEMAR. Edvard Munch og Eva Mudocci. *Kunst og Kultur*, 1973 pp. 209–36.

STANG, NIC. *Edvard Munch*. Grundt Tanum Forlag, Oslo 1971. Also English edition, Oslo 1972.

STANG, RAGNA. Gustav Vigeland. *Om Kunst og Kunstnere*, Oslo 1955. 46 letters to Sophus Larpent.

STANG, RAGNA. Mecenen Ernest Thiel og Gustav Vigeland. *Livets ansikter*. Exhibition catalogue, Stockholm 1975 pp. 76–9.

STEINBERG, STANLEY and WEISS, JOSEPH. The Art of Edvard Munch and its function in his mental life. *The Psychoanalytic Quarterly*, New York 3, 1954.

STENERSEN, ROLF E. *Edvard Munch. Nærbilde av et geni*, Gyldendal, Oslo 1946. *Edvard Munch: Close-up of a Genius*. Oslo 1969.

STENERUD, KARL. Edvard Munchs testamente. *Kunst og Kultur*, 1946 pp. 73–8.

STORSTEIN, OLAV. Hans Jæger. *Det norske Studentersamfunds folkeskrifter*, 18, 1935.

STRINDBERG, AUGUST. 'L'exposition d'Edvard Munch'. *La Revue Blanche*, Paris, No. 10: pp. 525–6, 1896.

STRINDBERG, AUGUST. *Strindbergs brev, XI, Maj 1895–November 1896*. Edited by Torsten Eklund. Bonniers, Stockholm 1969, p. 277.

STRUCK, HERMANN. *Die Kunst des Radierens*, Berlin 1908.

SUZUKI, MASAAKI. *Edvard Munch*, Tokyo 1977.

SVEDFELT, TORSTEN. Quickborn. *Bokvännen*, 1969 nr. 3.

SVENÆUS, GÖSTA. *Idé och innehåll i Edvard Munchs konst*, Gyldendal, Oslo 1953.

SVENÆUS, GÖSTA. 'Trädet på berget'. *OKK. Årbok* 1963 pp. 24–46.

SVENÆUS, GÖSTA. *Edvard Munch. Das Universum der Melancholie*, Lund 1968.

SVENÆUS, GÖSTA. 'Strindberg og Munch i Inferno'. *Kunst og Kultur*, 1969.

SVENÆUS, GÖSTA. *Edvard Munch. Im Männlichen Gehirn I og II*. Writings published by Vetenskaps-societeten in Lund, 1973.

THAULOW, FRITZ. *I kamp og fest*, Kristiania, København 1908.

THIIS, JENS. *Edvard Munch og hans samtid. Slekten, livet og kunsten, geniet*. 330 pp., Oslo, Gyldendal Norsk Forlag 1933. Abridged German edition 1934, see E. Büttner.

THIIS, JENS. 'Kunstutstilling i Köln'. *Kunst og Kultur* 1911/12, pp. 234–7.

THUE, OSCAR. 'Fra Albertine-striden'. Vol. 65. «*Samtiden*», Oslo 1956 pp. 662–70.

THUE, OSCAR. «Gustav Wentzel, Dagen derpå 1883» in *Trondhjems Kunstforenings Årbok 1962* pp. 6–13.

THUE, OSCAR. 'Edvard Munch og Christian Krohg'. *Kunst og Kultur* 56: 1973 pp. 237–56.

TIMM, WERNER. *Edvard Munch, Graphik*. Henschelverlag, Berlin 1969, 314 pp. *The Graphic Art of Edvard Munch*. London 1969.

TORJUSEN, BENTE. *Edvard Munch og den tsjekkiske Kunst* in M. M. 27/2 to 30/6–71. Catalogue.

TORJUSEN, BENTE. 'Edvard Munchs utstilling i Praha', 1905. *Kunsten idag*, 1971 H. 3 pp. 5–55. Also with English text.

TVETERAAS, TRYGVE. «Publikum i åttiårene». *Samtiden*, 1932 pp. 1–15.

VENDELFELT, ERIK. *Bengt Lidfors*, Lund 1962.

VIGELAND, EMANUEL. *Konkurransen om Den kunstneriske utsmykning av Universitetets nye festsal*, 1911. Gives V's own explanation of his design, p. 5 ff, Oslo 1911.

VRIESEN, GUSTAV. *Munch und die Brücke*. Die Schanze, Münster 1951.

VAA, DYRE. 'Om Munch'. *Farmands Julehefte*, 1968.

WARLOCK, PETER. *Frederick Delius*, revised ed. London 1952, pp. 49–52. Reprints Delius's *Recollections of Strindberg*.

WARTMANN, W. 'Edvard Munch, der Graphiker'. *Graphis*, Zürich. Jan.–Mar. 1945 pp. 3–27.

WENTZEL, KITTY. *Gustav Wentzel*, Oslo 1956.

WERENSKIOLD, MARIT. *De norske Matisse-elevene. Læretid og gjennombrudd, 1908–1914*, Oslo 1972.

WERENSKIOLD, MARIT. 'Die Brücke und Edvard Munch'. *Zeitschrift des deutschen Vereins für Kunstwissenschaft B. XXVIII*. No. 1–4, Berlin 1974 pp. 140–52.

WERENSKIOLD, MARIT. Tysk ekspresjonisme i Norden. «Die Brücke» stiller ut i København og Kristiania i 1908'. *Kunst og Kultur*, 1975 pp. 155–68.

WESTRUP, ZENON P. 'Jag har varit i Arkadien'. *Natur och Kultur*, Stockholm 1975.

WIKBORG, TONE. *Menneskeberget. Zarathustras Berg ?*, 1973. MS in M. M.

WILLOCH, SIGURD. *Edvard Munch raderinger*. With foreword by Johan H. Langaard. Oslo Kommunes Kunstsamlinger. *Munch-Museets skrifter* II. 29 p. 214 ill, Oslo. Johan Grundt Tanum, 1950.

WOLFF, THEODOR. «Bitte ums Wort». *Berliner Tageblatt*, XXI 12/11–1892.

WOLL, GERD. *Edvard Munchs Arbeiderfrise*. Master's thesis in art history, Universitetet i Oslo, august 1972. MS in M. M.

WOLL, GERD. Edvard Munch. *Arbetarskildringar* (Pictures of Workers). In catalogue of exhibition at Liljevalchs and Kulturhuset, Stockholm 1977 (Includes English text).

Index

NOTE: Italicized numbers are illustration numbers.
n. = note

Aars, Mr., 271
Abel's Art Gallery, Christiania, 86
Aker collection, 303n.
Alving, Mrs., 159
Amaldus, Hr., 289n.
Anarchism, 45, 48
Angerer, Hr., 296n.
Angstbilder, 288n.
Anker, Johan, 295n., 302n.
Archinard, M., 230
Arneberg, Hr., 302n.
Art Nouveau, 106, 183, 189, 195
Askeland, Jan, 291n.
Aspasia, 95
Aubert, Andreas, 45, 57, 60, 70, 169, 236

B. H. Schubothes Boghandels Forlag, Copenhagen, 288n.
Backer, Harriet, 236
Bäckström, Ragnhild, 293n.
Bahr, Hermann, 297n.
Bang, Eina, 286n., 288n., 299n., 301n.
Barcley, E., 289n.
Barlach, Ernst, 184
Baroccio, Ugo, 292n., 293n., 294n.
Baudelaire, Charles, 79, author of *Les Fleurs du Mal*, 79, *94*
Becker, Paula Modersohn, 285n.
Beckmann, Max, 300n.
Benesch, Otto, 275
Bergendahl, David, 285n.
Bergesen, Sigvald, 295n.
Bergh, Ludvig, 288n.
Bergh, Milly, 290n.
Bertrand, Harald, 288n.
Biedermeier style, 194
Bierbaum, Hr., 295n.
Bing's Salon de l'Art Nouveau, 183
Bisanz, Hans, 304n.
Bjølstad, Karen, 33, 36, *50*, 87, 98, 123, 124, 155, *165*, 169, 178, 187, 257
Bjørneboe, Jens, 287n.
Bjørnson, Bjørnstjerne, 52, 62, 82, 84, 185
Blaue Reiter, Die, 277
Bleyl, Fritz, 277
Blomberg, Erik, 303n.
Blomqvist's Lokale, Oslo, 120, 183, 253, 254
Böcklin, Arnold, 299n.
Bødtker, Sigurd, 70, *272*
Boe, Roy, 285n., 286n., 288n., 289n.
Bohemian movement, 45, 46, 48, 55, 57, 58, 67, 73, 82, 94, 109, 178, 257
Bonnard, Pierre, 130
Bonnat, Léon, 70, 72, *80*, 155
Bouvet, M., 289n.
Brandes, Georg, 45
Brenna, Arne, 287n., 288n.
Broby-Johansen, Rudolf, 45
Broch, Professor Olaf, 302n.
Brøgger, W. C., 302n.
Brücke, Die, 277–8
Burckhardt, Dr. Hans, 300n.
Busch, Günter, 285n., 287n.
Büttner, Erich, 138

Café Bauer, Berlin, 95
Capek, Josef, 283
Carl, Prince of Denmark, *see* Hoakon VII, King of Denmark
Carley, Lionel, 294n., 298n.
Carlsen, Aase, *see* Nørregaard, Aase
Cassirer's, Berlin, 303n.
Cézanne, Paul, 230, 232, 260, 282
Chopin, Frédéric François, 96
Christiania Theatre, Christiania, *8*, 31, 52
Classicism, 236, 240, 275
Colditz, Herman, author of *Kjaerka, a Studio Interior*, 46, 48
Corday, Charlotte, 109, 209, *266*
Corinth, Louis, 291n.
Cubism, 60, 133, 272–3

Dahl, Peter, 283
Dannenberger, Hr., 138
Daübler, Theodor, 184
Daumier, Honoré, 128
Dauthendey, Max, 160, *202*
David, Jacques-Louis, 31
Decadents, 79, *La Décadence* (periodical), 79, *Le Décadent* (periodical), 79
Dedekam, Hans, 51, 111
Dedichen, Georg M., 303n.
Dedichen, Henrik Th., 303n.
Dedichen, Dr. Lucien, 263, *336*
Degas, Edgar, 299n.
Dehmel, Richard, 96, 98
Deknatel, Frederick B., 81
Delius, Frederick, 96
Denis, Maurice, 285n.
Derain, André, 304n.
Determinism, 46, 48
Dietrichson, Lorentz, 235, 243
Digby, G. W., 300n.
Dioramalokalet, Oslo, 235, 250
Ditten, Hr. von., 300n.
Dorra, Henri, 290n.
Dostoyevsky, Fyodor, author of *The Idiot* and *The Brothers Karamazov*, influences on Munch, 111
Drachmann, Holger, 98, *120*
Durand-Ruel Gallery, Paris, 291n.
Düsseldorf school, 86

Edwards, Bella, 178, *229*
Eggum, Arne, 285n., 294n., 295n., 298n., 299n., 300n., 302n., 303n.
Eidem, Odd, 287n.
Eidsvold Monument, 220
Ekelund, Vilhelm, 146
Elias, Julius, 94, 127
Ensor, James, 282
Erichsen, Thorvald, 235
Eriksen, Børre, 214, 219, 236, 243, *305*, *307*
Esche, Frau, 186
Esche, Herbert, 186, 187, *235*
Essen, Siri von, 294n.
Expressionism, 106, *107*, 256, *263*, 272–3, 275–7, 282

Fauve movement, 271, 275, 277
Felsing, Hr., 296n.
Ferkel fraternity, Berlin, 96 ff.
Filla, Emil, 187, 276
Fisenne, Otto von, 286n.

Fjeld, Lars, 219
Fjeldstad, Lise, 293n.
Förster, Dr. Otto H., 302n.
Förster-Nietzche, Elisabeth, 228
Freia Chocolate Factory, Oslo, 258, *352*
Freie Berliner Kunstausstellung, 93–4
Freud, Sigmund, 79–80, 178
Frogner Park, Oslo, 250

Gad, Mette, 289n.
Gallen-Kallela, Akseli (Axel Gallen), 90, 96
Garborg, Arne, 45
Gauguin, Paul, 57, 59, 70, 80, 96, 230, 232, 282
Gauguin, Pola, 70, 271, 282
Gérard, Edouard, 183
Gerstl, Richard, 275
Gierløff, Christian, 26, 28, 206, 210, 213, 222, 227, 253, 276, *294*
Giotto, 253
Glaser, Curt, 184, 214
Glaspalast, Munich, 88
Gløersen, Inger Alver, 297n., 298n.
Goethe, J. W. von, 98, 184, 187, 195
Gogh, Vincent van, 187, 230, 232, 246, 260, 282, 28[
Goldstein, Emanuel, 16, 72, 73, 86, *88*, 184, 210, author of *Alruner (Mandrakes)*, 104
Gordon, Donald E., 304n.
Goya y Lucientes, Francisco José de, 128
Gran, Henning, 51
Grand Café, 45, 46, *119*, 213
Greve, Eli, 177, 209
Grieg, John, 288n.
Griesebach, Professor Eberhard, 278
Grisebach, Lothan, 302n.
Grosch, H., 294n.
Gulbransson, Olaf, 298n.

Haftmann, Werner, 291n.
Hagemann, Sonja, 293n., 301n.
Hagenlocher, Alfred, 304n.
Hals, Harald, 133
Halvorsen, Holst, 303n.
Hammer, Hr., 297n.
Hamsun, Knut, 74, *121*, article 'From the subconscio[life of the soul' in *Samtiden*, 107
Hanover, Emil, 294n.
Hansen, Oliana Olive, 287n.
Hansson, Ola, 96
Hartleben, Hr., 98
Hast, *see* Stenhamar, Haldis
Hatz, Felix, 254
Haugholt, Karl, 287n.
Haukland, Andreas, 300n.
Hauptmann, Ivo, 298n., 299n.
Hausenstein, Wilhelm, 300n.
Heber, Knut, 292n., 293n.
Heckel, Erich, 277, 278
Hedberg, Thor, 127
Heiberg, Axel, 297n.
Heiberg, Fru, 98
Heiberg, Gunnar, 48, *56*, 98, 115, 177, *272*
Heller, Reinhold, 285n., 288n., 290n., 291n., 292n., 294n., 295n., 299n.
Heilbut, Emil, 299n.
Heise, Carl George, 299n.
Helmer, Jan Groos, 288n.
Héran, Henri, *see* Hermann, Paul

rmann, Paul, 142
yden, August von, 292n.
yerdahl, Hans, 55
yerdahl, Hieronymus, 254
ell, Jensen, 289n.
ort, Oyvind, 288n.
aakon VII, King of Denmark, 303n.
odin, J. P., 258, 282
ofmann, Ludvig von, 107, 195
ofmann, Werner, 287n.
olterhöff, Adolph, 286n.
olmeboe-Bang, 288n.
olass, Odd, 301n., 303n.
oppe, Ragnar, 11, 20, 22, 23, 94, 107, 108, 133, 144, 146, 174, 253, 257, 258, 283
ost, Sigurd, 18, 19, 178, 212, 213, 219
ougen, Pål, 120, 159
uggler, Max, 300n.
uysman, Joris, 84

sen, Henrik, 89, 108, 119, 120, 127, 155, 156, 159, 185, 189, 213, 260, 266
le, Sverre, 289n.
npressionism, 45, 51, 55, 57, 59, 67, 80, 82, 84, 90, 184
he Impressionist (newspaper), 46, 48, 62
sen, J. J., 287n.

acobson, Dr. Daniel, 209, 210, 222, 267, 268, 271, 275
eger, Hans, 36, 45, 48, 51, 52, 53, 54, 60, 62, 64, 67, 70, 73, 86, 109, 177, 356, author of The Anarchist's Bible, 46, and From the Christiania Bohemians, 46, editor of The Impressionist, 46, 48, 62
apanese woodcuts, 62, 128
arl, Hakon, 40
ena University, 250
ensen-Hjell, Karl, 51, 57, 57, 58, 61, 228
ránek, Milos, 241
orgensen, Johannes, 295n.
oyeaux, M., 289n.
uell, Dagny see Przybyszewska, Dagny Juell
uell, H., 291n.
ugendstil see Art Nouveau
usti, Ludwig, 260, 275

ahane, Arthur, 160, 192
ammerspiele, Berlin, 189, 194
andinsky, Wassily, 278, 282
anow, Karl, 289n.
ant, Immanuel, 46
arsten, Ludvig, 210, 232, 263, 275, 295
avli, Arne, 298n.
essler, Count Harry, 96, 187, 195, 242
hnopff, Fernand, 291n., 292n.
ielland, Kitty, 297n.
ielland, Valentin, 289n., 290n.
ierkegaard, Søren, 94
indermann, Heinz, 299n.
irchner, Ludwig, 277
irkeby, Anker, 299n., 300n.
leis, Georg, 103
leppe, K. A., 219
limt, Gustav, 275
linger, Max, his graphic series, Eine Liebe, 103, 104, 127
okoschka, Oskar, 275, 283
ollmann, Albert, 127, 184, 186, 187, 214, 217, 236, 275
ollwitz, Käthe, 94, 127
ongsrud, Anders, 289n.
ongsrud, Hakon, 289n.
öpping, Professor Karl, 127
otalik, Jiři, 283
rafft, Stina, 219, 243
rag, Vilhelm, 76, 90
ristiania, E. M., 288n.
rohg, Christian, 52, 57, 58, 59, 62, 64, 73, 96, 98, 103, 104, 108, 172, 177, 213, 236, author of Albertine, 46, 55
rohg, Per, 55
ronprinzen Palais, Berlin, 275
rotkaja, 30, 283, 359

Kruse, Max, 90, 93, 189
Kruskopf, Erik, 300n.
Kunst og Ukunst (Art and Non-Art) Exhibition, Oslo, 278
'Kunstlerabend', 96
Kunstnernes Hus, Oslo, 273

Laage, Wilhelm, 277
Lafenestre, George, 290n.
Langaard, Ingrid, 286n., 289n., 290n., 292n.
Langaard, Johan H., 285n., 290n., 291n., 294n., 295n., 297n.
Lang, Wilhelm, 296n., 297n., 299n.
Larpent, Hr., 291n., 293n.
Larsen, Ellef, 219
Larsen, Gunnar, 303n.
Larsen, Mathilde (Tulla), 159, 172, 174, 177, 213, 226, 227, 228
Larsen, P. A., 298n.
Larsson, Sven, 304n.
Lassally, Berlin, 138
Leclerc, J., 288n.
Leibl, Wilhelm, 299n.
Leistikow, Walter, 90, 98, 107, 117
Lemercier, M., 296n.
Leonardo da Vinci, 111
Lerolle, M., 303n.
Letow, Einar, 302n.
Lidfors, Bengt, 292n., 293n.
Liebermann, Max, 90, 107, 127, 169, 183, 184, 232
Liljevalch's, Stockholm, 301n.
Linde, Brita, 299n.
Linde, Dr. Max, 127, 128, 130, 152, 186, 187, 188, 189, 190, 192, 211, 212, 223, 236, 239, 240, 248, author of Edvard Munch und die Kunst der Zukunft (Edvard Munch and the Art of the Future), 186, 187
Lindtke, Gustav, 288n., 299n.
Lindström, Aune, 292n.
Lochen, Ingeborg Motzfeldt, 285n., 289n.
Lochen, Kalle, 288n., 290n.
Lohmann-Seims, Isa, 292n.
Lund, Macody, 288n.
Lundström, Göran, 294n.

Macke, August, 276, 277
Maeterlinck, Maurice, 79, 120
Mallarmé, Stéphane, 79, 82, 93
Manés group of artists, 187, 275
Manet, Edouard, 58
Mann, Thomas, 96
Marc, Franz, 278
Mathiesen, Sigurd, 209, 210
Matisse, Henri, 230, 271, 275
Mayer, Rudolf, 296n.
Meier-Graefe, Julius, 84, 86, 99, 130, co-author of Das Werk des Edvard Munch, 96, 111
Mengelberg, Richard, 127
Mergaard, Hr., 290n.
Meyer, Eli, 243
Meyer, Hakon, 243
Meyer, Karl, 234, 243
Meyer, Ludwig, 60, 188, 234, 243
Meyers, Rasmus, Munch collection, 15, 73, 128, 132, 227, 291
Middelthun, Julius, 33, 155
Millet, Jean-François, 128
Moe, Jan Thurmann, 289n.
Mohr, Anna, 290n.
Mohr, Otto Lous, 301n., 302n.
Moore, Henry, 300n.
Moreas, Jean, 80
Moreau, Gustave, 80
Mudocci, Eva, 174, 178, 229, 230, 231, 232
Müller, Ingse Vibe, 222, 300
Müller, Titus Vibe, 222
Munch, Andreas, 33, 36, 37, 52, 67, 123
Munch, Dr. Christian, 31, 33, 36, 38, 48, 59, 67, 72, 76, 84, 86, 123, 124, 155, 172, 177, 178, 183, 257
Munch, Edvard
  unhappy childhood and its effect on his painting, 33, 34, 36, 43, 44, 60, 67, 103, 123, 169, 209;
  artistic education, 33, 55, 57, 59, 62, 67, 70, 72, 80, 82, 84, 103, 155, 199; self-portraits, 1, 2, 3, 4, 5, 6, 7, 11, 12, 13, 14, 15, 16, 17, 18, 19, 20, 22, 23, 24, 25, 26, 27, 28, 29, 30, 65, 110, 156, 178, 207, 209, 214, 217, 219, 228, 231, 250, 260, 263, 264, 271, 282-3, 299, 314, 324, 337, 345, 354, 357; preoccupation with death in his painting, 30, 33, 33, 34, 35, 36, 40, 43, 44, 51, 60, 67, 74, 81, 82, 84, 103, 104, 108, 109, 120, 121, 123, 124, 128, 148, 174, 177, 178, 183, 214, 250, 264, 265, 283, 324, 348, 349, 350; influence of the bohemian movement, 31, 45, 46, 48, 109, 178, 257; Frieze of Life, series of paintings, 34, 70, 76, 82, 84, 85, 86, 90, 98, 103, 104, 106, 107, 111, 112, 115, 123, 127, 133, 146, 155, 160, 170, 174, 183, 184, 223, 235, 236, 245, 253, 258, 260, 262, 273, 276, 278, the Liebe (Love) paintings within the series, 103, 104, 106, 107, 108, 111, 111, 112, 112, 114, 117, 121, 124, 125, 126, 127, 130, 131, 132, 133, 177, the From the Modern Life of the Soul paintings within the series, 107, 112; author of two pamphlets, The Origins of the Frieze of Life and The Frieze of Life, 45, 73, 121, 183; impressionistic style, 55, 57, 70, 80, 81, 82, 86, 90, 91, 94; naturalist influence in his painting, 55, 57, 60, 62, 64; affinities with Symbolism, 55, 57, 67, 70, 80-1, 108, 130, 170; travels to Paris and the south of France, 57, 59, 60, 62, 67, 70, 72, 73, 76, 79, 80, 81-2, 84, 84, 86, 91, 92, 96, 96, 97, 107, 195, 209, 214, 262, 275; travels to Berlin, 76, 80, 94-6, 127, involvement with the Ferkel fraternity, 94-6, 98, 108, 112, importance to his artistic development of the writers for Pan magazine, 112; anticipation of the techniques of Cubism, 60, 74, 133; influence of Japanese coloured woodcuts, 62, 78, 128; influence of Mysticism, 67, 73; influence of Neo-Impressionism, 72, 81, 82; his 'mood' or 'blue' paintings, 75, 76, 79, 86, 96; his pictures described as 'schmierereien' ('daubs'), 94; Madonna pictures, 98, 110, 115, 116, 161, 162, 163, 164, 174, 178, 190, 232; his 'soul' painting, 107; his 'thought painting' ('gedankenmalerei'), 108; influence of the writings of Ibsen, 89, 155, 156, 159, 186, 192, 210, 211, 212, 214, 215, 216, 217, 260, 266, 334, 349; other literary influences, 111, 112, 183, 250; projected series of portraits of writers, 188; paintings of children, 188-9, 210, 243, 244, 247, 256, 259, 260; the 'Linde portfolio', 188; the Linde Frieze, 189, 190, 194, 223, 236, 249, 252, 253, 254; the Reinhardt Frieze, 189, 192, 223, 243, 255, 258; the Bathers Triptych, 197, 199, 219, 245, 246, 246, 264; portrait painting, 61, 67, 101, 228, 230, 232, 263, 296, 298, 336; landscape painting, 29, 70, 73, 84, 107, 115-17, 134, 140, 169-70, 172, 174, 183, 188, 195, 197, 219, 220, 220, 221, 222, 222, 223, 223, 224, 228, 236, 237, 238, 240, 243, 252, 259-60, 282, 282, 283, 284, 309, 310, 311, 312, 332, 333, 334, 343, 344, 346, 347; animal studies, 211, 221, 259, 263, 325, 333; commission of murals for Oslo University, 213, 219, 222, 223, 227, 232, 235-50, 253, 262, 264, 302, 304, 308, 310, 311, 312, 313, 314, 315, 316, 318, 319, 320, 321, 322, 323; commission for the decoration of Oslo Town Hall, 253-4, 256, 258, 260, 271, 326; murals for the canteen of the Freia Chocolate Factory, Oslo, 258; themes from working class life, 221-2, 253-7, 327, 328, 329, 330, 331, 332; influence of Matisse on his late paintings, 271; influence of German Expressionism and French Cubism, 272-3, 346, 347; graphic work, 127-52, 155, 169, 195, 213, 260, 263-6, 271, 277, 278, 282, 283, landscapes, 130, 151, 165, 166, 265, 278, 342, the Alpha and Omega series, 130, 174, 210, 211, 214, 216, 269, 273, 279, 280, 281, plans to publish suite of engravings entitled The Mirror, 130; one of the founders of Expressionism, 106, 107, 263, 275-7, 282; the father of Die Brücke, 277-8; first one-man exhibition in Christiania, 67, 84, 89; second one-man exhibition in Christiania, 84, 86, 88, 89; exhibition at the Salon des Indépandants, Paris, 107, 169, 183, 206, and at Bing's Salon de l'Art Nouveau, Paris, 183; first exhibition in Berlin in 1892, 84, 86, 88, 90, 93, 98, 103, 262, exhibition of rejected works at the Freie Berliner Kunstausstellung in 1893, 93-4, 127, exhibition with the Secession movement in

Berlin in 1902, 98, 107, 112, 183–4, exhibitions in Berlin in 1913, 250, in 1926, 275, in 1927, 282; exhibition in Dresden in 1906, 271, 277; exhibition in Cologne in 1912, 93, 184, 230, 232, 250; exhibition in Copenhagen in 1893, 103; exhibition in Stockholm in 1894, 107, 111; exhibition in Prague in 1905, 195, 275–6, 277; exhibition in Zürich in 1922, 282; various exhibitions in Oslo and in Bergen, 120, 183, 213, 219, 250, 253, 254, 275, 282; made a Knight of the Order of St. Olav, 212, 213, 271; given the Grand Cross, 271; interest in contemporary politics, 256–8, *317*; paintings branded 'degenerate' by the Nazis, 276, 278, 282; importance in twentieth-century art, 282–3; reaction of the critics to his paintings, 57, 60, 64, 67, 70, 73, 86, 90, 93, 94, 98, 112, 115, 178, 183, 209, 213, 228, 236, 243, 250, 254, 257, 275, 282, 283

Munch, Inger, *36, 37, 45, 47, 57, 57, 67, 67, 70, 73, 81, 82,* 86, 124, *165,* 169, 177, *195,* 228

Munch, Jacob, 31

Munch, Johan Storm, 31

Munch, Laura, *36, 37, 46,* 67, 78, 124, 169, 177, 178, *232*

Munch, Laura Bjølstad, 31, 32, 33, *36, 37,* 67, 123, 124, 169, 178

Munch, P. A., 31, 33, 155, 236

Munch, Sophie, 31, 32, 33, *36, 37, 41,* 62, 67, 123, 124, 177, 178

Munthe, Dr., *86*

Munthe, Gerhard, 235, 250

Mustad, Else, 263

Mustad, Charlotte, 293n., 303n.

Mustad, Christian, 293n., 303n.

Myers, Bernard S., 304n.

Mysticism, 67, 73, 79, 80

Nabis, 80, 183

Nag, Martin, 293n.

Nash, John, 300n.

Natanson, Thadée, 298n.

Naturalism, 46, 55, 57, 59, 60, 62, 64, 67, 73, 79, 80, 88, 89, 90, 177, 283

Nay, Wilhelm, 303n.

Nergaard, Trygve, 285n., 286n., 288n., 294n., 297n.

Neo-Classicism, 236, 240

Neo-Impressionism, 76, 81, 82

Neo-Romanticism, 107

Nielsen, Hr., 289n.

Nietzsche, Friedrich, 96, 185, 187, 188, *237,* 250

Nilssen, Jappe, 15, 18, 46, 48, 187, 210, 212, 213, *213,* 214, 222, 227, 230, 256, 263, *292, 336*

Nolde, Emil, 275, 277

Norberg, Lorentz, 288n.

Nordenfalk, Carl, 288n.

Normann, Adelsten, 86, 89

Nørregaard, Aase, 228, *296, 298*

Nørregaard, Harald, 178, 228, *278*

Obstfelder, Sigbjørn, 51, *62,* 94, 96, 98, 107, 120, 146, 152

Old Aker Church, Christiania, *49,* 155

Open Air Academy, Modum, 57

Oslo Arbeidersamfunn, 287n.

Oslo Town Hall, 253–4, 256, 258, 260, 271, *326*

Oslo University, 213, 219, 222, 223, 227, 232, 235–50, 253, 262, 264, *302, 304, 308, 309, 310, 311, 312, 313, 314, 315, 316, 318, 319, 320, 321, 322, 323*

Østby, Leif, 60

Pan (periodical), 112, 130

Pastor, Willy, co-author of *Das Werk des Edvard Munch,* 111

Paul, Adolf, 90, 98, 100, 107, 108

Paul, Herman, 111

Peckstein, Hr., 303n.

Peladan, Josephin, 291n.

Pericles, 95

Peters, W., 301n.

Peterssen, Eilif, 235, 250

Piat, M., 290n.

Picasso, Pablo Ruiz y, 133, 184, 232, 275

Piero della Francesca, 253

Pisarro, Camille, 289n.

Poe, Edgar Allan, influence on Munch, 111

Pointillism, 82

Poulsson, Hr., 302n.

Preisler, Jan, *241*

Prestøe, Birgit, 256, 263, 266, 271, *338, 339, 340, 341*

Przybyszewska, Dagny Juell, 84, 86, 95, 96, *98, 101,* 228

Przybyszewski, Stanislaw, 84, 90, 95, 96, 98, 108, *122,* 144, 174, author of *Underveis,* 86, *The Vigil,* 102, 111, *Zur Psychologie des Individuums,* 96, *Satans Kinder,* 96, co-author of *Das Werk des Edvard Munch,* 111–12

Puvis de Chavannes, Pierre, 72, 80

Rathenau, Ernst, 287n., 297n.

Rathenau, Walther, 93, 230, 257, *291*

Rave, Paul Ortwin, 303n.

Ravensberg, Ludvig, 11, 33, 155, 213

Read, Herbert, 282, 283

Realism, 62, 67, 70, 79, 80, 82, 84

Redon, Odilon, 80

Reifenberg, Benno, 300n.

Reinhardt, Max, 159, 160, 189, 192, 223, 243

Reiss-Anderssen, Hr., 297n.

Rembrandt van Rijn, 133

Renoir, Pierre-Auguste, 130, 263

Revold, Reidar, 286n., 297n.

Revue Blanche, La (periodical), 130, 183

Rode, Helge, 210, 222, *293*

Rode, Ove, 290n.

Rodin, Auguste, 299n.

Roede, Fru, *306*

Roede, Johs., 272, 278, 283

Rohde, H. P., 223

Rohde, Johan, 86, 103, 222

Roll, Nini, 295n.

Romdal, Axel, 289n.

Rops, Félicien, 80, 84

Rosenberg, Adolf, 90

Rosicrucianism, 80

Rothers, E., 304n.

Rouault, Georges, 291n.

Rousseau, Henri ('Le Douanier'), 277

Royal Norwegian Society of the Sciences, 299n.

Rubek, Professor Arnold, 120

Salda, Franticek, 276

Sandberg, Christen, 230, *288, 306*

Sandøy, Haakon, 293n.

Sarvig, Ole, 291n., 295n., 296n.

Sawichi, Stanislaw, 293n.

Scharffenberg, Johan, 121, 123, 178

Schack, Gerhard, 296n.

Scheerbart, Paul, 108

Schefte, Rolf, 288n.

Schiefler, Gustav, 94, 130, 133, 134, 144, *152,* 198, 210, 214, 277, author of *catalogue raisonné* of Munch's graphic works, 127–8

Schiefler, Ottilie, *206*

Schiele, Egon, 275

Schleffler, Gustav, 292n.

Schlittgen, Hermann, 96, 100, *123,* 228

Schmidt, Werner, 292n.

Schmidt-Rottluff, Karl, 277, 278

Schmiereien, 94, 113

Schmoll, Professor, 299n.

Schou, Olaf, 213; Foundation, 285n.

Schreiner, Professor K. E., 11, 12, 15, 19, 22, 26, 121, 242, 253, 264, 278, 282, *355*

Schulte, E., 291n.

Scott, Walter, 33

Secession movement, Berlin, 90, 93, 98, 107, 112

Selberg, Ole Michael, 293n.

Servaes, Franz, 74, 222, 228, co-author of *Das Werk des Edvard Munch,* 111

Seurat, Georges, 82

Sherman, Ida, 289n., 292n., 302n.

Sinding, Chr, 288n.

Singlahlsen, Andreas, 288n.

Sjaelemeri, 288n.

Skarbina, Franz, 292n.

Skovgaard, Joachim, 235–6, 243

Skredsvig, Christian, 82, 90, 107

Smith, John Boulton, 294n.

Social Realism, 55

Socialism, 48, 258

Société Royale d'Encouragement des Beaux-Arts, Paris, 9

Sonderbund Exhibition, Cologne, 93, 184, 230, 2[

Sørensen, Aimar, 287n.

Sørensen, Henrik, 222

Sørensen, Hørgen, 289n.

Sørensen, Jørgen, 288n.

Spala, Vačlav, 187, 276

Springer, Jaro, 292n.

Stabell, W., 178

Stand-Lund, Fr., 302n.

Stang, Frederick, 302n.

Stavanger, Hr., 296n.

Stenersen, Gudmund, 289n.

Stenersen, Rolf E., 20, 169, Munch collection, *212, 240, 351*

Stenhamar, Haldis, 254, 262

Sterk, Inga, 219

Stern, Ernst, 159

Stilloff, Anders, 288n.

Støa, Kristofer, 221–2, *328*

Storstein, Olav, 287n.

Strindberg, August, 45, 84, 94, 95, 96, 98, 100, 1[108, *118,* 174, 183

Strøm, Halfdan, 288n.

Struck, Hermann, 127

Sturm, Der, 277

Suzuki, Masaaki, 287n., 297n.

Svedfelt, Torskn, 294n.

Svenaeus, Gösta, 250

Sven, Gösta, 292n., 299n.

Sverdrup, Johan, 58

Swedish Literary Society, 300n.

Symbolism, 55, 57, 67, 70, 79–81, 107–8, 283

Thaulow, Dr. Carl, 288n.

Thaulow, Frits, 55, 59, 60, 64, 79, 82, 88, his Oper Academy, 57

Thiel, Ernest, 16, 127, 185, 187, 209, 212, 219, 22[232, *238*

Thiis, Jens, 16, 23, 31, 45, 48, 51, 55, 57, 60, 96, 1[107, 155, 174, 184, 185, 187, 197, 202, 213, 22[222, 230, 235, 236, 240, 242, 243, 271, 272, 276, 278, *289, 301*

Thoresen, Axel, 289n., 291n.

Thormaehlen, Dr. Ludwig, 304n.

Threlfall, Robert, 294n., 298n.

Thue, Oscar, 287n., 288n.

Thygesen, Rudolf, 275

Timm, Werner, 295n., 296n.

Torgetsen, Thorbald, 288n.

Torjusen, Bente, 299n., 304n.

Törnquist, Arne, 253

Tostrup Building, Christiania, 84, 86, 89

Trondeheims Kunstforenings arbok, 288n.

Tunhold, Solveig, 288n.

Tveteraas, Trygve, 289n.

Uddgren, C. G., 160, 297n.

Uhde, Fritz von, 59, 88, 90

Uhl, Frida, 293n.

Vaa, Dyre, 301n., 303n.

Vaering, Ragnvald, 285n.

Valloton, Felix, 285n., 286n.

Velde, Henry van de, 186, 195

Vendelfelt, Erik, 293n.

Verein Berliner Künstler, Berlin, 86, 88, 89, 90, 93

Verlaine, Paul, 79

Vigeland, Emanuel, 235, 236, 246, 250, 275, 276

Vigeland, Gustav, 48, 96, 184, 187, 220, 250, 271, [

Vogel, Hugo, 292n.

Vogt, Nils Collett, 303n.

Vollard, Ambroise, his *Album des peintres graveurs* 130, 183

Vuillard, Édouard, 130

Walden, Herwarth, 277
Wang's, Oslo, 304n.
Warlock, Peter, 294n.
Wartmann, W., 296n.
Watkins, Peter, 293n.
Welhaven, J. S. C., 287n.
Wentzel, Gustav, 48, 60, 62
Wentzel, Kitty, 288n.
Werenskiold, Erik, 51, 57, 64, 70, 82, 235, 236, 250
Werenskiold, Mart, 303n., 304n.
Wergeland, Henrik, 287n.
Werner, Anton von, 90, 93
Westrup, Zenon P., 292n., 293n.
Whistler, James Abbott McNeill, 76, 81
Wikborg, Tone, 302n.
Vilhelm, Kaiser, 90
Willoch, Sigurd, 296n.
Villumsen, J. F., 86
Winones, A. H., 287n.
Wold-Torne, Oluf, 235
Wolff, Theodor, 90
Woll, Gerd, 254
Worringer, F., 283

Zetterberg, Nisse, 283
Zola, Emil, 46, 60
Zum Schwarzen Ferkel, Berlin, 95, 98, 112